A Murray, William Ashdowne

A Clear Display of the Trinity from Divine Revelation

With an impartial examination of some traditions concerning God, in systems contrived by councils, assemblies, and synods, and imposed upon mankind as articles of faith

A Murray, William Ashdowne

A Clear Display of the Trinity from Divine Revelation
With an impartial examination of some traditions concerning God, in systems contrived by councils, assemblies, and synods, and imposed upon mankind as articles of faith

ISBN/EAN: 9783337301576

Printed in Europe, USA, Canada, Australia, Japan

Cover: Foto ©Lupo / pixelio.de

More available books at **www.hansebooks.com**

A CLEAR

DISPLAY

OF THE

TRINITY,

FROM

DIVINE REVELATION:

WITH

An impartial Examination of some Traditions concerning GOD, in Systems contrived by Councils, Assemblies, and Synods, and imposed upon Mankind as Articles of Faith.

IN THREE PARTS.

I. The Divine Character of a Plurality in Deity proved.
II. The oeconomical Character of *Father*, *Son*, and *HolyGhost*, illustrated.
III. The Scholastic Doctrine of the Trinity examined.

To which is added, by Way of Preface,

An ADDRESS to Enquiring CHRISTIANS.

The whole written in an easy and familiar Manner.

By A. M. A LAYMAN.

Hear, O Israel, JEHOVAH, *our* ELOHIM, *is one* JEHOVAH. Deut. vi. 4.—*Whosoever shall confess that* JESUS *is the* SON OF GOD, *God dwelleth in him, and he in God.* 1 John iv. 15.—*Whether it be right in the Sight of God, to hearken unto* MEN *more than unto* GOD, *judge ye?* —*We ought to obey* GOD *rather than* MEN. Acts iv. 19.—v. 29.

LONDON:

Printed for the Author, and sold by G. Robinson, in Pater-noster Row; and W. Nicholl, in St Paul's Church-yard; G. Elliot, in the Parliament-Close, Edinburgh; and T. Slack, in Newcastle.
MDCCLXXIII.

AN
ADDRESS

To the free enquiring Christians of Great-Britian, who imitate the Example of the NOBLE BEREANS, *in receiving the* WORD OF GOD *with all Readiness of Mind, and searching the* SCRIPTURES *daily, whether the Doctrines taught by* MEN *are agreeable thereto.*

BRETHREN,

NOTWITHSTANDING all the discourgements that have been formerly in the way of free enquiry into religion, there are many of our fellow christians, especially in *Britain*, who now see it to be the duty and privilege of every individual christian, to enquire as far as he is able, into every thing that his religion requires him either to believe or practise: And if there be any, to whom providence hath given a capacity and opportunity of enquiring into truth, with more leisure and exactness than others, they should use the talents heaven hath blessed them with, tho' not merely for themselves, but for the instruction of others, who have not the same advantages which they have.

As christians should be exemplary for virtue and goodness, so they should be distinguished from a corrupt world, by a diligent search after *truth*, and an honest and open profession thereof, notwithstanding the difficulties and discouragements they are liable to upon that account, which, with purity and holiness of life,—universal love to mankind,— and patience under sufferings which they cannot honourably avoid, will recommend the *truth* and cause of their crucified master, who suffered before them in the cause of *truth*. By such methods, the doctrine of *Christ* prevailed in the hands of a few weak, inconsiderate men, without power, riches, or learning; in opposition to the leading interests of this world, in the hands of self-interested priests, powerful princes, proud philosophers, the wisdom of men, and the prejudices of the people, under the influence of superstition and heathen darkness.

A DILIGENT search after *truth* is the most commendable exercise of a christian. It is a precious treasure when found, and should be pursued for its own sake; listened to with attention, temper and charity; to it we should give an open ear, candid mind, and ingenuous heart. As it carries with it the evidence of its own divinity, we should pay it the respect it deserves, not only by an inward conviction, but an open declaration of its perspicuity, force, and efficacy. Every man that would be free, honest, and wise, has an intimate concern in the success of *truth*; and is under a moral obligation to contribute all in his power, to the success and service thereof.

As *truth* cannot be wrong in itself, so it cannot lead to any thing wrong. It is our indispensible duty to lie open to the evidence of *truth*, and lay aside every bias and prejudice that may hinder us to embrace it. Above all things it should engage our serious regards. *Truth* is the rule that GOD himself follows, he is engaged to defend it, and for this end sent his Son into the world to *bear witness to the truth*. All our comfort in life and death depends upon our knowing and embracing the *truth*.

BE not then discouraged, *Brethren*, in your diligent search

search after *truth*, and cordial embracing of it when found, because, perhaps, it agrees not with the received opinions of great men, whether ancient or modern; nor with schemes of religion, whether authorized by greater or lesser authorities, established in national churches, or adopted by dissenting parties; none of these is the rule of your faith. The scriptures alone claim that honour. Whatever is added, by human schemes or interpretations, should be peremptorily rejected as dangerous innovations.

As to the *Ancients*, whatever esteem others may have for them, you may certainly judge of what they taught with the same liberty, as of any other writers: Yea, the neglect of them can have no bad consequence, since the divine rule, which teacheth all that is necessary, is complete without them.

THE Fathers in the first three centuries, had no settled systems of religion but the scriptures, on which every one had his own speculations, which differed as much as in any age since. On the doctrine of the Trinity especially, they gave their imaginations great latitude, which appears from their expressions and explications of scripture on that point; so that it would be difficult to determine, what was the settled notions of these times, since they not only differed from one another, but with themselves. But at the fourth century, in the heat of furious zeal and opposition, among proud contending parties, the doctrine was reduced to articles, which were armed with sanctions, and the civil powers called in to enforce them, under the severest penalties; so that whom church authority could not convince, the secular power might compel, without any regard to scripture at all. Having assumed the power of dictating to fellow christians, there followed every kind of unchristian treatment towards dissenters from the schemes they had established, and persecution was carried on in the name of the LORD JESUS, the king of peace: And as it was necessary they should be thought to have the countenance and approbation

probation of heaven, inſtead of ſcripture authority, the doctrine of miracles, pretended to be wrought by themſelves or predeceſſors, was propagated, which iſſued in all the ſuperſtition and ſervile worſhip of the *Romiſh Beaſt.*

WHATEVER weight was laid upon miraclous powers in the firſt centuries, and continued in the Romiſh church, to make their other doctrines and practices paſs for truth; and whatever reverence our modern Doctors may pretend is due to the doctrines of the ancients on that account, it will appear evident to every impartial enquirer, that no argument can be taken from that quarter, to favour the ſchemes invented by the ancients, but what equally tends to ſupport and countenance all the impoſtors of the church of *Rome* ſince that time: Nor can any argument be drawn from this, or any other thing but the ſcriptures, to make any doctrine paſs for truth, but what takes juſt as much authority from revelation, which alone, without *any* other help, authenticates the truths we ought to believe in religion. 'Tis a ſtrange compliment Proteſtants pay to Papiſts, in their avowed adherence to human traditions, in oppoſition to the ſcriptures as the only rule of faith!

IN ſuch a deplorable ſituation was religion from the fourth century, for many hundred years under all the tyranny, ſuperſtition, ignorance, and craft of the *Beaſt*, that the advocates for human authority among Proteſtants, find little but what they are aſhamed of, till the reformation from popery. "The Reformers, as a late author ſays, gave a violent ſhock to popery, by ſeparating from the church of *Rome*, caſting off the Pope's ſupremacy and infallibility, tranſlating the ſcriptures into the vulgar tongues, and aſſerting them *alone* to be the only rule of faith and doctrine. But having been born and educated in the error and ſuperſtition of *popery*, we cannot ſuppoſe, at their firſt emerging out of that profound darkneſs, their minds were at once completely illuminated. Many groſs errors they rejected,
ſome

some they retained. But the grand miſtake was, after they had drawn ſchemes of faith from the ſcriptures, honeſtly no doubt, to the beſt of their abilities, either they or their followers, as if they had delivered the whole ſcripture truths without any mixture of error, erected thoſe ſchemes, tho' differing very much from one another, into rules, to be univerſally received."

IT ſeemed ſomewhat contradictory and very partial in in our Reformers from popery, that they ſhould teach the people to exerciſe their own judgments in rejecting the doctrines and worſhip of *Rome*; but at the ſame time, not allow them the exerciſe of their private judgments, in chuſing or refuſing the ſchemes of religion formed by themſelves.. It is true, the ſcriptures were permitted to be read, but only in the ſenſe of theſe ſchemes: Any that diſputed them, were loaded with party-names; and chriſtian profeſſors were again led to hate, to caſt out, and ſeparate from one another, on account of the difference of ſentiments; in which they could not but differ, ſince a free and peaceable ſtudy of GOD's word was not allowed them.

IN Proteſtant ſchools, they that were educated for the miniſtry, were taught the doctrine they were to preach, not from the holy ſcriptures, but from ſyſtems of divinity, after the model of the popiſh ſchool-men, and taken chiefly from them. Their abſtract metaphyſical notions, terms of art, and diſtinctions, were retained, and ſtill applied to chriſtian principles. Their ſeveral creeds and churches were eſtabliſhed by the ſecular power, and the magiſtrate required his people to believe after the particular confeſſion, or articles he eſpouſed. Subſcriptions to human ſchemes were demanded,—men were conſtituted judges of ſcripture doctrine for whole nations and communities, and conſcience was again made reſponſible to earthly tribunals. Worldly emoluments were annexed to a ſuppoſed right belief, and heavy penalties inflicted upon recuſants: Except when the

magi-

magistrate pleased on some occasions, and under certain limitations, to grant a TOLERATION. †

THIS was only a change of *Popes*, but the popery remained. For tho' they reformed in several valuable respects, in this they were more inconsistent than those they separated from; to renounce infallibility, and yet impose and persecute as infallible,—reject human authority, and in many cases plead and rest upon it,—permit the scriptures to be read, but not understood; or, which is the same, to be understood only in the sense of schemes formed and established by men.

To tell us that these schemes were formed by the ablest divines, is no ways to the purpose, and perhaps not altogether true. For if they had not only been *able* but *infallible*, they had no right or power to do what the divine Spirit had already done, and which no creature should ever have any hand in, after he had finished revelation as a rule of faith. They might be the ablest for the times they lived in, and yet but comparatively weak. For being educated at popish schools, in times of great ignorance with regard to the

scrip-

† IT seems strange, however it came into the heads of christians, who professed to make the scriptures the rule of their religion, to think that a civil magistrate could have any power either to *limit* or *tolerate* religion. He cannot *limit* it, for human sanctions, which can reach no further than outward appearances, cannot in the least influence what is solely attained by a man's own sentiments and choice. Had GOD designed the arm of magistrates to make christians, he would have endued them with penetration suitable for the knowledge and influence of hearts.

AND as for *toleration*, there is something extremely humbling in its emphasis; as the right of private judgment, the privilege of a man's understanding and determining for himself, is the unalienable charter of every rational creature attested by GOD that created him, who has put it beyond the power of any man upon earth to think or judge for him: Must it not then be strange to say, the magistrate indulges the man's weakness, in allowing him the exercise of an unalienable right and privilege?

scriptures, it cannot be suppofed that such as were newly come out of this situation, could be so perfect in what was in a manner new to them, as is commonly pretended. But however eminent they might be, the task was far too great for them, to compose and determine the precise rules of faith in their own words for all christians. It needs no more evidence to prove their pride and weakness, than that they imposed their own decisions upon the consciences of their fellow christians, concerning the faith and the practice of religion. This was to lead christians off the foundation and principle of religion, subjection, and allegiance to *Christ*, the LORD and Law-giver: And destroy that fundamental principle of the reformation, that the scriptures are a complete rule both of faith and practice; and as such, are clear and intelligible in all necessary points, to every private christian. Now, if the scriptures are a sufficient rule, we do not want men in any age as guides; and if they are clear, they are not necessary as interpreters. The enquiring christian cannot lose much by the neglect of them, as the scriptures teach every thing clearly, that is necessary either to be believed or practised.

WE shall grant that those who have gone before us, whether ancient or modern, were good, virtuous men; yet, for reasons that might be given, they might not see the truths that yet are obvious in revelation; and shall their knowledge be the precise standard of ours? What letters-patent, what special privilege of *divine authority* can they plead, to stop the progress of divine knowledge, and to engross our belief for all times to come? Or rather must the the truth GOD hath made known, be limited by any human understanding whatsoever? If they had known much less, was there any necessity upon us to seek for no more knowledge? And why might not they be under the same prejudices against examining for themselves as we are,—pay the same respect for the opinions of others,

that

that we are difposed to fhew for their's;—or imagined points of faith fufficiently fettled by predeceffors, whom they reverenced;—Or perhaps like many of us, hold fome truths fo facred, and fo far above human comprehenfion, as they durft not examine them;—Or fo clear by the interpretation of others, as to need no examination? Whatever one or more of thefe, or other unmentioned prejudices affected them, it is certain they were under the fame temptations to be biafed with others, at beft were fallible, and therefore fhould not have the honour due to *Chrift*, whom we are to follow as our mafter *alone*.

MEN, of whatever character or denomination, ancient or modern, whether many or few fince the Apoftles, are by no means the rule of faith. Ther is no chriftian can have any power to rule over other chriftians, as judge of their confciences and religion: And whoever ufurps fuch a power, muft be *Antichrift*, and puts himfelf in the *place of God:* And as much as any fubjects his underftanding and heart to any man or church upon earth, he is guilty of *idolatry*. No, Brethren, our Dear LORD forbids us to call any man mafter, and every chriftian has a divine warrant to examine and judge for himfelf. " 1 Theff. v. 21. Prove all things, hold faft that which is good. 1 John iv. 1. Believe not every fpirit, but try the fpirits whether they are of GOD. Phil. i. 9, 10. And this I pray, that your love may abound, yet more and more in knowledge, and in judgment, that ye may approve (try, *margin*) things that are excellent. Gal. i. 8, 9. If we or an Angel from heaven,—and again, if any man preach any other gofpel unto you than that ye have received, let him be accurfed." If the doctrines of *Angels* and *Apoftles* were to be examined before received, it muft be unaccountable ftupidity to receive, without examination, the dictates of any fince the Apoftolic times.

OUR LORD exprefsly taught the doctrine of private judgment. " Luke xii. 57. Yea, and why even of yourfelves judge

judge ye not what is right?" The *Jewish* Rabbies imagined that their dictates and traditions were as binding as the written law, but our Saviour bids the disciples " beware of this leaven, or corrupt doctrine of the *Pharisees*," and lets them know they had a right to judge for themselves. John v. 39. " Search the scriptures.—If any man have not the Spirit of *Christ*, he is none of his.—He that is spiritual, judgeth all things." And the Apostles followed their divine master, enjoining the same duty. " Judge in yourselves.—I speak as to wise men : Judge ye what I say. I John v. 10. He that believeth on the son of God, hath the witness in himself." It should read, " *holds the testimony for himself.*" Which points out the necessary connection betwixt a person's believing in the Son of God, and examining and knowing the testimony or record of God concerning his Son, on which his faith is built, *for himself.*

THE BEREANS were highly commended for searching the scriptures, to see if the *Apostles'* doctrine was agreeable thereto; and have the epithet of *noble* or *renowned*, and *honourable*, given them for so doing. Whereas the LORD finds fault with such as blindly follow the dictates of men, " Hof. v. 11, 12. *Ephraim* is oppressed, and broken in judgment ; because he willingly walked after the commandment. Therefore will I be unto *Ephraim* a moth, &c." The commandment here is that mandate of *Jeroboam*, with his corrupt council of priests and princes, to worship the calves at *Dan* and *Bethel*; which was not only sinful in them to appoint, but so in the people to comply with. Those who will follow men in matters of religion, may expect to meet with the judgments of God, whom they reject as their guide.

IT must be highly commendable for every christian to search the scriptures, and compare the doctrines of men, with the pure word of God. There is no way of finding the faith once delivered to the saints, but by diligent search into the word. In receiving doctrines by tradition, we make void the love and goodness of God, and involve ourselves in the guilt of the *Pharisees*, who made the commandments of God of no effect through their traditions. We are ready to blame the Papists for believing implicitly; but what are we better, if we take religion upon trust, without evidence from revelation itself?

It is a fault that prevails with most, that they neglect the study of the scriptures in general, and content themselves with a few scraps, the meaning of which they take from others, and consequently do not understand them; yet these they make the test of truth to them, and the ground of their principles, in contradiction to the whole tenor and scope of revelation. By much the greatest part of mankind, have no other evidence for their belief of *Revelation itself*, than general received opinion; what has been held by their fathers, and all their acquaintance, passes for truth, and produces resolutions and actions.

Truth is but one, it cannot be mouldered and defined as our prejudices, passions, temporal interests, or fancies would suggest: Nor can it be altered, mended, suppressed, or established, by nations, synods, assemblies, congregations, or the agreement of parties. It is not what a *divine* may invent, or a *society* approve; nor does it change to suit circumstances, as the times change. Like its author, it is unchangeably the same, in all ages and generations.

Truth was very early corrupted by ignorant and superstitious men, who, from self-conceitedness, were unsatisfied with the plainness of it: And it is still misunderstood in many particulars, by such as account themselves the true protestants, and most perfect reformers: Nor will any one find it in its original purity, but by a free, diligent, and impartial study of revelation, in which its genuine principles are certainly explained. And whatever pains it may cost, the discovery

very of a treasure so valuable as *native truth* is, will richly reward the free enquirer. But whatever assistance is used, the work itself, no other person can do for us, every christain must do it for himself, if he would have a religion that he can call his own.

BUT instead of taking religion from the Bible, if we take human systems and decisions, or our own conceits and suppositions for our guide, like one who has lost his way in the dark, and led by a false light, we will wander in the maze of error and delusion,—lose the beauties of *truth*,—and live unacquainted with that divine temper of soul,—that love, goodness, comfort, and holy courage, which the knowledge of the *truth* inspires the mind with, which, like the natural sun in the world, diffuses its genial light and heat through the soul and conversation of him, who is possessed of it. It creates a joy, which strangers to the exercise of searching the scriptures, do not intermeddle with, nor experience.

I CANNOT imagine how it should never enter into the minds of such as neglect to search the scriptures, how they think to answer to GOD at the great day, for turning over so many volumes of human compositions, while they, perhaps, never ONCE in their life, closely and seriously read over the Bible, which above all others, contains the most excellent knowledge; and which above all others, every christian is under the deepest obligation from GOD, and their own real interest, to study constantly, and know thoroughly.

IF any one would know the *truth*, he must certainly be acquainted with the rule of judging what is *truth*. That man's religion is uncertain and precarious, who is not acquainted with the scriptures. He may read books on religious subjects, and hear sermons without number; but how shall he know what is *truth* or error, while he neglects to bring them to the standard, by which alone they can be tried and known. He may judge of what one man says, by what he hath heard from another, whom he thought he could credit, which is far too frequently the cafe, but ftill he may receive error in place of *truth*; and it is the more likely, as by this kind of judging, he puts the doctrines of men in the place of GOD's word, by which alone doctrines can be tried. What opinion would we have of a man, who fhould fet himfelf up to determine the moft important caufes in the civil courts of a nation, while he was ignorant of the ftatute and ftanding laws of the nation, to which all judges muft have recourfe in their decifions? Would any one chufe to rifk a caufe that nearly concerned him in fuch hands? Much more inconfiftent and dangerous is it, for any profeffed chriftian to pretend to judge for himfelf, (which every one fhould do) without acquaintance with the laws and ftatutes of CHRIST's kingdom, which are the only criterion of *truth*.

WHATEVER is built upon the foundation, (for all pretend to make the fcriptures the foundation) muft be tried by the pure truth therein revealed, whether it be gold, filver, precious ftones, wood, hay, or ftubble, to which the Apoftle compares the doctrines of men. All muft be tried by the fire of *truth*, before we can know of what fort it is. What will not abide the trial, muft be rejected, tho' he whofe work it is, may be faved by the fame *truth*, which deftroys his work. " The fire fhall try *every man's work* of what fort it is.—If any man's work be burnt (as not fit to abide the trial) *he* fhall fuffer lofs, but he himfelf fhall be faved; yet fo as by fire." By that *truth* which deftroys his work.

WITHOUT judging by this rule, there can be no religion at all: For he that does not believe *truth* upon his own perfuafion that it is fuch, after trial and examination, does not believe, but only fays fo. Revelation is given to individuals, not to men merely as collective bodies; and he
who

who does not enquire and believe for himself, is an unbeliever of G*o*d's *word*, whatever foundation he otherwise rests his faith upon.

BUT as the books of scripture, which are perfectly adapted for all the purposes of man's salvation, and easy to be understood, are really the revealed will of GOD to men, what power or authority can frame the least supplement to them, especially contrary to the scope and tenor of the doctrines therein made known, without incurring the highest guilt, and being answerable for all the souls they mislead?

IT is a strange infatuation which thousands are under, who spend their time and parts in the study of other books, while they totally neglect, or but very superficially read the scriptures! It is a dangerous error in practice, to give the preference to the works of men, whether heathen or christian writers, ancient or modern, in point of frequent use and attention, while the scriptures have every thing that can recommend them to the daily study of a christian. Any one who has looked over the remains of ancient learning, philosophy, and the religion of nations; and has also but taken a cursory view of the Bible, must be filled with a strong prepossession in its favour, if he is not under the strongest infatuation. In the former, nothing is to be met with but folly and impertinence; no tolerable view of the Deity, none of the duty of man from good principle and true motives; none of the chief and peculiar felicity of man, in the enjoyment of the favour of GOD. But in this Book, the praises of GOD are every where to be met with, as one, spiritual, infinite, eternal, merciful, long-suffering, perfect, &c. The duty of man is placed where it ought, and his felicity described to consist in the enjoyment of GOD, through that medium which he in infinite grace and condescension hath provided and revealed to them. This is the spirit and language of the whole.

IF GOD had not revealed it, how could man have known that his sin could be pardoned ? Is there any thing in the light of *nature* to teach a man certainly, that the infinite, perfect, immutable, justice of GOD, will pardon, connive, or wink at sin, which is a transgression of the eternal law of order, in setting up another sovereign, without some cause, or consideration of infinite moment to interpose ? Or, could nature find out that there was truly the interposition of such a cause, as the atonement found out by infinite mercy, to satisfy immutable justice ? The whole that the wit of man can discover concerning the nature, ways, and will of GOD, must be acquired, not by imagining vainly what is proper or improper for him to be, or to do; but by contemplating what he has done, and the serious consideration of what he has revealed of himself in the scriptures.

IF we shall attempt to learn religion, from the various systems into which the contending parties among professed christians have manufactured it, and follow the intricate disputes they have maintained about it, we will in the issue lose our pains. For few are qualified for this search, or competent judges in it : And when the task were at an end, (if possible) we would still have christianity to learn, and might probably conclude, that religion had not been at the bottom among the disputants. But if we sincerely apply to the scriptures, we shall find christianity in its purity and simplicity, from the doctrines and practice of *Christ* and his Apostles, without any danger of being led aside by any bias in the rule itself.

IT is no reason why we should neglect the study of the scriptures, because the learned have differed so much about the sense of them ; but rather a reason why we should examine and judge for ourselves. Tho' they differ, it does not follow that truth is not clearly taught in scripture, or that it is impossible to find it. They have differed about the sense of ancient authors of every kind, however plain in them-

themselves: And the scriptures have the advantage in point of perspicuity, that no other book has the least right to, namely, that they were indited by the wisdom of GOD, for the general instruction of all mankind, in things necessary to be known and practised: And if they are not sufficiently plain for that purpose, it is a gross reflection upon the wisdom of GOD, as well as his goodness, who certainly can make his mind known as intelligible as one man can do to another, in such things as he requires every man to know; but this would be contrary to equity and justice, to require the knowledge of what he had not plainly revealed.

THE different comments on scripture, no ways affect the truth and evidence of christianity, as contained in revelation. Tho' all the different schemes of religion, contained in the whole group of bodies of divinity, and other human compositions contrived by men, should be called in question and proved false, christianity would by no means suffer by it; for this plain reason, because religion neither in whole, nor in part, is fundamental, as it stands manufactured in these human compositions, but as it is recorded in scripture, which would be the same, tho' the other were consigned to oblivion. Consequently, whatever differences there are, they no way affect christianity, but the human explications thereof. Differences among the learned, have often had this salutary effect, that they have occasioned enquiring minds, after being bewildered by human disputes, to look back to the scripture, where they have found the truth more clear than by all the laboured arguments of disputants, who by their subtility render things unintelligible to common capacities. But the truth remains in its native simplicity, and open to the view of every diligent and impartial enquirer in revelation.

AMONG all the inventions of the Devil, there never was one so well calculated to render the scriptures useless to tho the generality of christians, as the character commonly given them, that they are *dark*, *abstruse*, and *ill to be understood*. A more horrid falsehood cannot be uttered, nor a greater affront offered to the GOD of truth. Yet this is the foundation of all the pretended right of some dictating to others in matters of faith.—It hath been productive of all the schemes that have been imposed upon mankind—And, I may say, of all the blood that hath been shed among religious zealots and devotees to systems invented by men.—It is the very foundation of popery: For once admit the principle, and we are more than half way to *Rome*, where we will find ample provision made for this great defect in the scriptures, by having an infallible interpreter to depend upon; which is certainly necessary if revelation is so dark, as after diligent enquiry, the things belonging to salvation cannot be understood from them.

THAT the scriptures are not easily understood, if the sense of them is to be taken from the various explications that have been made of them, may be readily granted: But to maintain they are so in themselves, is subversive of the great end for which they were given to mankind. GOD hath provided for the salvation of the vulgar, by making his religion plain and easy to their understandings. It is an affront to our reason itself, to depend upon men for the meaning of that on which our salvation rests, who at the same time that they would be confided in as the trustees of the secret councils of heaven, in their great humility disclaim the character of infallibility, and so by their own consent, *may* deceive us in all that is dear to us.

SUCH as represent the scriptures to be mysterious, should shew what it is that GOD requires christians to believe, that is not clearly revealed in his word. There is not one text that will prove that any such article of religion exists. But if they should produce an article not clearly revealed, they have next to prove, that it is necessary fary to falvation, which they can never do, feeing it is not fo revealed; for all things neceffary are clearly revealed in the fcriptures, otherwife they could not make the man of GOD wife to falvation.

It is not only the groffeft reflection on the *wifdom* of GOD, who indited and impofed the fcriptures upon mankind as a rule of faith and practice, while they needed the affiftance of fome of the creatures who were to be ruled by them, before they could be intelligible to others: But alfo, upon the *goodnefs* of GOD, to command conformity to a rule, upon the pain of damnation, which was not in itfelf fo clear and plain as to be underftood by thofe who were bound by it; and that he is refolved to damn his creatures for want of capacities to know what he himfelf had made above their capacities.

It is a ftrange conceit men have of themfelves, and ftill ftranger opinion of their maker, that he fhould not fpeak in a book defigned for the inftruction of all, fo as to be underftood by them, whom he intended to inftruct by it! Does not GOD, who made man, know what will fuit their capacities, better than any number of men met in a fynod or council? Every attack upon the perfection of revelation, is an attack upon the perfections of GOD himfelf, and plainly faying, he is not fo capable to teach his creatures, as they are to teach one another.

No fooner did men think of dictating to others, than they propagated this opinion of the fcriptures, to which, in a great meafure, may be attributed all the ignorance that has prevailed among the generality of profeffed chriftians. The people being once perfuaded that the fcriptures are *dark*, and *above* their capacities, are eafily led away from the ufe of them to *other books*, which they think are neceffary to make them plain, and unfold the myfteries which they fuppofe are otherwife incomprehenfible to them.

(xviii)

To mend this supposed defect in the scriptures, some men have summed up religion in systems, and by authority imposed them upon whole nations, as tests of orthodoxy to the adult, and rules of religious education for youth, who, by their parents and tutors, are taught to lay up these summaries in their minds, as the only necessary truths to be known, which it is criminal to forget, or in the least to call in question. The ground-work being laid in their acquaintance with human directories, they are confirmed in their adherence to them, by being admitted to all the privileges of the church they belong to, by shewing a very superficial knowledge of what they have been taught in their childhood: From that time, they hold themselves bound to believe and maintain all the doctrines adopted by the church or party they belong to. Hence, they rest satisfied with what they have attained, and consequently are as wise at *sixteen* years old in religion, as at *sixty*, which is far too frequently the case: And if they use the scriptures, it is with a strong bias on their minds, in favour of what they have already received as undoubted truths; what is not agreeable to these, they pass over superficially, or pervert the obvious meaning of the texts, and force them into the service of their cause. Thus they take the very reverse method to finding the *truth*. For, whereas all doctrines should be tried by the scripture, before they are received as *truth*, they first receive the doctrines, and then make the sense of scripture agreeable to them. For the sense of scripture is neither more nor less, than what such men and books have said it is. Such searchers are not likely to find the *truth*, nor yet embrace it when it evidently appears. What is plain and easy to a free enquirer, is dark and obscure to them.

There are many, who under the influence of this bad opinion of the scriptures, that they are above their capacities, conclude themselves in great humility (as they think)

think) unfit to judge for themselves, and determine to be guided by certain *men* and *books*, which they approve of. Such persons do not remember, that at the same time they are so self-diffident, they are judging for themselves in a manner that requires greater qualifications, than learning religion from the word of GOD itself. For, is not the choice of such *men* and *books* an act of their judgment? And who taught such ignorant persons, as they reckon themselves, to judge so precisely, in so many things, where there was the greatest danger of being mistaken; and yet could not judge of doctrines laid down in the clearest manner, by the unerring wisdom of GOD?

THERE is one special consideration which merits universal attention; that as divine jealousy will not remit without punishment, the heinous crime of parents, who train up their children in religion by precept or example, without shewing them the evidences from the word of GOD in support thereof; so the plea of instruction and example made by children and posterity, will be a very insufficient apology for their having received principles of religion from their fathers, without using (when capable) their own understandings, in examining them by the word of GOD.

To the obscurity of the scriptures, there is commonly added another popular objection against people judging for themselves, viz. That by allowing every one to judge for himself, the greatest confusion would take place, heresies would abound, and there would be as many religions, as there are persons to judge. It is necessary therefore, that the learned in councils or assemblies, should reduce the true religion to certain heads, and require the conformity of the common people thereto, to preserve them from error and division, and to keep peace and good order among them.

SUCH precaution might be very commendable in a senate of a common-wealth, to contrive laws for the security of its peace, and prevent dangers that might rent and divide it: But to argue the neceffity of fuch methods in religion, is making it a political tool, to keep up the fpirit of obedience among the people. If allowing men to judge for themfelves, would naturally introduce difference in religion, and errors; then it muft be certain, that confent and agreement in religion, and keeping in the truth, flow from the conftraint of this liberty. Such a religion may do for papifts, but it is a fhame for proteftants to own it as their's. How would this maxim do in trade, phyfic, or philofophy? They would be reckoned infatuate, that would be fond of buying goods in the dark, where they could not examine their qualities: To take that for gold, which they were not allowed to try: To call that a fine face, which they were not allowed to come fo nigh as to know whether it was painted. This is the reafon why falfe religions have fo many followers, as that of *Mahomet*, becaufe none of its votaries dare examine it; and this objection infinuates, that the gofpel fhould be embraced for no better reafon.

THIS is paying a poor compliment to the chriftian religion, if it has not arguments in itfelf to prove the truth, and energy to influence the belief of it; but muft have auxilliary aid from men, whofe diminutive conceptions of it are fuch, as would almoft perfuade us, themfelves do not believe it. It is the honour of chriftianity, that it needs no foreign aid to vindicate it. The evidence is in itfelf, not in what men can frame to eftablifh it. The laws and rules in itfelf, are fufficient to preferve its friends from fuch important differences, as would overthrow the foundation of their hope, and manage leffer differences which are not of fuch confequence. To fuppofe any other way *more* fufficient, is to imagine that GOD fhall conftantly work a miracle in making fome men infallible to direct the reft; which in fact, is at the bottom of all that affumed power to form laws and rules, other than what are laid down in fcripture to direct men in religion.

AND it is much to be suspected, if their fear about differences in religion, be not rather a fear that men shall see the weakness of their pretensions to such power, and be led to take their religion from the scriptures alone, independent of their decisions, which to them would be of fatal consequence indeed; but is a genuine effect of people judging freely for themselves. All directors in religion have experienced this, and no wonder they are afraid of what would destroy their power of keeping the people solely under their direction.

BUT what if some men should abuse the privilege of judging for themselves, must means be used to prevent this, which are not of GOD's appointing? He hath no where told us of this remedy, that some men shall have power to dictate to others. Nor can even this remedy answer the end; for tho' the church of *Rome* pretend to be under an infallible guide, yet they cannot prevent differences in their communion: And what is more, differences abounded in the Apostles' times, who were really infallible in their dictates to the churches. GOD does not want either the power or policy of men to preserve the unity of his church, so far as he wills it should be preserved: GOD hath said there must be heresies, but men have said there must be none. What can be supposed more dangerous, than for men to put it out of their own power ever to correct an error, tho' of the most dangerous nature, by establishing it as a rule, never to acknowledge a fault in the system men have composed for them, and bind themselves by solemn oath, to defend every article, right or wrong, for ever? This is not only first supposing the system infallibly right; but for ever depriving themselves of the means to know the least error, in what they have once, with very little, or perhaps no examination, determined on. This is making GODS of men, and believing they can neither deceive nor be deceived. Such persons would do well to consider, before they risk too much, the import of that commination, " Thus saith the

LORD

Lord, curſed be the man that truſteth in man, and maketh fleſh his arm, and whoſe heart departeth from the Lord."

Allow me, *Brethren*, to cloſe the conſideration of this ſubject at this time, by a ſhort addreſs to thoſe people, who excuſe themſelves from the duty of ſearching the ſcriptures, and the uſe of means to enable them to judge for themſelves, by pretending that providence puts them in ſuch ſituations of life, that they have no time to uſe ſuch means, being obliged to labour and care for the neceſſaries of life. Thus the people excuſe themſelves, and the teachers are willing to admit it as ſufficient.

Be aſtoniſhed, O heavens, at the audacious reproach caſt upon the wiſdom and goodneſs of thy creator's *providence!* Who, O man, has been ſo cruel as to condemn thee to this ſlavery! Not the meek and compaſſionate Jesus, who bids us firſt ſeek the kingdom of God, and his righteouſneſs, and hath promiſed that all other things ſhall be added,— forbidden us to take *anxious* care for the things of this world, for we know not what a day may bring forth.—Not the *Apoſtle*, who directs us to ſeek thoſe things which are above,——to ſet our affections on things above, and not on things on earth. Ponder the divine queſtions, " What is a man profited, if he ſhall gain the whole world, and loſe his own ſoul? What ſhall a man give in exchange for his ſoul?" Pray, for what end was you ſent into the world? What is your moſt material concerns in it? Is it not to learn to know, and to do the will of your creator? Conſider, whether all the time God hath given you, hath been well uſed, before you charge God fooliſhly. What became of the time of child-hood and youth, when God hath ſo ordered it, that man is unfit for work and care, pointing it out as the time for inſtruction? Why was you not taught the doctrines of the goſpel, and the grounds of the chriſtian religion then? Let parents, teachers, and yourſelves ſhare the guilt of this neglect: God's *providence* is clear.—What have you done on all the

Sabbath

Sabbaths you have had, in which, by the laws of GOD and the land we live in, we cease from labour? Here is one *seventh* of your life free of the entangling excuse. Add to the former, all the days and hours spent in feasting, gaming, drinking, sporting, pleasures of different kinds, and perhaps a great deal in indolence and sloth, it will be found the highest injustice in men, to complain for want of time, who can spare so much to superfluous, trifling, and often wicked purposes. When that time, which is now devoured in vain pursuits, anxious or inordinate cares, idle extravagancies, and vicious pleasures, is restored to you, you will have enough to answer all the calls of religious enquiry. You will prosecute your callings with christian diligence, and find the sweetest refreshments; in such days and hours as you appropriate to the momentuous concerns of an everlasting state.

☞ A s to the following work, be assured, *Brethren*, that to assist you in the further exercise of that commendable duty of enquiry after *truth*, I have spent some time in illustrating from revelation, some points in religion, which the generality of professed christians seem either to neglect the right understanding of, or by certain means have mistaken notions about: And as the right knowledge of GOD, is the true foundation of all the right understanding we can have in religion, I thought proper, *first*, to present to your consideration, what I find revealed concerning GOD. This I have done in the *first* and *second* parts: But as my sentiments on that subject, do not coincide with the common established doctrine in the schemes of religion, adopted by professed christians, it was therefore necessary to examine these, that the reasons may appear why I differ from them. This makes a *third* part.

I HAVE not said any thing more in any of the parts than *truth* obliges me, according to the most serious view I can at present take of it; and I hope no consideration whatever

shall

shall prejudice me so far, as to make me deny or dissemble, what the conviction of my own mind from the word of GOD requires me to confess. I have made revelation *alone* the rule of my judgment, not any opinions or schemes of men. Notwithstanding, I do not maintain, that I have every where either fully or infallibly given the sense of revelation; the weakness and imperfections of the man will appear in all his endeavours, to set things of this kind in a clear light, however honest and impartial he may be. But I am satisfied, you will not find any of these subtle arts commonly employed, either to colour a bad cause, or perplex a good one. Intricate refinements, forced constructions, and evasive distinctions, are carefully avoided. Plain reasoning, founded on scripture evidence, and adapted to plain and honest minds, is studied through the whole. But if any of my readers are so wedded to any particular scheme, as to think it sinful to offer any further light on the subject, they may let this book alone: For I can assure them, it is not adapted to any scheme, further than I judged they agree with revelation.

But as to you, my *Brethren*, who dare think closely and freely, I hope you will accept in good part what is well meant. If you receive any profit, return thanks to GOD, to whom alone all praise is due: But if you judge that I have fallen short of the *truth*, or mixt it in any particular; in this case, you will mind the common rule of justice, to do to me, as reason and revelation will tell you, I ought to do to any of you, were you the author, and I the reader. I do not thus bespeak my readers, because so scrupulous with regard to consequences as many are. I not only chuse to seek, but to speak the *truth*: And it breeds comfort upon every new reflection, that divine providence hath preserved me from these servile restraints, in which many are involved from particular connections, the view of preferment, and the supposed sweets of an ambitious life. When any *truth* begins to open, I am not upon the reserve, lest I should push

the

the discovery too far, a caution strictly attended to by such as are trained up in the trammels of a church, whose religion is all settled in a system, which the light of truth is ready to expose as derived from error, or superstition; and imposed upon many, to serve the interests of a few. Such are commonly fired with rage against those who discover truth, and persecute under pretence of glorifying GOD. But whatever others may think on this subject, I content myself with the discharge of my duty to you, *Brethren*, by a free declaration of my sentiments, and indulge the same liberty to every one else: But you must not be surprized, if I leave the common tract of interpreters, even the most admired for orthodoxy;—as I freely decline any regard to them as a *Rule* in believing for myself, or shewing to others the truth taught in the *word of* GOD.

HENCE, you need not think it strange, that I have cited no human authorities for proof of any thing advanced: These I have purposely neglected; *first*, because human authorities have been so frequently ensnaring to readers, by determining their judgment according as the men or books were, or were not their favourites. With such readers, a favourite author is of more weight than several plain texts, and therefore they are in danger of receiving error for the sake of good company: Also, because human authorities cannot prove any truth in religion. If they are added to scripture texts, it insinuates that the scripture is not sufficient without them. If they are used alone, it is either that they are expected to have more effect upon the reader than scripture; or because there are not any texts that will prove the point, which is enough to bring both it and the human authorities under suspicion. I confess there are several borrowed sentiments in the following work: But as I have to the best of my knowledge, adopted nothing but what is agreeable to scripture, it is no matter of moment to the reader whose they are, if he finds them to be *truth*.

I MUST

I MUST also notice, that tho' one text is sufficient to prove any doctrine, if it is plainly expressed or implied in it: Yet I have often added several texts to prove one point, because the same text does not always appear to be so conspicuous a proof of the same point to different persons; and partly to shew how copiously the scriptures prove such doctrines, when the evidence is collected into one point of view, and to leave them as much as possible beyond doubt.

I FREQUENTLY read the text otherwise than it is in our English translation. The reader will observe the different reading is generally put in parenthesis, if not more fully pointed out. If he find upon examination, that the common translation is nearer the original than my alterations, he will do well to keep by it; but if otherwise, I hope the freedom I have used this way will be acceptable to him; and with other things that may appear new at first sight, be fairly examined, and candidly interpreted. "*Prove all things, hold fast that which is good.*"

I HOPE the reader will take care not to lose sight of the leading sentiments intended to be conveyed, through the variety of incidental ideas, introduced either to illustrate the general subject, or elucidate particular texts: Nor on account of the terms in which some things are expressed. With regard to the last of these, I have taken all the care I could, not to use ambiguous or mystical terms; and have explained such as might appear dark to some: Yet in the third part especially, where the systematic doctrine of the Trinity comes to be examined, I was under the disagreeable necessity of using the systematic terms, which, perhaps, may occasion the inattentive or prejudiced reader to suppose, that in some instances, I am not consistent with myself. What appears to be of this kind, I hope the reader will interpret, if possible, agreeable to the leading sentiments of the book. But if any *real* inconsistency is found, let it be

set

fet to my account,—the fault is mine,—I pretend not to be perfect :—The truth I contend for, is, I am fully perfuaded, clear of all inconfiftency or felf-contradiction

NOTWITHSTANDING the difficulties that attend the inveſtigation of a ſubject, where the ſcriptures have been generally miſapplied,—the learned much divided,—involved in intricacy and contradiction by eſtabliſhed ſyſtems,—and ſuppoſed by the bulk of mankind to be under the veil of ineffable myſtery: Yet, leaving human conjecture, we turn to the word of GOD, as the only guide, with humble confidence, being perſuaded that He hath not left that truth in impenetrable darkneſs, which He hath made neceſſary for us to know and underſtand: More we do not expect to find: And if we are ſo happy as to point out to the candid reader, the clear and determined ſenſe which the Spirit of GOD hath conveyed on this ſubject, (which by his aſſiſtance we hope to do) our labour will not be in vain. But let GOD have the praiſe; "*who hath choſen the fooliſh things of this world, to confound the wiſe,—the weak things of this world, to confound the mighty,—that no fleſh ſhould glory in his preſence,—as it is written, he that glorieth, let him glory in the* LORD,—*who hath hid thoſe things from the wiſe and prudent, and revealed them unto babes: Even ſo, Father, for ſo it ſeemed good in thy ſight.*"

CONTENTS.

INTRODUCTION.——*But two ways of knowing God.—Our notions of Spirit all negative.—Revelation the only rule.—Speculations of the schools unnecessary.—The general intention of the work.*

PART I.

SECT. I. p. 7. *Texts that prove there is but* one God. *—One Almighty and Omnipotent,—Infinite,—Eternal and Unchangeable.—*One Being *to be worshipped.*

SECT. II. p. 11. *That there is a* DIVINE PLURALITY. *—*JEHOVAH *and* ELOHIM *not properly translated.—*ELOHIM *a plural.—False ideas of it as a plural removed.—The word* GOD *not a proper translation of it.—True import of* ELOHIM. *—Other nouns that express a plurality.—Texts which seem to limit the divine plurality to* Three.*—Difficulties concerning a divine plurality removed.*

SECT. III. p. 27. *The proper Deity of the* LORD JESUS CHRIST *and the* HOLY GHOST *proved from express scripture—Name* JEHOVAH *ascribed to—*LORD *in the most absolute sense—The name* GOD.*—Rom.* ix. 5, *considered.— The texts considered where* CHRIST *is distinguished from* GOD *by the copulative* AND*—Creation work ascribed to—Inditing Revelation——Author of the divine law——Breakers thereof tempt Christ and the Spirit—Omnipresence ascribed to—Dwelling in the saints—Holiness—Fountain of life—Absolute power —Raising the dead—All spiritual and divine operations.— Evidence in scripture language unavoidable.*

SECT IV. p. 40. *The Deity of* JESUS CHRIST *further proved from* 26 *arguments, formed by comparing one text with another, whereby it appears, that all the* names, titles, perfections, works, *and* worship *ascribed to the Supreme Being are attributed to him: And* 16 *arguments deduced in the same manner, to prove the Deity of the* HOLY GHOST.*—Ideas implied in the phrase* SPIRIT-JEHOVAH.

SECT. V. p. 58. *A further illustration of the proper Deity of Jesus Christ, from the scope of several passages of scripture.—As he made all things, he must govern them.—Revelation a history of the church.——He who appeared in the Old Testament*

ment is called GOD, JEHOVAH, &c.——*That it was Christ, a general argument for.*——*Two objections answered.*——*The phrase* Angel of the Lord *should have been* ANGEL-JEHOVAH.—— Angel *joined with* ELOHIM, *reason for.*——JESUS CHRIST, *the* ANGEL-JEHOVAH,——ALMIGHTY GOD, *and* KING OF ISRAEL, *whom they worshipped.*--*Image of God, after which man was made, respects dominion.*——JESUS CHRIST, *the* Angel, *and* God, *mentioned by* Jacob *in blessing* Joseph's *sons*—*The* Angel *in whom the name of* God.——*What meant by the* name of God.—*Opinion of the ancients.*—CHRIST *gave the law at* Sinai——*Appeared to* Joshua *and* Manoah.——*Judgment of* Jews *and ancient christians.*——*Difficulty of* CHRIST *speaking of and to himself, removed.*——*What is said of* JEHOVAH *in the Old Testament, applied to* CHRIST *in the New.*—Holy one of Israel, *who*—*General rule to interpret such passages.*—*The name* JESUS *frequent in the Old Testament.*—*Passages in the New Testament, which prove that Christ existed as the* GOD *and* KING *of the church in the Old.*——*Names of Christ that imply this*——*Worshipped under the Old Testament*—*Under the New.*—*Utility and advantages of this truth, to the right understanding of the scriptures.*——*Exalts Christ in his wisdom, power, love, care, and condescension.*

P A R T   II.

SECT. I. *p.* 106. *The term* OECONOMY *explained.*——*A beautiful passage in* Isaiah *explained.*—*God's perfections, and relation to men, only known in* Christ.—*The revealed distinction of Father, Son, and Spirit, does not destroy the unity of Deity.* —*Unity and plurality pointed out in* JEHOVAH ELOHIM.—— ELOHIM *of great importance among the* Jews—*Implies relation.*—*General view of the terms* Father, Son, *and* Holy Ghost.—*Of the term* Father,—*often includes all that is called* GOD.—*Jesus Christ called* Father.—*The meaning learned by analogy.*—*General ideas of Paternity.*—*God a Father to saints*— *To Jesus Christ.*——*Why called* heavenly Father.—*Difference betwixt Old and New Testament worship.*—Spirit *and* truth, *what.*

SECT. II. *p.* 129. *Scripture ideas of* sonship.—*Lineal descendants*—*That which proceedeth from another*——*Successors in government.*——Adam *and* Angels *called sons of God, why.*—*Magistrates, why.*——*Some called children of death.*—— *Inferiors, and such as were taught and adopted, called sons.*—— *Wicked called sons of men,*—*the world,*---*the* Devil,---*darkness and disobedience,*---*wrath and the curse,*---Belial *and perdition.*

dition.——*Saints sons of God, how.---Chosen, &c.---of light,---wisdom,---promise,---resurrection, &c.*——*General ideas of sonship applied to Christ.---Begotten, born, a child, first-born, how, submission,---obedience, honouring and manifesting his father's name.---* BEN, *its meaning.---* NIN, *the meaning.---Christ, Corner stone, how.*——*His sonship includes more than being begotten.---All ideas of sonship imply inferiority, &c.*

SECT. III. p. 140. *Christ called son of man, why.*——*Common reasons defective.----Others so called, why.----Christ called* Son *of* GOD, *importance of.----The meaning---denotes excellency,---respects his offices---Put for Messiah.---Ten arguments to prove his sonship to be oeconomical.* (1) *From the various ideas of sonship, as derivation, subordination, dependence, submission, a distinct being, building his father's house, transmitting his name to posterity. The name of God represented by the life of Christ.* (2) *As son of man notes relation to man; his being called Son of God, points out his sublime relation to God.* (3) *From the meaning of Old Testament passages, where he is called Son.* Psa. ii. 7. *particularly considered---Not applied to Christ's resurrection in the New Testament.* (4) *From texts in the New Testament, that are exegetic of the term son of God.* (5) *From the same things being predicated of him under the name* Jesus Christ, *as under the title* Son of God.---*Head of the church, all things made and upheld by him, sent, born of the virgin, author of the gospel, his faith justifies sinners, his blood made peace, object of faith, fellowship with him, died, rose from the dead, was exalted, shall judge the world.---The Apostles expresly affirm that* Jesus Christ *is the* Son of God---*Not figurative expressions.* (6) *From the character he takes to himself when inditing the epistles to the seven* Asian *churches.* (7) *From his being called the image of the invisible God,---as he is man,---as* EMMANUEL,---*in his dominion as God's ambassador and representative.* (8) *From the necessity of believing in him, as the* Son of God.---*All religion practical,---no mysteries in things necessary,---oeconomical sonship clear.* (9) *There must be that in his sonship directly suitable to the sinful state of mankind.---Pure Deity has no relation to mankind.---All we know of God in Christ.----God out of Christ not scripture doctrine.* (10) *Sonship of Christ the ground of our adoption;---necessary sonship makes our's so,---destroys the sovereign love of God.---No analogy betwixt saints' sonship, and a necessary sonship in Christ.*——*Objection from the difference betwixt Christ as a* Son, *and a servant, answered. Called a servant, how.---Absolute Deity*

has

has no relation to creatures.---We should not too critically distinguish the names and titles of Chrift. *Objection from* Chrift *and* Son *being mentioned together, anfwered.* Chrift *and* Son *the fame object of worſhip.---Whether* Chrift *is a term of office.---When joined with* Son *of God, the meaning.---Relative character of* Chrift, *the ſum of religion.---Keys of the kingdom of heaven, what.---No ambaſſadors of* Chrift *now; nor ſucceſſors of the Apoſtles.*

SECT. IV. *p. 192. Of the title* WORD *as applied to* Chrift.---*Schoolmen's notions void of ideas:---In what ſenſe applied in ſeveral texts.---The meaning of the term* LOGOS,---*oeconomically uſed throughout the ſcriptures---By it the Jews meant the* Meſſiah.

SECT. V. *p. 205. The term* Holy Ghoft *oeconomical. ---Proofs for eternal proceſſion conſidered.---Proceſſion from the Son rejected.---Scripture meaning of the* Holy Ghoſt *and* Spirit *of* God---*Illuſtrated from the* appellations *given him.---Holy* Spirit, Spirit *of* God, *of truth, adoption, freedom, wiſdom, revelation, life in* Chrift, *judgment:---From his* Miſſion: *What it does not include---The import of---how oeconomical.* Works *of the* Spirit *oeconomical.* Works *relating to* Chrift *before and after his coming---*Bearing witneſs *to him, how.----The manner and time*---Glorifying *of him, how,---In the greatneſs of the gift, confirming the truth of his reſurrection, wiping off the ignominy of his life and death, proving all accuſations falſe, erecting a kingdom for him, and bringing ſubjects into it, conforming them to his image, ſhewing them the greatneſs of his merit, love, &c. enabling them to ſuffer for him, and perfecting them for glory. The goſpel, the favour of death unto death, and life unto life, how. Other parts of the* Spirit's *work briefly mentioned. Inferred that all his work is oeconomical---The great agent in the goſpel oeconomy.*

PART III.

INTROD. *p. 232. Inventions of men uſeleſs in religion--Their opinions made the ſtandard of the ſenſe of ſcripture.---Contrivers of ſyſtems not conſiſtent,---every conſequence not to be imputed to them.---The part to be examined.---An extract from a popular ſyſtematic---The ideas therein relate to heathen mythology.*

SECT. I. *p. 243. (1) Of the terms* Firſt, Second, *and* Third---*No foundation in ſcripture for.---The terms edifying in an oeconomical ſenſe.---The order of operation does not teach the order of ſubſiſtence---If ſo, the* Arians *right.---Bad effects*

of

of such doctrine. (2) *No such different internal distinctions as the scheme asserts.---Contrary to the sameness of perfection.---Communication implies mutability and derivation.---A derived Being a mere creature.---Most glaring absurdity in the scheme.---No prior or posterior, inferior or superior in Deity.---Presumption to determine more of God than is revealed.---The nature of God not a subject of definition.*

SECT. II. *p.* 253. *Common notion of* Christ's *sonship considered---Six arguments against.---*(1) *Term* GOD *generally includes the divine three.---Difficulty in the common scheme.---Arian doctrine in it.* (2) *Of one divine person, being from another.---Every effect posterior to its cause.---Every effect hath a beginning.---Filiation is an effect.----Self-existence, what.* (3) *Eternal generation no part of religion, because mysterious.---If truth, it requires express revelation.---*(4) *Son of God, and Messiah, of the same import.---Christ, nor his Apostles, never mention eternal generation,---no part of the counsel of God,---not profitable to christians.* (5) *Texts which mention* Christ *as a* Son, *and cannot mean his* Deity.---(6) *Every human scheme which favours error more than truth should be rejected.---Common orthodox scheme favours the* Arians,---*Terms inconsistent,---Begets prejudices in weak minds,----more than twenty self-contradictions in it.*

SECT. III. *p.* 273. *The general arguments in favour of the systematic doctrine of the Trinity, especially eternal generation, particularly answered.*

SECT. IV. *p.* 295. *Passages from both the Old and New Testament alledged in favour of the human scheme, and particularly eternal generation, fully considered ; and the whole shewed to be in favour of the oeconomical characters of* Father, Son, *and* Holy Ghost.

CONCLUSION.----*p.* 341. *Containing several general observations.*

ADDENDA.---*p.* 350. *Shewing, that the name* JEHOVAH *has a relation to the church, in several particulars.*

⁂ Not to swell the contents too much, many useful particulars are omitted in them, which the attentive reader will find in perusing the book. In the two last sections, many texts are explained and illustrated, which are only mentioned here in general.

INTRODUCTION.

THERE are but two ways by which we can attain to any knowledge of God. In the great volume of creation, or the works (including the providence) of God, he hath manifested himself in such a manner, as to leave every rational spectator inexcusable who shall doubt of his existence, or set up any creature before, or besides the creator as the object of their reverence and esteem. This the Apostle teaches the *Romans*, when he says, " The invisible things of Him (God) are clearly seen, being understood by the things that are made, even his eternal power and God-head (Deity); so that they are (that they may be) without excuse."

BUT, tho' by reasoning from the works of creation, we come to the knowledge of the existence of a first cause; yet, by this way, we can never come to have any direct or simple idea of God. The greatest length we can go, is, to remove from our notions of the creator, all the imperfections we find among creatures, and attribute to him, all their perfections or good qualities: And, that the Supreme Being we thus conceive of, may be as *spiritual* as may be, we particularly attribute to him the perfections of our *minds*; and after all, conclude that these are in him in the *abstract*, but not so in

A us.

us. This is only saying, the perfections in the Supreme Being are of a different *species* from our's, and so cannot admit of *comparison* in any degree. By all our reasoning, we cannot *positively* determine any thing concerning *spirit:* The notions we have thereof are all *negative*. We may call it an *immaterial substance*, something that is not matter; which is the same as to say, we know nothing about it. How adequate the conceptions of mankind might have been of God, from the contemplation of created objects if they had remained innocent, I shall not pretend to know: But it is evident beyond dispute, that the works of creation are utterly insufficient to direct mankind to that knowledge of God, which is necessary for them in their *fallen* or *sinful state*. Therefore, God, of his unbounded goodness, hath mercifully supplied the great defect, by giving mankind a *verbal revelation* of his character, every way suited to the state and weak capacities of sinful men.

This revelation of God is contained in the Old and New Testaments, which, taken together, is the *rule*, the *only rule*, to us in all things concerning faith and salvation. When we approach these *sacred oracles* for instruction, we should be stript of all prejudice and prepossession to received opinions from men, and be ready to receive what the *divine author* doth teach, upon his own authority only, which is sufficient testimony to the truth of every thing contained therein. And with respect to the *manner* of some things which may be mysterious, we ought humbly to keep within the verge of divine revelation, and not venture to sound the depths of divine mysteries, (that is, things *unrevealed*) by the short line of our finite understandings, which is infinitely too short to measure the height and depth of the

secret

secret things of the Most High. Here it is more becoming the christian to adore and admire, than curiously to search and enquire. It is no ways necessary in religion to know what God hath not been pleased to reveal.

ONE particular doctrine, the reality of which God hath been pleased to reveal, tho' the *manner* of it continues a secret, is, that he himself is ONE, and that he is THREE. The *truth* of this is indisputable, if we can credit *his* testimony who has revealed it to us: But if we reject his authority in this instance, we may with equal propriety refuse it in every other part of revelation, and so render it wholly useless to us as a rule of either faith or practice. If God hath told us that it is so, the obligation to believe it is binding upon us, tho' the *manner how it is* remains only proper for his own infinite mind to investigate.

BUT there is a very wide difference between what is revealed in scripture, and the nice speculations of the schools concerning the doctrine of the Trinity. The schoolmen, who abounded in wit and leisure, have been very speculative and acute in starting a great number of subtilties concerning it, which no christian is bound to trouble his head about; much less is it necessary for him to understand those niceties, which we may reasonably presume those who invented them, did themselves never thoroughly understand; and, least of all, is it necessary to believe them. The modesty of christians is contented in divine things, to know what *God* hath said concerning them, and has no curiosity to be *wise above what is written.* What God reveals is enough in these matters; but if any will venture to say more, every other man surely is at liberty to believe as he sees cause.

As our knowledge of God in this world is more properly conversant about what he is *not*, than what he is in himself; the utmost care should be taken in all our conceptions of God, to remove every thing that is not agreeable to what he hath made known of himself in his own word; which is all we can know of him with certainty, and of real use to us, on this side the full enjoyment of himself in glory.

Tho' there is much difficulty at present, to ascertain the full and true import of the several titles whereby the Great Creator of heaven and earth is designed, in any language; yet, this we may venture to say we are sure of, that they never were intended to give us a clear and full comprehension of the divine nature, or the precise *manner* in which the Supreme Being doth exist. This is what even the most glorious and extensive finite reason can never possibly comprehend to perfection. It must then follow as a necessary consequence, that the words in all languages by which it has been endeavoured to be explained, must be as defective as our comprehensions are.

Were it possible for us fully to comprehend all the properties which necessarily distinguish the Supreme Being from all beings, and to have adequate words to express our conceptions, it is likely dissentions on this head would be at an end. But as this, in the nature of things, is not to be expected; and as many, by attempting it in words of their own conceiving, have but darkened counsel with words without knowledge, the best way is, to confine ourselves to the holy scriptures, and say no more of God, than he hath been pleased to teach us. But as to the *manner* of his existence, I do not find from revelation that he hath taught us any thing at all.

When

When *Moses* asked him what was his name, he answered by a word I AM, or, I WILL BE; which does not convey any notion of the manner how he existed, (as has been often pretended); tho' it implies absolute existence, as well as irresistable power to accomplish what he had promised, or was pleased to do. But this does not in the least degree favour the empty speculations that have been framed concerning the nature and existence of God. His nature being infinite and incomprehensible, the mode of his existence must necessarily be above the investigation of every finite capacity. Here all analogy and comparison are utterly useless and trifling.

TWO things in general are intended in the following work.

First, *To draw out to the consideration of the enquiring christian, a brief connected view of what the scriptures say concerning the Trinity,* or the THREE *that are* ONE.

Secondly, *To shew how little regard is due from christians, to the subtle distinctions invented among men concerning that subject.*

THE first of these, for the reader's ease, and greater distinctness, I shall divide into two parts, and each of the parts into sections, as the matter treated of shall require.

PART FIRST.

IN this firſt part, I ſhall endeavour to ſhew plain ſcripture evidence for theſe three particular points:

Firſt, THAT there is but ONE GOD.

Secondly, THAT there is a PLURALITY in GOD, and that it is limited to THREE.

Thirdly, THAT EACH of the THREE hath aſcribed to him in ſcripture the NAMES and PERFECTIONS proper only to GOD. Or that the NAMES and PERFECTIONS proper only to DEITY are COMMON to THREE that ARE ONE.

SECT. I.

THE firſt thing undertaken is, *to prove that there is but one* GOD.

HERE I might tire the reader's patience, by a long train of arguments, commonly advanced to prove that there *can* be no more than *one God*: But
as

as I have engaged to keep to *scripture evidence*, and this being a point never questioned by any denomination of christians, let it suffice to name a few texts concerning the *unity* of God, and the perfections peculiar to him for proof of it. (*a*) " I am the LORD (JEHOVAH) and there is *none else*, there *is no* GOD *besides me*. (*b*) *Thou, even thou art* JEHOVAH *alone*. (*c*) That men may know, that thou *whose name alone is* JEHOVAH, art the *most high over all the earth*. (*d*) Know ye that the LORD he is GOD, it is he that made us. (*e*) Who shall not fear thee, O LORD, and glorify *thy name*, for thou *only* art holy. (*f*) And there are diversities of operations, but it is the *same* God, *who worketh all in all*. (*g*) The *same God over all*, is rich unto all that call upon him. (*h*) Hear, O *Israel*, the LORD our GOD is ONE LORD. (*i*) Now a mediator is not a mediator of one, but GOD *is one*. (*k*) We know that an idol is nothing in the world, and that there is *none other God but one*. To us there is but *one* GOD, the father, *of whom are all things*. (*l*) For thou art great, and dost wonderous works: *Thou art God alone*. (*m*) But the LORD is the *true* GOD, he is the *living God*, and an everlasting king. (*n*) For there is *one* GOD, and one mediator between *God* and *men*, the man *Christ Jesus*. (*o*) Thou believest that there is *one* GOD; thou dost well.

WHERE the perfections peculiar to *Deity* are mentioned in scripture, the *unity* thereof is either expressly taught, or necessarily understood; excluding in the plainest terms every idea of a *plurality of Gods*.

REVE-

(*a*) Isa. xlv. 5. (*b*) Neh. ix. 6. (*c*) Psa. lxxxiii. 18. (*d*) ibid c. 3. (*e*) Rev. xv. 4. (*f*) 1 Cor. xii. 6. (*g*) Rom. x. 12. (*h*) Deut. vi. 4. (*i*) Gal. iii. 20. (*k*) 1 Cor. viii. 4. 6. (*l*) Psa. lxxxvi. 10. (*m*) Jer. x. 10. (*n*) 1 Tim. ii. 5. (*o*) Ja. ii. 19.

(8)

REVELATION gives us a clear account of *one Being* who is ALMIGHTY and OMNIPOTENT.—(*p*) " *I am the almighty God*; walk before me, and be thou perfect. (*q*) *I am God almighty*; be thou fruitful and multiply. (*r*) And they rest not day and night, saying, holy, holy, holy, *Lord God almighty, which was, and is, and is to come.* (*s*) And I heard as it was the voice of a great multitude, saying, *alleluia*: for the *Lord God omnipotent reigneth.* (*t*) He doth according to *his will* in the army of heaven, and among the inhabitants of the earth: And none can stay his hand, or say unto him, what *dost thou?* (*u*) Whatsoever the *Lord pleased*, that did he in heaven and in earth, in the seas, and in all deep places. (*v*) *He* maketh all things, stretcheth forth the heavens *alone*, and spreadeth abroad the earth *by himself.* (*w*) Upholdeth all things by the word of *his power.* (*x*) *God* who quickeneth the dead, and calleth those things that be not as tho' they were."

———— INFINITE.—Which includes INCOMPREHENSIBLENESS, IMMENSITY, and OMNIPRESENCE. (*y*) " Canst thou by searching find out God? Canst thou find out the Almighty to perfection? High as heaven, what canst thou do? Deeper than hell, what canst thou know? (*z*) How little a portion is heard of him? The thunder of his power who can understand? * Behold God is great, and we know him not, neither can the number of his years be searched out. Heaven, and the heaven of heavens cannot contain *thee*,—(*a*) who hath measured the waters in the hollow of his hand, and meted out heaven with a span, and comprehended the dust
of

(*p*) Gen. xvii 1. (*q*) ibid. xxxv. 11. (*r*) Rev. iv. 8. (*s*) ibid. xix. 6. (*t*) Dan. iv. 35 (*u*) Psa. cxxxv. 6. (*v*) Isa. xliv. 24. (*w*) Heb. i. 3. (*x*) Rom. iv. 17. (*y*) Job xi. 7, 8. (*z*) ibid. xxvi. 14, and xxxvi. 26. * 1 Kings viii. 27. (*a*) Isa. xl. 12, 22.

of the earth in a meafure, and weighed the mountains in fcales, and the hills in a balance.—He fitteth upon the circle of the earth, and the inhabitants thereof are as grafshoppers ;——that ftretcheth out the heavens as a curtain, and fpreads them out as a tent to dwell in.—(*b*) Great is the Lord, and of great power: His underftanding is infinite,—greatly to be praifed; and his greatnefs is unfearchable. —(*c*) Am I a God at hand, faith the Lord, and not a God afar off? Can any hide himfelf in fecret places that I fhall not fee him? Do not I fill heaven and earth? faith the Lord.

——— ETERNAL.—*Without* BEGINNING, END, *or* SUCCESSION.—(*d*) "From everlafting to everlafting thou art God.—(*e*) Thou, O Lord, fhalt endure for ever, and thy years fhall have no end.—(*f*) One day is with the Lord as a thoufand years, and a thoufand years as one day."

——— UNCHANGEABLE.—(*g*) "I am the Lord, and change not.—(*h*) The father of lights, with whom is no variablenefs, neither fhadow of turning.——(*i*) The fame yefterday, to-day, and for ever."

THERE are many texts which point out the *one divine Being* to be ALL-SUFFICIENT, ABSOLUTELY GREAT, GOOD, and INDEPENDENT on any other being in his *perfections* and *operations*. He is the creator of heaven and earth, with all that they contain,—the preferver of all—by him all things confift—in him they live, move, and have their being—he opens his hand liberally, and fatisfies

B   the

(*b*) Pfa. cxlvii. 5, and cxlv. 3. (*c*) Jer. xxiii. 23, 24. (*d*) Pfa. xc. 2. (*e*) ibid. cii. 12, 27. (*f*) 2 Pet. iii. 8. (*g*) Mal. iii. 6. (*h*) Jam. i. 7. (*i*) Heb. xiii. 8.

the defire of every thing that lives—his kingdom ruleth over all—he is the governor among the nations—the one law-giver, who is able to fave and to deftroy—there is none good but one, *that is* GOD.

Now, as it is abundantly evident from thefe texts, (and reafon alfo teacheth us) that there is but *one firft caufe*, and *ultimate end* of all things—*one infinite, eternal, unchangeable Being*—*one almighty* and *omnipotent*, whom no being can oppofe or refift—*one*, who *created* and *uniformly governs* all things to *one* certain end—*one*, who poffeffes all thefe perfections which the fcriptures attribute to Deity. I fay, fince there *can* be but *one Being*, who is the author of all things, and the *ultimate end* of them, it muft follow, that there is but *one* divine Being, who is to be *worfhiped* as the *fupreme object of all religious adoration*—*one*, who is the *chief good* and *center* of happinefs—who is to be ferved and loved with all the *heart, foul,* and *ftrength*, and confequently but *one* God. Hence, every one who credits revelation, (with thofe who do not, I have no bufinefs at this time) may join with *David* in faying, (*k*) " O *Lord*, there is *none like thee*, neither is there *any God befide thee*, according to all that we have heard with our ears.

(*k*) 1 Chro. xvii. 20.

SECT. II.

THE next thing promised, was to shew that the scriptures teach us there is a DIVINE PLURALITY, and that it is limited to THREE.

INFINITE wisdom and divine prudence, appear conspicuously in the revelation of the scripture character of GOD. A divine plurality is copiously pointed out, and at the same time the divine unity every where strictly taught and maintained.

THIS would have appeared with brighter evidence, if the Translators of the Bible into *English* had given us the words JEHOVAH and ELOHIM where they occurred, without any translation: Or told the *English* reader, how he should know when the words LORD and GOD, which they have translated them by, had JEHOVAH and ELOHIM for their originals. But as they have given us these words, not only from JEHOVAH and ELOHIM, but from other original words of another meaning, the reader not only loses the peculiar beauties pointed forth in those words that LORD and GOD are taken from; but is bewildered in seeking the scope and meaning of many passages where they are promiscuously used: Whereas, if a distinction had been preserved in the translation, or the words expressed from the original, and the sense of them once pointed out in the *margin*, *contents*, or *otherwise*, the Old Testament would have appeared a more intelligible book to the enquiring *English* reader, or hearer, than it has often done.

ONE, among many instances which might be given,

given, is that text which should read, (*l*) " Hear, O Israel, Jehovah, our Elohim, is one Jehovah." Which is rendered, " Hear, O Israel, the Lord our God is one Lord."

It does not affect my present argument, how much difficulty the *English* reader of this text will be in, to know whether the word Lord here be taken from Jehovah, which is peculiar to Deity; or from Adoni, which implies *lordship, dominion,* or *government,* and is not peculiar to God alone; tho' by retaining the word Jehovah, as in several other texts, it would have been evident. What especially concerns my purpose, is the evidence of a *divine plurality* so plain in the face of the text, had it not been obscured, or rather quite lost, by using the word God, which is by no means a proper translation of the word Elohim.

Nor need I here stay to prove that Elohim is of a *plural* signification. This is acknowledged by the *Jews*, who best knew the meaning of their own language; and likewise by christians, who know the *Hebrew*, and are under no temptation to impose a false meaning upon it. Any thing that has been advanced to the contrary is so trifling, as to be unworthy of notice. Even the impartial *English* reader will readily see, that the very sense of the phrase necessarily leads him to seek for a *plural* interpretation: For if the word Elohim in the text be of a *singular* signification, then the word *God*, by which it is translated, will evidently point out the *unity* of the divine Being, and so would introduce an insipid repetition of the same thing. The text would convey no other idea, than that the *one divine*

divine Being, is the *one divine Being*. It muſt appear to be a low conceit of the conſummate wiſdom of God, to imagine that he would give us a revelation of ſo ſmall conſequence. For if the word ELOHIM is ſingular, the text is no more than a revelation that ONE is ONE. But as it is demonſtratively evident that ELOHIM is of a *plural* ſignification, it muſt follow, that the word GOD cannot convey a ſuitable idea of the ſenſe of this expreſſion uſed here by the divine ſpirit.

THE true ſenſe of this term, if attentively conſidered, is of great importance in the preſent argument of proving a *divine plurality*, which it puts beyond diſpute. It is alſo a key to open many paſſages of ſcripture, which, without the right underſtanding thereof, appear dark, and ready to be miſapplied.

BUT as there are ſeveral falſe ideas, which ſome may perhaps affix to the word ELOHIM as a plural, it will be therefore neceſſary to remove theſe, that the true ſenſe may appear with more evidence to be the *only one*, and of that conſequence it really is, for the right underſtanding the character of GOD given us in revelation.

1. As ELOHIM is a *plural*, it cannot be a general name to denote the *one divine Being*, ſuch as the word GOD is; nor can this be a proper tranſlation of it, for theſe two reaſons: *Firſt*, As ELOHIM is plural, it muſt of neceſſity convey the ſame idea to the *Hebrews*, that GODS do to *Engliſhmen*; which introduces a palpable contradiction into revelation, that the divine Being ſhould conſtantly teach therein, that there is only one GOD; and yet wherever he ſpeaks of himſelf, to call himſelf GODS.

It

It is a poor shift to alledge, that the author of revelation took up with the word which he found in use among men, to convey the idea which the word GOD doth to us. For, besides that it will be hard to say what that idea was, or how they came by it, previous to revelation: The plural termination would still so perplex the idea of *unity* he was inculcating, that had all the subtle *Doctors* and metaphysical divines, which have been since the Apostles days, existed at that time, their whole fund of definition could not have furnished a *salvo*.

BUT *secondly*, Another reason why the divine Being would not adopt a plural word to denominate himself by, is the remarkable proneness of these ages to *polytheism*. Would not boundless wisdom and goodness carefully avoid every word or phrase that favoured their corrupt bias? A bias which was so offensive to him, and which cost his people so dear, on account of their obstinacy in that very point: Or would he not only use the plural word, which carried such a snare in it, but have embarrassed the idea of unity still more, by constructing it with plurals, both verbs and nouns? May we not venture to determine it is impossible?

2. NOW, as ELOHIM cannot be a name that stands for the unity of the divine Being; neither can it be a word substituted to express the different characters of *Father*, *Son*, and *Holy Ghost*, in which the divine Being has manifested himself in revelation. These are so distinguished by the different lights in which omnipotence is displayed by each of them, that *one* common name is not sufficient to convey an adequate idea of these distinctions.—' They are designed to be kept always intelligibly distinct

distinct in the conceptions of mankind; whereas a *common name* can convey no separate views of their peculiar characters and operations.

3. NEITHER can the name ELOHIM import all, or any of the *perfections or attributes* common to each of the *three* who are *one*; for that would infer all that might be said of the impropriety of the word GODS. And sure nobody would chuse to say infinite WISDOMS, or infinite GOODNESSES, any more than they would say GODS. Whether we express attributes separately or complexly, it still runs us up (when we consider it with attention) to the same idea of a plurality of beings, possessed of these perfections: And strongly insinuates, that there are more than *one* to be worshiped and adored.

AND since none of these can be the signification of the word ELOHIM, there is only one we can possibly rest in, which is, that in its signification it refers to a TRANSACTION common to all the *three* who are *one*; and must be a common designation of all the THREE, as stated in that TRANSACTION. I say, a transaction (for it cannot allude to attribute or perfection) common to all the three, and which they themselves acted in with regard to one another. I say with regard to one another; because all their actions towards men, are applicable to one or other of the different relations they manifest themselves in to us.

AND this TRANSACTION, so plainly intimated in divine revelation, is the basis of the whole future manifestation of the divine glory discovered to, and applied for the benefit of man. And as the word ELOHIM intimates the *obligation* of that *transaction* among the divine three, so it always suggests the character.

racter of GOD in revelation to us in that view, as the moſt comfortable, and at the ſame time, awful light in which he can ſtate himſelf to mankind; and may with ſome propriety be expreſſed by the *Engliſh* word, the SWEARERS, † which, on the whole, makes an undeniable argument for a *divine plurality.*

THE ſtrength of this argument in favour of a *divine plurality*, will appear ſtill more conſpicuous, from the different forms of conſtruction in which the word ELOHIM is found in revelation. The manner of ſpeaking the ſeveral penmen have uſed, lead naturally into the notion of a *divine plurality*. This is moſt remarkable in *Moſes*; a great part of whoſe writings are evidently deſigned to guard againſt *polytheiſm*, or a *plurality of Gods*, which the

Jews

---

† The genius of the *Hebrew* language is ſuch, that ſignificant words are always framed from roots which have ſome certain and fixed idea, and thereby convey a determinate meaning. The root *Elah*, means an *oath* or *adjuration*, an execration made to affect the breaker of a covenant. And as the ſingular admits of this meaning, *one* that hath taken upon him an oath, the plural, *Elohim*, muſt denote more than one under that obligation, or entering into covenant or agreement together.

This idea may ſeem ſtrange at firſt view, but it will become more familiar, if we conſider that on many occaſions in ſacred writ JEHOVAH is ſaid to *ſwear*,—to *ſwear* by himſelf for conformation of future events, to create abſolute certainty, and reliance on his promiſe. And ſince JEHOVAH repreſents himſelf in this light, as binding himſelf by *oath* to the performance of his promiſes, it need not ſeem ſtrange, that he calls himſelf the *God bound by oath*, engaged by mutual obligation to fulfil his promiſes.

This plainly accounts for the ſcripture phraſeology of joining *relatives* to the term *Elohim*.—Why JEHOVAH deſcribes himſelf as the *Elohim* of *Abraham*, *Iſaac*, *Jacob*, &c. and why his people call him *my*, *thy*, *our*, *their* ELOHIM. And if JEHOVAH is pleaſed to repreſent himſelf under the obligation of a covenant, for the benefit of mankind; ſurely the addreſſing him under the term *Elohim*, denoting the notion of *Fœderatores*, muſt command their ſerious attention,—raiſe their moſt thankful ſentiments of his mercy and goodneſs,—ſtrengthen their confidence in his favour,—and at the ſame time, warn them of the great danger of tranſgreſſing his divine laws.

Jews were far too fond of: Yet his ſtile in manifold inſtances plainly conveys the idea of a *divine plurality*. The firſt appellation he gives to God, is plural, (*a*) "ELOHIM BARA," (GODS *created*); and in the ſhort hiſtory of the creation, repeats it about thirty times, beſides ſeveral hundred times more in his other writings.

IT need not be imagined, that it was for want of a *ſingular* name, that he was obliged to uſe this *plural*; he might have taken JEHOVAH, which has no *plural*, or ELOAH, the ſingular of ELOHIM, the laſt of which he uſes in ſome inſtances: But as he generally makes uſe of the plural ELOHIM, it certainly was to convey ſome idea of a *divine plurality*.†

AND tho' ELOHIM is in ſeveral texts joined with a ſingular verb, no doubt to guard againſt the notion of a plurality of GODS: Yet, it is many times in conſtruction with *verbs, adjectives*, and *participles, plural*. (*b*) " And it came to paſs, when the GODS (according to the ordinary tranſlation of ELOHIM) cauſed me to wander from my father's houſe.—(*c*) And he (*Jacob*) built there an altar, and called the place *El-Bethel*, becauſe there the GODS (ELOHIM)

(*a*) Gen. i. 1. (*b*) Gen. xx. 13. (*c*) ibid. xxxv. 7.

† Since ELOHIM has a ſingular, which is ſometimes uſed in ſcripture, it would be ſtrange in the ſacred writers, commonly to uſe the plural out of choice, and not of neceſſity, if there was not ſome particular inſtruction intended to be conveyed by it as a plural; and that a word more fit to miſlead than inform, ſhould be uſed by God in his written inſtructions to men.—ELOHIM is owned to be a plural by the *Jews*, who ſince their captivity in *Babylon*, have the idea of plurality in the greateſt contempt; and in their tranſlations make a very ridiculous diſtinction, by rendering the ſame ſpecific word in the ſingular, when they think it relates to the true God, and plural, when it relates to the idols which were the objects of the *Pagan* worſhip.

(ELOHIM) appeared to him. *(d)* What nation is there so great, that *have Gods* (ELOHIM) who *are* so near unto them? *(e)* What one nation in the earth is like thy people, even like *Israel*, whom the *Gods* (ELOHIM) sent to redeem for a people to himself? *(f)* For who is there of all flesh, that have heard the voice of the *living Gods* (ELOHIM) speaking out of the midst of the fire, and lived? *(g)* Ye have perverted the words of the *living Gods* (ELOHIM.) *(h)* But the Lord is the true GOD; he is the *living Gods* (ELOHIM.) *(i)* And *Joshua* said unto the people, ye cannot serve the LORD; for he is an holy God, (that is, the *holy* GODS (ELOHIM) is he.) *(k)* Verily there is a God that judgeth in the earth. *(Gods*, ELOHIM, that judge.) To these might be added, that expression so frequent in scripture, "The LORD thy GODS," (JEHOVAH ELOHEKA.)

T H E R E are several other *nouns* besides ELOHIM, that are to be understood of the being of GOD, which, being expressed in the plural, must imply a *divine plurality*.—*(l)* "I neither learned wisdom, nor have I the knowledge of the holy, *(holy ones.)* *(m)* Where is God my maker, *(makers.)* *(n)* If I be a master, (if I am *masters.)* *(o)* Remember now thy creator, *(creators.)* *(p)* Let *Israel* rejoice in him that made him, (in his *makers.)* *(q)* For thy maker is thy husband, the Lord of Hosts is his name." Here both *maker* and *husband* are plural.

T H E plural expressions used in revelation by God, when speaking of himself, do further prove

a *divine*

(d) Deut. iv. 7. *(e)* 2 Sam. vii. 23. *(f)* Deut. v. 26. *(g)* Jer. xxiii. 26. *(h)* ibid. x. 10. *(i)* Jos. xxiv. 19. *(k)* Psa. lviii. 11. *(l)* Pro. xxx. 3. *(m)* Job xxxv. 10. *(n)* Mal. i. 6. *(o)* Eccl. xii. 1. *(p)* Psa. cxlix. 2. *(q)* Isa. liv. 5.

a *divine plurality*.—(*r*) And *God* (ELOHIM) said, let *us* make man in OUR image, after OUR likeness. (*s*) And the LORD GOD said, (JEHOVAH ELOHIM said) behold the man is become like ONE OF US.† (*t*) And the Lord God said, let *us* go down and there confound their language. (*u*) I heard the voice of the Lord, saying, whom shall I send, and who will go for us? (*v*) Produce your cause, faith the Lord? let them bring forth, and shew us what shall happen,—let them shew the former things, that we may confider them, &c."

IF it is possible for language to convey the idea of *plurality*, these texts in the above pages certainly do it. And as they are all spoken of the *divine Being*, beyond contradiction, they prove a *divine plurality*. Such as deny it, will find it impossible upon any other plan, to reconcile the texts with common sense, or shew what other idea can be formed from the plural expressions used in them.

INDEED, against the evidence of a *divine plurality*, from the last cited texts, it has been objected, by such as are no friends to the doctrine, that it is only a *figurative* way of speaking, taken from the custom of kings in Eastern countries, who used to express themselves in the *plural*, to shew their dignity. THIS

(*r*) Gen. i. 26. (*s*) ibid. iii. 22. (*t*) ibid. xi. 6, 7. (*u*) Isa. vi. 8. (*v*) ibid. xli. 22, 23.

† The expression in this text is so distinct and unambiguous, as no force of figure or example can twist it to the *Jewish* construction. *One of us*, necessarily implies more than one. The enemies to a *divine plurality* are terribly put about for a meaning to this text. They say JEHOVAH is speaking to the *angels*, bringing them upon a level with himself. Although this did not imply an absurdity, which it does, there is no reason to imagine he does so here, since he no where else so in scripture does so, and the plural word ELOHIM immediately preceding, determines who the *us* were, and forbids the application of that pronoun to any other beings.

THIS objection is without foundation. For, can any one suppose that GOD would borrow his manner of speaking from a *king*, before *any man was upon earth!* But if this, however absurd, we should grant to be possible, yet the objection is not to the purpose. For tho' a king may say US and WE, common sense tells us, that there is not the least propriety in saying ONE OF US, when he speaks of himself; the phrase is destitute of meaning, if there is not more than *one* supposed. Therefore, this manner of expression, (*w*) "The LORD GOD said, behold the man is become as ONE OF US," must either be void of sense, or it must imply a *divine plurality*; the first, no christian will alledge, if the latter be true; then all the other texts, as they are in a stile similar to this, must be admitted as fair proofs of the same doctrine.

I might have illustrated this point, from a number of testimonies in revelation; but as the texts brought together in the next section, equally prove this point, with that which they are brought in vindication of, I shall only add here, a very few texts, to prove that this *divine plurality* (for ought we can learn to the contrary) in scripture, is limited to THREE.

(*x*) " HOLY, *holy, holy*, is the LORD *of hosts.*" (*y*) *John* applies this text to *Jesus Christ*, and (*z*) *Paul* applies it to the *Holy Ghost*; from which, if the passages are carefully considered and compared, it will appear, that the *divine plurality* is intended by the repetition of the word *Holy* in the text, as well as by the same repetition of it in the (*a*) revelation to St *John*; and its being repeated just

so

(*w*) Gen. iii. 22. (*x*) Isa. vi. 3. (*y*) John xii. 41. (*z*) Acts xxviii. 25. (*a*) Rev. iv. 8.

so often, and *no more*, in both places, seems to teach us, that the *plurality* implied in it is *limited to three*. (*b*) I will pray the FATHER, and he shall give you ANOTHER COMFORTER, that *He* may abide with you for ever: Even the SPIRIT OF TRUTH. (*c*) How much more shall the blood of CHRIST, who through the ETERNAL SPIRIT, offered himself without spot to GOD, purge your consciences from dead works, to serve the living God? (*d*) The LORD direct your hearts unto the love of GOD, and the patient waiting for CHRIST." The *Spirit* is called the *Lord* here, as well as by (*e*) *Ezekiel*. (*f*) " Go and teach all nations, baptising them in the name of the FATHER, the SON, and the HOLY GHOST. (*g*) There ARE THREE that bear record in heaven, the *Father*, the *Word*, and the *Holy Ghost*. (*h*) The grace of our *Lord Jesus Christ*, and the love of *God*, and the communion of the *Holy Ghost*, be with you all. *Amen*."

THIS point also, is not only manifest from the above texts, but from those cited in the beginning of the next section. I shall not therefore enlarge upon it here: But before I proceed, I hope the reader will allow me a little to reason the case, upon their own principles, with such as reject the doctrine I have been endeavouring to prove, because they cannot comprehend and describe the manner and reason of it.

THE greatest difficulty concerning the Trinity is, that we cannot account upon philosophic principles, how one simple infinite nature can act in three personal identities, with equal glory. But the

---

(*b*) John xiv. 16, 17. (*c*) Heb. ix. 14. (*d*) 2 Thesso. iii. 5. (*e*) Ezek. viii. 1, 3. (*f*) Matt. xxviii. 19. (*g*) 1 John v. 7. (*h*) 2 Cor. xiii. 14.

the ground of this difficulty lies, in reasoning from what we know of a nature that is finite and limited, to one that is infinite and incomprehensible, and beyond the reach of definition. The nature of men is the same, yet personal identity is various, according to the number of individuals; and if human nature was *infinitely simple,* we do not know but one nature, and one power, might act in all the individuals. It is not inconsistent with any rule of reason, that a nature which is infinite and simple, may act in a plurality of distinct identities without division. If it is infinitely simple, it cannot be divided, and if it is infinitely powerful, holy, just, and good, it is no absurdity to say, it may act in distinct persons, and be one according to the simplicity of nature. The word *nature,* when applied to God, must (according to the rules which revelation affords us to judge of that blessed Being) be understood in the most simple and absolute sense, removing from our thoughts, all the gross ideas which our acquaintance with corporeal things suggest to our minds. If we can by reason conceive, that there is an immaterial and infinite nature, it is no way unreasonable to suppose that nature capable to act quite beyond all the rules which we have learned from our observations of *limited* natures.

However, it must be unreasonable to reject the *divine testimony,* which affirms that God is *one,* and expresseth himself by a *plurality,* and in each claims the same honour, worship, and reverence, and assumes the same names and attributes; because we cannot account for the manner of such an union and distinction. We may conceive of the most difficult thing concerning the Trinity, as a *matter of revelation,* if it is affirmed therein, as well

as

as any other doctrine, *i. e.* we may conceive that God has informed us that it is true. But if by conceiving thereof be meant, that we shall know the manner and reasons how it is true, that is quite another thing, and natively tends to profanity; the same as to say, we will not credit the Almighty, 'till we be as wise as himself; and that it is necessary for us to be Gods, before we believe that there is one. We can just as little conceive of the manner how God exists at all, as we can conceive how he exists in a plurality, and if we will not believe his existence, 'till we know the manner of it, we must be *Atheists* for ever.

There are some who deny the doctrine of the Trinity, because they cannot understand it, who yet pretend to know several things as difficult to understand; as for instance, that a creature made the world, and himself also. If *Jesus Christ* made all things, which they dare not deny, since the Apostles have told us so often in so plain terms, and he himself be a creature as they affirm, then he is the maker of himself, which is as inconceivable as any point concerning the Trinity.

That the divine *three* are *one*, is demonstrable from scripture, in as much as the divine attributes and perfections are ascribed to the *three*, who, if possessed of divine perfections, must be possessed of the divine nature; for there is no separating the divine nature and perfections; and as the divine nature is but *one*, consequently they must be one God.

I do not pretend to prove from reason, that God is *three* and *one*, this would be foolish; for no man can prove *a priori*, that such a thing must be in God.

It

It muſt be proved from revelation, and if it is found there, every man that owns revelation is divine, is obliged to acquieſce in what God ſays of himſelf, unleſs he is ſo preſumptive as to pretend to know the infinite Being better than he does himſelf.

Nor do I pretend to tell *how*, and in what reſpects God is *three* and *one*. The beſt anſwer I ſuppoſe that could be given to this queſtion is, that God has not revealed it, and therefore no man can tell. Words have been uſed, and we are obliged to uſe them ſtill, to expreſs this matter, not ſo much for their propriety to the ſubject, as for want of better, and for the ſake of diſcourſe; as that there are three, commonly called *perſons*, in one *eſſence* or nature. But, we have no notion of *Perſon* or *Eſſence* as to God, and ſo no notion of either *Trinity* or *Unity* in this ſenſe. Notwithſtanding, we muſt not refuſe, on this or any other account, our aſſent to what God aſſures us is true, as to the reality of the thing itſelf, tho' not in the words which men have deviſed to expreſs it in. Should we do this, we might with equal propriety deny that God made the world, for we cannot tell *how* he created all things of nothing: Nor can we tell *how* God is immenſe without extenſion, or eternal without ſucceſſion, or growing older. *How* ſpirits work on bodies,—nor *how* our ſouls are united to our bodies? Yet to deny all theſe, and many other things which we know are real, tho' we cannot comprehend or deſcribe the manner or reaſon of them, were to commence ſceptics, or rather mad men. God may oblige us to believe the exiſtence of this or that thing, and give us no account *how*, or in what manner it does exiſt. If God tell us that *Jeſus Chriſt* is God and

man,

man, in a true and proper fenfe, we are to believe the reality of it as a truth, tho' he tells us not the manner, or wherein the unity confifts. We are not told that he is God and man, in the fame refpect, but that he is God and man, tho', in different refpects, which is no contradiction, and therefore *reafon itfelf muft be fatisfied*.

THERE are fome who pretend to found their fcheme of religion upon reafon, and maintain that nothing is to be admitted but what they can affign a reafon for: Or rather what agrees with the ideas they have formed for themfelves. The *humble* chriftian agrees with them as far as right reafon goes; but believes that there are things of which he neither has, nor can have adequate ideas: That fome things may be true, tho' he does not juftly know *how* or *why* they are fo; and for the truth of fuch things as do not depend upon reafon, or fall within his knowledge and inveftigation, he muft depend upon fuch evidence, as is fufficient to induce the belief of any matter of fact.

WHEN we confider how little we know of *matter*, which we fee, feel, and tafte, and on which fo many experiments have been tried by the wit of the greateft geniufes, which have been certainly believed for fome time, but denied and fucceeded by others: How little we know of the *mechanifm* of ourfelves, or the fyftem we are in: And how much lefs of the nature of our own fouls, or of any other fpirit, except the little we feel tranfacting in us. When we farther reflect, how infinitely above our comprehenfion the *Deity* muft be; can we view without aftonifhment, the prefumption of thofe

thofe men, who, by their knowledge, would define the nature and manner of exiftence of the incomprehenfible Deity,—peremptorily decide what God is, or what he is not, and make their definitions the teft and ftandard to others of divine things.

 H E N C E, the doctrine of the Trinity is rejected by many, becaufe of the difficulty of comprehending the *how* and *wherefore* in it, as commonly expreffed in the fyftems, which carry fome more than the appearance of contradiction in the terms, and make no fmall difficulty to conceive what is meant to be believed. But this apparent or real contradiction, is not owing to the revelation of that doctrine, from which the knowledge of it fhould be taken; but to the folly and vanity of church *Doctors*, who, puffed with too great an opinion of their own parts, would pretend to define what revelation does not; and coin terms not ufed in fcripture, to exprefs their imperfect conceptions. To thefe terms, and the application of them, the difficulty of believing the doctrine is chiefly owing. But on this, I fhall fay no more in this place, as I fhall have occafion more particularly to handle it afterwards.

SECT. III.

HAVING shewed from scripture evidence, that there is but ONE GOD—That there is a DIVINE PLURALITY;—and so far as we can understand the scope and meaning of many passages in revelation, the *plurality* so plainly taught, is *limited* to THREE. I now come to the next thing proposed for this *first* part, which was to shew, that to *each* of the *divine three*, is ascribed in revelation the NAMES and PERFECTIONS proper *only* TO GOD. Or, that the NAMES, PERFECTIONS, WORKS, AND WORSHIP, *proper only to Deity, are common to the* THREE who are ONE.

BUT as no professed christian calls in question the proper *Deity* of the *Father*, it would answer no valuable end, to spend time in using arguments to prove it. The proper *Deity* of the *Lord Jesus Christ*, and of the *Holy Ghost*, I shall endeavour to prove:

First, By a collection of scripture texts, in which the *names, attributes, perfections,* and *works*, that are proper only to *supreme Deity*, are ascribed to the *Lord Jesus Christ,* and to the *Holy Ghost.*

Secondly, By comparing one text with another, and deducing the necessary conclusions for the demonstration of that truth.

Thirdly, I shall prove the *proper Deity* of the *Lord Jesus Christ*, by some more general arguments, taken from the scope of some parts of scripture which have a relation to that subject.

FOR the *first* of these, I hope the reader will impartially consider the following texts.

THE *Supreme Being* is distinguished in revelation from all creatures, by the name JEHOVAH. (*a*) " Thou, whose *name alone* is JEHOVAH, art the *most high* over all the earth. (*b*) *Thou*, even *thou*, art LORD (JEHOVAH) *alone*."

THE *Lord Jesus Christ* is called JEHOVAH. (*c*) " This is the *name* whereby *He* shall be called, the LORD our righteousness." Rather as in the margin, JEHOVAH TSIDKENU.

THE *Holy Ghost* is called JEHOVAH. (*d*) " The LORD (JEHOVAH) took me, and the SPIRIT lift me up. (*e*) The SPIRIT of the LORD (the SPIRIT JEHOVAH) came upon *Sampson*,—the LORD (JEHOVAH) departed from him. (*f*) The SPIRIT of the LORD (the SPIRIT JEHOVAH) is upon me, for the LORD (JEHOVAH) hath anointed me, &c."

THE name LORD in an absolute sense in the New Testament, is proper only to *Deity*. (*g*) " The same LORD over all, is rich unto all that call upon him."

THIS is given to *Jesus Christ*. (*h*) " For unto you is born this day, in the city of *David*, a *Saviour*, who is *Christ* the LORD."

(*i*) " Now the LORD is that spirit.—We are changed

(*a*) Psa. lxxxiii. 18. (*b*) Neh. ix. 6. (*c*) Jer. xxiii. 6. (*d*) Ezek. viii. 1. 3. (*e*) Judg. xv. 14.—ibid. xvi. 20. (*f*) Isa. lxi. 1. (*g*) Romans x. 12. (*h*) Luke ii. 11. (*i*) 2 Corin. iii. 17, 18.

changed from glory to glory, as by the LORD, the spirit." *Margin.* ‡

—— To the *Spirit.* (*k*) " For who hath known the mind of the LORD ? (*l*) Who hath directed the SPIRIT ?"

THE name GOD, in a proper sense, belongs only

(*k*) Rom. xi. 3, 4. (*l*) Isa. xl. 13.

‡ Some readers will be surprised that I apply this text to *Jesus Christ*, which has been universally applied to the *Holy Ghost*, and reckoned by the orthodox on the Trinity, an incontestable proof of his Deity ; whereas, it is plain from the scope, that the *Holy Ghost* is not intended by the term *Spirit*, in any part of the chapter ; nor should it be understood personally, as is commonly supposed. From the 6th verse, the Apostle shews the excellency of the New Testament dispensation, which he calls the *Spirit* that giveth life, above the Mosaic dispensation, which he calls the *Letter* that killeth. To those who looked no further than the outside, or the external part of that dispensation, without regard to the *Spirit*, intent, and gospel signification thereof, it was *death*— " circumcision is that of the heart, in the *Spirit*, and not in the *Letter*." The law, without *Christ*, who is the end of it for righteousness to them that believe, is *death*, a killing *Letter* : But the *law* of the *spirit of life, in Christ Jesus*, makes free from the law of sin and death. The spirit of life—the spirit that quickeneth, is the truth concerning *Christ*, who is the substance of the whole Mosaic dispensation, which the Apostle calls *figures, shadows,* &c. But the substance is *Christ*, the last *Adam*, who is a quickening Spirit. After he had compared the *letter* with the *Spirit*, he tells the *Corinthians*, " Now the *Lord* is that *Spirit* : And where the *Spirit*, the *Lord* is, (there is no possessive in the text) there is liberty." And who the *Lord* is, he tells them immediately after, " We preach *Jesus Christ, the Lord*." He speaks of the Mosaic œconomy, as under a veil, which made it difficult to look to the *end* of that which is abolished : " But we (under the New Testament) all with open face, beholding as in a glass, the glory of the *Lord (Jesus Christ)* are changed into the same image, from glory to glory, by the *Lord, the Spirit.*" Tho' the ceremonial dispensation, established at *Sinai*, had much outward pomp, yet it had "*no glory,*" that is, very little in comparison of the "*glory that excelleth,*" in the new dispensation, wherein *Christ* in all his fullness is revealed in more clear, powerful, and extensive manner, as the *Spirit* of the old, and the *Lord* of the new dispensation, in the most proper and spiritual sense, therefore with the greatest propriety called, " the *Spirit, the Lord*, and the *Lord, the Spirit*."

only to Deity. (*m*) "Thou shalt have no other GODS before me. (*n*) Thus saith the Lord, *besides me* there is no GOD. (*o*) For there is *one* GOD, and there is *none other but he.* (*p*) There is none other GOD but *one*.—But to us there is but *one* GOD."

THIS name is often given to *Jesus Christ*. (*q*) " And *Thomas* answered and said unto HIM *(Jesus) my Lord, and my* GOD. And the *Word* was GOD. (*r*) GOD was manifest in the *flesh.* (*s*) But unto the *Son,* he saith, thy throne, O GOD, is for ever and ever. (*t*) For unto us a *Child* is *born,* unto us a *Son* is given, and the government shall be upon *His* shoulders: And his name shall be called, wonderful counsellor, the MIGHTY GOD. (*u*) Whose are the fathers, and of whom as concerning the flesh CHRIST came, *who* is *over all,* GOD, *blessed for ever.* Amen. * (*v*) And we are in him that is true, even in his Son, *Jesus Christ. This* is the *true God,* and

(*m*) Exo. xx. 3. (*n*) Isa. xliv. 6. (*o*) Mark xii. 23. (*p*) 1 Cor. viii. 4, 6. (*q*) John xx. 28. ibid. i. 1. (*r*) 1 Tim. iii. 16. (*s*) Heb. i. 8. ((*t*) Isa. ix. 6. (*u*) Rom. ix. 5. (*v*) 1 John v. 20.

* This is so plain a proof of the proper Deity of our *Lord Jesus Christ,* that one must be surprised, how any can impose so much upon reason and common sense as to deny it, by saying, that it is not *Jesus Christ* that is here intended, but God the Father, mentioned (as they say) in the foregoing verse; whereas nothing is said of the Father, from the beginning of the chapter; nor the word God so much as mentioned. Indeed, the translators have supplied the word God in the context, but it is of no manner of use, which any one may plainly see at first reading the passage. The Apostle is pointing out the great privileges of his countrymen, to whom, says he, pertained the adoption—the glory—the covenants—giving of the law—the service—the promises.—And then adds, as the most distinguishing privilege,—" *of whom as concerning the flesh* CHRIST *came,* WHO *is over all,* GOD, *blessed for ever. Amen.* It is not common sense to say, the relative *who* refers to any but Christ mentioned immediately before; for there is not another, that with the least propriety, it can refer to.

and *eternal life*. (*w*) For this is good and acceptable in the fight of GOD our SAVIOUR. (*x*) According to the commandment of GOD our SAVIOUR. (*y*) That they may adorn the doctrine of GOD *our* SAVIOUR in all things. (*z*) After that the kindness and love of GOD *our* SAVIOUR appeared. (*a*) Looking for that bleſſed hope, and the glorious appearing of the GREAT GOD and (*even*) our LORD JESUS CHRIST. (*b*) *Paul*, an Apoſtle of *Jeſus Chriſt*, by the commandment of GOD our *Saviour*, and (*even*) the LORD JESUS CHRIST our hope. (*c*) *Simon Peter*, a ſervant, and an Apoſtle of *Jeſus Chriſt*, to them that have obtained like precious faith with us, through the righteouſneſs of GOD, and (*even*) our *Saviour* JESUS CHRIST. (*d*) And denying the ONLY TRUE GOD, and (*even*) our Lord Jeſus Chriſt." †

(*w*) 1 Tim. ii. 3. (*x*) Tit. i. 3. (*y*) ibid. ii. 10. (*z*) ibid. iii. 4. (*a*) ibid. ii. 13. (*b*) 1 Tim, i. 1. (*c*) 2 Pet. i. 1. (*d*) Jude 4.

† In the four laſt cited texts, as well as in ſeveral others, where our tranſlators have given us the *copulative* AND, it could be wiſhed they had uſed another word inſtead thereof, both nearer the original, and more favourable to the *Deity* of our *Lord Jeſus Chriſt*. In the texts which I have cited, before theſe four, the Apoſtles apply the title GOD to our Lord Jeſus, the *Saviour*, without any copulative to diſtinguiſh them, ſo that none can doubt it is *Jeſus Chriſt* they mean. And even in theſe texts, where the terms *God* and *Jeſus Chriſt* are ſo diſtinguiſhed as in our tranſlation, there is enough to convince any one that ſhall conſider the texts impartially, that it is the ſame divine perſon who is meant.

It is not the *Father*, but *Jeſus Chriſt*, who the ſcriptures ſay ſhall make the *glorious appearance* at the laſt day. The word tranſlated, *appearing* in the firſt of the four texts, is other five times uſed in the New Teſtament, and always applied to *Jeſus Chriſt*: Whereas the *Father* is always conſidered as inviſible. Beſides, *Chriſt* is emphatically called the *hope* of his ſaints; which two words being joined together in the text, limits the term *Great God* to *Jeſus Chriſt*, whoſe appearing the ſaints hope and long for,— and who (ſays the Apoſtle in the very next verſe) " Gave himſelf for us, that he might redeem us from all iniquity." This puts it beyond diſpute, that *Jeſus Chriſt* is called the *Great God*, and not the *Father*, as is commonly ſuppoſed, and which inattentive readers may eaſily be led to think, from the word *and* being put betwixt

THE Holy Ghost is also called GOD. (e) " But *Peter* said, *Ananias*, why hath *Satan* filled thine heart to lie to the HOLY GHOST ? Thou haft not lied

(e) Acts v. 4, 3.

twixt *Great God* and *Jesus Christ*, which would point out *two*, whereas there is but *one* intended in the text.

The same Greek word Καὶ, which is here rendered *and*, is in many other places, by the same translators, rendered *even*. Rom. viii. 23. " And not only they, but ourselves also, which have the first fruits of the Spirit, EVEN we ourselves, &c. 1 Cor. xv. 24. He shall have delivered up the kingdom to God, EVEN the Father. 2 Cor. i. 3. Blessed be God, EVEN the Father, &c. 2 Cor. x. 12. Which God hath distributed to us, a measure to reach EVEN to you." Had Καὶ been rendered *and* in these and other texts, it would have made them wholly unintelligible; and there is no reason why it should be so here, if it is not to favour an argument against the Deity of *Jesus Christ*, in the hands of such as are no friends to that doctrine.

BY considering the other three texts, we will see equal reason to conclude, that *God* and *Jesus Christ* ought not to be distinguished as they are. At *whose commandment* did *Paul* become an Apostle ? Through *whose righteousness* do we obtain salvation ? And *who* does *Jude* say the scoffers of his time denied ? Not that there was a *God*,—which must be the sense, if the copulative be admitted; but they denied the truths taught by the Apostles, concerning the character and kingdom of *Jesus Christ*. Now, since the things predicated in the texts, are constantly applied to *Jesus Christ* in other scriptures, what reason can be assigned, why the Apostles should apply them to any *other*, in these texts under consideration.

Besides, admitting the copulative *and* in these and other texts conveys a very strange idea of what is predicated of the *Great God* and *Jesus Christ*, as if there were *one* appearing of the *Great God*, another of *Jesus Christ*,—*One* commandment of the *Great God* to make *Paul* an Apostle, another of *Jesus Christ*.— *One* righteousness of *God*, another of *Jesus Christ*, and so of all the texts where it is found. Whereas the appearing, commandment, righteousness, denying, &c. mentioned in the texts, is but *one* appearing, &c. therefore it must be one and the same subject or person they are predicated of.

Such considerations kept in view, in reading many passages of the New Testament, would make the scope and meaning of them abundantly more clear; and set the proper Deity of *Jesus Christ* in the plainest point of view that language can possibly express it : But otherwise, the texts are either pressed as arguments against the Deity of *Christ*, or at least, subject to the criticisms of such as are no friends to it.

lied unto *men*, but unto GOD. ‡ (*f*) All scripture is given by inspiration of GOD. (*g*) But holy men of *God* spake as they were moved by the HOLY GHOST. (*h*) Know ye not, that ye are the temple of GOD, and that the SPIRIT of *God* dwelleth in you? If any man defile the temple of GOD, him shall *God* destroy; for the temple of GOD is holy, which temple ye are. (*i*) Know ye not, that your body is the temple of the HOLY GHOST?"

CREATION WORK is proper only to GOD. (*k*) "The LORD he is GOD, it is he that made us. (*l*) Thou, even thou, art LORD *alone*, thou hast made heaven, the heaven of heavens, with all their host, the earth, and all things that are therein, the seas, and all that is therein. (*m*) *He that built all things is* GOD."

BUT CREATION WORK is ascribed to JESUS CHRIST. (*n*) "All things were made by him (the Word); and without *him* was not *any thing made* that was made. (*o*) By *him* (JESUS CHRIST) were all things *created* that are in heaven, and that are in earth, visible and invisible, whether they be thrones or dominions, or principalities, or powers: All things

E were

(*f*) 2 Tim. iii. 16. (*g*) 2 Pet. i. 21. (*h*) 1 Cor. iii. 16, 17. (*i*) ibid. vi. 19. (*k*) Psa. c. 3. (*l*) Neh. ix. 6. (*m*) Heb. iii. 4. (*n*) John i. 3. (*o*) Col. i. 16, 17.

‡ The antithesis is here betwixt *man* and *God*;—and *Ananias* lied unto *God*, because he had lied unto the *Holy Ghost*; who, by the plainest inference, (if the Apostle spoke good sense) is there‑ fore *God*. Had it not been thus, the Apostle would have said, "Thou hast not lied unto the *Holy Ghost*, or, to the *Holy Ghost* only, but unto *God*." If the Holy Ghost is *not* God, the Apostle is certainly culpable for writing so uncautiously; for any man of common sense, whose mind is not prejudiced, and reads only to know the truth, must necessarily conclude from this and other texts, that the Holy Ghost is *God*. To interpret them otherwise, needs a great deal of criticism and learned pains, and after all, the in‑ terpretations appear to the unprejudiced very unnatural and forced.

were *created by him and for him. And he* is before all things, and by *him* all things *confift*."

———— A N D to the *Spirit*.—(*p*) "The SPIRIT of GOD (* the SPIRIT GOD) hath *made me*, and the breath of the Almighty hath *given me life*."

T H E *Author of divine revelation, is* GOD. (*q*) "GOD fhall *reveal* even this unto you. (*r*) GOD,— who *fpake* in time paft unto the fathers, by the prophets. (*s*) *Thus faith* the LORD of Hofts."

B U T this is attributed to *Jefus Chrift*.—(*t*) "For I neither received it of men, neither was I taught it, but by the *revelation* of JESUS CHRIST. (*u*) Since ye feek a proof of CHRIST *fpeaking* in me, which to you ward is not weak, but is mighty in you. (*v*) *Thefe things faith the* SON OF GOD."

———— A N D to the *Holy Ghoft*.—(*w*) "It was *revealed* unto him by the HOLY GHOST. (*x*) It is not ye that *fpeak*, but the HOLY GHOST. (*y*) *Thus faith the* HOLY GHOST."

T H E *divine law* hath its *authority from* GOD. They who break it *tempt* GOD.—(*z*) "So then with the mind, I myfelf ferve the *law of* GOD. (*) There is *one law-giver*, who is able to fave, and to deftroy. (*a*) Ye fhall not tempt the *Lord* your *God*."   THE

(*p*) Job xxxii. 4. (*q*) Phil. iii. 15. (*r*) Heb. i. 1. (*s*) Ifa. i. 24. (*t*) Gal. i 12. (*u*) 2 Cor. xiii. 3. (*v*) Rev. ii. 18. (*w*) Luke ii. 26. (*x*) Mark xiii. 3. (*y*) Acts xxi. 11. (*z*) Rom. vii. 25. (*) Sam. iv. 12. (*a*) Deut. vi. 16.

* In this text, as well as feveral others, (which we will have occafion to notice afterwards) there is no poffeffive pronoun to denote a relation to any other; which makes it a clear proof that the *fpirit is God* ; and that creation work is properly afcribed to him.

THE same is said of *Christ.*—(*b*) " Bear ye one another's burthens, and so fulfil the *law of Christ.* (*c*) Neither let us *tempt Christ,* as some of them also tempted, and were destroyed of serpents."

—————— OF the *Spirit.*—(*d*) The *law* of the *spirit of life* in *Christ Jesus,* hath made me free from the law of sin and death. (*e*) How is it that ye have agreed together, to *tempt* the *spirit of God?*"

ETERNITY is a perfection proper. *only* to *God.*— (*f*) " Even from everlasting to everlasting, thou art God. (*g*) The *eternal God* is thy refuge, and underneath are the everlasting arms."

—————— Attributed to *Jesus Christ.*—(*h*) " Unto us a child is born, unto us a son is given,—and his *name* shall be called—the *everlasting Father,* (the *father of eternity.*) (*i*) I (the redeemer) am the *first,* and I am the *last.* (*k*) I am *Alpha* and *Omega,* the *beginning* and the *ending.* (*l*) *Jesus Christ,* the *same* *yesterday,* and *to-day,* and *for ever.*"

—————— To the *Spirit.*—(*m*) " How much more shall the blood of *Christ,* who through the *eternal Spirit* offered himself without spot unto *God.*"

IMMENSITY is another perfection proper only to *Deity.*—(*n*) " Can any hide himself in secret places, that I shall not see him? saith the *Lord:* Do not I fill heaven and earth? saith the *Lord.*"

THIS

(*b*) Gal. vi. 2. (*c*) 1 Cor. x. 9. (*d*) Rom. viii. 2. (*e*) Acts v. 9. (*f*) Psa. xc. 2. (*g*) Deut. xxxiii. 27. (*h*) Isa. ix. 6. (*i*) ibid. xliv. 6. (*k*) Rev. 1. 8, and 21, 13. (*l*) Heb. xiii. 8. (*m*) ibid. ix. 14. (*n*) Jer. xxiii. 24.

This is also attributed to *Jesus Christ*, who is —(*o*) " head over all things to the church, which is his body, the fullness of him (*Christ*) that *filleth all in all.*"

———— To the *Spirit.*—(*p*) " Whither shall I go from thy *Spirit*? Or whither shall I fly from thy presence? If I ascend up into heaven, *thou* art there: If I make my bed in hell, behold, *thou* art there, &c."

He that is *present* with all the saints, and *dwelleth in them*, is *God*. (*q*) " Ye are the temple of the *living God*; as *God* hath said, I will *dwell in them*. (*r*) *God* is *in you* of a truth."

But *Jesus Christ dwelleth in them*.—(*s*) " Know ye not your ownselves, how that *Jesus Christ is in you*, except ye be reprobates? (*t*) That *Christ* may dwell in your hearts by faith."

———— To the *Spirit.*—(*u*) " Even the *Spirit of truth*, he *dwelleth* with you, and shall be *in you*. (*v*) But if the *spirit* of him that raised up *Jesus* from the dead, *dwell in you*: He that raised up *Christ* from the dead, shall also quicken your mortal bodies, by his *spirit* that *dwelleth in you.*"

———— God *only is holy*.—(*w*) " Who shall not fear thee, O *Lord*, and glorify thy name? for *thou only art holy.*

———— This perfection is ascribed to *Jesus Christ*.

(*o*) Eph. i. 22, 23. (*p*) Psa. cxxxix. 7, 8. (*q*) 2 Cor. vi. 16. (*r*) 1 Cor. xiv. 15. (*s*) 2 Cor. xiii. 5. (*t*) Eph. iii. 17. (*u*) John xiv. 17. (*v*) Rom. viii. 11. (*w*) Rev. xv. 4.

Chriſt.—(*x*) " But ye denied the *holy one*, and the juſt. (*y*) Theſe things, ſaith *he* that is *holy*, he that is true." Even *Jeſus Chriſt* who indited the epiſtles to the ſeven churches.

———— And to the *Holy Ghoſt.*—(*z*) " But ye have an unction from the *holy one*, and ye know all things."

God only is the *fountain of life.*—(*a*) " That thou may'ſt love the *Lord* thy *God*—for he is thy *life.* (*b*) The Father raiſeth up the dead, and quickeneth them."

This is attributed to *Jeſus Chriſt.*—(*c*) " When *Chriſt* who is our *life,* ſhall appear, then ſhall ye alſo appear with him in glory. (*d*) Even ſo, the *Son quickeneth* whom *he will.* (*e*) But ye denied the holy one, and the juſt,—and killed the *prince* (margin, *author*) *of life.*"

———— And to the *Spirit.*—(*f*) " The body is dead, becauſe of ſin ; but the *ſpirit is life,* becauſe of righteouſneſs. But if the *Spirit* of him that raiſed up *Jeſus* from the dead, dwell in you ; he that raiſed up *Chriſt* from the dead, ſhall alſo *quicken* your mortal bodies, by his *ſpirit* that dwelleth in you. (*g*) It is the *Spirit* that *quickeneth.*" †

God only is poſſeſſed of abſolute unlimited
power.

(*x*) Acts iii. 14. (*y*) Rev. iii. 7. (*z*) 1 John ii. 20. (*a*) Deut. xxx. 20. (*b*) John v. 21. (*c*) Col. iii. 4 (*d*) John v. 21. (*e*) Acts ii. 14, 15. (*f*) Rom. viii. 10, 11. (*g*) John vi. 63.

† If by the term *Spirit,* in any of theſe texts, be meant the *truth* rather than the *Holy Ghoſt,* (ſee Note, p. 29) this will by no means weaken the evidence in favour of his divinity, ſo manifeſt in many other texts, where he is clearly meant.

power. He only can *raife the dead*.—(*h*) " Power belongeth to *God*. (*i*) Thou haft made the heavens and the earth by thy *great power*; and there is nothing too hard for thee. (*k*) *God* hath both *raifed up* the *Lord*, and will alfo *raife us up* by his *own power*."

———— Attributed to *Jefus Chrift*.—(*l*) " Moft gladly therefore will I rather glory in my infirmities, that the *power* of *Chrift* may reft upon me. (*m*) Deftroy this temple, and in three days *I will raife it up*. But he fpake of the temple of his body."

———— To the *Spirit*.— (*n*) " To make the *Gentiles* obedient by word and deed, through *mighty figns* and *wonders*, by the *power* of the *Spirit* of *God*. (*o*) *Chrift* being put to death in the fleih, but *quickened by the Spirit*."

ALL *fpiritual* and *divine operations* muft be *from God*.—(*p*) " There are diverfities of operations, but it is the *fame God*, that *worketh all in all*."

THE Apoftle faith,—(*q*) " But *Chrift is all in all*." And adds, (*r*) " But all thefe worketh that *one* and *felf-fame Spirit*, dividing to every man feverally as *he will*."

FROM thefe, and many others, that might have been collected, it is plain from *fcripture teftimony alone*, that the fame *attributes, perfections, and works*, which are proper *only to Deity*, are afcribed to the
Lord

(*h*) Pfa. lxii. 11. (*i*) Jer. xxxii. 17. (*k*) 1 Cor. vi. 14. (*l*) 2 Cor. xii. 9. (*m*) John ii. 19, 21. (*n*) Rom. xv. 18, 19. (*o*) 1 Pet. iii. 18. (*p*) 1 Cor. xii. 6. (*q*) Col. iii. 11. (*r*) 1 Cor. xii. 11.

Lord Jesus Christ and the *Holy Ghost*. And as the evidence is in scripture language, (without comment) and so not liable to the weakness or misapplication that often attends evidence, which depends upon human consequences, drawn from scripture by men; I do not imagine, how it is possible to avoid the force of so necessary a conclusion from them, as, that *Jesus Christ*, and the *Holy Ghost*, are *truly* and *necessarily God*.

IT may be observed here, as I hinted above, that these texts thus collected, do not only prove the proper Deity of the *Lord Jesus*, and the *Holy Ghost*, but also clearly point out the truth of a *divine plurality*, and not obscurely that it is limited to *three*. And as the scriptures so copiously ascribe divine *names*, *perfections*, and *works* to a *plurality*, and yet peremptorily, and in the clearest terms assert, that there is but *one God*, that is one divine Being, possessed of these *names* and *perfections*, and no where give the least hint concerning the *manner* of this plurality and *unity*, or how the divine *three* are *one*: It becomes all christians to check the first emotions of curious inquiry into what is not revealed concerning this subject. That these *three* are *one* we know, because revealed, but *how*, we know not.

SECT.

SECT. IV.

BUT as it was propofed in the beginning of the laſt ſection, to prove the *Deity* of our *Lord Jeſus Chriſt*, and the *Holy Ghoſt*, by comparing one text with another, and deducing the neceſſary concluſions, I ſhall make that the ſubject of this ſection; and *firſt* begin with theſe arguments of this kind, which prove the *proper Deity* of the *Lord Jeſus Chriſt*.

ISAIAH ſaith,—(*s*) "Mine eyes have ſeen the *King*, the LORD OF HOSTS." *John* ſays, this was CHRIST whom *Iſaiah* here ſpeaks of.—(*t*) "Theſe things, ſaid *Eſaias*, when he ſaw HIS *glory*, and ſpake of HIM." Therefore JESUS CHRIST is the LORD OF HOSTS.

(*u*) "THUS ſaith the LORD (JEHOVAH) the *king of Iſrael*, and his redeemer (GOAL) the LORD OF HOSTS, I am the *firſt*, and I am the *laſt*, and beſide me there is no GOD." He who is the *redeemer* (GOAL) the *firſt* and the *laſt*, is JEHOVAH, the LORD OF HOSTS, beſide whom there is no GOD: But JESUS CHRIST is the *redeemer*,—(*v*) "In whom we have *redemption* through his blood." And the titles *firſt* and *laſt* he takes to himſelf:— (*w*) "I am *Alpha* and *Omega*, the *beginning* and the *end*, the *firſt* and the *laſt*." Therefore he is JEHOVAH, the LORD OF HOSTS, and *beſide him* there is no GOD.

(*x*) "I am JEHOVAH, and beſide me there is no Saviour." But *Jeſus Chriſt* is the *Saviour*.—(*y*)
"Grow

(*s*) Iſa. vi. 5. (*t*) John xii. 41. (*u*) Iſa. xliv. 6. (*v*) Eph. i. 7. (*w*) Rev. xxii. 13. (*x*) Iſa. xliii. 11. (*y*) 2 Pet. iii. 18.

"Grow in grace, and in the knowledge of our Lord and Saviour *Jesus Christ*." Therefore *Jesus Christ* is JEHOVAH.

(*z*) "SANCTIFY the LORD OF HOSTS *himself*, and let *him* be your *fear* and *your dread*. He shall be for a *sanctuary*, and for *a stone of stumbling*, and for a *rock* of *offence* to both the houses of *Israel*." He who was to be a stumbling stone, and a rock of offence, *Isaiah* calls the LORD OF HOSTS, and bids the children of *Israel sanctify* (*honour, worship, and magnify*) *him*, and make *him* their *fear* and *dread*. *Fear* is here put for the *object* of fear, which is GOD; but the Apostles *Paul* and *Peter*, apply this expresly to CHRIST. (*a*) "They stumbled at the *stumbling stone*; as it is written, behold, I lay in *Zion*, a *stumbling stone*, and *rock of offence*; and whosoever believeth in *him* (*Christ*) shall not be ashamed." (*b*) "Unto you therefore who believe *he* (*Jesus Christ*) is precious; (an *honour*, as in the margin) but unto them who are disobedient, the *stone* which the builders disallowed, the same is made the head of the corner, and a *stone of stumbling*, and a *rock of offence* to them who stumble at the word." Therefore JESUS CHRIST is the LORD OF HOSTS— is to be *sanctified*, (*worshipped* and *magnified*) and is the *true object* of *religious fear* and *reverence*.

THAT glorious and magnificent description in the ninety-seventh Psalm, is of one, who in several parts of it is called (*c*) JEHOVAH,—and *worship* commanded to be given to *him*. (*d*) "Worship him all ye Gods." But the Apostle (*e*) says, it was the SON OF GOD who is spoken of in that

F sacred

(*z*) Isa. viii. 13, 14. (*a*) Rom. ix. 32, 33. (*b*) 1 Pet. ii. 7, 8.
(*c*) ver. 1, 5, 8, 9, 10, 12. (*d*) ver. 7. (*e*) Heb. i. 6.

sacred hymn: Therefore *he* is JEHOVAH, *to whom divine worship* is due, and *of whom* the glorious things in that Pfalm are faid, proper to none but the *true God*.

ANOTHER majeftic defcription we have in the hundred and fecond Pfalm, where feveral divine afcriptions are given to JEHOVAH, which cannot with any propriety be applied to *any other*,—as *divine worship—eternity—infinite power*—and *unchangeableness*. *(f)* " But thou, LORD, (JEHOVAH) fhalt *endure for ever*, and thy remembrance unto *all generations*. The heathen fhall *fear* the *name* of the LORD, (JEHOVAH) and all the kings of the earth *thy glory*. Of old haft *thou* laid the foundations of the earth: And the heavens are the work of *thy hands*. They fhall perifh, but *thou fhalt endure*: Yea, all of them fhall wax old like a garment; as a vefture fhalt *thou* change them, and they fhall be changed. But *thou art the fame*, and *thy years fhall have no end*." But the Apoftle giving the character of CHRIST to the *Hebrews* (*g*) tranfcribes thefe verfes, and applies the contents of them to *him*: Therefore, after the Apoftle, we may fafely conclude, that the *name* JEHOVAH, with all the *perfections* attributed to *him* in that Pfalm, are properly applicable to our LORD JESUS CHRIST.

(*h*) " The LORD (JEHOVAH) is my *fhepherd*." The Pfalmift fays, his *fhepherd* is JEHOVAH: But JESUS CHRIST affirms of himfelf, that *he* is the *fhepherd*;—(*i*) " I am the good *fhepherd*: The good *fhepherd* giveth his *life* for the fheep." Therefore JESUS CHRIST is JEHOVAH. Here it may be proper

---

(f) ver. 12, 15, 25, 26, 27. (*g*) Heb. i. 10, 11, 12. (*h*) Pfa. xxiii. 1. (*i*) John x. 11.

proper to add, that *Chrift* calls the church his (*k*) *fheep*, and *Peter* calls them the (*l*) *flock of God*: Therefore *Chrift is God*.

(*m*) " THY *maker* is thy *hufband*, (the LORD OF HOSTS is his *name* :) and thy *redeemer* the *holy one of Ifrael*, the GOD of the *whole earth fhall he be called.*" The *hufband* or *bridegroom* of the church, and her *redeemer* is here called the LORD OF HOSTS, and the GOD (*Elohim*, or *Judge*) of the whole earth : But JESUS CHRIST is *hufband* or *bridegroom*, and *redeemer* of the church;—(*n*) " The *hufband* is the head of the wife, *even as Chrift* is the head of the church. (*o*) Let us be glad and rejoice, and give honour to him : For the *marriage* of the *Lamb* is come, and *his wife* hath made herfelf ready. (*p*) Come hither, and I will fhew thee the *bride*, *the Lamb's wife*. (*q*) *Chrift* hath redeemed us from the curfe of the law,—(*r*) in whom we have *redemption* through *his blood*. (*s*) Ye were not redeemed with corruptable things, as filver and gold, but with the precious blood of *Chrift*." Therefore JESUS CHRIST is the LORD OF HOSTS, the GOD *of the whole earth*.

(*t*) " THE LORD GOD of the *holy Prophets fent his Angel*, to fhew unto his fervants the things which muft shortly be done." The *Angel* mentioned here, is the *Angel* of the LORD GOD : But he is the *Angel* of JESUS CHRIST, and *fent by him*. (*u*) " I JESUS, have *fent mine Angel* to teftify unto you thefe things in the churches." Therefore JESUS is the LORD GOD of the *holy Prophets*.
To

(*k*) John xxi. 16. (*l*) 1 Pet. v. 2. (*m*) Ifa. liv. 5. (*n*) Eph. v. 23. (*o*) Rev. xix. 7. (*p*) ibid. xxi. 9. (*q*) Gal. iii. 13. (*r*) Col. i. 14. (*s*) 1 Pet. i. 18, 19. (*t*) Rev. xxii. 6. (*u*) ibid. 16.

To which we may add, (*v*) " And *Thomas* answered and said, *my* LORD and *my* GOD."

(*u*) " AND thou, child, shalt be called the prophet of the HIGHEST: For thou shalt go before the face of the LORD, to prepare *his* way." Here *John* is called the prophet of the LORD, and of the HIGHEST, whose way he was sent to prepare: But it was before JESUS CHRIST that *John* was sent, to prepare *his* way. (*x*) " *Jesus* began to say unto the multitudes concerning *John*, this is he of whom it is written, behold, I send my messenger before *thy face*, who shall prepare *thy way* before *thee*." Therefore JESUS CHRIST is the LORD—the HIGHEST.

(*y*) " HE (*John*) shall be great in the sight of the LORD; and many of the children of *Israel* shall he turn to the LORD their GOD, and he shall go before HIM." He whose forerunner *John* was, is here called the LORD GOD *of Israel*; but it was JESUS whom *John* came before and bare witness to. (*z*) " *John* seeth JESUS coming unto him, and saith, behold the Lamb of *God*, who taketh away the sin of the world. This is *he* of whom I said, *after me cometh* a man who is preferred before me." Therefore JESUS is the LORD GOD *of Israel*.†

(*a*) " I

(*v*) John xx. 28. (*u*) Luke i. 74. (*x*) Matt. xi. 7, 10. (*y*) Luke i. 15, 16, 17. (*z*) John i. 29, 30.

† To illustrate the former arguments, let it be considered, that *John* the *Baptist*, the forerunner of *Christ*, was prophesied of by *Isaiah*, whose words are cited by *all the Evangelists*, and expressly called *his* when applied to *John* the *Baptist*. Matt. iii. 3. Mark i. 3. Luke iii. 4. John i 23. Now, *Isaiah* says, chap. xl. 3, 9. 10, 11. " The voice of him that crieth in the wilderness, (where *John* preached) prepare the way of the LORD, (JEHOVAH) make straight in the desart, a high way for *our* GOD.—O *Jerusalem*, that bringest good tidings, (thou that tellest good tidings to *Jerusalem*, margin) say
unto

(a) "I am *Alpha* and *Omega*, the *beginning* and the *ending*, faith the LORD, which *is*, which *was*, and which *is to come*, the ALMIGHTY." Every character in this text proves the *Deity* of the *speaker*; but that JESUS CHRIST is the *speaker*, is plain from his own testimony in the same paragraph. (b) "And I (*John*) turned to see the voice of *him that spake with me*. And in the midst of the seven candlesticks, one like unto the *son of man*,—and when I saw *him*, I fell at his feet as dead: And he laid his right hand upon me, saying unto me, fear not, I am the *first* and the *last :* I am he that *liveth*, and *was* DEAD; and, behold, I live for *evermore*, *Amen*; and have the keys of hell and of death." Therefore the characters in the text belong to JESUS CHRIST, and prove his *Deity* beyond all dispute.

(c) "GOD was in *Christ*, *reconciling* the world to *himself*." Here *God* is the *reconciler*, and that to *himself* : But *Jesus Christ* is the *reconciler*.—(d) "You that were sometimes enemies, hath he (*Jesus*) *reconciled* in the body of his flesh through death." Therefore *Jesus Christ* is 'GOD, the object of whom the *reconciliation* was made.

(e) "WHO can *forgive sins* but GOD *only ?*"— But CHRIST can *forgive sins*. (f) "Even as CHRIST *forgave you*, so also do ye." Therefore he is GOD.

IT

---

unto the cities of *Judah*, behold *your* GOD. Behold, the LORD GOD will come with a strong hand, and his arm shall rule for him: Behold, his reward is with him, and his work before him. He shall feed his flock like a shepherd : He shall gather the lambs with his arm, and carry them in his bosom, and shall gently lead them that are with young." All this can be applied to no other than JESUS CHRIST, the bishop of souls, and good shepherd of the sheep; it is therefore *he* who through this passage is called JEHOVAH—the LORD GOD—the GOD *of Israel*.

(a) Rev. i. 8. (b) ibid. i. 12, 13, 17, 18. (c) 2 Cor. v. 19. (d) Col. i. 21, 22. (e) Mark ii. 7. (f) Col. iii. 13.

IT is GOD *only* that *searcheth the heart.*——— (g) " *Thou,* even *thou only, knoweth the hearts of all the children of men.*" But JESUS CHRIST is the *searcher of hearts.*—" (h) " Thefe things faith the *Son of God,*—All the churches fhall know that *I am he, who searcheth the reins and hearts.*" Therefore he is GOD.

THE Pfalmift fays, it was the (i) LORD GOD that *ascended on high,* and led captivity captive. But the Apoftle (k) fays, it was CHRIST that did fo: Therefore he is the LORD GOD.

(l) " IN that day, faith the LORD, (JEHOVAH) they fhall look on *me* whom they have *pierced.*" But it was JESUS CHRIST who was *pierced.* (m) " One of the foldiers with a fpear *pierced* his fide, that the fcripture fhould be fulfilled,—they fhall look on *him* whom they have pierced." Therefore JESUS CHRIST is JEHOVAH.

THE *blood* which was the price of the church's redemption, is called the *blood of God.* (n) " Feed the church of GOD, which he hath *purchased* with his *own blood.*" But this was the blood of JESUS CHRIST.—(o) " And the four and twenty elders fell down before the Lamb, faying, thou art worthy to take the book, and to open the feals thereof: For thou waft *slain,* and haft *redeemed* us to God by thy *blood.*" Therefore he is GOD.

(p) " THE *life* was manifefted, and we have feen it, and bear witnefs, and fhew unto you *that eternal*

(g) 1 Kings viii. 39. (h) Rev. ii. 18, 23. (i) Pfa. lxviii. 17, 18. (k) Eph. iv. 7, 8, 9. (l) Zach. xii. 4, 10. (m) John xix. 34. (n) Acts xx. 28. (o) Rev. v. 8, 9. (p) 1 John i. 2.

eternal life which was with the Father, and was manifested unto us." It is certain that in this text, *Jesus Christ* is called *that eternal life*; let us then fee, what another title the fame Apoſtle adds to this. (*q*) " And we are in him that is *true*, even in his *ſon* JESUS CHRIST, this is the TRUE GOD, and (but more agreeable to the original *even the*) ETERNAL LIFE." This title the *eternal life*, is in both texts given to *Jeſus Chriſt*, agreeable to many other of the fame import in ſcripture, which the greateſt ſtretch in criticiſm cannot interpret otherways: it muſt then follow, if the Apoſtle wrote truth, that JESUS CHRIST, who is the *eternal life*, is the TRUE GOD.

THE Apoſtle affixes the fame idea to being *born of Chriſt*, and being *born of God*, and ſpeaks of them as the fame privilege to the faints, conveying the fame ſenſe. (*r*) " Every one that doth righteouſneſs, is *born of him*, (*Chriſt* the perſon ſpoken of in the context.) (*s*) Behold what manner of love the Father hath beſtowed upon us, that we ſhould be called the *ſons of God*." The inference is plain, that in the Apoſtle's ſenſe *Jeſus Chriſt* is God.

THE like concluſion is evident from what this fame Apoſtle ſays, (*t*) " Hereby perceive we the love of GOD, becauſe he laid down *his life* for us." *God* in this verſe, is the proper antecedent to the relative *his*, and points out on the face of the text, that *he* was *God*, who laid down his life for us; but this was *Chriſt*, therefore *he* is GOD.

(*u*) " LOOKING for, and haſtening to the coming

(*q*) 1 John v. 10. (*r*) ibid. ii. 29. (*s*) ibid. iii. 1, 9. (*t*) ibid. iii. 16. (*u*) 2 Pet. iii. 12.

ing of the *day of God.*" The same that *Peter* calls the *day of God,* *Paul* calls the *day of Christ.* (*v*) " That ye may be sincere, and without offence 'till the *day of Christ.*" Therefore he is GOD.

UNCHANGEABLENESS is proper only to JEHO-VAH.—(*w*) " I am JEHOVAH, I CHANGE NOT." But JESUS CHRIST is *unchangeable.*—(*x*) " JESUS CHRIST, the *same yesterday, to-day, and for ever.*" § Therefore *he is* JEHOVAH.

MOSES says, the children of *Israel* (*y*) *tempted* JEHOVAH: The Psalmist says, (*z*) they *tempted the* MOST HIGH GOD: But the Apostle *Paul* says, it was (*a*) CHRIST *they tempted.* Therefore CHRIST must be JEHOVAH the MOST HIGH GOD.

(*b*) " Now unto *him* that is *able* to keep you from falling, and to *present* you faultless before the presence of his glory, with exceeding great joy, to the *only wise God our Saviour,* be glory and majesty, &c." Here it is the *only wise God,* who is able to *present* us before the presence of his glory; but the Apostle *Paul* says, *Christ* shall do this.— (*c*) " That *he* (*Christ*) might *present it* (*the church*) to
himself

(*v*) Phil. i. 10.   (*w*) Mal. iii. 6.   (*x*) Heb. xiii. 8.   (*y*) Exod. xvii. 2.   (*z*) Psa. lxxviii. 56.   (*a*) 1 Cor. x. 9.   (*b*) Jude 24, 25. (*c*) Eph. v. 27.

§ This text the *Arians* interpret of the doctrine, not of the person of *Jesus Christ*; because to preach *Christ* in several other texts, means to preach the doctrines of *Christ*; hence, say they, " this text points out *Jesus Christ*, as the same saviour, and his gospel the same to them of old,—to the Hebrews then,—and would be the same to all generations that were to come." Even in this sense, by an easy consequence, it is a clear proof of the Deity of *Jesus Christ*, as it proves that he governed the world in general, and the church in particular, in all ages, which none but the supreme *God* could do. This, I shall prove at large in the sequel.

himself a glorious church, not having spot or wrinkle, or any such thing." Therefore he is the ONLY WISE GOD *our Saviour*, to *whom* (in the words of the Apostle) we ascribe *(d)* " *glory and majesty, dominion* and *power*, both now and ever. Amen."

MANY more texts might have been compared in support of the proper *Deity* of the *Lord Jesus Christ*; but I thought it best to take only such under this head, as when compared, the inference would be obvious at first sight to the meanest capacity.

THE reader will now suffer me, in the same manner, to prove the proper *Deity* of the *Holy Ghost*, by a few plain examples from scripture.

THE same LORD OF HOSTS that *Isaiah* saw, *said unto him*, *(e)* " Go and tell this people; hear ye indeed, but understand not, &c." But the Apostle saith expressly, that these were the words of the HOLY GHOST. *(f)* " Well *spake* the HOLY GHOST by the Prophet *Isaiah*, saying, go unto this people, and say, hearing ye shall hear, and shall not understand, &c." Therefore the HOLY GHOST is the LORD OF HOSTS.

THE people of *Israel* is often in the Old Testament said to *resist* and rebel against JEHOVAH: But *Stephen* says, it was the HOLY GHOST they *resisted*. *(g)* " Ye stiff-necked, and uncircumcised in heart and ears, ye do always *resist* the HOLY GHOST: As *your Fathers did*, so do ye." Therefore the HOLY GHOST is JEHOVAH.

G THE

(*d*) Jude ver. 25. (*e*) Isa. vi. 9. (*f*) Acts xxviii. 25, 26. (*g*) ibid. vii. 51.

THE spiritual *birth* is the work of GOD. (*h*) "Whatsoever is *born of God*, overcometh the world. (*i*) To them gave he power to become the *sons of God,*—who were *born* not of blood, nor of the will of the flesh, nor of the will of man, but *of God*." But this is the work of the SPIRIT.— (*k*) " Except a man be born of water, and of the SPIRIT, he cannot enter into the kingdom of God. That which is *born* of the flesh, is flesh; and that which is *born* of the *spirit*, is spirit." Therefore the SPIRIT is GOD.

HE whom *Christ* teacheth us to pray to as our *heavenly Father*, is the *object of worship*, and must be GOD. But he must be our *Father*, of whom we are *begotten* and *born*, in the stile of scripture, and that is the SPIRIT, as the last article proves: Therefore the SPIRIT is included in the term *Father*, as the *object of worship*, and consequently must be GOD.

TO GOD only are we to *pray*, who alone hath power to send forth labourers into his harvest.— (*l*) " Pray ye therefore the LORD *of the harvest*, that he would *send forth* labourers into his harvest." But the HOLY GHOST sends them forth. (*m*) " So they (*Barnabas* and *Paul*) being *sent forth* by *the* HOLY GHOST." Therefore he is the *object of prayer,*—the LORD *of the harvest*,—and must be the *true* GOD.

HE is the *Supreme Being*, whom the Saints have worshipped under the divine titles of LORD and GOD.—(*n*) " Then he (*Simeon*) *blessed God*, and said, Lord

---

(*h*) 1 John v. 4. (*i*) John i. 12, 13. (*k*) ibid. iii. 5, 6. (*l*) Matt. ix. 38. (*m*) Acts xiii. 4. (*n*) Luke ii. 28, 29.

Lord now letteſt thou thy ſervant depart in peace, according to *thy word.* For mine eyes have ſeen *thy ſalvation.*" But it was the *word* of the HOLY GHOST he here ſpeaks of.—(*o*) " It was *revealed* unto him (*Simeon*) by the HOLY GHOST, that he ſhould not ſee death, before he had ſeen the *Lord's Chriſt.*" Therefore the HOLY GHOST, who is here worſhipped under the ſacred titles of LORD and GOD, is the *Supreme Being.*

THE *calling* and *work* of the Apoſtles were under the ſole direction of GOD.—(*p*) " No man taketh this honour to himſelf, but he that is *called of God.*" But this *calling* and *work* were under the direction of the HOLY GHOST.—(*q*) " The HOLY GHOST ſaid, ſeparate ME, *Barnabas* and *Saul*, for the *work* whereunto *I have called them.*" Therefore the HOLY GHOST is GOD.

HE who qualified the Apoſtles, and firſt propagators of chriſtianity, with ſuch a diverſity of extraordinary *gifts* of (*r*) *wiſdom—knowledge—faith—working of miracles—healing all diſeaſes—prophecy—diſcerning of ſpirits—interpretation of tongues—and ſpeaking divers kinds of languages* to the *different kinds of people* where they came, muſt be not only *omnipotent,* or he could neither beſtow the *gifts*, nor ſupport *them* to whom they were given in the due and regular exerciſe of them; but he muſt be *omnipreſent* alſo; at the ſame time preſent in all places, however diſtant: This the Apoſtle ſaith, is (*s*) " the *ſame* GOD that worketh all in all ;" and at the ſame time ſays, (*t*) " But all theſe *worketh* that *one* and the *ſelf-ſame* SPIRIT, dividing

to

(*o*) Luke ii. 26. (*p*) Heb. v. 4. (*q*) Acts xiii. 2. (*r*) 1 Cor. xii. 4,—12. (*s*) ver. 6. (*t*) ver. 11.

to every man severally as HE WILL." Therefore the SPIRIT is GOD *omnipotent*, and *every where present*.

IF the last cited texts are compared with what the Apostle saith,—(*u*) " *God* also bearing them (the Apostles) witness, both with signs and wonders, and with divers miracles and gifts of the *Holy Ghost*, according to *his own will*." It will shew the strength of the former argument in another point of view, *viz*. That the same things are done by the *will* of the SPIRIT, that are said to be done by the *will* of GOD: It must follow, that as they have but *one will*, they are but *one* God.

THE scriptures were indited by God.—(*v*) " All scripture is given by inspiration of God." But it was the HOLY GHOST that *inspired* the penmen who wrote the scriptures.—(*w*) " Holy men of God, spake as they were *moved* by the HOLY GHOST." Therefore he is GOD.

GOD only is the author of all *spiritual comfort*.—(*x*) " Blessed be GOD,—the GOD of all comfort; who comforteth us in all our tribulations." But the HOLY GHOST is *the comforter*, in whose comfort the churches *rest*.—(*y*) " But the *comforter*, which is the HOLY GHOST, whom the Father will send in my name, he shall teach you all things. (*z*) Then had the churches *rest*,—walking in the fear of the *Lord*, and in the *comfort* of the HOLY GHOST." Therefore he is GOD.

IT is GOD that *dwelleth* in believers.——
" Who-

(*u*) Heb. ii. 4. (*v*) 2 Tim. iii. 16. (*w*) 2 Pet. i. 21. (*x*) 2 Cor. i. 3, 4. (*y*) John xiv. 26. (*z*) Acts ix. 31.

(*a*) " Whosoever shall confess that *Jesus* is the son of God, GOD *dwelleth in him*, and he in *God*. (*b*) GOD is *in you* of a truth." But it is the SPIRIT that *dwelleth* in believers.—(*c*) " The SPIRIT *of God dwelleth in you*. (*d*) The SPIRIT of Truth *dwelleth* with you, and shall be *in you*." Therefore he is GOD.

IT is GOD who *teacheth* the saints.—(*e*) " They shall be all *taught of* GOD." But it is the HOLY GHOST that *teacheth* them.—(*f*) " Not in the words which man's wisdom teacheth, but which the HOLY GHOST *teacheth*." Therefore he is GOD.

THE Apostle says, (*g*) "It was the long-suffering of GOD, that waited in the days of *Noah* :" But *Moses* says, (*h*) " It was the SPIRIT that did *strive* with the men of that generation." Therefore the SPIRIT is GOD.

NONE but one *infinitely wise* can know the deep things of the counsel and purpose of *God*.— (*i*) " O the *depth* of the riches, both of the wisdom and knowledge of *God !* How *unsearchable* are his judgments, and his ways *past finding out !* For who hath known the *mind* of the LORD, or who hath been his *counsellor* ?" But this the SPIRIT can do.—(*k*) " The SPIRIT *searcheth all things, yea, the deep things of* GOD. The things of GOD knoweth no man, but the SPIRIT of *God.*" Therefore the SPIRIT is *infinitely wise*, and so must be GOD.

THE

(*a*) 1 John iv. 15. (*b*) 1 Cor. xiv. 25. (*c*) ibid. iii. 16. (*d*) John xiv. 17. (*e*) John vi. 45. (*f*) 1 Cor. ii. 13. (*g*) 1 Pet. iii. 20. (*h*) Gen. vi. 3. (*i*) Rom. xi. 33, 34. (*k*) 1 Cor. ii. 10, 11.

THE Apostles say, (*k*) It was GOD,—the LORD GOD, the *maker* of heaven and earth, the sea, and all that therein is: who *spake* by the mouth of his servant *David*. But *Peter* says, (*l*) it was the *Holy Ghost* that spake by the mouth of his servant *David*: Therefore these divine names and works are properly attributed to the *Holy Ghost*, from which it is manifest that he is the true and supreme * GOD.

To conclude these arguments for the Deity of the Spirit, I must let the reader know, how plain and indisputable this truth would have appeared, if all the texts where the phrase *spirit of God*,— and *spirit of the Lord*, occurs, had been properly translated. We have generally the word *of*, which denotes possession; put betwixt Spirit, and *Lord* or *God*, which possessive commonly in *English* signifies *property*, and implies subordination of one to another, if applied to *different persons*. And if one *person* only be supposed, then the phrase *his Spirit*, signifies *his mind* or *power*. These ideas seem most natural, when such expressions are applied to *God* as *his Spirit*, the *Spirit of God*, which, without the help of a figure, cannot so evidently prove the proper Deity of the *Spirit*, when such possessives are used; but must rather refer to the *œconomical* character

---

(*k*) Acts iv. 24, 25. (*l*) Acts i. 16. Also compare Luke i. 68, 70, with Acts xxviii. 25.

* Because so many have used the phrase *supreme God*, as peculiarly applicable to the Father, implying, that the Son and Spirit are *subordinate Gods*; I have sometimes chosen this term, to shew that they have an equal title to this, and every other character which implieth Deity. If it be used *inclusively*, or when applied to *one*, not *exclusive* of the other *two*, I see no manner of danger therein, more than in the term *Great God*, ‡ which, if applied to *one exclusively*, would also infer the other *two* to be *lesser Gods*.

‡ *Tit*. ii. 13. *Rev*. xix. 17.

character of the *Spirit*, in the difpenfation of *God*, when the word *Spirit* is confidered *perfonally*, or fomething diftinct from GOD: But otherwife, the expreffion *his Spirit*, or the *Spirit of God*, will only point out the *mind*, *power*, or fome other attribute of *God*. Thefe ideas have been induftrioufly improved by the enemies to the proper Deity of the *Spirit*, as the ftrongeft arguments they could find againft it.

BUT a little attention given to the texts, rendered *Spirit of God*,—the *Spirit of the Lord*, would have faved *them* the labour of difputing about words; and the orthodox the trouble of defending that truth from expreffions which they accommodate to it by the affiftance of figures very aukwardly applied, and which, the caufe itfelf needs no affiftance from, if the poffeffives are left out of the text, which they really ought to be. Hence fuch texts as the following, fhould read, (*m*) "The SPIRIT GOD (RUACH ELOHIM) moved upon the face of the waters. (*n*) And *Pharoah* faid unto his fervants, can we find fuch a man as this, in whom is the SPIRIT ELOHIM? (*o*) The SPIRIT GOD hath made me. (*p*) The SPIRIT JEHOVAH refts upon me. (*q*) The SPIRIT, the LORD JEHOVAH, is upon me, for JEHOVAH hath anointed me to preach good tidings." In like manner, we might mention above a dozen places, where fuch expreffions are ufed without any poffeffive. It is therefore beyond contradiction, that *Spirit* and *God* are the fame, where they are joined in thefe texts, throughout the Old Teftament. This idea fets the *Deity* of the *Spirit* in the cleareft point of view.

It

(*m*) Gen. i. 2. (*n*) ibid. xli. 38. (*o*) Job xxxiii. 4. (*p*) Ifa. xi. 2. (*q*) ibid. lxi. 1.

It is a general rule in all languages, that two names or words, not diftinguifhed by any article, prepofition, or other word, commonly belong to the fame thing.

The not attending to this, has been the occafion of many foolifh and unworthy conceits concerning the *Spirit*. Hence, a very learned and ingenious critic, tho' he cites the words in Gen. ii. 2, in *Hebrew* characters, which is Ruach Elohim, and tells us, that it is fo in many other places, yet makes this obfervation thereon, " That as *Elohim* is plural, it fhews that he (the Spirit) proceeds from more perfons than one." On this he builds the proceffion of the *Holy Ghoft* from the *Father* and the *Son*. A very ftrange foundation indeed!

As *Ruach* is in the fingular number, and *Elohim* is plural, as we proved above, the one muft imply the fingular character of Deity, as the *one* infinite eternal *Spirit*: And *Elohim*, a plural, muft be viewed in that relative light in which *God* hath revealed himfelf to men.

I muft again put the reader in mind, that I by no means pretend to tell the modus of divine exiftence, or anfwer that curious queftion, which fome may afk here, " How can thefe things be?" I find revelation joins Elohim, a *plural*, and Ruach, a *fingular*, to point out the fame divine *Being*; but how this plurality fubfifts in *Deity*, becaufe not revealed, I leave to infinite intelligence; but that it is fo, remains a truth while thefe words ftand in the Bible, Jehovah Elohim,—Ruach Elohim.—Thefe three are one.

Having now proved, *firft*, by a collection of
scripture

scripture texts, that the names, attributes, perfections, and works, proper only to *Deity*, are ascribed to the *Lord Jesus Christ*, and the *Holy Ghost*.

AND *secondly*, demonstrated the truth of their *Deity*, by comparing one text with another, from which the conclusions are both easy and strong in favour of the point.

I shall next, as proposed, illustrate the truth of *Christ's* proper *Deity*, by considering the scope of several passages in revelation, which have a relation to that subject.

SECT. V.

IF it can be made appear from scripture, that our *Lord Jesus Christ* created all things,—governed the world in general, and the church in particular, both under the Old and New Testaments,—was manifested by all the god-like appearances under the Old Testament to the Patriarchs and Prophets, and under the New to the Apostles;—did all the mighty works we read of among his ancient people, the *Jews*,—assumed the names and titles, and claimed the worship and homage due only to *God:* And whom not only the *Jews* worshipped as their *God* and king,—but whom christians on earth, and both saints and Angels in heaven do account worthy to receive all worship, honour, glory, and praise. If these things are evident in scripture, none that credit revelation can doubt, that he is the TRUE GOD.

THAT *Jesus Christ* created all things, was proved from several plain texts, in page 33, and were it necessary, many more might be added. And as we must admit it as a truth, from such abundance of divine testimonies, that all things were made by *Jesus Christ*, it must be undeniably true, by a very natural consequence, that he is the ruler and governor of them all. For the very notion of creature existence, implies in it a dependence upon the will and government of the creator. And if we suppose the creature to be rational, and consequently under a *law*, then its existence as such denotes not only dependence upon the will of the creator, but that it is accountable to him as the law-giver, ruler, and judge. Creator and creature are relative terms, and imply the necessity

of

of rule and government : Unlefs we could imagine (which would be contradictory, if not blafphemous) that the creator fhewed fo much wifdom in the making of creatures, without any defign to rule and govern them : Or, in fhort, that he was not able to manage the things he had made.

SEEING then it is infallibly true, that by the immediate agency of the divine *word* (*Jefus Chrift*) all things were made ; *He* muft be the immediate ruler of the world in general, and of Angels and men in particular. This will be further manifeft, from a confideration of the fcripture account of *his* character, who governed the church in all ages.

AND here we are in a great meafure *confined* to the rule and government of the church : Becaufe revelation is a hiftory not fo much of the world, as of the church, and takes no more of the affairs of the world into the account, than is neceffary fome way or other to compleat the hiftory of the church. So that the *Bible* in general, may be called *God*'s hiftory of the church in all ages. And it hath thefe two properties, which no other hiftory can pretend to, *firft*, that all the facts are infallibly related by him who was an eye witnefs, and directed the whole. *Secondly*, this hiftory is not confined to paft facts, which all others muft be, but extends to all future periods, to the end of time, with the fame exactnefs as if they were paft. Yet, from the account we have of the church, we learn, that he who guided and governed it by his wifdom and power, alfo ruled the world in general, tho' in very different refpects.

I DO not propofe to take under confideration, all
the

the remarkable things which occur in the government of the church; this would be to transcribe almost the whole Bible; only a few instances, to make it evident, that *Jesus Christ* was the sole director of every thing pertaining to it in all ages.

It is evident beyond dispute, that in a great number of appearances, recorded in the Old Testament, whether in a bright cloud,—flame of fire,—or as a man, who is often called Angel, he who spake assumed the highest names and characters of Deity. And the spectators, as well as the sacred penmen or historians, call him GOD, JEHOVAH, &c. ascribe such perfections,—and give him such homage and worship, as are due to none but Almighty *God*. It must then be equally true, that it was *God* who spake, whether in the cloud, in the fire, or in the man, who is so often called Angel.

That it was not a common Angel is plain, for he challenges divine worship, which no created Angel ever did. We have many instances of the appearance of other Angels, sent upon particular errands, both in the Old and New Testaments, as ministers in the affairs of providence; yet none of these ever assumed divine titles, nor would they allow any kind of worship to be given them; much less did they challenge the names and honour due only to *God*. On the contrary, they declared themselves special messengers sent by divine authority,—expressly refused divine worship, when through mistake offered them,—and prefaced their embassies, with a *thus saith the Lord*. This is a manifest discrimination betwixt their character and him, who, in all his appearances, bears the titles and receives the worship which belong to *God*.

It

IT is likewise evident from the scope of scripture, and agreed to by every denomination of christians in general, that *God* under the character of *Paternity*, or he whom the scriptures call the *Father*, hath throughout the whole dispensation of revelation, always maintained the character of the *invisible God*, " whom (says the Apostle) no man hath seen, or can see." Or as our Saviour affirms, " Not that any man hath seen the *Father*,—ye have neither heard *his* voice at any time, nor seen his shape." As we cannot in the least degree call in question so plain a testimony concerning the *Father*, by the *Son*, " who only knows the *Father*, and can reveal him," we may safely conclude, it was not the Father that made these appearances which are recorded in the Old Testament.

AND as to the *Holy Ghost*, he never appeared (that we read of) as a man, or acted as an external messenger; his work in the divine œconomy being internal upon the mind, according to what we can learn from revelation concerning him under that name.

BUT as the scriptures represent *Jesus Christ* as the *image* of the *invisible God*,—his *express image*,— the *brightness* of his glory,—in whom the Father dwells,—the *revealer* of the Father,—the *word* of God, by whom he is *manifested* and made known, as a man doth his mind by his words,—we have good ground to conclude, from these general considerations, that whatever divine messenger we read of in the Old Testament that appeared to good men, (by whatever manner of appearance) to whom the name of GOD in a proper sense, or JEHOVAH is ascribed; or to whom these good men paid worship and homage, due *only to God:* This messenger

messenger may with all safety be owned to be the *true God*, tho' he uses such names as to us may seem to imply inferiority, or rather † *condescension*; and at the same time, to be the *Logos*, or *word of God*, who under the New Testament is known by the name *Jesus Christ*.

THESE things kept in view, it will plainly appear to any attentive reader of the Bible, that he who appeared on various occasions under the sacred titles of GOD, JEHOVAH, GOD-ALMIGHTY, and received the worship of the saints, is no other than the LORD JESUS CHRIST.

BUT before I shew from particular instances, that these appearances are applied to him in the New Testament, it will be necessary to remove an objection or two, raised against this doctrine in general, by such as are afraid of the force of it, in proving the proper Deity of *Jesus Christ*.

THEY

---

† When we at any time speak of *inferiority* as applied to *Jesus Christ*, we should take care not to lose sight of his *condescension*, which has been too little attended to in the controversy with those, who will allow him to be no more than an *inferior God*. Tho' he *condescended* to become man, and acted in an *inferior* character, this did not change his *divine* character, (which our divines have given too much occasion to conceive, by the terms they have used on this subject) but only shewed his *grace* and *condescension*. He assumed a form when he was manifest in flesh, which he had not before, but remained the same unchangeable JEHOVAH. The very *heathens* seem to have understood this notion of *condescension* in *their Gods*: For when *Paul* and *Barnabas* had cured the impotent man at *Lystra*, they cried, "The *Gods are come down to us in the likeness of men*." They wondered at so great *condescension*, but never imagined that their *Gods* had *less* divinity, or were *less* to be worshipped for the change of their form: For they still gave them their highest titles, *Jupiter* and *Mercurius*; and their high *Priest*, with the people, were ready to worship them, in the most solemn manner their religion could express. But among christians, there are many who will not allow the *Deity* to be manifest in the flesh, in grace and *condescension*, without denying him *supreme* worship, and the character of the *true God*.

They do not deny that it was *Jesus Christ* who made these appearances, and they dare not deny, that the titles and worship due to *God* are given to him; but not satisfied that he should have such honour, in a *proper sense*, they endeavour to account for his assuming these divine honours in an *improper* and *figurative sense*, as a *messenger*, *ambassador*, or at most an *inferior God*, sent and authorized by the Great God. Hence they argue with great assurance, "That as ambassadors among men may speak in the same manner, and receive the same honour, as those in whose name they come; so *Jesus Christ*, consistent with his being a creature of high rank, might, as a representative or deputy, clothed with authority from the supreme God, and representing his sacred Majesty, assume the names, and receive the worship due to *God*."

Ans. This argument is not only weak, but quite foreign to the point. The antecedent, or first proposition, is not true in fact. No examples can be found of any ambassador assuming his master's titles. He who had such presumption, must be possessed of a larger share of pride than *Rabshakeh* himself, who said, "Thus saith the *great king of Assyria*,—my master sent me to speak these words." But according to the objection, he would have said, "*I am the king of Assyria.*" Whatever pride *Nuncios*, *Legates*, and *Ambassadors* may otherwise shew, none of them presume to say, *I am the Pope of Rome*,—*I am the king of Britain*,—or, *I am the king of France*.

But tho' the first proposition were true, which it is not, yet there is not the least connection betwixt it and the latter. For tho' ambassadors among men were to assume their master's titles
and

and honour, there is some proportion, but in the other case there is none. Here the distance is really infinite betwixt the greatest creature, and the great *God*. In the one case, it would be a misdemeanor betwixt man and man: But in the other, it would be the highest sacrilege, and would lead directly to the most abominable idolatry, in giving the worship due to *God* to any creature. We may venture to say, it is impossible that *God* would indulge men in any such mistake. And if to the impossibility of the supposition, we add the absolute security *God* hath given us, that he will by no means do so, it may certainly, at least, blunt the edge of such unguarded zeal, in favour of an argument every way so unworthy of the character of *God*, who has expressly declared, "Thou shalt worship the *Lord* thy *God*, and him only shalt thou serve. Thou shalt worship no other *God*, for the *Lord* thy *God*, whose name is jealous, is a jealous *God*. I am JEHOVAH, that is my name, and my glory will I not give to another."

GOD, who well knew how ready the *Jews* were to be taken with appearances, and fall into idolatry, guards them against it in the strongest terms. This seems to be one reason why there were no appearances in human shape to them, while in the wilderness, tho' the appearances both before and after that were so, that they might have no foundation of framing images of *God*. But in all the appearances, whether in human shape, or as an Angel, the titles and worship of JEHOVAH were claimed, and freely given by *Abraham*, *Moses*, and others, so that we may justly conclude, he who appeared was *God*, in the most *true* and *proper sense*.

BUT

But there remains another general objection, which is, that the fiery bush,—the flame on *Sinai*,—the pillar of cloud, and fire in which God appeared, may be called God and Jehovah, with the same propriety, as the man or Angel in whom God appeared.

Anf. Here it must be remarked, that neither the bush, fire, cloud, the man or Angel, in which God appeared, is called God or Jehovah, but as they include the idea of *Deity* that dwell in them. And tho' all the motions and gestures of the symbol of God's presence, in which he appeared for the time are ascribed to God; yet these symbols of his presence are never called God, when considered alone; but only as they included the divine inhabitant. As *David* said of the Ark, " God is gone up with a shout."—When the Ark moved, *Moses* said, " Arise, Jehovah, and let thine enemies be scattered." And when it rested, he said, " Give rest, Jehovah, unto the many thousands of *Israel*." Which could not be meant of the Ark, but of the God whose presence it represented, and who is said to dwell upon it. The Dove-like appearance which descended upon *Christ* at his baptism, is called the *Holy Ghost:* But it cannot be imagined that the Dove was God, the Spirit; but only a symbol of his presence. And so the fire and cloud, which appeared on *Mount Sinai*, in the tabernacle, and temple, were only designed as symbols of God's presence, as he tells *Moses*, " Lo, I come to thee in a thick cloud." *Exo.* xix. 9. I will appear in the cloud upon the Mercy's seat. *Lev.* xvi. 2.

The names that express *Deity*, are not used on these occasions in a *figurative* and *metaphorical* sense, as both the objections would insinuate; but in a true and divine sense, applied to GOD *himself*, considered in such a habitation as he for the time made use of as a symbol of his presence, whether it was a cloud, or fire, the Angel, or the man.

BUT in which ever one of these, it seems evident from the narratives of the appearances, that the *angelic medium* was always used, which moved and spake through what was corporeal in the appearance. For the names JEHOVAH, GOD, and ANGEL, are used promiscuously; and it is said sometimes the one appeared, spake, &c. and sometimes the other, in the very same appearance. But it is never said the bush, fire, cloud, or flame spoke, but only GOD, or the Angel in them. By which it appears, that the *Angel*, and not the cloud or fire, assumed the divine characters. What makes this perfectly clear, is the distinction which *Moses* makes betwixt the pillar of cloud, and the divine inhabitant.—(a) " And the LORD went before them by day *in* a pillar of cloud, to lead them in the way; and by night *in* a pillar of fire, to give them light." Compare this with what he says a little after.—(b) " And the *Angel* of *God*, which went before the camp of *Israel*, removed, and went behind them; and the *pillar* of *cloud* went from before their face, and stood behind them." These two things are plain here, *first*, that the pillar of cloud is not called the *Lord*, nor the *Angel*, they are mentioned as different; the *Lord* is said to be *in* the pillar of cloud, and the Angel and cloud are expressed in much the same language, with a copulative, pointing out they are not the same. *Secondly*, that the LORD (JEHOVAH) who

---

(a) Exo. xiii. 21. (b) ibid. xiv. 19.

who is said to lead *Israel* in the one text, is called the ANGEL in the other.

THIS is further evident from the appearance made to *Moses* in the burning bush, where it is said, (c) "And the *Angel* of the LORD *appeared* unto him in a flame of fire, out of the midst of the bush,—and GOD called to him out of the midst of the bush,—and said, I am the GOD of thy father, the GOD of *Abraham*, the GOD of *Isaac*, and the GOD of *Jacob*. And *Moses* hid his face, for he was afraid to look upon GOD." In the beginning of this passage, he is called *Angel*, in the other parts of it, the LORD GOD, JEHOVAH, the GOD of *Abraham*, *I am*, &c. And the very same who appeared in the bush, and on *Mount Sinai*, who assumed these divine titles, and worship, *Stephen* expressly calls the *Angel*.—(d) "The *Angel* which appeared to him (*Moses*) in the bush,—this is he that was in the church in the wilderness, with the *Angel* which spake to him in *Mount Sinai*." By an impartial reading of the narrative, it will be plain, that JEHOVAH, who appeared in the bush,—gave the law on *Mount Sinai*, and led the people in the wilderness, is the same with the *Angel*, so often mentioned in the history, and referred to by *Stephen*.

AMONG many particular passages that might be brought to prove this, to the above, I shall only add *Jacob's* account of it.—(e) "The *Angel* of God spake unto me in a dream, saying, *Jacob*: And, I said, here am I, and he said,—I am the GOD of *Beth-el*, where thou anointed the pillar." And when

(c) Exo. iii. 2 to 6. (d) Acts vii. 35, 38. (e) Gen. xxxi. 11,—13.

when he was blessing *Joseph*'s sons, he said, *(f)* " God, before whom my father *Abraham* and *Isaac* did walk, the God that fed me all my life long unto this day, the Angel which redeemed me from all evil, bless the lads." In both places God and *Angel* are spoken of as the same. Nay, the *Angel* expressly calls himself the *God* of *Beth-el*.

But, because not only the gentlemen whose objections I have been considering, but others who are esteemed orthodox interpreters of scripture, have exercised their talents of criticism, in attempting to prove that the *Angel* mentioned in the last text, is a created one, not the same, but an inferior being to *God*, who is mentioned in the same text; I hope the reader will have me excused, while I endeavour to rescue the text from such a manifest imposition.

Joseph having brought his two sons before his father, the aged Patriarch opens the interview, with a recapitulation of the appearance and promises which *God Almighty* made to him at *Luz*, which place he called *Beth-el*, (or the house of God) on that solemn occasion.—*(g)* As God had there promised to multiply his seed, he takes this unexpected event as a pledge of the complete fulfilling thereof. " I had not (says he) thought to see thy face: And lo, God hath shewed me thy seed." And being filled with a sense of God's abundant goodness to him, he proceeds to supplicate for the same blessings to *Joseph*'s sons, which had been promised to himself. Now it cannot be supposed, that he would invocate any other than the same *Almighty God*, who had promised, and so far above

(f) Gen. lxviii. 15, 16. *(g)* ibid. xxviii. 19.

above his expectations, already performed his promises unto him.

It should also be carefully attended to, that upon the visitation at *Beth-el*, *Jacob* vowed to God, saying, " If God will be with me, and will *keep me* in the way that I go, and will give me *bread to eat*, and raiment to put on; so that I come again in peace to my father's house: Then shall the Lord be my God." And here he acknowledgeth the receipt of what he then prayed for, saying, " The God that *fed me* all my life long unto this day, the *Angel* that *redeemed* me from all evil, bless the lads." The same God he had vowed to, and expected protection from, that had fed him, and redeemed him from all evil, he now addresses in favour of the lads; which proves the Angel to be the same with God in the preceding clause, and the *God Almighty* who appeared to *Jacob* at *Beth-el*.

But this is still more manifest from the construction of the language *Jacob* uses. For the words here translated God and Angel, have each a *demonstrative* prefixed before them, which points them out to be the same, whereas had they been different, of necessity there would have been a *copulative* betwixt them. " *That God, that Angel*, that fed me, and redeemed me," must point at the same object. But had it been " the God that fed me, *and* the Angel that redeemed me," it would have pointed out different objects. Many critics read *Peter*'s short confession of faith,— " Thou art *that Christ*, *that* son of the living God." None will deny that *Peter* meant the same person in both; and so the object of *Jacob*'s
addrefs

address must be the same, seeing the demonstratives are prefixed.

And not only so, but the verb here used is singular, which would be a manifest impropriety, if there were two intended so very different as the *Almighty God*, and a *created Angel*. Could we suppose the absurdity which some maintain, " of joining them together in an address;" yet, to make it sense, it would read, " may *they* bless:" But to join two so very different Beings together, and then say, " may he bless," is wholly incongruous.

Further, if we suppose the *Angel* here a created one, it will make *Jacob*'s prayer to be very irreligious. For that which the Angel is said to do, is only proper for God. To deliver his people from all evil, is what he has promised, and what they daily pray for, as expressed in our *Lord*'s summary, " Deliver us from all evil. Many are the afflictions of the righteous, but the Lord delivereth them out of them all." This is what they neither expect from, nor pray to *any Angel* to do. Indeed those of the Popish persuasion, in which Angel worship is included, may: And it is most likely that this notion, with many others, have been taken without examination from *their* systems, who must hold this to be a created Angel, the better to support Angel worship.

It is admirable how any can imagine, that *Jacob* would give to any mere creature the sacred title of his *Redeemer*, seeing it is that which the saints glory in, as proper to God only; and what he challengeth as his peculiar prerogative. " O *Lord*, (faith *David*) my strength and my *Redeemer*. Thus faith the *Lord*, your *Redeemer*. As for our *Redeemer*,

deemer, the *Lord* of Hosts is his name. O *Lord*, our *Redeemer*, thy name is from everlasting." (Our Redeemer from everlasting is thy name, *Margin*.) It would be robbing God to give the glory of this title to any creature.

We may justly conclude, that *Jacob* had the same object of worship in view, when blessing *Joseph* and his sons, that he had immediately after when blessing *Joseph* among his other sons; there he ascribes all to God, saying,—(*b*) "His hands were made strong by the mighty God of *Jacob*; even by the God of thy father, who shall help thee; and by the Almighty, who shall bless thee."

I shall only add here, that the *Angel* mentioned in this passage, is the same with the God before whom *Abraham* and *Isaac* did walk, which phrase implies the whole of their religion; as it is said of *Enoch*, " he *walked* with God." It is the same *Angel* that appeared to *Jacob* in *Padanarum*, and said, I am the God of *Beth-el*: The same redeeming Angel that answered him in his afflictions: To whom he cried for help at the meeting of his brother *Esau*. The same that *fed* and *led* him and his posterity. The Angel that *Isaiah* calls God's presence, who in his love saved them, and in his pity redeemed them,—who bare and carried them all the days of old,—delivering them from all evil, and increasing them into a multitude in the earth, which was the answer of *Jacob's* prayer in the text: And on the whole, proves that the *Angel* mentioned here, is the same object with *God*, whom he addresses under these two names.

There is one thing I have to mention here, which

(*b*) Gen. xlix. 24, 25.

(72)

which will put the general point I am pleading for, entirely beyond all difpute. And I am furprized, that none of all the difputers for the divinity of *Chrift*, ever took any notice of it, *viz.* That wherever the word *Angel* is joined with JEHOVAH, there is no *poffeffive* prefixed to them in the *Hebrew*. What we have tranflated *the Angel of the Lord*, is the ANGEL JEHOVAH, which certainly proves them to be the fame. And through all the Old Teftament it is fo, when they are joined together. For the reader's fatisfaction, the following texts may be confulted in the original, which he will find without any poffeffive fign.

GEN. xvi. 7, 9, 10, 11. Chap. xxii. 11. Num. xxii. 23, 24, 25, 27, 31, 34, 35. Judg. ii. 1, 4. Chap. xiii. 3, 16, 18, 20, 21. Chap. v. 23. Chap. vi. 11, 12, 21, 22. 1 Kings xix. 7. 2 Kings i. 3, 15. Chap. xix. 35. 1 Chro. xxi. 12, 15, 18, 30. 2 Sam. xxiv. 16. Pfa. xxxiv. 7. and xxxv. 5. Zech. i. 11, 12. Chap. iii. 5, 6. Chap. xii. 8. with feveral others.

THO' there be no poffeffive fign prefixed to *Angel*, when joined to JEHOVAH, yet there is, when it is joined with * ELOHIM, which is tranflated GOD. This may point out to us the humble dependent character, in which the Meffiah acted as the *meffenger of* ELOHIM, which is a plural. Notwithftanding, fince the word *Angel* is joined with JEHOVAH, without the poffeffive fign, it fhews that his ftate of dependence was *voluntary*, and that he lofes no claim to fupremacy by that voluntary dependence: It fairly points out, that our *Saviour*,
the

---

* Exo. xiv. 19. 1 Sam. xxix. 9. 2 Sam. xiv. 17, 20. Chap. xix. 27. In Judg. xiii. 6. it wants the poffeffive.

the *Angel*, or *meſſenger* for us, was never leſs than JEHOVAH, and that in both characters, as to their ſignification to his church, he is equally related to them. But when *Angel* is joined with ELOHIM, it ſhews that the ANGEL JEHOVAH humbled himſelf to be a meſſenger by œconomy of ELOHIM to guilty men, to inſtruct them in heavenly wiſdom. In the character of the ANGEL JEHOVAH, our Saviour ſhews his *one-neſs* or *unity*, as *Emmanuel*; but in the character of the ANGEL of ELOHIM, he ſhews his partnerſhip in the ſcheme of man's redemption with the Father and Holy Ghoſt. We may therefore conclude, that as *Chriſt*'s name, as the *Angel* or meſſenger, and that of JEHOVAH conſtantly ſignify the ſame perſon, in the Old Teſtament, the *Meſſenger* and JEHOVAH muſt be one, that is, *Jeſus Chriſt* the *meſſenger* is JEHOVAH. And tho' he be the *meſſenger of* ELOHIM, in the way of partnerſhip in the ſcheme of man's ſalvation, yet as *Emmanuel*, he aſſumes one of the ſupreme titles that is attributed to Deity in ſcripture.

As there are but two texts, Gen. xxviii. 12, and xxxii. 1. where the word *Angel*, as a *plural*, is joined to JEHOVAH, in which it is *hoſt* or *armies*, there is no fear of miſtaking the meaning for want of the poſſeſſive. When *Angel* is joined with *Berith*, or covenant, it has the poſſeſſive, Mal. iii. 1. Perhaps for the ſame reaſon that it is ſo when joined with ELOHIM.

HAVING thus far cleared the ſubject, I come now to ſhew that JESUS CHRIST was this ANGEL JEHOVAH,—this GOD,—the ALMIGHTY GOD,—the KING OF ISRAEL, whom they *worſhipped and adored*. It would be far too tedious to conſult the narrative of all the appearances he made in the Old Testament, and shew how they may, or really are applied to him: Or enter particularly into all the arguments that might be advanced in proof of this point. I shall only select a few, which I presume, if impartially considered, may not only serve as a key to the rest, but to the scope of the Old Testament.

I NEED not stay to prove that *Jesus Christ* was that image of GOD, after which man was created; this is manifest from the text itself, compared with the New Testament character of *Christ*, as the image of GOD. But this we must observe, that as the image after which man was made, in a particular manner referred to that dominion man was endowed with over the lower creation; it must necessarily infer that *Jesus Christ*, the image of GOD, after which he was made, had a real and universal dominion over all things. And it seems as evident that GOD appeared to man at first in his own shape, which could not fail to convince him, that even as to his body he was made in the image of GOD, that is, in such a form as GOD did at that time, and would frequently after assume, in order to converse with men. This he did with *Adam* while innocent, and also after he sinned,—with *Cain*, who is said to go out from the presence of the *Lord* after the dialogue betwixt GOD and him,—to *Abraham, Jacob, Joshua, Gideon, Manoah, Ezekiel, Daniel*, and several other of the Prophets. This could be no common Angel, for he is always called JEHOVAH,—not the Father, nor the Spirit, for reasons given above; therefore it must have been *Jesus Christ*, who made these appearances in human form, yet called the LORD GOD, as a prelude of

his

his appearance in real flesh in the fullness of time, whom the Apostle says, was GOD manifested in the flesh.

WHEN he who appeared is promiscuously called GOD and ANGEL, it is plain that *Jesus Christ* is meant. In that instance of *Jacob* blessing *Joseph*'s sons, it was proved that *God* and *Angel* are the same, and it is equally conspicuous that *Jesus Christ* is meant by both, from the terms which *Jacob* expresses himself in, which are only applicable to *Jesus Christ*, in the common language of revelation.

"THE *Angel*," or messenger, this is emphatically applied to *Christ* by *Malachi*.—(*a*) " The *Lord*, whom ye seek, shall suddenly come to his temple: Even the *messenger of the covenant*, whom ye delight in." The Angel that *redeemed me*," *my kinsman redeemer*. This is a name peculiar to *Christ*, of whom that institution of *redemption* by *kinsmen* among the *Jews*, was a shadow. *Job*, who lived in these ancient periods with *Jacob*, makes an excellent discovery of the same character of *Christ*.— (*b*) " I know, faith he, that my redeemer liveth, (I know my kinsman redeemer) and that he shall stand upon the earth." (The omega shall rise from the earth.) This is certainly applicable to none but *Christ*, whose *day* both *Jacob* and *Job*, (as well as *Abraham*) saw afar off, and was glad.

IT is further evident that *Christ* is meant in the text, from his character of a *shepherd* being so plainly expressed in it. This *Christ* himself challengeth as his office, in a peculiar manner.—" I am

(*a*) Mal iii. 1. (*b*) Job xix. 25.

am the good shepherd." The Psalmist and Prophets often speak of him under this name.— " The *Lord* is my shepherd. He shall feed his flock like a shepherd." And *Jacob* calls him " the mighty of *Jacob*, the *shepherd*, the stone of *Israel*." *Jacob*, and his seed, are denominated the *flock* of *Christ*. " Thou leddest thy flock, by the hand of *Moses* and *Aaron* ;" which privilege, *Jacob* on his death-bed very thankfully acknowledgeth his part of: ." The GOD, before whom my fathers *Abraham* and *Isaac* did walk,—the GOD that *fed me* all my life long unto this day,—the *Angel* that redeemed me from all evil." It is hence evident, that *Jesus Christ* led and guided *Abraham* and his posterity in all their peregrinations, and it is he whom they worshipped as their *God* and *king*.

GOD said to *Moses*, (c) " Behold, I send an *Angel* before thee, to keep thee in the way, and to bring thee into the place which I have prepared. Beware of him, and obey his voice; provoke him not, for he will not pardon your transgressions, for *my name is in him*" (in the midst of him.) This, with what remains of the paragraph, comes in so abruptly in this chapter, without connection with what goes before or follows it, that some are of opinion, it properly belongs to the 33d chapter, where *Moses* is begging of GOD to let him know how the people should be guided into the land he had promised them. GOD tells him " his presence should go with them," and here he promises to send his *Angel* to lead them, in whom his name is. Now, as his *presence* must mean *himself*; so the *name* of GOD is put for himself by the Psalmist, " The *name* of the GOD of *Jacob* defend thee." And

(c) Exo. xxiii. 20, 21.

And as his *name* was in the *Angel*, it muſt intimate a real in-dwelling of Deity in him. There can no reaſon be given, why *Chriſt* might not have Deity dwelling in him in his *angelic* character, as well as after he became fleſh, when it is ſaid, " in him *dwelleth* all the fullneſs of the *God-head* (Deity) *bodily*." That is, in him who now had a real body.

By the *name of God*, we are to underſtand that deſcription he hath given of himſelf in revelation, whereby he is known to men; and this is only in *Jeſus Chriſt*, whoſe character is the ſum of revelation. The name of GOD is ſo in him, as he can be known only by him. This *Chriſt* affirms himſelf. " No man knoweth the Father, but he to whom the *Son* doth reveal him." *Malachi* ſays, " The *name* of the *Lord* ſhould be great among the *Gentiles*; and that in every place incenſe and a pure offering ſhould be offered up unto his *name* by the heathen." This muſt refer to the clearer and more general diſcoveries of *Jeſus Chriſt* in the goſpel, and the homage and worſhip given to him by the great number of *Gentile* converts to chriſtianity. When *Chriſt* prays the Father to " glorify his *Name*,"—it ſeems to be of the ſame import as when he prays that he would " glorify his Son." In this ſenſe may that part of the ſummary of prayer, which *Chriſt* dictated to his diſciples, be underſtood. " Our Father who art in heaven, hallowed be thy name, (thy *Chriſt* who is *thy name*, as by him thou art manifeſted to us) Thy kingdom come;" which is under his adminiſtration as the king and law-giver thereof.

THIS *Angel*, who is called the preſence of GOD, in whom his name is, *Iſaiah* calls the Saviour,

our, and adds, "In all their afflictions he was afflicted, (or in all their straits they were not besieged) the *Angel of his presence* saved them: In his love and in his pity, he redeemed them,—and carried them all the days of old." This is the same of whom *Malachi* speaks,—" The LORD, whom ye seek, shall suddenly come to his temple; even the *messenger* (which is the meaning of the word *Angel*) of the covenant whom ye delight in." This is none other than *Jesus Christ*, the same who is called the *Angel of God's presence*, in whom *his name is*, who had the power and prerogative of GOD in pardoning or retaining the people's sins at his pleasure, and who claimed the titles, authority, and worship of *Almighty God*.

I MUST confess, that the account we have from *Eusebius* gives room to think the *ancients* were of a different opinion concerning this *Angel*, who is promised to lead *Israel* into *Canaan*; which is, that as *Moses*, by divine authority gave the title of *anointed* to *Aaron*, as a type of *Christ*, the great high priest; so upon *Joshua's* defeating the *Amalikites*, whose name before was *Oshea*, he added the first letter of *Jehovah* to his name, pointing him forth as an eminent type of *Christ* in his regal office, as JEHOVAH the *Saviour*, by his name *Joshua*, which is the same with *Jesus a Saviour*: And also in his remarkable conquest of *Israel's* enemies, and bringing them into the promised land. And when our *Lord* was to assume flesh, he received this name *Jesus* by commission from heaven, in allusion to so eminent a type of him, as a Saviour. Therefore they conclude, that the *Angel* promised to lead *Israel*, is no other than *Joshua* or *Jesus* (as he is oftener than once called in the New Testament)

ment) the fucceffor of *Mofes*, whom the people were commanded to obey, becaufe he bare the fame name, that he himfelf was to be known by, when he fhould actually appear in flefh. And whereas it is faid, "He will not pardon your tranfgreffions," (or let your rebellion go unpunifhed) It points out *Jofhua* having only the executive power of laws already made, committed to him; and that he would not have that accefs as a temporary mediator, which *Mofes* had of coming into the prefence of GOD, to fave them from punifhment when they had finned.

IF this, rather than the other, be chofen as the fenfe, it makes the point I am proving equally ftrong: As by taking the *Angel* in this fenfe, then *Jefus Chrift* is the *God* that promifes to fend the *Angel*, and favour the people with his prefence, if they would obey him.

A VERY little confideration will lead any one to fee, that it was *Jefus Chrift* who gave the law, and made that auguft and folemn appearance on *Mount Sinai*, claiming the divine authority of giving laws to *Ifrael*, under the facred titles of JEHOVAH *their* GOD. In the epiftle to the *Hebrews*, the Apoftle fays,—(*d*) "See that ye refufe not him that fpeaketh: For if they efcaped not who refufed him that fpake on earth, much more fhall not we efcape, if we turn away from him that fpeaketh from heaven: *Whofe voice then fhook the earth:* But now *he* hath promfed, faying, yet once more I fhake not the earth only, but heaven alfo." This fhaking of the earth refers to the convulfions of *Mount Sinai*, at the giving of the law. It is *Jefus*, the
mediator

(*d*) Heb. xii. 25, 26

mediator of the New Testament, whom he is here speaking of, as is most clear from the context, " *whose voice* (says he) *shook the earth*, &c." The promise mentioned is also referred to him. " *He* (*Jesus*, for there is no other antecedent to this relative) hath also promised, &c." The words of the promise are taken from *Haggai*, (e) Who tells us, it was the LORD GOD that said so; but the Apostle says it was JESUS. It is therefore manifest that JESUS, the mediator of the New Testament, is JEHOVAH the GOD of *Israel*, who gave the law on *Mount Sinai*,—and the LORD GOD, mentioned by *Haggai*.

IT will make this argument more conspicuous, if we consider him who is said *to speak on earth*, to be *Christ* in his angelic character under the Old Testament: (Not *Moses*, as commonly supposed) And he who speaks from heaven, the same *Jesus Christ* in his glorious exaltation as a *Son*, at the Father's right hand. The antithesis then will not be betwixt *Christ* and *Moses*, but betwixt the character of *Christ*, under the more obscure dispensation of the Old Testament, and the clear discoveries of his grace and power as an ascended king and lawgiver. The Apostle's scope in the passage, is not to compare *Moses* and *Christ*; but the *darkness* and *awfulness* of the dispensation of the *law*, compared to a yoke of bondage; with the *freedom* and *spirituality*, the *clearness* and *sweetness* of the *gospel*: And having proved that the excellencies and privileges of the one, are superior to the other, as to *evidence*, the one being dark and cloudy, the other clear and perspicuous. As to *extent*,—the former being confined to the *Jews*, and a few proselytes of the *Gentiles*; the latter extends to the whole world,— its

(*e*) Hag. ii. 6.

its converts are out of all nations, &c. As to *worſhip*,—the one being a yoke, the other spiritual and easy: The one excels the other also in the *plenitude* and *efficacy* of the *gifts* bestowed. The Apostle having made the difference so plain, he then makes a very natural conclusion, that therefore the obligation to attend the duties required, were in proportion to the privileges bestowed, and the danger of contempt heightened accordingly.

WHICH ever way the reader inclines to take this part of the Apostle's argument, it holds true, that JESUS is the LORD OF HOSTS, who shook the earth in that tremendous manner when he gave the law,—and he whom *Moses* and the people feared and worshipped on that solemn occasion.

HE who appeared to *Joshua* on the banks of *Jorden*, calls himself the " Captain of the LORD's hosts;" and by this title, intimates for his encouragement, that as he had protected the people in the wilderness, so now he appeared ready armed to lead them against the formidable nations, which he had formerly promised to drive out before them. This character is so much the same with the " Captain of salvation," given to *Chriſt* in the New Testament, that none can doubt it was he who appeared to *Joshua*.

HE also appeared to *Manoah*, and called himself by a *name*, which, by the Prophet *Isaiah*, is given to *Jesus*. (*f*) " Why askest thou after my name (faith he to *Manoah*) seeing it is WONDERFUL?" as in the margin. (*g*) " His *name* (even the child that should be born, and the son given) shall be called WONDERFUL."

FROM

(*f*) Judg. xiii. 18. (*g*) Isa. ix. 6.

From these examples, it is plain that it was *Jesus Christ*, who made the appearances, and claimed the honours of Deity. And were it necessary, we might, to the testimony of the Apostles and Prophets, add the suffrage of the ancient *Jews* and christian Fathers, who ascribe these expressions of scripture to the *word of God*,—the *Memra* or *Logos*,—and often to the *Messiah*, where he is represented in a visible manner conversing with men, or coming to save them. Now, among the ancient *Jews*, the *Memra* or *Logos*, (that is the *word of God*) often signifies God *himself*,—something *in and of God*,—some *divine principle* belonging to the *essence of God*, whereby he transacts his affairs with creatures: It also with them signified a *glorious Spirit*, superior to all angels, *in whom God put his name*,—*in whom he resided* in a peculiar manner, as in a *habitation*, which they called the *Shekinah*. Both these ideas may be united in the *Messiah*. However, it is certain, that these scriptures, where God is represented in a visible manner, eminently, as a Saviour to his people, have been interpreted concerning *Christ*, by ancient *Jews*, christian Fathers, and the Apostles themselves. From which we may conclude, that proper Deity is included in his character: For these * ancient *Jews* and sacred writers,

---

* The *Jews* supposed something very extraordinary and divine in the *letters* which make the word Jehovah, and the highest profanation for *any* to pronounce them, but the *high-priest* once a year; they therefore never wrote or pronounced the word, but substituted the word Adonai instead of it. And this conceit they carried so far, as to imagine that whoever could pronounce them truly, might work miracles, and controul nature at pleasure. Hence they pretend to account for the power our Saviour had to work miracles by this forged story; that he gaining admission into the temple, stole the name Jehovah, rightly wrote and pointed, as it should be pronounced, and by virtue of this divine secret wrought his miracles, and might have wrought as many as he would.

writers, had such an awful sense of the transcendent excellency of the Great GOD, and of his jealousy for his own name and honour, that they would not dare to attribute his most sublime titles, characters, and glories to any mere creature, or to any thing which had not true and proper Deity.

THEREFORE to deny these glorious titles, JEHOVAH, LORD GOD, the GOD *of Israel*, &c. to belong to *Christ*, or to interpret them into such a diminutive sense as may belong to a created being, without unity to Deity, is to deny the most plain and obvious sense and meaning of both the *sacred writers* and *ancient Jews*.

BUT I must remove another difficulty, which some perhaps will reckon insurmountable on this plan. " He who sustains the character of GOD under the Old Testament, often speaks of *another* of an inferior character, and promises to send *him*, which is no other than *Jesus Christ*. Now if *Christ* be the speaker, he must speak of *himself*,—promise to send *himself*, &c."

THE difficulty here is far from being insuperable, if one thing is duly attended to, that wherever he is promised, as the *seed of the woman*,—of *Abraham* or *David*,—as the *righteous branch*,—a *son*, or *servant*,—or whatever other name, they all refer to that part of his œconomical character, in which he appeared to be inferior to GOD, in that state of humiliation he had to undergo for the salvation of mankind. There is therefore no incongruity in his assuming the majesty of *Deity*, and yet foretelling his transactions in that low and abased character, which he was to appear in as the servant of GOD, and Saviour of men. This idea will appear

strange,

strange, perhaps, to them who have not accustomed themselves to read the Old Testament in that view: But a little serious attention will reconcile them to it as a truth, which is intelligible and plain in itself.

LET such only consider these passages of the Old Testament, where *Jesus Christ* under the title of JEHOVAH makes promises, and foretels events concerning what he would do for the church in future times, which he *(Jesus Christ)* performed and fulfilled in his own person, and are expresly applied to him in the New Testament. This will clearly shew, that while he was sustaining the majesty of *Deity*, as the GOD and king of *Israel*, and speaking of another, (as it would appear at first sight to the inattentive reader) that it was himself under another character, in which he was to appear for the fulfilling the great purposes of GOD concerning mankind. A few examples will make this abundantly evident.

(*h*) " AND ye shall know that I am the LORD your GOD,—I will pour out my Spirit upon all flesh, and your sons and your daughters shall prophesy,—and whosoever shall call on the name of the LORD (JEHOVAH) shall be delivered; for in *Mount Zion* and in *Jerusalem* shall be deliverance, as the LORD hath said; and in the remnant whom the LORD shall call." The Apostle *Peter* applies the whole of this to that extraordinary effusion of the Spirit at Pentecost, which *Christ* had promised that *he* would send when he went away. And *Paul* expresly applies what is said by JEHOVAH in *Joel* to *Jesus Christ*. Having mentioned these words,—
" Who-

(*h*) Joel ii. 27,—32.

(*i*) "Whosoever shall call on the *name of the Lord, shall be saved,*" he presently accommodates them to him who brought glad tidings of good things to both *Jews* and *Gentiles,* in whom they should believe, which can be no other than (*k*) *Jesus Christ.*

AFTER the Psalmist had given a summary of GOD's wonderful works among the children of *Israel,* he says, (*l*) "This is the hill GOD desireth to dwell in; JEHOVAH will dwell in it for ever: The chariots of GOD are twenty thousand,—the LORD is among them as in *Mount Sinai,*—thou hast ascended on high, thou hast led captivity captive, and received gifts for the rebellious also, that the LORD GOD might dwell among them." This in the very words of the Psalmist is applied to (*m*) *Jesus Christ* by the Apostle.

(*n*) "JEHOVAH reigneth, let the earth be glad,—confounded be they that serve graven images: Worship *him* all ye GODS." This passage points out the glory of the *Gentile* nations, when salvation should be brought to them by *Jesus Christ,* and their idolatry destroyed by the success of his gospel. Then the commandment is to the GODS to worship *him.* It no ways affects the present argument, whether the GODS mentioned here, are Angels, or princes of the *Gentiles;* it is plain, that whether or both be meant, they are commanded to worship JEHOVAH that reigneth. But the Apostle interprets this of *Christ,* (*o*) and applies the very words of the Psalmist to him.

AGAIN,

(*i*) Rom x. 12, 13. (*k*) Com. Isa. lxi. 1, 2. with Luke iv. 17, 18, 19. (*l*) Psa. lxviii. 7,—18. (*m*) Eph. iv. 7,—11. (*n*) Psa. xcvii. 1,—7. (*o*) Heb. i. 6.

AGAIN, the Pſalmiſt foretelling the glory of that time, when *Jews* and *Gentiles* ſhould be one church under *Chriſt*, ſays, (p) "The heathen ſhall fear the *name* of the LORD, and all kings of the earth thy glory: The LORD ſhall declare his *name* in *Zion*, and his praiſe in *Jeruſalem*, when the people are gathered together, and the kingdoms (of the *Gentiles*) to ſerve the LORD. Of old haſt thou laid the foundations of the earth, and the heavens are the work of thy hands; they ſhall periſh, but thou art the ſame, &c. This is alſo applied to (q) *Chriſt* by the ſame Apoſtle.

IT is univerſally acknowledged, even by the *Jews*, that the 2d Pſalm is a deſcription of the kingdom and government of the *Meſſiah*. And as kings and governors are there required to yield obedience to him, or be puniſhed for rebellion againſt him, their ſovereign, it is evident; he is not only king in *Zion*, but governor over the heathen to the utmoſt ends of the earth. The way the ſeventy render this paſſage, makes it more plain. (r) "But I am appointed king under him, upon his holy hill of *Zion*, to make known the conſtitution of JEHOVAH: For JEHOVAH hath ſaid unto me, &c." From which it appears, that all government was then in the hand of *Chriſt*, as well as it is now, which he affirms himſelf. "The Father judgeth no man; but hath committed all judgment (government) unto the *Son*."

THE Pſalmiſt ſays,—"Thou art my king, O GOD, command deliverances for *Jacob*." Pſa. xliv. and in the ſame Pſalm adds, "For thy ſake we are

---

(p) Pſa. cii. 15, 16,—25. (q) Heb. i. 10, 11, 12. (r) Pſa. ii. 6, 7.

are we killed all the day long, we are counted as sheep for the slaughter." *Paul* cites these words, when he is shewing how impossible it was to separate him and the believing *Romans* from the love of *Christ*. Which shews that he who was the GOD and *king* of *Israel*, is the same *Jesus Christ*, for whose sake the saints in *Paul*'s time suffered tribulation, distress, persecution, &c. Rom. viii. 35, 36.

IT is obvious to every attentive reader, that one of the most striking descriptions we have concerning GOD in revelation, is given by *Isaiah*, (s) Whose glory, saith he, filled the earth,—whom seraphs adored as LORD of the whole earth,—who is called the king, the LORD of hosts. Yet this is applied in the plainest terms to *Jesus Christ* by *John*, (t) " These things said *Isaias*, when he saw *his glory* and spake of him."

(u) " THE wilderness, and the solitary place shall be glad, the desart shall rejoice and blossom as the rose, the glory of *Lebanon* shall be given to it, the excellency of *Carmel* and *Sharon*, they shall see the glory of the LORD, and the excellency of our GOD. Your GOD will come with a recompense, *he* will come and save you. The ears of the deaf shall be unstopped, and the eyes of the blind shall be opened, &c." This plainly refers to the miracles wrought by *Christ*, and so applied by himself. (v)

(w) " BEHOLD, I will send *my* messenger, and *he* shall prepare the way before *me*: 'And the *Lord*, whom ye seek, shall suddenly come to *his* temple:

Even

(s) Isa. vi. 1, 2, 3, 4, 5. (t) John xii. 41. (u) Isa. xxxv. 12. (v) Matt. xi. 4, 5. (w) Mal. iii. 1.

Even the messenger of the covenant, whom ye delight in: Behold, he shall come, saith the LORD OF HOSTS." This text is a demonstrative proof of what I am pleading for, and a fair answer to the objection proposed above. For without admitting that he who is spoken of, is also the speaker, it is impossible to make it good sense, or agreeable to the scope of revelation. The *messenger* or *Angel* of the covenant, is no other than the *Lord Jesus*, whose way *John* was sent to prepare; yet the LORD OF HOSTS says, "I will send MY messenger, and he shall prepare the way before ME." Therefore the natural meaning is, that the LORD OF HOSTS is declaring how soon he would appear in the character of the MESSIAH, who had been often promised to the *Jews*, and whom they were at this time waiting and wishing for.

I SHALL only add one instance more to this purpose. The eleventh chapter of *Isaiah* is a glorious description of the character and kingdom of the *Messiah*, there called the stem and root of *Jesse*. But after we are told what great things he would do in his church, by the SPIRIT JEHOVAH resting upon him; in the 12th chapter (which should not have been divided from the former, if the sense had been attended to by him that divided them) we are told, what the church would say in consequence of such privileges. "Behold, GOD, my *salvation*: I will trust, and not be afraid; for JEHOVAH, JEHOVAH, is my strength and song, he also is become my *salvation* (JESUS). Therefore with joy shall ye draw water out of the wells of salvation." This is the great change! He who bore the character of JEHOVAH, is become JESUS *the saviour*, whose promises, character, and work, are wells of salvation, out of which his people shall

shall for ever draw water with joy. The conclusion is, " sing to JEHOVAH; for he hath done excellent things: This is known in all the earth. Cry out and shout, thou inhabitant of *Zion:* For great is the *holy one of Israel* in the midst of thee." By JEHOVAH becoming JESUS, he loses neither the titles nor glory due to JEHOVAH. This being so plain here, and in many other passages, that it will be hard to find what profitable use can be made of them, if they are taken in a different point of view.

IT seems pretty evident to me, that he who is so often called the *holy one of Israel*, is the *Lord Jesus Christ*. The epithet *holy one*, is frequently given him in both Testaments. In view of his sufferings and death, he says, (*x*) " My flesh shall rest in hope, for thou wilt not leave my soul in hell; neither wilt thou suffer thine *holy one* to see corruption." This is not spoken of *David*, for *Peter* expressly tells us, that it was spoken (*y*) " of the resurrection of *Christ*." And *Paul* says, " it could not be said of *David*, who fell asleep, was laid unto his fathers, and saw corruption: But he *(Jesus)* whom GOD raised again, saw no corruption. Thou spakest in vision to thy *holy one*, and saidst, I have laid help upon one that is mighty, &c." The sequel of the Psalm, and the use the Apostle makes of the passage, shew that *Jesus*, *David's seed*, is here intended. (*z*) " I know thee who thou art, the *holy one of God*. But ye denied the *holy one*, and the just. But ye have an unction from the *holy one*." This was the son of GOD, who is so designed: Now, *son of God*, and *king of Israel*,
M were

(*x*) Psa. xvi. 9, 10. *(y)* Acts ii. 27, 31. ibid. xiii. 35, 36, 37. Psa. lxxxix. 19. (*z*) Mark i. 24. Acts iii. 14. 1 John ii. 20.

were titles of the same person. Hence the *Jews* upbraided our LORD upon the cross, " if thou be the *son of God*, come down from the cross: If he be the *king of Israel*, let him come down from the cross." Perhaps some of the same multitude, who a little before cried Hosanna, blessed is the king of *Israel*, &c. *Nathaniel* is express to this purpose, " Rabbi, thou art the *son of God*, thou art *the king of Israel*." The *son of God* is *the king of Israel*, who is the same with the *holy one of Israel*; for these are frequently given as titles of the same person, and even in the same verse, " I am the *Lord*, your *holy one*, the creator of *Israel*, your king." With this title is also joined that of *redeemer*, which determines who we are to understand by the *holy one of Israel*. (*a*) " Thus saith the *Lord*, the *redeemer of Israel*, his *holy one*. For thy maker is thy husband, (the *Lord* of hosts is his name) and thy *redeemer*, the *holy one of Israel*." The Psalmist says, they tempted GOD, and limited the *holy one of Israel*; and the Apostle says, it was *Christ* they tempted. These things considered, put it beyond doubt, that by the *holy one of Israel*, is meant the *Lord Jesus*, the king and governor of the *Jewish Theocracy*.

FROM which it must follow, that all the characters that are joined with this, as belonging to the same person, properly belong to the *Lord Jesus*. As the name *Jehovah*. (*b*) " Thus saith *Jehovah*, the *holy one of Israel*, and his maker, &c. As for our redeemer, the *Lord of hosts* is his name, the *holy one of Israel*. The heathen shall know that I am the *Lord*, (JEHOVAH) the *holy one of Israel*."

He

(*a*) Isa. xlix. 7, and liv. 5. '(*b*) Isa. xlv. 11, and xlvii. 4. Eze. xxxix. 7.

He was the object of *Ifrael*'s worſhip.—(c) "Unto thee will I ſing with the harp, O thou *holy one of Ifrael*." He was their defence, hope, and ſtay.— (d) " For the LORD is our *defence*: And the *holy one of Ifrael* is our king." Againſt him they ſinned in all their departures from the laws he had given them:—(e) " They provoked the *holy one of Ifrael* unto anger. They have caſt away the law of the *Lord of hoſts*, and deſpiſed the word of the *holy one of Ifrael*." This argument, if properly conſidered, will amount to a ſtrong proof of the *Deity of Jeſus Chriſt*, in as much as he was the GOD and governor of *Ifrael*, who had given them laws, and puniſhed them for their frequent rebellions,—whoſe holy preſence they could not endure when diſpoſed to ſin, and therefore cry, " cauſe the *holy one of Ifrael* to ceaſe from before us."

THESE are but a few of the many inſtances that might be given, to which, thoſe in the laſt ſection relating to the ſame ſubject may be added, to ſhew that he who ſpeaks, or is ſpoken of by the ſacred writers, and is called JEHOVAH, LORD GOD, the GOD *and king of Ifrael*, &c. is no other than JESUS CHRIST: For as the ſame things which are ſpoken *of*, or *by him* in the Old Teſtament, under theſe ſacred titles, are applied to *Jeſus Chriſt* in the New Teſtament, it muſt be *him* who bears theſe titles in the Old. And by a ſerious and impartial attention, we will find, that in all the Old Teſtament, eſpecially the Pſalms, and ſome of the Prophets, wherever JEHOVAH, GOD, or any other term by which the ſupreme Being is expreſſed, there is ſomething predicated of him, that is either

expreſsly

(c) Pſa. lxxi. 22 (d) ibid. lxxxix. 18. ſee alſo Iſa. x. 20,— xii. 16,—xvii. 7,—xxix. 19,—xli. 44. (e) Iſa. i. 4.—v. 24. ſee chap. xxx. 11, 12.—xxxi 1.

expresly applied to *Christ* in some other text, or is a part of his character and office in the œconomy of grace and providence. Take for instance, all those epithets given to JEHOVAH of a *rock, refuge, redeemer, deliverer, defence, shepherd, shield, strong hold, saviour, helper, healer, light, leader, guide, holy one, horn of salvation, hope, inheritance, law-giver, judge, king,* &c. all which are so many parts of *Christ*'s character. And hence, by a *general rule*, which must hold, if the scriptures are intelligible, the whole Old Testament will be found a description of the character and works of JESUS CHRIST.

THAT wherever there is any part of a Psalm, or other passage, applied to *Jesus Christ* in the New Testament, as spoken either *of,* or *by him* in the Old Testament, then, not only the whole of that Psalm, or other passage, but every other Psalm or passage, that is parallel to those which are expresly applied to *Christ*, must as certainly be spoken *of*, or *by him*, as that which is expresly applied *to him*. If the subject be the same, or has a relation thereto, the person must be the same who speaks, or is spoken of. This is the true *analogy of faith*, to lead into the scope and sense of scripture, with respect to *him* who is the leading subject of the whole.

WHAT I have been endeavouring to illustrate, would have appeared perfectly clear, if the word rendered *salvation* in the Old Testament, had been read JESUS, which it really is. As for example, *Isaiah* says,—*(f)* " The LORD JEHOVAH is my strength and song, he also *is become my salvation*, (JESUS). *(g)* " In that day shall this song be sung

in

(*f*) Isa. xii. 2. (*g*) ibid. xxvi. 1.

in the land of *Judah*, we have a strong city, salvation will GOD appoint for walls and bulwarks." Keep out the words *God* and *for*, which are only supplements of the translator, and it reads,— "*Salvation* (JESUS) will appoint walls and bulwarks." It would have been as plain in such texts, of which there is a great number, that JESUS was JEHOVAH the *king of Israel*, as that he died and rose again, appear in the gospels. The most stubborn prejudice could not then have denied, that he had an existence before he was conceived of the virgin,—or believed him to be only an inferior Deity. While the Old Testament could scarcely be opened any where, but they might find him spoken of in characters suitable only to ALMIGHTY GOD,—Ascriptions which obviously point out Deity, agreeably blended with others, which imply his character and office as the redeemer and Saviour of men. Thus, as EMMANUEL, he is as certainly, tho' not with the same *degree* of clearness, described in the Old Testament, as in the New, and in such terms as cannot be applied with any propriety to any other but JESUS CHRIST.

I SHALL now only mention a few texts from the New Testament, which prove that *Jesus Christ* existed as the GOD and king of the church, under the old dispensation,—the guide and hope of his people in all ages.

WHEN our LORD told the *Jews*, that " Abraham rejoiced to see his day : And he saw it, and was glad ;" They reckoned it impossible, and told him, " Thou art not yet fifty years old, and hast thou seen *Abraham* ?" Yea, replied our *Lord*, " before *Abraham was*, I AM." He does not deny, that as a man, he appeared to be less than fifty years old,

old, but at the same time asserts his *pre-existence before Abraham*, and in the same words, which he did under the title of JEHOVAH, the *God of Israel*, to *Moses*, whom he commanded to say, "I AM hath sent me unto you." And as *Christ* oftener than once calls himself so, after he appeared in flesh, it cannot be doubted that he is the I AM that spoke with *Moses*.

And this is further clear from what the Apostle says of *Moses*, that " he choose rather to suffer affliction with the people of GOD, than to enjoy the pleasures of sin for a season ; esteeming the reproach of CHRIST greater riches than all the treasures of *Egypt*." In what sense *Moses* going with the people of GOD, can be called the *reproach* of CHRIST, without admitting the truth I am pleading for, I cannot understand. The reproach of *Christ* has always been the same. Those who bear it, must forsake their attachments to the leading interests of this world. As *Moses* forsook the treasures of *Egypt*, so the Apostle exhorts the *Hebrews* to go forth unto *Christ* without the camp, bearing his reproach.

THE *Corinthians* are admonished not to tempt *Christ*, as some of the *Israelites* did in the wilderness, which certainly supposes that CHRIST was their leader. *Peter*, speaking of the salvation which the ancient believers looked and longed for, says, " The Prophets (from *Adam* to that period) prophesied of the grace that should come, searching what manner of time the spirit of CHRIST which was in them did signify, when it testified before hand the sufferings of CHRIST, and the glory that should follow." The same *spirit of Christ*, that taught the Apostles in the New Testament, inspired

spired the Prophets in the Old. Hence, *Christ* is the author of all the religion we have in the Bible: The sole guide of those who were the chosen instruments of publishing it: The universal shepherd of the church,—this is his character in both testaments: The door by which Prophets, as well as Apostles, Old as well as New Testament saints have entered into the fold,—by whom they were saved, conducted, and instructed in the knowledge of GOD. From the first to the last saint on earth, their knowledge of GOD must come through this medium,—" *Christ the power of God, and the wisdom of God.*" The power of GOD, in creating all things, and governing them,—in pardoning, sanctifying, supporting, and comforting his people in all ages.—The wisdom of GOD; not only as he is perfectly acquainted with the whole will of GOD; but as he hath revealed and made it known to men. Hence, said to be " made of GOD unto us wisdom. In him dwell all the treasures of wisdom and knowledge," personally and œconomically. He is not only possessed of infinite knowledge and understanding, whereby he can view the whole length and breadth of the mind and will of GOD, in the most perfect manner: But infinite wisdom and prudence, to execute the purposes of GOD in creation, government, and redemption, with unerring fitness and skill; whereby he brings the will of GOD to the view of intelligent creatures; and for this reason is so often called in scripture the WORD or LOGOS *of God*, a name by which the *Jews* knew him who governed the world in general, and the affairs of their church and nation in particular; and to whom, in the New Testament, is ascribed, the creating and disposal of all things.

THE

THE Apostle's description is so plain and full, that it's surprising any should refuse to assent to this truth. He tells us, that all things in heaven and earth were made by him, and for him: And adds, " he is before all things, and by him all things consist. And he is the head of the body, the church; who is the beginning, the first-born from the dead, that in all things he might have the pre-eminence, for it pleased the Father that in him should all fulness dwell."

IN favour of this cause, several other names which are given to *Jesus Christ*, may be applied with great propriety. As *Alpha* and *Omega*,—the *beginning* and the *ending*,—the *first* and the *last*. All these, I humbly conceive, have an immediate respect to his creating and governing all things,—his managing all the dispensations of GOD, and bringing them to a glorious conclusion at last.

THE word AMEN, which will bear no translation, and is therefore the same in all languages, is of the same import with " *the truth*," a designation which *Christ* appropriates to himself, denoting that he is the author, as well as the scope of all the truth contained in revelation.

THE attentive consideration of the first twelve verses of *John*'s gospel, will convince any one of the truth I have been illustrating. *Jesus Christ*, who is there called the *Word*, is described as having existence WITH GOD before any thing else existed, and his giving existence to all things,—being the *light* and *life* of all in general,—his ancient relation to the *Jewish* nation, who are called *his own*,—his divine power in giving the right and privilege of adoption to these who are made the children

dren of GOD. That all thefe are faid of him, before his appearing in flefh, is plain from the narrative itfelf, and the way this paragraph is clofed, by adding, "And the *word* was made FLESH, and dwelt among us, and we beheld his glory, &c." To add this, had been a manifeft impropriety, if the things formerly faid, had not referred to a time prior to his being made flefh. Befides, it is further added, "No man hath feen GOD at *any time*; the only begotten Son, which is in the bofom of the Father; he hath declared him." This plainly fhews, that all the knowledge ever any had of GOD, in *any period* of time, came by him, who, fince he affumed flefh, is commonly called the *Son of God*.

I AM perfuaded the impartial reader will be fatisfied from fo many fcripture teftimonies, that *Jefus Chrift* not only made the world, but hath governed all things, and the church in particular in all ages,—did all the mighty works, and affumed all the titles due only to GOD.

I SHOULD more particularly prove, that the faints under both Teftaments worfhipped him as their GOD and King. Having proved that he was the GOD, and king of *Ifrael*, it follows, that they worfhipped him as fuch: Nay, they were exprefsly prohibited from worfhipping any other than the *holy one*, who is called the *creator of Ifrael*, and *their king*,—*their redeemer*,—*the king of glory*,—*the king, the* LORD *of hofts*,—*the king of Zion*. All which are applied to *Jefus Chrift*, who owns himfelf to be the *king* of the *Jews*: And approves of *Nathaniel*'s addrefs, "Thou art the *Son of God*, thou art the *king of Ifrael*." The proper enjoyment of

thefe

these titles, by right, gives him the justest claim to the worship and praises of *Israel*.

WHAT evasion will be found, if instances are produced of the prophesies concerning the worship that should be given to GOD, literally fulfilled in him; and the most solemn acts of worship immediately directed to him? The Psalmist says, "Out of the mouth of babes and sucklings hast thou ordained strength, because of thine enemies, &c." This was fulfilled in the most striking manner in the praises of the children, who cried, "Hosanna to the son of *David*." Which honour being envied by his enemies, the *Jews*, he refers them to this prophecy in the Psalms, as fulfilling in their presence.

AFTER the Psalmist, in a most animating description, had shewed the beauty and grace of the church, and the majesty of her *king*, he adds, "The *king* shall greatly desire thy beauty: For he is *thy Lord*, and *worship thou him*."

WHATEVER relation that magnificent description in the 72d Psalm may have to *Solomon*, as the title would insinuate, I shall not determine; but it is certain, the ascriptions are such as will only suit a character that is truely divine. The perpetual and universal dominion, mentioned therein, is only applicable to *Christ*, whose "dominion is an everlasting dominion, and whose kingdom ruleth over all." And what is said concerning the bringing of presents, and offering gifts by eastern kings, was literally accomplished at his birth, when the sages from the (*b*) east presented their gifts, and *worshipped him*. "O COME,

(*b*) Matt. ii. 11.

(c) "O come, let us worship and bow down: Let us kneel before the Lord (Jehovah) our maker: for he is our God, and we are the people of his pasture, and the sheep of his hand: to-day if ye will hear his voice, &c." If the character of a *shepherd*, so plainly implied here, is reckoned not sufficient to limit the *worship* to *Jesus Christ*, it will certainly put it beyond doubt, when the Apostle applies the passage expressly to him. (d)

In the New Testament, we find divine worship given him by saints, both in earth and heaven. I shall not take notice of all the instances of worship and homage given him by the people, when they were under surprize from the greatness of his miracles: This, perhaps, would be reckoned by some too low a kind of worship, to argue the Deity of the object from: But I shall select an example or two of divine worship solemnly directed to him; one is, that remarkable instance of *Stephen*, who, when his enemies were stoning him to death, could venture his departing soul, with every concern of his, in eternity, to the care of *Jesus Christ*, and with his last breath, addressed him in solemn prayer, in behalf of himself and his murderers. (e) "And they stoned *Stephen, calling upon*, and *saying, Lord Jesus receive my Spirit*. And he kneeled down, and cried with a loud voice, *Lord*, lay not this sin to their charge." I have omitted the word *God* in this text, because it should not be there; and the *English* reader will see that the translators, who supplied it, have been so fair as to put it down as a supplement. But for what reason it should be there at all, is more than any
friend

(c) Psa. xcv. 6, 7. (d) Heb. iii. 7, 8. and iv. 7. (e) Acts vii. 59, 60.

friend to the Deity of *Jesus Christ* can account for, as it weakens the evidence in the text for *Christ* being the object of *Stephen's* worship, which is so conspicuous without it, as the greatest enemy to *Christ's* divinity cannot deny it, if he will admit that *Luke* spoke good sense. His words are literally thus, " And they stoned *Stephen, crying, Lord Jesus receive my Spirit.*"

ANOTHER plain text to this purpose is, what *Peter* concludes his second epistle with. " Grow in grace, and in the knowledge of our *Lord* and Saviour *Jesus Christ: To whom be glory, both now and evermore. Amen.*" †

AND the inhabitants of heaven do also account the *Lamb* worthy of divine adoration.—*(f)* " And I beheld in the midst of the throne, a *Lamb*, as it had been slain,—and when he had taken the Book, the four Beasts, and four and twenty Elders *fell down before the Lamb*, having every one of them harps, and golden vials full of odours, which are the prayers of the saints,—saying, with a loud voice,

---

(f) Rev. v. 6.—14.

† Acts i. 24. " Thou, LORD, who knowest the hearts, shew whether of these two thou hast chosen, &c." That it was *Christ* who is here solemnly addressed seems plain. (1st.) From his challenging the same perfection of knowing the reins and the hearts, Rev. ii. 23, 27. which is here attributed to him. (2d.) From the subject of the petition, viz. the appointing an Apostle, which was his office as *Lord* and *head* of the church, and whom *Paul* tells us, had called him and all the other Apostles to their offices.

There are many other texts, which point out the worship of *Christ*, a few of them I shall here cite. Matt. xxviii. 19. Luke xxiv. 51, 52. John v. 22, 23. Acts ix. 13, 14, 21.—15, 17. 1 Cor. i. 2. Acts xix. 13,—iii, 6.—vii. 59. 2 Cor. xii. 8. Phil. ii. 10, 11, 19. Col. iii. 11.—17. 2 Thess. ii. 16, 17. 1 Tim. i. 12. 2 Tim. iv. 18, 22. Tit. i. 4. Heb. i. 6. 2 Pet. iii. 18. Rev. v. 6. 8, 9, 10, 12, 13.—vii. 10.

voice, worthy is the *Lamb* that was flain, to *receive power*, and *riches*, and *wifdom*, and *ftrength*, and *honour*, and *glory*, and *bleffing*,—and the four Beafts faid, *Amen*. And the four and twenty Elders *fell down and worfhipped him that liveth for ever and ever.*" Thefe laft words are part of the character *Chrift* took to himfelf in the firft of the Revelations; and therefore we may conclude, it is he who is meant, when they are fo often repeated in that book, and always with the higheft worfhip, adoration, and praife afcribed to him, both by angels and men.

AT the clofe of thefe revelations, *Jefus*, the divine author of them, certifies *John* concerning the accomplifhment of the events.—(*g*) " He who teftifieth thefe things, faith, furely I come quickly." To which *John* replies in a moft folemn addrefs, which every one who is longing for the coming of their LORD will join him in, *Amen*. *Even fo*, " come LORD JESUS."

WERE it not that this fection is too long already, the utility and advantages of this truth might be fhewed to the right knowledge of revelation, and the practice of religion. It renders many texts plain and agreeable to the general fcope of fcripture, which have been tortured with unnatural expofitions, and been reckoned unintelligible, without the affiftance of figures and metaphors, as *prolepfes* (fpeaking of things before they were done) or *catachrefes*, (calling GOD a man, angel, meffenger, captain, &c. without actual union to human nature) which not one of a hundred that read the Bible knows any thing about. It makes an
agreeable

(*g*) Rev. xxii. 20, 21.

agreeable connexion betwixt the Old and New Testament, and brings the scope of both into an easy point of view; and consequently recommends the duty of searching the scriptures to the unlearned part of mankind. The multiplicity of interpretations by commentators, and their contrariety, have not only incumbered the sense of many passages; but given adversaries occasion to insult, as if the Bible was a volume of absurd and inconsistent things, which must discourage many sincere inquirers after truth.

WHEREAS the scheme of revealed truth, particularly what relates to *Christ*, is harmoniously connected; and the further light we get into any part of his character, never fails to shed divine brightness over all the other parts taken in connexion: The terms which express the character of *Christ* become familiar and plain, which have appeared dark, if not unintelligible. When we read of the *light, fire, bright cloud*, &c. in which GOD spake,—of his being *light*,—of his *face, presence, glory*, the *power of God*, the *wisdom of God*, and many others, we know what idea should be prefixed to them, as various parts of *his* character, who has managed all the dispensations of providence, grace, and mercy to the children of men.

IT tends greatly to exalt the character of *Christ* in our conceptions, as it spreads a lustre over all the parts of his glorious administration, in the various transactions recorded in revelation. The more we are acquainted with his government, the more just honour will we put upon him: And be more compleatly furnished with answers to the adversaries of his proper Deity,—support this part of our christian profession,—vindicate the honours of

our

our blessed *Lord*,—invite such as have opposed it through the prejudice of education, and others who are ignorant through inattention to embrace the truth.

It must also raise our views of his wisdom and and power to admiration. There have been many mighty monarchies upon earth, but none in a proper sense could ever be called universal; but that of *Jesus Christ*, who has without interruption been supreme ruler over all. He alone continued to reign in spite of death itself, which puts a period to the rule of other monarchs. In infinite wisdom, and uncontroulable power he has managed all nations, in all their various vicissitudes that have been upon earth, without neglecting the interests of every individual in the universal system. And tho' the reasonable part of his subjects have always acted as free agents, yet, by the providence of this supreme ruler, every thing has been so directed, as to answer the great ends of his government, which extends to the most minute actions. Nor hath the change of times or circumstances,—opposition greater or lesser, ever made the least defect in the unalterable principles on which he carries on his government, as well over the intellectual powers of the mind, as the external actions of the body.

His paternal love and care over his church, appear in most lively colours, through all the periods of his administration : Counterplotting *Satan*, the declared enemy of his people, by means every way suited to their salvation and safety,—raising up one Prophet after another,—and frequently honouring them with appearances and manifestations

tions of himself for their direction and comfort. Thus actually rejoicing in the habitable parts of the earth, and delighting to converse with the sons of men: And in the fulness of time, condescended so low, as to divest himself of the *form* of God, the glorious *Shickinah*, in which he appeared, spoke, and acted in the character *of God*; and take upon him the *form* of a servant,—make himself of no reputation, and submit to the ignominious death of the cross. Here the *Devil*, and the powers of this world, his combined enemies, were permitted to wreck all the premeditated vengeance which their hellish cunning could invent, or their tyranny could execute. Notwithstanding, he shewed their wisdom to be folly, and their power impotence; he triumphed over death, the *Devil*, and all his agents: Rose from the dead,—established upon the foundation of his own blood, the unerring plan of his future government, and perpetual reign over a kingdom of kings and priests; who shall for ever triumph in him as their king, who hath taken unto him his great power, and doth, and shall for ever reign.

PART

PART II.

SECT I.

IN this second part, I shall endeavour to shew that the *names*, or relative characters, FATHER, SON, and WORD, HOLY GHOST, or SPIRIT, are descriptive of the distinct parts they sustain in the DIVINE OECONOMY,‡ revealed in the *sacred word*.

O   THE

‡ The word œconomy, so frequently used in this work, especially in the two last parts, is compounded of two *Greek* words, οικος, which signifies a *house*, and νομος, which signifies a *rule* or *law*. In its sense, it is a scriptural phrase, used by GOD himself, Eze. xliii. 10, 11, 12. "Thou son of man, shew the *house* to the house of *Israel*,—shew them the *laws* thereof,—and all the *ordinances* thereof. Behold, this is the LAW OF THE HOUSE," OECONOMY, or what GOD hath revealed concerning his house, the church. The ideas commonly prefixed to it in *English* are, (1) The management or government of a family or house. (2) Good husbandry, or frugality in expence. (3) The method used in governing or ruling. (4) The disposition or arrangement of the parts of a work. (5) The taking measures rightly for giving a fabric a convenient form. When I speak of the *divine œconomy*, I include the most of these ideas, as far as they have any relation

THE divine scheme of religion, which is only known by revelation, was gradually opened up from one period to another throughout the Old Testament. At different times GOD furnished his people with fresh discoveries concerning himself. Every age was blest with some new revelation of his character, which, like the morning light, shined more and more, until the noon-day glory, manifested in the New Testament, by the sun of righteousness, the LORD JESUS CHRIST: Whose coming was foretold in every age, from the time that the original pair resided in paradise, to the preaching of *John the Baptist*, his immediate fore-runner.

AMONG the many sublime things, said by the Prophets concerning him, and the peculiar advantages that should attend the dispensation of his gospel, I have often admired the beauty of *Isaiah*'s descriptions; in one of which, when speaking of the privileges the kingdom of *Christ* should enjoy, he says,

---

lation to what GOD hath revealed concerning the order and government of his works in general, and the church in particular, which in scripture is called *his house*: Or the whole of GOD's revealed dispensation concerning Angels and men: And by OECONOMICAL, I understand, what belongs to the regulation or management of that dispensation. Hence this term, in its signification, points out the terms *Father*, *Son*, and *Holy Ghost*, *as relative names*, *graciously assumed in sovereign condescension in carrying on the great plan revealed by God in his word*: And is opposed to the common notion of these names, being *natural* or *necessary*, and *essential* in Deity, which at once destroys the freedom and sovereignty of GOD in all his dispensations, which have any relation to these names.

This much I thought necessary, for the sake of such readers as might not be acquainted with the meaning of the word OECONOMY, and in what sense it is applied to this subject. And, I earnestly desire the reader, before he goes further, to have a clear conception of the idea designed by the use of the word, and carry it along with him attentively, in the further consideration of this work.

says, (a) "It shall blossom abundantly, and rejoice, even with joy and singing; the glory of *Lebanon* shall be given into it;. the excellency of *Carmel* and *Sharon*." Then he introduces a surprising climax! Not only should the substance of the most lively shadows among the *Jews* be the privilege of this kingdom, even their temple and consecrated things, which they boasted of as the glory of *Lebanon*, *Carmel*, and *Sharon* : But, as if these were small things, he ascends to the quintessence of excellency and glory.—" They shall see the glory of the LORD (JEHOVAH) the *excellency* of our GOD (ELOHIM)." A more glorious discovery than the most striking appearance of the *Jewish* temple. They should see him who is the divine *medium*, that represents all the infinite perfections of JEHOVAH,—" They shall see the glory of JEHOVAH." Him, whose character and work exhibit the glorious relations in which the *divine three* are made known to the church :—" They shall see the excellency of ELOHIM."

WHEN we consider *Jesus Christ* as the *medium* of that knowledge we have of the divine perfections, our ideas are confined to the notion of *unity* : For we cannot suppose more than *one* possessed of infinite perfections or attributes. So that whatever we learn of divine perfections manifested in *Christ*, leads us to the unity of JEHOVAH, who alone is *infinite*, *unchangeable*, and *eternal*. But when we learn the revealed relations GOD stands in to us, which are also made known in *Christ*, revelation leads us to the knowledge of a *plurality* pointed out in the word ELOHIM, and clearly expressed in three particular *relative* names or *characters*,

(a) Isa. xxxv. 2.

racters, which confine our ideas to the notion of a *plurality*. To each of the three, revelation ascribes a particular work, in the execution of the divine purposes concerning men. In this Oeconomy there is an inequality of character, a manifest subordination among the divine three, which must be limited to the NAMES they bear,—the WORK which revelation assigns to each, in the plan of redemption,—or to the RELATION each stands in to mankind, as the objects of that redemption.

IN this respect, we may safely, being agreeable to revelation, consider a superiority and inferiority among the three, who, with relation thereto are called *Father, Son,* and *Holy Ghost.* Notwithstanding, this revealed distinction does by no means destroy the unity of *Deity*; nor does this œconomical subordination destroy the equality of the divine three; that is conspicuously supported throughout the scriptures, which ascribe to each the *names, attributes, works,* and *worship,* proper only to *Deity,* and which would be derogatory to the wisdom and honour of GOD, to allow any being but what is purely divine.

WITH respect to these, the wisdom of GOD is peculiarly displayed, in the manner of scripture phraseology, and in no instance that I remember more than in the phrase, so very common in the Old Testament, LORD GOD, or JEHOVAH ELOHIM: Which at the same time points out a *plurality* in the word ELOHIM, and the *equality* of that plurality, by being expressed in the *same term.* This would be very incongruous, if there were the least *inequality* among these implied in the term. And all is consistent with the *unity* of *Deity,* expressed in the word JEHOVAH. So that the divine *unity, plurality,*

plurality, equality, or *samenefs,* are all pointed out in the expreſſion JEHOVAH ELOHIM. But the reader will ſuffer me to clear this a little further, as it has an immediate relation to the ſubject in hand.

As it is very certain that the plural ELOHIM is not uſed by chance, but is the fruit of *choice,* and ſo muſt be ſignificant, the greateſt care is taken in ſcripture to prevent *polytheiſm* from being grafted on an expreſſion which ſeems ſo naturally to lead to it. Therefore that text, " Hear, O *Iſrael,* JEHOVAH, our ELOHIM, is ONE JEHOVAH," was to be of the greateſt moment among the *Jews:* They were to lay it up in their heart,—cauſe their children to learn it,—write it on the poſts of their houſes, and front of their gates,—wear it as a ſign upon their arms, and frontlets between their eyes,— ſo important, that all their laws were uſhered in with it. And the value of this precept to that people, appears further from what our LORD ſays of it, when interrogated, Which was the *firſt* and *greateſt* commandment? he readily gave the preference to this, as the firſt and higheſt of the law, " Hear, O *Iſrael,* JEHOVAH, our ELOHIM, is ONE JEHOVAH."

Now, as the noun JEHOVAH is ſingular, and has no plural, there was not the leaſt occaſion for ſo ſolemn a declaration, that JEHOVAH is *one,*—is no *plural,* if it were not for the plural word ELOHIM, which might lead into a miſtake; to prevent which, this ſolemn declaration was given, and ſo many inſtructions concerning the importance of it, that they might never forget, tho' there were diſtinct ELOHIM, yet but *one* JEHOVAH; which is allowing a plurality, but not of diſtinct Deities, for JEHOVAH is *one.* Tho'

Tho' the unity of JEHOVAH is expressly settled by this, and many other texts, yet we read of distinct agents to whom the name and perfections of JEHOVAH are ascribed; as the *Name* JEHOVAH, the *Word* JEHOVAH, the *Angel* JEHOVAH, the *Spirit* JEHOVAH. And however unwilling the *Jews* and some others are to see the particular emphasis in the plural ELOHIM, it is most certain, the word itself carries some idea in it, descriptive of some *character*, some *relation*, the being described by that name bears to man. This is plain from the use made of it in scripture, where the relatives *my, thy, our, their, his,* &c. are commonly joined with ELOHIM.

As the word implies *relation*, it should have been translated by some word that pointed out that sense. But it is rendered by GOD or GODS, which, as far as we know by the derivation, carries no idea of relation to us, or to any being else. If the word GOD is used as a sound only, to raise the idea of the infinite, eternal Being, without any significant meaning in itself; then the applying that word by the relatives, *my, thy, his, their,* &c. is improper; for the eternal Being, absolutely considered, has no more relation to one, than another. If the term ever had any signification of relation originally, it has been lost before the *Septuagint* translation. Nor do we know any meaning the *Saxon* word GOD has, but to denote the supreme Being. ELOHIM should either have been translated by a word that signified *relation*, or retained the *Hebrew* term, rendering it *totidem literas*, giving the same letters in the translation as are done in proper names. If this would have partly left men in the dark, it would have been still safer than to be so misled by an authority which is too implicitly followed. Tho'

THO' a divine plurality is very clearly pointed out in the Old Testament, in a variety of expressions, which cannot be properly interpreted otherwise: Yet this is one glory peculiar to the New Testament, that this plurality are clearly distinguished by the different names, FATHER, SON, and HOLY GHOST, which appears necessary in the further execution of the divine plan, at the commencement of that period, and gives the clearest discovery to men, of the distinct parts they acted with relation to men, in the great transaction agreed among the ELOHIM.

HE, who, in the *New* Testament, is known by the name *Jesus Christ*, did under the *Old* govern all things, particularly the *Jewish Theocracy*, assuming the names and glory of JEHOVAH, the GOD, *king*, and *holy one of Israel*. And as to what is said concerning the humble character he afterwards assumed, it is expressed in *promises, prophecies, figures*, or *shadows*, which respected some future time, and were all fulfilled in him, whose character and offices taken together, is the substance of the New Testament.

WHEN the fulness of time was come, for him to act that part in the divine œconomy, so full of wonder and unspeakable condescention, he became flesh,—subjected himself to the meanest circumstances,—the lowest abasement,—the greatest reproach and contempt,—and endured the most bitter sufferings: Or, as the Apostle finely expresses this astonishing part of his conduct, as the great pattern of humility to christians in all ages. (*b*) "Let this mind be in you, which was also in CHRIST

CHRIST JESUS: Who being in the *form of God,* thought it not robbery to be *equal with God :* But made *himself of no reputation,* and took upon him the *form of a servant,* and was made in the *likeness of men :* And being found in *fashion as a man, he humbled himself,* and *became obedient unto death, even the death of the cross.*" Thus he appeared in the humble character of the obedient SON and SERVANT of GOD, *who,* from that period, in the divine œconomy, sustains the name of the *Father of our Lord Jesus Christ,* and our *Father* in him.

As to the *Holy Ghost,* in the Old Testament he is generally called the SPIRIT JEHOVAH ; but under the New, his character is clearly pointed out in the great business of man's salvation, by the *appellations, mission,* and *works,* ascribed to him as a distinct agent from the *Father* and the *Son.*

THUS, this great point is represented in revelation, in which we are certified, that it shall continue so, 'till the sacred drama is finished on the theatre of this world, when *Jesus Christ* shall deliver up his great charge to GOD the Father, his œconomical administration being come to an end; then says the Apostle, " when all things are *placed in order,* (as the text should read) GOD shall be all in all."

WERE these, and other sentiments of the same kind, pursued to their proper length with true christian prudence, and an impartial attention, the clouds of human inventions that have darkened this doctrine for ages past, would soon dispel, and the minds of inquirers be satisfied from revelation, where GOD hath expressed it in such terms, as were every way agreeable to the different parts of the

great

great plan he was carrying forward, and sufficiently clear to convey all the ideas concerning it, which he intended thofe in the early, or us in the latter periods of time fhould know.

But inftead of being fatisfied with the ideas which revelation affords, it has been common for fuch as have handled this fubject, to devife other rules of interpretation than are found there, confequently, their conclufions are of the fame kind with the premifes they are built upon,—*human conjecture.*

As the names *Father, Son,* and *Holy Ghoft,* import and define fomething relating to the adorable *three* ; it has been commonly, as well as zealoufly maintained for many ages, by thofe who are too much attached to human compofitions, " That thefe names are given to defcribe to us in what manner three divine perfons exift in one God-head : Or, to fhew fomething natural, neceffary, and effential to each of them as divine perfons, that is not proper or applicable to the other perfons, as they fubfift in God-head."

But thefe propofitions are not only unfcriptural, but unintelligible in the conceptions of mankind; as there is nothing in revelation or nature to regulate our inquiries of fuch a kind, or ground any conclufions upon. God has never revealed that incomprehenfible myftery of his nature, or the manner of his exiftence to creatures. And it is more than probable, that, if God fhould pleafe to make a revelation thereof, we could not be capable to underftand it, unlefs he would at the fame time think fit to beftow on us fome new powers or faculties of the mind, which we want at prefent.

The

The nature of the *union*, and *distinction* of the *plurality* in Deity as to the *manner*, is utterly unknown to mankind.

There is no necessity for men to wade in the depths of mystery for knowledge, where God has given no rule to direct them. The terms *Father, Son*, and *Holy Ghost*, are plain intelligible characters, in which the divine Three have discovered themselves, to describe in what manner they have acted in executing the divine purposes, and particularly in carrying on the plan of redemption. This will appear evident, from the consideration of the scripture account of these terms, *Father, Son*, and *Holy Ghost*, distinctly viewed.

In all the texts where *Father, Son*, and *Holy Ghost*, or any two of them, are mentioned as distinct from each other, if the scope is attended to, it will appear, that they are not distinguished as being of a different *nature*, or with respect to their Deity;—or in the least to teach us the manner of their *existence*; but only in consideration of the several parts they are represented as sustaining in the creation, government, redemption, and sanctification of mankind.

The word *Father*, as applied to God in general, is a figurative term, expressing the relation between the great creator of all things, and his creatures: But can prove nothing concerning the *manner* in which the creator exists. If the term *Father* was an essential, internal character, peculiar to one, to denote the particular manner of his personal and divine subsistence in Deity, (as is supposed) then this term would be proper to *one only*, exclusive of the other two. But revelation teacheth us,

that

that in many places where the term *Father* is ufed, *all* that is divine muft be included, and not a word to point out one *only* of the divine three; but refers to GOD as the maker and conferver of his creatures, in which fenfe it belongs to all the three, who, in this refpect, are *one*.

OUR LORD teaches his difciples to addrefs the divine Being, under the character of *Father*,—(*a*) " Our *Father*, who art in heaven." It cannot be denied, that all that is divine, and properly the object of worfhip, is included in the word *Father* here; but *Jefus Chrift*, and the *Holy Ghoft*, are included in the object of worfhip; therefore, they muft be included in the term *Father* in this, as well as in the following texts.—(*b*) " Have we not all *one Father*?—(*c*) But to us there is but one GOD, the *Father*, of whom are all things.—(*d*) " One GOD and *Father* of all, who is above all, and through all, and in you all.—(*e*) Shall we not much rather be in fubjection unto the *Father* of fpirits, and live?"

JEHOVAH, as an evidence of his boundlefs grace and benevolence, hath condefcended to come under the endearing relation of a *Father*, in a fpecial manner, to his elect children.—(*f*) " And will be a *Father* unto you, and ye fhall be my fons and daughters, faith the LORD ALMIGHTY.—(*g*) But ye have received the fpirit of adoption, whereby we cry, *Abba, Father*." He is alfo a Father to the man *Chrift Jefus*, which he manifefted in fixing his love upon him.—(*h*) " Behold, my fervant, whom
I up-

(*a*) Matt. vi. 9. (*b*) Mal. ii. 10. (*c*) 1 Cor. viii. 6. (*d*) Eph. iv. 6. (*e*) Heb. xii. 9. (*f*) 2 Cor. vi. 18. (*g*) Rom. viii. 15. (*h*) Ifa. xlii. 1. com. with Matt. xii. 18.

I uphold, mine elect, in whom my soul delighteth." This is applied to *Christ* by *Matthew*.

But if we find that *Jesus Christ* bears the name *Father*, it will certainly prove, that it is not peculiar to *one*, and so cannot in any sense be descriptive of the manner he subsists in Deity. It was proved above, that *Jesus Christ* governed the church in the wilderness, of whom *Moses* says,— (*i*) " Is he not thy *Father* that bought thee ? hath he not made thee, and established thee ?" *Isaiah* is express to this purpose.—(*k*) " Unto us a child is born, unto us a son is given, (which is no other than *Jesus Christ*) and his name shall be called,— the *everlasting Father*. (*l*) Doubtless thou art our *Father*,—thou, O Lord, art our *Father*, our redeemer, thy name is from everlasting." The *Alpha* and *Omega* (*Jesus Christ*) assumes the character of *Father*, when he says,—(*m*) " He that overcometh, shall inherit all things, and I will be his God; and he shall be my *Son*." In like manner it is said,—(*n*) " They are the *children* of God, being the children of the resurrection." But *Christ* says, " I am the resurrection and the life." Therefore he is their God and *Father*, and they are *his children*. Hence it appears, that the term *Father*, is not given to distinguish one from another, as they subsist in Deity: But is rather a term of relation between God and man, which will be very evident, by considering in what sense God is called a *Father* in scripture.

The sense of the term *Father*, as applied to God, must be learned by analogy, or we can have
no

(*i*) Deut. xxxii. 6. (*k*) Isa. ix. 6. (*l*) ibid. lxiii. 16. (*m*) Rev. xxi. 7. (*n*) Luke xx. 36.

no knowledge thereof at all. This is one great evidence, how far the divine Being hath condescended to the weak capacities of men, in making himself known to them in a language which hath analogy to what they know among themselves. And tho' the analogy in many respects is but faint, yet where there is none, ideas must fail, and inquiries should cease, in such terms as *Father*, applied to GOD. What knowledge we pretend to more, if it is not revealed in so many plain words, is mere uncertainty, and cannot be reckoned any part of that system of necessary truth which GOD intended to teach us.

GOD is called a *Father*, because he is the creator of all things; he brought them into being and existence,—preserves them by his power,—and sustains them by his bounty.—(*a*) " For in him we live, and move, and have our being; for we are all his offspring. (*b*) Have we not all one Father? Hath not one GOD created us all? (*c*) He maketh his sun to rise on the evil, and on the good, and sendeth his rain on the just, and on the unjust."

As children bear the image of their Father, so GOD made man in *his image.*—(*d*) " For man is the image and glory of GOD. (*e*) In the image of GOD made he him."

THEY are called *Fathers* in scripture, who were the first inventors of things which were for the general benefit of mankind. This idea may with great propriety be included in the character of GOD as a *Father*, who, through infinite wisdom, found out a method to save sinners,—renew

his

(*a*) Acts xvii. 18. (*b*) Mal. ii. 10. (*c*) Matt. v. 45. (*d*) 1 Cor. xi. 7. (*e*) Gen. i. 27.

his image in them,—and restore them to the enjoyment of his favour, which they were so unmeet for by sin,—and all consistent with the absolute strictness of his law, and the divine purity of his revealed perfections.

BESIDES such general ideas of paternity, it will be found, that there is no property or affection which fathers, as such among men, are endowed with, that is not ascribed to GOD, as the Father of his children, which he hath chosen in *Christ Jesus*. Respect must be had here to the great difference there is betwixt a property or affection in men, and the same thing as it is applied to GOD. But where the scriptures lead, we may safely follow.

THEY are called FAHTERS, who adopt children into their family, and give them the title and privilege of children; in this respect GOD is called a FATHER.—*(f)* " Blessed be the GOD and Father of our *Lord Jesus Christ*,—who hath predestinated us into the *adoption of children* by *Jesus Christ* to himself, according to the good pleasure of his will, &c. *(g)* Behold what manner of love the Father hath bestowed upon us, that we should be called the *sons of* GOD.—*(h)* And will be a FATHER unto you; and ye shall be my *sons* and *daughters*, saith the LORD Almighty."

HE is their FATHER, as he *begets* them again by the energy of truth,—makes them to bear his *name*,—and conforms them to the image of his *only begotten son*.—*(i)* " Blessed be the GOD and Father of our *Lord Jesus Christ*, who, according to his

---

(f) Eph. i. 3,—5. *(g)* 1 John iii. 1. *(h)* 2 Cor. vi. 18. *(i)* 1 Pet. i. 3.

his abundant mercy, hath *begotten us again* unto a lively hope, by the refurrection of *Jefus Chrift* from the dead. (*k*) Of his own will *begat he us* with the word of truth. (*l*) And I looked, and lo, a Lamb ſtood on *Mount Zion*, and with him a hundred and forty and four thouſand, having *his father's name* written in their foreheads. (*m*) He that overcometh, I will write upon him the *name of my* God,—new *Jeruſalem*, which cometh down out of heaven from my God : *And* my new name."

As a Father he feeds them with ſpiritual food. —(*n*) " My *Father* giveth you the true bread from heaven."

He has the *love* of a Father to them; and permits them to have the freedom and fellowſhip of children with him.—(*o*) " If a man love me, he will keep my words, and my *father* will love him." (*p*) The *Father* himſelf *loveth* you. (*q*) Truly our *fellowſhip* is with the *Father*, and with his ſon *Jeſus Chriſt*."

He bears with their weakneſſes, and forgives their offences.—(*r*) " And I will ſpare them as a man ſpareth his *ſon* that ſerveth him.—(*s*) Your heavenly *Father* will alſo *forgive* you."

He has the *ſympathy, care*, and *tenderneſs* of a *father*.—(*t*) " Like as a Father *pitieth* his children : So the Lord pitieth them that fear him. (*u*) Even the very *hairs* of your head are all numbered. (*v*) A Father of the *Fatherleſs*, and a judge of the widow, is God."

He

(*k*) Jam. i. 18. (*l*) Rev. xiv. 1. (*m*) ibid. iii. 12. (*n*) John vi. 32. (*o*) ibid. xiv. 23. (*p*) and xvi. 27. (*q*) 1 John i. 3. (*r*) Mal. iii. 17. (*s*) Matt. vi. 14. (*t*) Pſa. ciii. 13. (*u*) Luke xii. 7. (*v*) Pſa. 68. 5.

H E is acquainted with all their wants, and giveth them all neceſſary things.—(w) "Your heavenly FATHER *knoweth* that ye have need of all *theſe things*. (x) How much more ſhall your FATHER, who is in heaven, give *good things* to them that aſk him."

H E *correɛts* them in love when they offend.— *(y)* "What ſon is he whom the FATHER chaſteneth not? (z) I will viſit their tranſgreſſions with the *rod,* and their iniquities with *ſtripes*."

H E is a *pattern* to all his children.—(a) "Be ye therefore perfect, even as your FATHER who is in heaven is perfect."

H E challengeth paternal authority and reſpect. —(b) "If I be a FATHER, where is mine honour?"

H E inſpects the deportment of his children, and rewards them accordingly.—(c) "Thy FATHER who ſeeth thee in ſecret, himſelf ſhall *reward* thee openly."

H F provides an *inheritance* for them,—gives it *freely* to them,—and makes them all *meet* for the enjoyment thereof.—*(d)* "Come, ye bleſſed of my FATHER, inherit the kingdom prepared for you. (e) It is your FATHER's *good pleaſure* to give you the kingdom. (f) We give thanks to the FATHER, who hath made us *meet* for the inheritance of the ſaints in light."

H E

(w) Matt. vi. 32. (x) ibid. vii. 11. (y) Heb. xii. 7. (z) Pſa. lxxxix. 32. (a) Matt. v. 48. (b) Mal. i. 6. (c) Matt. iv. 6. (d) ibid. xxv. 34. (e) Luke xii. 32. (f) Col. i. 12.

HE hears their humble prayers, and anſwers them.—(*g*) " As touching any thing that they ſhall aſk, it ſhall be done for them of my FATHER, who is in heaven. (*h*) How much more ſhall your heavenly FATHER give the holy ſpirit to them that aſk him."

HE is the object of their worſhip.—(*i*) " After this manner therefore pray ye: Our FATHER, who art in heaven. (*k*) The true worſhippers ſhall worſhip the FATHER in ſpirit and truth: For the FATHER ſeeketh ſuch to worſhip him."

THESE, and many other privileges they enjoy, through the *well-beloved* SON *of* GOD, by whom they have the knowledge of their FATHER, and in whom they approach acceptably to him.—(*l*) " No man knoweth the FATHER but the SON, and he to whom the SON will reveal him.—(*m*) I am the way, the truth, and the life; no man cometh unto the FATHER but by me. (*n*) Through him we have acceſs by one ſpirit, unto the FATHER."

WITH reſpect to *Jeſus Chriſt*, the ſcripture repreſents GOD as a FATHER, in his being GOD's *firſt-born*,— † his image,—the *head* of all his ways,— the repoſitory of all his purpoſes,—in the *ancient love* he had to him,—the choice he made of him, and all the elect in him.—(*o*) " Giving thanks to the

† By reſemblance and repreſentation, for it is a contradiction in terms, to ſay a *Son* as ſuch, can be the *image* of his *Father* as ſuch: Filiation is no image of *Paternity*; they are ſpecifically different, and can no more be the image of one another, than light can be the image of darkneſs.

(*g*) Matt. xviii. 19. (*h*) Luke xi. 18. (*i*) Matt. vi. 9. (*k*) John iv. 23. (*l*) Matt. xi. 27. (*m*) John xiv. 6. (*n*) Eph. ii. 18. (*o*) Col. i. 12, 13, 15.

the FATHER,—who hath tranflated us into the kingdom of his *dear* SON (*marg.* the SON *of his love*)—who is the *image* of the invifible GOD, the *firft-born* of every creature. (*p*) I will make him, my *firft-born*, higher than the kings of the earth. (*q*) But thou, *Bethlehem Ephratah*, though thou be little among the thoufands of *Judah*, out of thee fhall *he* come forth unto me, that is to be ruler in *Ifrael:* Whofe *goings forth* have been from of old, from everlafting." (*r*) This is applied to *Chrift* both by *Matthew* and *John*. (*s*) The LORD poffeffed me in the beginning of his ways, before his works of old. I was fet up from everlafting, from the beginning, or ever the earth was, —then I was by him, as one *brought up with him:* And I was daily his delight, rejoicing always before him. (*t*) Bleffed be the GOD and Father of our *Lord Jefus Chrift*, who hath bleffed us with all fpiritual bleffings in heavenly places, *in Chrift*. According as he hath *chofen us in* HIM, before the foundation of the world. (*u*) According to the eternal purpofe, which he purpofed in *Chrift Jefus* our LORD. According to his own purpofe and grace, which was given us *in Chrift Jefus*, before the world began."

WITH refpect to *Chrift*'s birth of the virgin, and appearance in this world in flefh.—(*v*) " The HOLY GHOST fhall come upon thee, and the power of the higheft fhall over-fhadow thee: Therefore, alfo that holy thing which fhall be *born of thee*, fhall be called *the* SON *of* GOD. He fhall be great, and fhall be called *the* SON *of the higheft*. (*w*) And the word was made flefh, and dwelt among

---

(*p*) Pfa. lxxxix. 27...(*q*) Mic. v. 2. (*r*) Matt. ii. 6. John vii. 42. (*s*) Prov. viii. 22.—31. (*t*) Eph. i. 3, 4. (*u*) ibid. iii. 11. (*v*) Luke i. 2, 5, 35. (*w*) John i. 14.

among us, (and we beheld his glory, the glory as of the *only begotten* of the FATHER) full of grace and truth."

As a Father commits the charge of all his affairs to his *only* SON; so the Son of GOD is made governor over all things.—(*x*) " The LORD (JEHOVAH) hath said unto *me*, thou art *my* SON, this day I have begotten thee. Ask of me, and I will give thee the heathen for *thine inheritance*, and the uttermost parts of the earth for *thy possession*. (*y*) Unto us a SON is given,—and the government shall be upon his shoulders:—of the increase of his government and peace, there shall be no end. (*z*) All things are delivered unto me of my Father. (*a*) The FATHER judgeth no man, but hath committed all judgement (government) to the SON. The Father loveth the SON, and hath given *all things into his hand*."

As a FATHER, he owns and makes known *Jesus Christ as his* SON. (*b*) " This is my beloved son, in whom I am well pleased. (*c*) *Simon Peter* said, thou art *Christ* the SON of the living GOD. *Jesus* answered,—flesh and blood hath not revealed it unto thee, but my Father, who is in heaven."

As a Father, he *sent* the Son to fulfil his will in accomplishing the work of redemption,—prepared him for that great work,—supported and instructed him therein,—and rewarded him after it was finished.—(*d*) " I came down from heaven, not to do mine own will, but the *will* of him that *sent me*.

(*x*) Psa. ii. 7, 8. (*y*) Isa. ix. 6, 7. (*z*) Matt. xi. 27. (*a*) John v. 22. ibid. iii. 35. (*b*) Matt. iii. 17. (*c*) ibid. xvi. 16, 17. (*d*) John vi. 38.

me. (*e*) Wherefore when he cometh into the world, he faith, ſacrifice and offering thou wouldſt not, but a *Body* haſt thou *prepared me:* Then, ſaid I, Lo, I come to do *thy will*, O GOD. (*f*) Say ye of him, whom the Father hath *ſanctified*, and *ſent* into the world, thou blaſphemeſt; becauſe, I ſaid, I am the SON *of* GOD. (*g*) He ſhall cry unto me, thou art my FATHER, my GOD, and the *rock* of *my ſalvation*. I have found *David, my ſervant:* With my holy oil have I *anointed him*, with whom my hand ſhall be eſtabliſhed: Mine arm ſhall alſo *ſtrengthen* him. (*h*) I do nothing of myſelf; but as the Father hath *taught* me, I ſpeak theſe things. (*i*) He humbled himſelf, and became obedient unto death, even the death of the croſs, wherefore GOD alſo hath *highly exalted* him, and given him a name above every name; that at the name of *Jeſus* every knee ſhould bow, &c."

To theſe we might add manifold inſtances, where *Chriſt* addreſſes GOD as his FATHER, in behalf of himſelf,—his friends,—and his enemies. We might turn to *Paul's* epiſtles for illuſtration of this ſubject, where one thing is remarkable, that in his ſalutations at the beginning of every epiſtle, he carefully ſupports the diſtinction betwixt GOD as a FATHER, and *Jeſus Chriſt* as a SON. And to conclude all, tells us, that when he ſhall have finiſhed the whole adminiſtration, which GOD hath entruſted him with, *as his* SON, and brought all whom the Father gave him to glory, then he ſhall deliver up the kingdom to GOD his FATHER, and GOD ſhall be all in all. The executive part of the divine oeconomy being finiſhed,—there is no further

---

(*e*) Heb. x. 5, 6. (*f*) John x. 36. (*g*) Pſa. lxxxix. 26, 20, 27. (*h*) John viii. 28. (*i*) Phil. ii. 8, 9, 10.

further use for the oeconomical authority and subjection, the superiority and inferiority implied in the *paternal* and *filial* characters.*

FROM the whole, I may venture to affirm, that there is not one idea which can with any propriety be prefixed to the term FATHER as applied to GOD, in the whole revelation, but what has a plain reference to the *works* of GOD, either in *creation, providence,* or *redemption.*

IT may perhaps be of use to some of my readers, to give the reason that seems most probable to me, why GOD as a FATHER is always said to be *in heaven,* or called the *heavenly* FATHER. This is a sacred phrase, I am afraid, tho' very often repeated in the New Testament, yet but very little understood. It not only teaches us, that as *Jesus Christ* is *now* in heaven, who is the true medium of all our intercourse with GOD,—our worship being only of a right kind, when directed through

---

* I must here observe, that by not considering the scope and import of the Apostle's expressions in 1 Cor. xv 28 the text hath been improved as an argument against the proper Deity of the Lord *Jesus Christ*. The Apostle is there speaking of the state of *Christ's* kingdom, after the resurrection, when he as mediator, into whose hand *God's* chosen were given to redeem, govern, and bring to glory, shall deliver them without spot to GOD: And as there shall be no more occasion for his ministry in this world, he shall deliver up his service, and GOD shall be all in all. The text reads literally thus, "Then shall the SON be placed in order to him, subduing all things, or, placing all things in order, that GOD may be all in all," *i. e.* without such an oeconomical administration as was necessary in this world. But if it is still urged that SON and GOD are different; I may also insist that GOD and FATHER are also different; for the words read in verse 24, "GOD *and* the FATHER," according to our ordinary translation of Και, which would infer, that the kingdom must be delivered up to one who is GOD, and another who is *Father*, and would make as clearly against the Deity of the *Father* as the *Son*. But by considering it as above, the text is clear, and free of that ambiguity which it is commonly clouded with.

through *him*, and all the privileges God bestows upon us come in the same channel,—and therefore our praises and prayers should be directed to our Father *in heaven*, since *he* is there, in whom they are acceptable.

But it hath a special reference to the difference in point of excellency there is betwixt *Old* and *New* Testament *worship*. The former, according to the Apostle's estimate, consisted in meats, and drinks, and divers washings, and carnal ordinances imposed upon them, until the time of reformation. He calls them weak, beggarly elements of *this world*, under which the *Jews*, like children, were held in bondage: Figures for the time then present,—patterns, and shadows only of heavenly things,—confined to an earthly tabernacle, and temple made with hands, where the worshippers were obliged to attend, and if unavoidably absent, or at the greatest distance, to perform their worship with their faces toward that place.

Under the latter, the worship is *spiritual, unlimited*, and *heavenly*; not wrapped up in dark signs, figures, and shadows; not confined to times, places, a particular nation, and external modes. He who is the spirit of all *Jewish* worship, the substance of all the signs and shadows being come, and having fulfilled all the ancient promises and prophecies concerning him, has opened a way into the holiest of all, through his own blood,—taken down the partition,—so that believers, who are a holy priest-hood in every time, place, and nation, offer up spiritual sacrifices, acceptable to God through *Jesus Christ*, who has entered into heaven itself, now to appear in the presence of God for us.

The

THE church *now*, is called the *heavenly Jerusalem*, in opposition to the *earthly Jerusalem*, the seat and center of worship among the *Jews*. Hence, says the Apostle, (*k*) "Ye are not come to the mount that might be touched, and that burned with fire, nor unto blackness and darkness, and tempest, &c. But ye are come unto *Mount Sion*, and unto the city of the living GOD, the *heavenly Jerusalem*, &c." To the same purpose our Saviour tells the *Samaritan* woman, that neither on *Mount Samaria* should the *Samaritans*, nor yet at *Jerusalem* should the *Jews* worship: "But that the hour cometh, and *now* is, when the true worshippers shall worship the FATHER in *spirit* and *truth*."

THE *spirit* and *truth* here, does not mean, as is commonly supposed, that they should worship in their *hearts* and in *sincerity*, (true worshippers always do so) in opposition to worshipping with the *body*, and in *hypocrisy*; was this the sense, it might then be inferred from our *Saviour*'s words, that none of the Old Testament saints worshipped GOD with their *hearts*, and in *sincerity*; and that christians are not to worship GOD with their *bodies*; whereas they are commanded to "serve GOD with their *bodies* and *spirits*, which are his,—and to present their *bodies* living sacrifices, holy, and acceptable to GOD, which is their reasonable service."

BUT *Christ* here teaches, that christians were to worship the *Father in him*, who is the *spirit* of all the signs and shadows, and the *truth* of all the promises and prophecies in the Old Testament, with respect to holy *times*, *places*, and *things*. The Father having declared himself well-pleased *with him*,
all

(*k*) Heb. xii. 18,—22.

all their worship must be *through him, by whom they have access with boldness to the throne of grace*. (*l*) " The LORD is that SPIRIT ; And where the SPIRIT the LORD is, there is *liberty*. (*m*) The *testimony* of *Jesus* (the doctrines concerning him in the New Testament) is the SPIRIT of *prophecy*," (what was foretold of him in the Old Testament.)

AND as *he* who is the *head*, and representative of the *whole* church, (that is, the saints both in heaven and earth) is in heaven, and every privilege that pertains to them as such, is heavenly,—their birth,—the image they are formed after,—the blessings they enjoy,—their calling,—their inheritance—their conversation,—their hopes,—their affections and desires,——the country they are travelling to, (for here they are strangers and pilgrims) and since all the acts of their worship must be directed through the heavenly medium,——him who is their ascended LORD, no wonder if the New Testament represents their FATHER, who bestows all these blessings upon them, and whom they love and adore, as *in heaven*, and so frequently calls him their *heavenly* FATHER.

(*l*) 2 Cor. iii. 17. (*m*) Rev. xix. 10. see note, pa. 29.

SECT.

SECT. II.

I SHALL now confider the fcripture fenfe of the term SON, as applied to the *Lord Jefus Chrift*. It is fhewed above in feveral particulars, in what fenfe GOD is called the FATHER of *Jefus Chrift*. And as FATHER and SON are *correlates*, that is, one that ftands in an oppofite relation to another, any impartial and unprejudiced reader may eafily conceive in what fenfe *Jefus Chrift* is called the SON *of* GOD.

BUT as I am pretty certain that the greateft part of my readers, through the prejudice of education, and a bias in favour of other notions concerning this point, will, on that account, not fo readily fee the conclufion concerning the *fonfhip* of *Chrift*, which natively flows from the fcripture account of GOD as a FATHER: For that reafon, I fhall be obliged to open this fubject in a more particular manner, that no room may be left for entertaining prepoffeffed opinions, fo contrary to the fcripture account of that great article of the chriftian faith.

AND, let me beg my reader to diveft himfelf as much as he can of any bias in favour of party opinions formerly received, that he may impartially weigh the evidence from revelation, againft the traditions of men; and I make no doubt which fide he will be determined to take, as he will plainly fee, the opinions of men in this matter are attended with too little evidence to reft an article of faith upon, fo interefting, and of fo great confequence to himfelf.

ALLOW

ALLOW me then, *first*, to give a very brief account of the several ideas relative to the term SON, as applied to *other things* in scripture than *Jesus Christ*, which will in a great measure lead to a more distinct notion concerning the use of the term, as applied to *him*.

BESIDES the ideas of *lineal descendants*, whether immediate or more remote, even to the third and fourth generation of a man's seed, who are commonly called his *sons*, there are several other ideas of sonship in scripture.

IN eastern stile, the inhabitants of a city or country were called the *sons* or children of that city or country. This is frequent in the Old Testament.

THAT which *proceeded from* another thing, whether animate or inanimate, was called the *son* of that it proceeded from, and always denotes derivation. In this sense, the *sparks* are called the *sons of the burning coal.*—(a) And *sons* are called branches or boughs. (b) " *Joseph* is a fruitful bough. (c) The *branch* thou madest strong for thyself,— the *son* of man thou madest strong for thyself. (d) And there shall come out a rod out of the stem of *Jesse*, and a branch out of his roots."

A SUCCESSOR in government, was called the *son* of him or them who went before him.—(e) " How say ye unto *Pharoah*, I am the *son* of the wise, the *son* of ancient kings."

ADAM

(a) Job v. 7. (b) Gen. xlix. 22. (c) Psa. lxxx. 15, 17. (d) Isa. xi. 1. (e) ibid. xix. 11.

ADAM is called the *son of God*, becaufe he was made after his image, and had his being immediately *derived* from him without the inftrumentality of human generation. For much the fame reafon are *Angels* called the *sons of* GOD, being created by GOD a dignified rank of beings, endowed with excellent fpiritual powers and perfections, not derived from each other by fucceffion, but immediately brought into being by GOD himfelf.

MAGISTRATES are called *sons* of the moft high, becaufe of the power and authority they are raifed to, that in fome refpect is the image of GOD's power and government, which makes them a terror to evil doers, and a praife to them who do well.

SUCH as were appointed to death are called *sons*, or children of death.—(*f*) "Preferve thou thofe that are appointed to death. (*g*) Hear the groanings of the prifoner, to loofe thofe that are appointed to death." In both texts, it reads as in the margin, *sons* or children of death, as doth alfo that which *Saul* faid concerning *David*,——(*h*) "Wherefore now fend and fetch him unto me, for he fhall furely die." He is a *son* of death.

WHEN a *superior* would exprefs his love and regard to an *inferior*, he commonly addreffed him in the language of a *father*, by calling him his *son*. In like manner, when an *inferior* would exprefs his dutiful affection and fubmiffion to one he acknowledged his *superior*, he did it by calling him *father*.

THE term fon is alfo ufed to point out the fubordinate character of fuch as were under the care

of

(*f*) Pfa. lxxix. 11. (*g*) ibid. cii. 20. (*h*) 1 Sam. xx. 31.

of others for instruction: So *Eli* calls *Samuel* his *son*; and others were called *sons* of the Prophets. For much the same reason, *Paul* calls *Timothy* and *Philemon*, whom he had converted to the truth, his *sons*. And to point out the useful, submissive, and obedient character of *Timothy*, he says of him, (*i*) "As a *son* with his *father*, he hath served with me in the gospel."

WHEN one was adopted into another family, he was then called a *Son*. Thus *Moses* is called the *son* of *Pharoah*'s daughter. It also signifies one that *builds up his father's house*,—and *transmits his name* down to posterity. But these I shall have occasion to notice afterwards. I shall next mention several ideas of *sonship*, applied to the *wicked* and the *saints*, peculiar to their different characters in scripture.

THE wicked part of mankind are called *sons* and *children* of *men*. The *commandments* of *men*, being the matter of their faith, and the rule of their worship. The *sinful customs of men*, the pattern they imitate. And the *praise* of *men*, their highest end.

———— OF the *world*.—They are not born from above. They wallow in the wickedness of the world,—chuse it for their portion,—*its* pleasures are their highest felicity,—and their chief study is to fulfil the lusts and desires thereof.

———— OF the *Devil*.—They bear his image, being thoroughly qualified with the wickedness he introduced into the world,—resemble him in malice and subtilty,—and cheerfully imitate, serve, and

---

(*i*) Phil. ii. 22.

and obey him as a *son* his *father*.—Our LORD says of them, " Ye are of your father the Devil, and the lusts of your father ye will do."

———— OF *darkness* and *disobedience.*————Their minds are in ignorance of the truth. Their works are the shameful works of darkness. Their hearts are enmity, and their actions a scene of rebellion and treachery against GOD.

———— OF *wrath* and the *curse.*—By nature they are heirs of wrath, and by their wicked deeds they merit the vengeance of GOD. They are a curse upon earth, and accursed for ever in the world to come.

———— OF *Belial.* Of *perdition.*—*Without law*, *useless, unprofitable,—abandoned to crimes,*—lost to every sense of real good,—run headlong to destruction, and are for ever lost.

THE scripture character of saints as *sons* and children of GOD.—As they are the early objects of his love,—chosen and predestinated in *Christ Jesus*, his well-beloved son, to the *adoption* of *sons*, and to be fellow heirs with him of the same inheritance.—(*h*) " Having predestinated us unto the *adoption of children* by *Jesus Christ* to himself. (*i*) And if children, then *heirs;* heirs of GOD, and joint heirs with *Christ*."

———— As they are converted by the power of the truth,—begotten again,—made sons of GOD, real members of his spiritual family,—have the image of their heavenly father drawn upon them

through

(*h*) Eph. i. 5. (*i*) Rom. viii. 17.

through the energy of the spirit,—and entitled to innumerable privileges.—(*k*) " As many as received him, to them gave he power to become the *sons of God*. (*l*) Ye have received the spirit of adoption, whereby we cry, *Abba*, *Father*. (*m*) Beloved, now are ye the *sons of God*, and it doth not yet appear what ye shall be; but we know, that when he shall appear, we shall be like him, for we shall see him as he is."

——— Children of *light*.—Begotten of God the fountain of light,—possessed of a true and distinct knowledge of God their father, by the pure light of his word,—walk in the light of his countenance, the path that shines more and more unto the perfect day,—shine as children of the light, and the light of their good works shines before men, 'till they are made meet for the inheritance of the saints in light.

——— Of *wisdom*.—That is of *Christ*, who is the *wisdom* of God made known to men. His seed they are, who travailed for them in bloody agonies unto death,—bequeaths to them the fruits of his purchase,—and in consummate *wisdom* guides them to glory, where he shall with delight see them as his *seed*, the travail of his soul, and shall be satisfied.

——— Of the *promise*.—By which they are quickened, gathered, comforted, strengthened, restored, and infallibly *secured* of the enjoyment of God their father for ever.

——— Of the *resurrection*.—By the truth of *Christ*'s *resurrection* they are begotten again, and confirmed in

(*k*) John i. 12. (*l*) Rom. viii. 15. (*m*) 1 John iii. 2.

in the faith and hope of their own glorious refurrection, to enter upon the full poffeffion of their inheritance as *fons* of GOD.—(*n*) " Bleffed be GOD, who according to his abundant mercy, hath begotten us again unto a lively hope, by the refurrection of *Jefus Chrift*."

THE faints are alfo called *fons* and children of the *free woman*—of *Zion*,—of *Jerufalem*,—of the *kingdom*, &c. pointing out the *freedom, honour, peace, fafety, glory,* &c. of the church of *Chrift*, in which they are born, nourifhed, inftructed, and prepared for the kingdom of their father, which was prepared for them before the foundation of the world.

I NOW come to mention fome general ideas of fonfhip applied to *Jefus Chrift* ; one is, that of his being BEGOTTEN.—(*o*) " Thou art my fon, this day have I begotten thee. (*p*) The word was made flefh, and dwelt among us, (and we beheld his glory, the glory as of the only begotten of the father) full of grace and truth."

ANOTHER general idea included in his fonfhip, is his being called a *child*, and faid to be *born*.—— (*q*) " Unto us a *child* is *born*. (*r*) That holy thing that fhall be *born* of thee, fhall be called the *fon of* GOD."

HE is called the *firft born*.—The *firft born* among the ancient *Jews* had a primogenial right to particular privileges in the family. So *Chrift* is called the *firft born*, not only with refpect to *priority*, or being *before* all others that are called fons of GOD, this

---

(*n*) 1 Pet. i. 3. (*o*) Pfa. ii. 7. (*p*) John i. 14. fee alfo John i. 18. and iii. 16, 18. 1 John iv. 9. (*q*) Ifa. ix. 6 (*r*) Luke i. 35. fee alfo Acts iv. 27, 30. Matt. ii. 2. John xviii. 37.

this he alſo is, "the *firſt born of every creature:*" But he is called ſo with reſpect to *excellency* and *dignity*. (*s*) "I will make him my *firſt born,* higher than the kings of the earth." A right of *inheritance*, *prieſt-hood*, and *government* over his brethren.—(*t*) "God hath in theſe laſt days ſpoken to us by his *ſon,* whom he hath *appointed heir of all things.* (*u*) *Jeſus Chriſt,* the firſt begotten of the dead, and the prince of the kings of the earth. (*v*) And he is the head of the body, the church, who is the beginning, the *firſt born* from the dead; that in *all things he might have the pre-eminence.*"

The *firſt born* of old, in whoſe ſtead God made choice of the *Levites,* had not only a double portion of inheritance, power, and pre-eminence above their brethren, but were particularly loved and honoured of their fathers, had reſpect and ſubmiſſion from their brethren, and miniſtered in holy things for the family. So *Jeſus Chriſt,* the *firſt born of* God, had the ſpirit without meaſure given him,—was declared to be the peculiar *favourite* of God,—had the *government* of all things committed to him,—Angels and men commanded to *worſhip* him,—and conſtituted the great *high-prieſt* over the houſe of God, by no leſs ſolemnity than the *oath of* God conſecrated for evermore.

Submission, *obedience,* and *reſignation* to the *will* of the father, is one idea inſeparable from the character of a dutiful *Son.* In this reſpect, the Son of God was the moſt perfect pattern.—(*w*) "*Jeſus* ſaith unto them, my meat is to do the *will* of him that ſent me, and to finiſh his work. (*x*)

I ſeek

(*s*) Pſa. lxxxix. 27. (*t*) Heb. i. 1, 2. (*u*) Rev. i. 5. (*v*) Col. i. 18. (*w*) John iv. 34. (*x*) ibid. v. 30.

I seek not mine own will, but the will of the father who hath sent me. (*x*) Tho' he was a *Son*, yet learned he *obedience*, by the things which he suffered. (*y*) O Father, if it be possible, let this cup pass from me; nevertheless, *not as I will, but as thou wilt*. (*z*) Lo, I come to do *thy will*, O GOD."

IN honouring and glorifying his *Father*, he has given us the most finished example.—(*a*) " I honour my Father,—I seek not mine own glory. (*b*) I have glorified thee on earth: I have finished the work thou gavest me to do."

HE manifests and makes known his Father's *name*, *glory*, and *love* to his younger brethren.—(*c*) " I have manifested thy *name* unto the men whom thou gavest me. I have declared unto them thy *name*, and will declare it: That the love wherewith thou hast loved me, may be in them, and I in them."

AMONG many other general ideas of sonship, applied to *Christ* in scripture, I shall only mention other two. The word BEN, which in the Old Testament language signifies a *Son*, comes from a word that signifies to *build up*, and the *Greek* word which answers to it in the New Testament, is rendered *Son* for the same purpose, because a *Son builds up his Father's house*. This idea of sonship is properly applied to the *son of* GOD, who *builds up* or edifies the church, which is the house of GOD, his heavenly Father. He is the foundation, the edifier,

S the

(*x*) Heb. v. 8. (*y*) Matt. xxvi. 39. (*z*) Heb. x. 7. (*a*) John viii. 49, 50. (*b*) ibid. xvii. 4. (*c*) and xvii. 6, 8, 26.

the supporter, and chief corner stone † of this building of GOD.

ANOTHER similar idea is included in the word NIN, which also signifies a *Son that transmits his father's name down to posterity*. This is expressly applied to the *Son of* GOD,—(d) " *He shall be as a son to continue his father's name for ever.*" And he himself says, (e) " I will *declare thy name unto my brethren*, in the midst of the church will I sing praise unto thee.—(f) *I have declared unto them thy name, and will declare it.*"

Now, from several of these scripture ideas of sonship, as applied to *Jesus Christ*, especially the two last, it is clear that they have not the least relation to *begetting* in any sense the word can be taken in. It must then be true, that the scripture account of *Christ's sonship*, includes more in it than we can learn from his being *begotten*. AND

(d) Psa. lxxii. 17. mar. (e) Heb. ii. 12. (f) John xvii. 26.
† It is an idea too limited, (and not worthy the subject, that because *Christ* is called in a general way the *corner stone*, in the singular number) to suppose, that he is compared to some one stone in some corner. When the Apostle mentions it, Eph. ii. 20. he is comparing the church in general to a vast temple, and says, it was founded on the doctrines of the Prophets and Apostles jointly; consequently, he means the church in the most comprehensive sense, taking in all good men in all ages, from the beginning to the end of time : And so must speak of *Christ* in his relation to the church, in a sense that is equally large and comprehensive. Corner stones in great edifices, unite and join together the walls on all sides, below, and above ; cement, strengthen, and adorn the whole building, from top to bottom. Thus only can we form any genuine notion of *Christ*, being compared to corner stones. He is the foundation, corner, and finishing part of the superstructure. That expression of GOD to *Job*, " Whereupon are the foundations of the earth fastened ? Or, who laid the corner stone thereof ?" must denote the finishing of its creation : So *Christ* being called the corner stone of the church, when compared to a building, must denote that he is the strength, security, glory, and perfection of the whole in all times: Which, since his appearing in flesh, he has made more conspicuous to all men. The reader may consult 1 Pet. ii. 6, 7. Isa. xxviii. 16. Psa. cxviii. 22. Acts iv. 11. Luke xx. 17. Mark xii. 10. Matt. xxi. 42. Job xxxviii. 6.

AND it is alfo evident from a due confideration of the *whole* of thefe fcripture ideas of *fonſhip*, that either *derivation*, *dependence*, *fubordination*, or *inferiority*, is neceſſarily implied in every notion that can be conceived of it, from any one inſtance fingly, or the whole taken together. I may therefore venture to affirm, that there is not one idea of *fonſhip* confidered *as ſuch* in the Bible, but what points out the *inferior* character of that perfon or thing it is applied to, with refpect to the oppofite or *ſuperior* character of that perfon or thing they are faid to be *ſons* of. Whatever they may be in other refpects, the fenfe in which they are called *ſons*, confines the idea (according to the fcope of revelation, and the beſt conceptions we can have of it) to the notion of *inferiority*. One may be an equal or fuperior in other refpects, but in that part of his character, in which he is a *Son*, he is certainly *inferior*. As for example; a magiſtrate, as fuch, is equal to thofe in the fame ſtation, and fuperior to fuch as are under his government; but as he is called a *ſon* of the *moſt high*, in that refpect he is *inferior*. As a *magiſtrate*, he may be fuperior to his natural Father, but as a *ſon* he is inferior to him. And with refpect to *Jeſus Chriſt*, the fcripture holds him forth to be JEHOVAH, GOD OVER ALL, as was proved above; but all the ideas which revelation affords us of his character *as a ſon*, imply *inferiority:* And therefore by the light of the divine word, we are led to view his *fonſhip* in another character than *pure Deity*. Which brings me to a more direct and particular anfwer to this-queſtion, in what fenfe JESUS CHRIST, in fcripture, is called the SON OF GOD.

SECT

SECT III.

THE *Lord Jesus Christ*, while in this world, generally spoke of himself under the title of the *son of man*. I do not remember that he is called so by any other, except the *Psalmist, Daniel, Stephen,* and *John*. (*a*) " Let thy hand be upon the man of thy right hand, upon the *son of man,* whom thou madest strong for thyself. (*b*) And behold, one like the *son of man,* came with the clouds of heaven,—and there was given him dominion and glory, that all people, nations, and languages, should serve him. (*c*) Behold, I see the heavens opened, and the *son of man* standing on the right hand of GOD. (*d*) And I looked, and behold, a white cloud, and upon the cloud one sat, like unto the *son of man,* having on his head a golden crown, &c. (*e*) And in the midst of the seven candlesticks, one like unto the *son of man,* clothed with a garment down to the foot, &c." The magnificent descriptions that are given him, who is called *son of man* in these texts, leave the reader of them at no loss to know that it is *Jesus Christ,* as an exalted mediator, who is meant through the whole.

NOTWITHSTANDING the sacred penmen were so sparing in giving this title *son of man* to *Jesus Christ,* he seems to delight particularly in it himself; for we seldom find that he calls himself by any other name. As this part of his conduct is worthy of regard, it may teach us, who have his character fully exhibited in revelation, what honour he chused to put upon his ancestors according

---

(*a*) Psa. lxxx. 17. (*b*) Dan. vii. 13. (*c*) Acts vii. 56. (*d*) Rev. xiv. 14. (*e*) ibid. i. 13.

ing to the flesh,—and the truth of his being descended from *them* in whom he was promised. It may shew his great love and regard to *man*, when he so frequently calls himself the *son of man*. It points out the great depth of his humility, in being clothed with flesh: And implies the reality of his humanity. But tho' some of these may appear to us good reasons for his assuming that name, especially the two last, which are commonly sustained as the *only* reasons; yet I can see no reason at all for his calling himself so often the *son of man*, to shew that he was *really* man, as this could be of no advantage to those he conversed with; for in his life time here, none doubted that he was *real* man, and but very few thought him any thing more than a *mere man*, and none of the best sort neither.

BUT I think there remain greater reasons for *Christ* having used this title, the *son of man*, so frequently. By it he leads naturally back to the first promise of himself, in which he, the *most eminent Son of man*, was promised as the *seed of the woman*, for the grand purposes of destroying the works of the *Devil*, and bringing redemption to his chosen. By assuming this name, he shewed himself to be the *true Messiah*, now come to set up that kingdom which should never be destroyed, whom *Daniel* describes under the character of the *son of man*. He, by it, directs the hearers to the consideration of himself as the *second Adam*, now come to restore what the *first Adam* lost to himself, and his seed.

UNDER this character, the *son of man*, the *Lord Jesus* has the pre-eminence above all that ever did, or shall bear that title; as in him dwells all the fulness of Deity,—with respect to the wonders of his extraordinary conception,—the singular

graces

graces he was endowed with above all the sons of men,—the admirable works he performed, which none other could do,—the offices he sustained, and the commission he bore,—together with the names, privileges, dignity, and glory, conferred upon him: In all which, and many other respects, he is the *chief of the sons of men,*—the choicest work of GOD.

SOME of the Prophets, as *Ezekiel* and *Daniel,* have the title *son of man* given them, whether to point out the dignity and eminence of these Prophets, in any particular respect; Or, to put them in mind of their frailty and low original, to keep them humble amidst so many visions, and such near intercourse with GOD, I shall not determine. But it is remarkable, that tho' *Ezekiel* in his prophecy, is called the *son of man* about a hundred times; yet he is never called THE *son of man,* which *Jesus Christ* is called, near a hundred times in the gospels; which certainly points out his singular eminence above all others under that title.

THE *Lord Jesus Christ,* in revelation, is also very often called the SON OF GOD: And in the New Testament, this part of his character is represented to be so important,—so much weight laid upon the proper or improper use of it, that it nearly concerns every christian, to endeavour with the utmost diligence, to attain the right understanding of the true sense and meaning thereof. This can only be had by a careful and impartial enquiry into revelation itself.

WHATEVER may be the various opinions of others concerning this term, as applied to *Jesus Christ,* I am satisfied that he is called the SON OF GOD, as he is the *glorious, divine* EMMANUEL,—

the

the *promised* MESSIAH, and ALL SUFFICIENT SAVIOUR, *chosen, anointed,* and *sent of* GOD, for the SALVATION *of men.* Here I include these three things: The *excellency* of the PERSON, EMMANUEL, who is GOD and MAN: His *designation* to the *office of* SAVIOUR: And his *fitness* and *sufficiency* to *finish* the *great work of Salvation.*

BEFORE I enter upon the proof of the above proposition, I shall mention some texts where the title *son of God* is given him, to point out the *excellency of his Person,* and some others his *office,* which will tend to clear the terms I have used.

'TIS certain that *Jesus Christ* is called the *son of God,* in a sense far *superior* to all others who are called his *sons*; because he has a nearer relation and resemblance to GOD; hence he is called *his own Son, only begotten Son,—beloved Son,—first born,—the image of the invisible God,—*and the *brightness of his glory.* Tho' all these expressions imply *derivation* and *dependence,* ideas inseparable from the common sense of the terms; yet, they also denote the excellency of the *Person,* and his resemblance to GOD, with the peculiar relation and endearment he is under above all others.

THE title *Son of God,* seems likewise to have a respect to the excellency of his *Person,* when joined to the word *Messiah* or *Christ,* (which are the same in sense) as descriptive of the *Person* who bore that official name.—" *Peter* answered and said, thou art *Christ,* the *Son* of the *living God.*" And the highpriest, when adjuring *Christ* to a confession, said, " Tell us whether thou be *Christ,* the *Son of God.*" To the same purpose is that which *Martha* says, " I believe that thou art *Christ,* the *Son of God.*"

THERE

THERE are also many texts, where the title, *Son of God*, has a respect to his *office*, as the promised *Messiah*, the *Saviour*; not excluding the excellence of his person, which rendered him fit for the office he was appointed to. This is plain from what he replied to the *Jews*, who charged him with blasphemy for assuming the title *Son of God*.—" Do ye say of him whom the Father hath *sanctified*, and sent into the world, thou blasphemest; because, I said, I am the *Son of God*?" His being *sanctified* and *sent* by the Father, He makes a sufficient ground to entitle him to the name *Son of God*. It is said of *John the Baptist*, that he, " saw and bare record that this is the *Son of God*." Which must be meant of the *promised Messiah*. " *Nathaniel* said, Rabbi, thou art the *Son of God*, thou art the *king of Israel*." As the *Messiah* was promised as a *king*, the *Jews* looked for him in that character; and here *Nathaniel* owns *Jesus* to be the very *Person*, *Messiah the king*. When *Jesus* asked the man whose eyes he had opened, " dost thou believe on the *Son of God*?" It must mean *Messiah*, the *Saviour*, for in that character only he was the object of the man's faith; which is evident from the reply he made to the man who asked him who the *Son of God* was? *Jesus* said, " thou hast both seen him, and it is he that talketh with thee." When the Apostle says, " We know that the *son of God* is come," it must mean the *promised Messiah*, who was appointed of GOD the Saviour of men.

IT might be also observed, that there are several texts where *son of God* is joined with *Jesus* or *Christ*, in which the name *son of God* is put for the *Messiah* or *Saviour*, and the terms *Jesus* or *Christ* do not signify character or office, but the particular name by which he was known among the *Jews* as a *man*,
and

and diftinguifhed from other men. Hence the *Ethiopian Eunuch* fays, " I believe that *Jefus Chrift*, is the *fon of God* ;" And *Luke* tells us, that *Paul* " preached *Chrift* in the fynagogues, that he is the *fon of God.*" That is, that the man commmonly called *Jefus*, is the *promifed Meffiah*, the *Saviour*. This fenfe of fuch texts is the more evident, if it is confidered, that the great queftion betwixt the *Jews* and *chriftians*, was not concerning the proper *Deity* of our Saviour, or whether *Jefus* of *Nazareth* was the true and eternal God ; but whether he was the *promifed Meffiah*, the Saviour of the world. But I only hint thefe things here, as I fhall have occafion to confider fome of them more fully afterwards. This much was neceffary to free the terms from ambiguity, and diftinguifh the ideas included in that fenfe, which I think the title, *fon of God*, is applied to *Jefus Chrift* in fcripture.

I SHALL next endeavour to prove, by a number of particular arguments, that it is the *true* fenfe and meaning, which our Saviour and the facred writers defigned to convey to chriftian difciples in all ages : And the only fenfe in which it is poffible for them to underftand that phrafe, as applied to *Chrift*, agreeable to the fcope of revelation, or their own fpiritual edification.

1. T H E *firft* argument in favour of this fenfe of *Chrift*'s fonfhip, may be taken from the various ideas of fonfhip mentioned above. The common notion of *Chrift* being a *Son*, as he is God, does not agree with any fenfe fonfhip is taken in among men, nor can any idea that revelation affords, be juftly connected therewith : Except that one of human fonfhip be infifted on, that a *fon* is of the fame *nature* with his *father*, which in this cafe,

T would

would make *two Gods*, as we shall see afterwards. But when we consider *Christ* in his character as *Emmanuel,* the *promised Messiah*, the *sent of God*, and *Saviour of men*, engaged in the great work of their *salvation*, there is not one idea of sonship, that I can remember either in scripture or the common acceptation of mankind, but what is perfectly reconcileable to him as the *son of God:* But as it would be too prolix to consider every idea of sonship in this light, I shall only take two or three, which will serve as a key for all the rest.

Derivation is one idea of *sonship*, which is necessarily implied in his being *begotten of God*, and his *first born:* And with respect to the offices he bears, the scriptures plainly shew that they are *derived* from God, as he was *chosen, appointed, sent,* and *authorized* by God.

Likeness, is another idea of *sonship*, in which respect he is the *image of God*,—the only *medium* of all the knowledge we can have of God; but this idea is intirely confined to his complex character, as we shall see afterwards.

Subordination, dependence, and submission, are manifest in his character *as a son*. Hence he says, " The *Father* is *greater* than I,—I *live by the Father*,—The *Son can do nothing of himself*,—I must be about my *Father's business*,—The *Father* who *sent me*, he doth the works." All these prove his character to be inferior *as a Son*.

The Son is a *distinct individual being* from the Father. This idea is just, when applied to *Christ* in his oeconomical character as a *Son*, which is

clear

clear from his praying *to the Father*,—and faying, " I feek not mine *own will*, but the *will* of the Father that fent me. Not *my will*, but *thine* be done." The will of God is but *one*, yet here are *two wills*, diftinct from each other, mentioned. If the will of the Father, be the will of God; and the will of the Son, diftinct from the Father's, the Son muft be a diftinct being from the Father, or he could not have a diftinct will and confcioufnefs from the Father, as the above expreffions of his plainly prove he has. Now, we muft either conclude that he is a *Son*, in an occonomical fenfe, in which it is neceffary for him to have a diftinct will: Or, we muft maintain that there are *two Gods*, each poffeffed of diftinct powers of willing and confcioufnefs.

ANOTHER fcriptural idea of *fonfhip*, is one that *builds up his Father's houfe*. We can be in no doubt in what fenfe this is applicable to the *fon of God*, as it muft be limited to his official character as the Saviour of men. God tells *David*, by *Nathan*, " I will fet up thy feed after thee,—and I will eftablifh his kingdom. *He fhall build an houfe for my name*, and I will eftablifh the throne of his kingdom for ever. I will be his *Father*, and he fhall be my *Son*." The whole of this undoubtedly refers to the promifed feed of *David*; and whatever refpect it had to *Solomon*, the particulars mentioned, are ftrictly true of none but the *fon of God*, who is alfo called the *fon* and *feed* of *David*, whofe kingdom and reign is for ever. Of this we are abfolutely certain, fince the Apoftle hath applied the words exprefsly to the *fon of God*, when proving *his* character to be more excellent than the Angels, becaufe God had faid of him, " I will be *his Father*, and *he* fhall be *my Son*." That is him, of whom it was faid, " *He fhall build a houfe for my name*,

name, &c." A short, but clear description of the distinct parts the *Father* and *Son* sustain in the oeconomy of redemption.

The *Son of God* rears *such* a superstructure, in *such a way*, and with *such materials*, as shall eternally exalt the glory of his Father's *love*, *wisdom*, *mercy*, and *grace*. He laid the foundation in his own blood, which he gave as a price to redeem them who were children of wrath,—dead in trespasses and sins,—enemies to God in their minds by wicked works,—walking after the lusts of the flesh, and fulfilling the desires thereof: By the powerful efficacy of his word, he gathers them out of all nations,—quickens and sanctifies them by his spirit, and so makes them polished living stones in the spiritual building of God, which is wholly intrusted to his care, as the great architect of this fabric of mercy, which is begun, carried on, and finished to the eternal praise of God, by him "who is faithful in all things over this his own house, as a Son."

I shall only mention one idea more of *sonship*, which is that of one *transmitting his Father's name down to posterity*. To what was said above on this, I shall just add, that as the name of God, is in his son *Jesus Christ*, so it is made known by him.* We can have no saving knowledge of God, but as revealed in *him*, who is not only the *medium* of our *knowledge*, but the *means* of our *access* to God. He is

---

* Psa. xci. 14. which we have translated,— "Because he hath known my name,"—reads literally,— "I will set him on high, because *he hath made my name known*." A promise respecting the exaltation of *Christ*, after glorifying his Father in his humiliation upon earth. The life of *Christ*, was a visible representation of the name of God, and the clearest display of the divine perfections. That power by which he did so many stupendous works, was the almighty power of God: He gave the clearest display of
divine

is with the greatest propriety called, "the *image of the invisible* GOD. No man knoweth the Father, but he to whom the *son doth reveal him*." When *Philip* wanted to see the *Father*, *Jesus* said to him, " Have I been so long time with you, and yet sayest thou, shew us the *Father?* He that hath *seen me*, hath *seen the Father*. No man cometh to the Father, but through him." All this is certainly said of him as the mediator betwixt GOD and men.

FROM the consideration of these, and other ideas of *sonship*, being so clearly applied to *Jesus Christ* as *Emmanuel*, the *all-sufficient Saviour of men*, it amounts to *one* good argument, that in *that* sense he is called the *Son of God*.

2. IT may be observed as another argument, that as he is called the *son of man*, to point him out to us as the *Messiah*, signifying his *relation to men* in an eminent sense, as the promised seed of the woman, and chief of all the sons of men: So he is called the *Son of God*, as he is the *Messiah*, including that *sublime relation to* GOD, by which he is in a more eminent sense, the *Son of God*, than any other who are called so.

THE first promise that was made of the *Messiah*, was,

divine benevolence or good will to men, in living and dying for them: He went about always doing good, diffusing his god-like kindness in the greatest acts of compassion, sympathy, and tenderness: He gave a most striking exhibition of the mercy of GOD, in forgiving his most inveterate enemies, and shedding his own blood for their salvation: He shewed the purity and holiness of GOD in real life: In short, all the revealed perfections of GOD were conspicuously manifested in his life, death, and satisfaction; in him, "mercy and truth met together, righteousness and peace have kissed each other."

was, as the *seed of the woman*, who should bruise the serpents head, that is, destroy his *power*. Now his being called the seed of the woman, must have a near relation to the title *son of man*: But this promise concerning him, is said to be fulfilled by him, as the *Son of God*; for *John* says, " The *Son of God* was manifested to *destroy the works of the Devil*." He, as the *son of man*, was promised to do this great work, and as the *son of God* he actually finished it; which evidently shews they have both a respect to him as the *Messiah*, the Saviour of men.

Perhaps some will think this argument not conclusive, because he is not called *son of man* in the first promise, and therefore it has not a relation to his being the *Messiah*. But there is abundance of texts to support the idea; as for example, (*f*) " Let thy hand be upon the man of thy right hand; the *son of man*, whom thou madest strong for thyself." Whether the first clause refers to the atonement he was to make, or the support that should be given him in the work,—and the settling of his kingdom and glory after it, I need not here enquire, as it cannot be doubted that the *Messiah* is meant, that *son of man*, on whom God has devolved the care of man's salvation, " I have laid help upon one that is mighty; I have exalted one *chosen out of the people*."

Daniel says, (*g*) " I saw,—and behold, one like the *son of man*, come with the clouds of heaven,—and there was given to him dominion, and glory, and a kingdom, &c.". This so plainly refers to the *Messiah*, as it needs no comment.

THE

(*f*) Psa. lxxx. 17. (*g*) Dan. vii. 13.

(*h*) "THE people answered him, we have heard out of the *law*, that *Christ* (*Messiah*) abideth for ever: And how sayest thou, the *son of man* must be lifted up? Who is this *son of man*?" The *Jews* had no notion of any other *son of man*, in that dignified sense the Prophets had spoken of him, than the *Christ* or *Messiah*, whom they had heard of out of the *law* or Old Testament: And they seem surprized, that any thing should be said of him *as* the *son of man*, that was not consistent with what they had learned of the *Messiah*, whom they expected.

(*i*) "IT is written of the *son of man*, that he must suffer many things, and be set at nought." This includes all that is said in the Old Testament concerning the sufferings of the *Messiah*, who is here called the *son of man*: And in many other instances *Christ* applies to himself, under the title *son of man*, what was said of him as the promised *Messiah*. But these are sufficient to prove, that the title *son of man*, in that eminent sense it was applied to our Saviour, points him out as the *Messiah*, implying his relation to man: So his being called *son of God*, points him out in the same character, including his peculiar relation to GOD, above all that are called his sons.

3. THIS sense of *Christ's* sonship, may be proved from the few hints that are given in the Old Testament concerning the *Messiah*, under the title of a SON. These are either under some shadow or type; or they are spoken prophetically concerning some part of his oeconomical character,—his incarnation,—resurrection from the dead,—or his kingdom, exaltation, and government: And we have the most certain rule of interpreting these passages,

as

(*h*) John xii. 34. (*i*) Mark ix. 12.

as they are all applied to him in the New Testament. That which the Apostle cites from *Samuel*, as a proof of *Christ*'s character being more honourable than Angels, because he was called a SON, I have considered above, where it appears in what sense it is applied to him. To much the same purpose is that promise concerning him in the *Psalms*.—(*k*) " He shall cry unto me, thou art *my Father*, my GOD, and the rock of my salvation : Also, I will make him my *first born*, higher than the kings of the earth." Where his *filial dependence* upon GOD, as his *Father*, is pointed out in the strongest light, and the confidence he should have as a SON, in going through the arduous work of man's salvation : Also, the great dignity conferred upon him after it was finished.

ISAIAH tells the house of *David* of a very remarkable sign, which JEHOVAH would give them. —(*l*) " Behold, a virgin shall conceive, and bear a SON, and shall call his name EMMANUEL." This is expressly applied to *Jesus Christ*, with respect to his appearing in flesh as the Saviour of mankind, by the concurrent testimonies of *Matthew* and the Angel *Gabriel*, who said to *Joseph* concerning *Mary*, " She shall bring forth a SON, and thou shalt call his name *Jesus* : For he shall save his people from their sins." Now (says *Matthew*) all this was done, that it might be fulfilled which was spoken of the *Lord*, by the Prophet, saying, behold, a virgin shall be with child, and shall bring forth a SON, and they shall call his name EMMANUEL, which being interpreted, is GOD WITH US." It is too evident to need explication, that in this instance,.
the

(*k*) Psa. lxxxix. 26, 27.   (*l*) Isa. vii. 14.

the fonſhip of *Chriſt* is reſtricted to his complex character EMMANUEL, the SAVIOUR *of men.*

IN the other inſtance where *Iſaiah* ſpeaks of him, as the *child born,* and the *Son given,* he ſays,—(m) " The government ſhall be upon his ſhoulders,— of the increaſe of his government and peace there ſhall be no end, upon the throne of *David,* and upon his kingdom, to order it, and to eſtabliſh it with judgment and with juſtice, from henceforth even for ever." We cannot refuſe the juſtneſs of that application, in a very ſimilar deſcription, which the Angel gave *Mary* of the SON ſhe ſhould bring forth.—(n) " The Angel ſaid, fear not, *Mary,* behold, thou ſhalt conceive in thy womb, and bring forth a SON, and ſhall call his name JESUS. He ſhall be great, and ſhall be called the SON of the HIGHEST; and the LORD GOD ſhall give unto him the throne of his Father *David:* And he ſhall reign over the houſe of *Jacob* for ever; and of his kingdom there ſhall be no end." The name he was to bear, implies the ſalvation he was to procure. It was given as a reaſon why he was called JESUS, becauſe, ſaid the Angel, " he ſhall ſave his people from their ſins." By the appointment of heaven, this was his *proper name.* But the term *Son* here, as in all other places where it is uſed, is deſcriptive of a character, in which is contained a number of diſtinct facts, and it is ſometimes applied to one part of the character, and ſometimes to another. In this paſſage, it is appropriated to the exalted ſtate of kingly government, which GOD would raiſe him unto, after finiſhing the great work of redemption. It ſo plainly reſpects him in his occonomical

---

(*m*) Iſa. ix. 6, 7.   (*n*) Luke i. 31, 32, 33.

nomical character, that to apply it to any other sense, would be a manifest abuse of the passage.

As to that passage in the *Proverbs*,—(o) " What is his name, or what is his son's name?" (which hath been so often perverted, by making it a proof of *Christ*'s sonship, as he is God) I think it is evident from the scope of it, that it has no relation to *Christ* at all; but a question of the same kind with some others in scripture, " who (that is, what man) hath ascended up to heaven, &c. what is his name, and what is his son's name?"

Nor do I think *Nebuchadnezzar* meant any thing concerning *Jesus Christ*, the *Messiah*, when in the height of his surprize, he says,—(p) " Lo, I see four men loose, walking in the midst of the fire,—and the form of the fourth is like the *son of God*." Any one but tolerably acquainted with the Bible only, will see that it was the manner of speaking in the eastern countries, to call almost every thing *Father, Son*, or *Daughter*. Hence, for a proud or wicked man, we read the *son of pride*, the *son of wickedness*; and for mighty men, the *sons of the mighty*. It is also observable, that the term God, is often used to heighten the idea of the thing spoken of, as, " *the trees of God*, &c." Why then might not *Nebuchadnezzar*, at the sight of so glorious a person, call him the *son of God*, or one whose glory was above the appearance of men,—one of a more divine and God-like form than the other three, whom he afterwards calls the *Angel* or *messenger* of the God of *Shadrach, Meshach*, and *Abednego*. This was like the language of a heathen king, who supposed that men might be *deified*, for he calls him

(o) Pro. xx. v. 4. (p) Dan. iii. 25.

him a *man* as well as the *other*, but more like the notion *he* had of a GOD. It cannot be imagined with any probability, that this idolatrous prince knew any thing of *Chriſt*, tho' ſome would have him know more than many of his Aſtoples did, all the time *Chriſt* was among them.

THERE is one text more in the Old Teſtament, which claims our particular attention, becauſe currently interpreted of the *ſon as he is God*, which is directly contrary to the ſcope of the paſſage itſelf, and the uſe which the Apoſtles make of it in the New Teſtament.—(*q*) " I will declare the decree, the LORD hath ſaid unto me, thou art my SON, this day have I begotten thee." It is evident, that the general ſcope of this *Pſalm*, is a prophetical deſcription of the character of the *Meſſiah*, in ſome things particularly relating to his *ſufferings*, *reſurrection*, *kingdom*, and *conqueſt* over his enemies.

THE *raging of the heathen, and vain imaginations of the people*, are expreſsly applied by (*r*) *Peter* and *John* to *Herod*, *Pontius Pilate*, the *Jews* and *Gentiles*, that were gathered againſt CHRIST. Theſe Apoſtles interpreted this Pſalm, with reſpect to the counſel and determination of GOD, concerning what ſhould happen to CHRIST. When the Apoſtle would convince the *Jews*, that the ſame JESUS, whom they had condemned and crucified, was the *Meſſiah* promiſed to the fathers, he ſays,—(*s*) " We declare unto you glad tidings, how that the promiſe that was made unto the fathers, GOD hath fulfilled the ſame unto us their children, in that he hath *raiſed up* JESUS again : as it is alſo written in the ſecond Pſalm, " *Thou art my Son, this day have I begotten thee.*"

(*q*) Pſa. ii 7. (*r*) Acts iv. 25.—29. (*s*) ibid. xiii. 32, 33.

thee." Now, to deny that by the SON in this text, is meant the *Messiah*, is in plain terms to say, that the Apostle, or the Spirit by which he was inspired, did not understand the meaning of it; seeing it is so expressly applied to him in that character, yea, brought as a proof of his being the MESSIAH: And not only here, but in other places, it is accommodated to the same purpose. It is certainly sufficient to limit human curiosity, when the matter is determined so explicitly by a divine interpreter.

THE text itself is the language of the SON, who says,—" I will declare the decree, the LORD hath said unto me, &c." Now the Apostle tells us, he became our high priest in pursuance of this decree, (*t*) " No man taketh this honour to himself, but he that is called of GOD, as was *Aaron:* So also, *Christ* glorified not himself, to be made an high-priest; but he that said unto him, thou art my SON, this day have I begotten thee." What kind of reasoning would this be for an Apostle, if the *sonship* in the text referred to the *manner* of his divine existence, under which consideration, he could not be *set apart, appointed, consecrated, or perfected;* nor could any office be prescribed to him. But the Apostle affirms all these of the SON, mentioned in the text, and therefore he must be so designed with reference to his oeconomical character.

CHRIST must certainly be considered under the same character in the 7th, as in the 8th verse of this Psalm, where it is said, " Ask of me, and I shall give thee the heathen for thine inheritance, and the uttermost parts of the earth for thy possession."

(*t*) Heb. v. 4, 5.

feſſion." To *aſk* and *receive* an inheritance and poſſeſſion, are terms quite agreeable with his inferior character, as *Meſſiah*: But abſolutely inconſiſtent with *Deity*. As GOD, he has an original right to all creatures, the heavens and earth are his, and all they contain.

THE word DAY in the text, is ſuppoſed to mean *eternity*; and ſo the SON is concluded to be an *eternal* SON. The beſt reaſon I could ever hear for this conjecture was, that ſome men have thought ſo. But the Apoſtle ſurely thought otherwiſe, when he applies the text to things done in *time*: And alſo joins it with another ſimilar paſſage, which is ſpoken in the future time, and very much elucidates this, " I *will* be to him a *Father*, and he *ſhall* be to me a *Son*." This cannot mean either *eternity*, or the pure *Deity* of *Chriſt*. Beſides, there is not one inſtance where the phraſe *to-day* ſignifies eternity in all the word of GOD.

MANY commentators apply the text to the *reſurrection* of *Chriſt*, from what the Apoſtle ſays, Acts xiii. 32, 33. " The promiſe which was made unto the fathers, GOD hath fulfilled the ſame unto us their children, in that he hath raiſed up *Jeſus* again; as it is alſo written in the ſecond Pſalm, Thou art my Son, this day have I begotten thee." Tho' the application of it to *Chriſt*'s reſurrection equally favours my argument; yet, I think by cloſe attention to this paſſage, it will be found, it rather refers to the ſending of *Chriſt* in the fleſh, as the fulfilling of thoſe promiſes made to the fathers.

THE Apoſtle had been giving the *Jews* at *Antioch*, a demonſtrative account of *Jeſus* being the
true

true *Messiah* promised to the fathers, in which he introduces the testimony of *John the Baptist*,—charges his death upon their countrymen, proves his resurrection from the testimony of living witnesses, and then tells them that these things were foretold by promises to the fathers, which were now fulfilled to them, *viz.* The promise of the coming of *Christ*, ver. 33. GOD hath fulfilled the *same* (that very promise made to the fathers, mentioned in the foregoing verse) unto us their children, in that he hath *raised up Jesus*, (*again*, this word the original will not bear) as it is written in the ·second Psalm, " thou art my Son, this day have I begotten thee." The promise of his *resurrection*, he adds the very next verse.—" And as concerning that he *raised him up from the dead*, no more to return to corruption, he said on this wise, I will give you the sure mercies of *David*, &c." The first *raising up* here, must refer to his coming in the flesh, as expressed in the 23d verse, " Of this man's (*David*) seed, hath GOD, according to his promise, *raised* unto *Israel*, a *Saviour Jesus.*" The words " *unto us their children,*" seem to limit it to that sense. Whereas had it been meant of the resurrection, why is it added immediately, " And as concerning that he *raised him up from the dead,*" if in the former verse, he had meant the resurrection? He rather seems to add these words, on purpose to distinguish this last *raising up* from the former. Moreover the words " *as concerning,*" point out another subject than the foregoing, whereas the former part of the 34th verse is superfluous, if the 33d meant the *resurrection* of *Christ*. Besides, the word here translated *raised up*, in other texts, signifies to *raise up seed*. " I will *raise* unto *David* a righteous branch.—I will *raise up* thy *seed* after thee,

thee, which shall be of thy sons, and will establish his kingdom.—I will *raise him up* a faithful priest.—And *raise up seed* to thy brother.—That of the fruit of his loins, according to the flesh, he would *raise up Christ* to sit on his throne.—A Prophet shall the Lord your God *raise up* unto you of your brethren, like unto me."

As to the other two places where this text from the second Psalm is cited, they have no relation to the *resurrection of Christ*, distinct from other parts of his character. It is therefore plain, from the use the Apostle makes of this text, that it refers to the general character of the *Messiah, as the son of God*, which name, as foretold in the Old Testament, was particularly given him, when he appeared in flesh upon the important errand of man's salvation.

Thus, I think it is abundantly evident, that all the texts in the Old Testament, which speak of *Christ* as a Son, are in the New Testament, applied to him in his oeconomical character; which makes one strong argument for his sonship being taken in that sense. But I proceed to a

4th General argument, taken from several texts, which seem *exegetical* or explanatory of the term *son of God*, as applied to *Christ* in the New Testament, and which cannot be interpreted any other way than as having a relation to his oeconomical character.—The first I shall mention, is that declaration of God concerning his Son at his baptism, which was repeated at his transfiguration. *"This is my beloved* Son, *in whom I am well pleased, hear ye him."* Three very comprehensive sentences, and all agreeable to the present purpose. In general, God, in

the

the character of the *Father*, expresses his delight and satisfaction in *Jesus Christ* his *Son*, as he stood intrusted with the great concerns of men's salvation, and the obligation to obedience from them, on account of that oeconomical relation. The *relation* and *love* of GOD to *Christ*, is expressed in the first clause. "*This is my beloved* SON." In the second, are implied the relation the redeemed stand in to GOD, and the love he bears to them *in his son*, as mediator. "In whom I am well pleased." Which is similar to that expression, "I am pleased for his righteousness sake;" which righteousness the *Son* having finished, and the *Father* accepted on their behalf, a new relation is constituted betwixt GOD and them, as the foundation of their duty required in the last clause, "hear ye him."

WE are under necessity to include the notion of *Christ* as *Mediator* and *Redeemer*, in the character of *Son* in this text, or it is impossible to make good sense of it. How else can we account for GOD's being well pleased with sinners *in him?* Is it not for what he has done for them as *Mediator* and their *Redeemer?* Or where shall we find ground for any particular immediate obedience to the *Son* more than to the *Father?* If he be considered to be GOD, as he is a SON, he cannot be the medium of our acceptance with GOD,—nor the object of any particular duty distinct from the Father, except we admit the notion of *two* GODS.

PETER tells us that the "*Lord Jesus Christ* received from GOD honour and glory, when this voice came to him from heaven." How this can be true, if he is a SON, as he is GOD, is not easily accounted for: That is, how he could receive honour and glory *as* GOD, by GOD owning him to be be *his* SON! But it is easy to conceive how he might receive honour and glory in his inferior character as GOD's *servant,*—the promised *Messiah*, by being so solemnly owned to be the " *beloved son of God, in whom he was well pleased.*"

AND as it is with *Christ, as Mediator*, that GOD is well pleased, it must be in that sense, he is here called *his beloved* SON. This is further clear from a parallel text,—(*u*) " Behold *my servant*, whom I uphold, mine *elect*, in whom my soul delighteth: I have put my spirit upon him, he shall bring forth judgment to the *Gentiles*, &c." All this, with several other things that are in the context, certainly belong to him *as Mediator*. The term *servant*, as applied to him, is the same with *Messiah*, and that of *Elect. Matthew* renders (*v*) " *Beloved in whom I am well pleased,*" when he applies the passage at large to *Christ*, which is the same with the text we are considering, and shews them to be of the same import.

AND whereas we are commanded to *hear the* SON, it is plain in what sense we are to understand that title, from an ancient prophecy of *Christ* by *Moses*.—(*w*) " The LORD thy GOD will raise up unto thee a Prophet from the midst of thee, of thy brethren, like unto me, *him shall ye hear.*" The (*x*) Apostle tells us, that this was foretold of *Jesus Christ*. From these considerations it is indisputable, that his being called the *beloved Son* in the text, is meant of his complex character as *Mediator, the Saviour of men.* In him as the *beloved son of God*, are we accepted, having made peace through the blood

---

(*u*) Isa. xlii. 1. (*v*) Matt. xii. 18. (*w*) Deut. xviii. 15. (*x*) Acts iii. 22.

blood of his crofs. He is the great Prophet and teacher of his people, whom they are to " hear in all things whatsoever he shall say unto them." For " GOD, (says the Apostle) in these last times hath spoken to us by his SON."

We have heard the testimony of the Father concerning *Christ's sonship*; the next instance shall be a short commentary upon this term from his *own mouth*. Having cured a man that was born blind, whom the *Jewish rulers*, through their blindness, had excommunicated for receiving his cure on the sabbath, and saying, that his physician was a Prophet, and had cured him by the power of GOD. Our LORD, to shew the regard he has to those who are persecuted for telling the truth, found out the man, and opens more fully his character unto him. " He said unto him, dost thou believe in the *son of God?* He answered and said, *who is he*, LORD, that I might believe on him? And *Jesus* said unto him, thou hast both *seen him,* and it is *he that talketh with thee.*"

OUR Saviour very rarely, if in any instance but this, expressly called himself the *son of God*. But here he does it in such a manner, as the meanest capacity may understand that his *human nature* must be included in his own description of himself as the *son of God*. Whoever is so possessed with prejudice as to deny this, do in effect say, that our LORD either gave such a description of his *sonship* to the man, as he could have no ideas of,—could understand nothing about, and so imposed upon him: Or, that the lips of truth told the man a plain and undisguised falshood, by saying, in answer to the man's question, " Thou hast both *seen him,* (*the son of God*) and *it is he that talketh with thee.*"

IT

It is very remarkable to our purpose, how the *Ethiopian Eunuch* came to the knowledge and belief of the *son of God*. Having read that prophetical account of *Christ*'s sufferings,—(y) " He was led as a sheep to the slaughter, and like a lamb dumb before his shearers, so opened he not his mouth, &c." He asked *Philip* who the Prophet was there speaking about? We are told that *Philip* from that text, preached JESUS unto him, and from the evidence of the truth, that JESUS was the person spoken of, he desired to be baptized. *Philip* told him he might, if he believed with all his heart. " He answered, I believe that JESUS CHRIST is the SON OF GOD." The *Eunuch* had been at *Jerusalem* to worship, where he, no doubt, had been told the current news of the nation at that time, concerning *Jesus* and his followers; but it is plain, he did not understand his character as the *Saviour*, till *Philip* informed him of the accomplishment of these prophecies which he had been reading, in the sufferings, death, and resurrection of *Jesus*, as the *Messiah* and *Saviour* of men. This knowledge was the ground of the faith which he expressed, " That *Jesus* (the man of whom he had heard among the *Jews*, and whose real character *Philip* had now informed him of) was the *son of God* ;" the promised *Messiah*, whose sufferings he had been reading, but did not know who to apply them to. This must be the sense of the passage, or we can find no connection betwixt *Philip*'s preaching *Jesus* unto him, and his believing on the *son of God* : Nor could his confession of such faith in any other sense give him a right to baptism, the badge of the christian religion.

CHRIST

(y) Isa. liii. 7, 8.

CHRIST having finished the work of redemption on the cross,—risen from the dead, and about to ascend to heaven as the representative of his redeemed seed, he says to *Mary*,—(z) " Go to *my brethren*, and say unto them, I ascend unto *my Father*, and *your Father*, and to *my God*, and *your God*." Here *Christ* as a SON, not only intimates his relation as the covenant head to his people, as covenant children, in their united relation to GOD, as their GOD and *Father :* But it is manifest, that he speaks of himself in the same oeconomical consideration, when he says MY GOD, as when he says MY FATHER. And as the one respects him as EMMANUEL, engaged in the work of redemption, so must also the other. This is indisputably true, as well as plain, from the two phrases being joined not only here, but in what is said concerning his confidence in GOD, when engaging in the work of salvation.—(*) " He shall cry unto me, thou art MY FATHER, MY GOD, and the *rock of my salvation.*"

5. IF it can be made appear, from what is said concerning our Saviour in the New Testament, that the same things are predicated of him under the title SON, as under the names JESUS and CHRIST;—that the names *Jesus Christ* and *Son*, are used promiscuously as synonimous terms, when any thing is affirmed of him that relates to the oeconomy of salvation : It will certainly prove, that as the names *Jesus* and *Christ* are *oeconomical*, that the title *Son* must be so also, since they are used indifferently without distinction, that is, the same things which are said of *Jesus Christ* in one place, are said of the *Son* in another, *& contra*. This, I shall

(z) John xx. 17.   (*) Psa. lxxxix. 26.

shall illustrate by several examples, from which it will appear, that by the terms -*Jesus Christ* and *Son*, in the New Testament language, we have presented the same object of *faith*, *hope*, and *confidence*.

To give all the texts at large which relate to this subject, would be to copy a great part of the New Testament. I shall only select some that respect the capital doctrines of christianity, write out one for proof of each particular, and leave others equally to the purpose, to be compared by the reader at his leisure.

CHRIST is called the head of the church.—(a) "*Christ* is the *head of the church*: And he is the Saviour of the body." So is the Son,—(b) "Giving thanks to the Father,—who hath translated us into the kingdom of his *dear Son*,—*he is the head of the Body, the church*, who is the beginning, the first born from the dead."

ALL things were made, and are upheld by *Jesus Christ*.—(c) "But to us there is but one GOD, the Father, of whom are all things, and we in him; and one *Lord Jesus Christ, by whom are all things, and we by him.*" Applied to the Son.—(d) "For by *him* (GOD's dear SON, the antecedent in the context) were all things created that are in heaven, and that are in earth, visible and invisible, whether they be thrones or dominions, or principalities or powers: All things were created by him, and for him. And he is before all things, and by him all things consist."

JESUS

(a) Eph. v. 23. (b) Col. i. 12, 13, 18. also com. Matt. xxiii. 8, 10. with Heb. iii. 6. (c) 1 Cor. viii. 6. (d) Col. i. 16, 17. also com. Eph. iii. 9. with Heb. i. 2.

JESUS CHRIST was *sent* into the world for man's falvation.—(*e*) " This is life eternal, that they might know thee, the only true GOD, and *Jefus Chrift*, whom thou haft *sent*."—The SON of GOD was *sent*.—(*f*) " When the fulnefs of the time was come, GOD *fent forth his* SON, made of a woman, made under the law."

HE is called *Jefus Chrift*, who was born of the virgin.—(*g*) " Behold, thou fhalt conceive in thy womb, and bring forth a Son, and *fhalt call his name* JESUS.—Unto you is born this day, in the city of *David*, a Saviour, which is *Chrift* the LORD." He is called the SON *of* GOD.—(*h*) " He fhall be great, and *fhall be called the* SON *of the higheft*. That holy thing which fhall be born of thee, *fhall be called the* SON *of* GOD."

JESUS CHRIST is the author of the gofpel. (*i*) " I am not afhamed of the *gofpel of Chrift*." So is the SON.—(*k*) " GOD is my witnefs, whom I ferve with my Spirit, in the *gofpel of his* SON."

BY the *faith* of *Jefus Chrift*, finners are juftified. —(*l*) " Knowing that a man is not juftified by the works of the law, but by the *faith of Jefus Chrift*, even we have believed in *Jefus Chrift*; that we might be juftified by the *faith of Chrift*." By the *faith of the* SON *of* GOD they live.—(*m*) " The life which I now live in the flefh, I live by the *faith of the* SON *of* GOD."

IT

(*e*) John xvii. 3. (*f*) Gal. iv. 4. alfo com. Acts iii. 20. Rom. i. 3. 1 Tim. i. 15. with Acts iii. 26. 1 John iv. 9, 10, 14 John iii. 17. Rom. viii. 3. (*g*) Luke i 31. and ii. 11. (*h*) ibid. i. 32, 35 fee Matt. i. 21, 23, 25. and ii. 4. (*i*) Rom. i. 16. (*k*) ibid. i. 9. fee Mark i. 1. (*l*) Gal. ii. 16. (*m*) ibid. ii. 20.

It was the *blood of Jesus Christ* that made peace with God, and purgeth away sin,——(*n*) " The blood of *Jesus Christ*, his Son, cleanseth us from all sin.". It is called the blood of God's *dear* Son.— (*o*) " In whom we have redemption through *his blood*, even the forgiveness of sin,—having made peace through the blood of his cross."

Jesus Christ is the object of the saint's faith.—*(p)* " Believe in the *Lord Jesus Christ*, and thou shalt be saved." So is the Son.—(*q*) " He that believeth on the Son, hath everlasting life."

They have fellowship with *Jesus Christ* as the Son *of* God.—(*r*) " Our fellowship is with the Father, and with *his Son Jesus Christ*. God is faithful, by whom ye were called into the fellowship of his *Son Jesus Christ*."

It was *Jesus Christ* that *died* for sinners.—(*s*) " When we were yet without strength, in due time *Christ died* for the ungodly." A little after the Apostle says,—(*t*) " When we were enemies, we were reconciled to God by the *death of his* Son."

It was *Jesus Christ* that rose from the dead.— (*u*) " He seeing this before, spake of the resurrection of *Christ*. This Jesus hath God raised up, whereof we all are witnesses." Applied to the Son.—(*v*) " Declared to be the Son *of* God with power,

---

(*n*) 1 John i. 7.　(*o*) Col. i. 14, 20.　(*p*) Acts xvi. 31.　(*q*) John iii. 36. also com. Acts x. 36, 43. and xix. 4. with 1 John iii. 23. (*r*) 1 John i. 3.　1 Cor. i. 9. com. Col. ii. 6. with 1 John v. 12. (*s*) Rom. v. 6.　(*t*) ibid. v. 10. com. 1 Cor. i. 23.　Rom. xiv. 9. 1 Thess. iv. 14, with Rom. 8. 32.　(*u*) Acts ii. 31. 32.　(*v*) Rom. i. 4. com. Rom. xiv. 9.　Col. iii. 1.　Eph. i. 20. with 1 Thess. i. 10.

power, according to the Spirit of holiness, by the resurrection from the dead."

JESUS CHRIST is exalted at GOD's right-hand, having all power and authority given unto him.—(w) " Wherefore GOD hath highly exalted him, and given him a name which is above every name: That at the name of JESUS every knee should bow, of things in heaven, and things in earth, and things under the earth; and that every tongue should confess, that JESUS CHRIST is LORD, to the glory of GOD the Father." The same glory and dignity is attributed to the SON.—(x) " GOD hath in these last days spoken unto us by his SON, whom he hath *appointed heir of all things*,— upholding all things by the word of his power, when he had by himself purged our sins, sat down on the *right-hand of the majesty on high*.—Unto the Son he saith, thy throne, O GOD, is for ever and ?ever; a sceptre of righteousness is the sceptre of thy kingdom."

JESUS CHRIST shall come in great glory to judge the quick and the dead.—(y) " In the day when GOD shall judge the secrets of men by *Jesus Christ*, according to my gospel." Now our LORD tells us himself, that (z) " The Father judgeth no man; but hath *committed all judgment to the* SON."

WHAT puts this matter wholly beyond dispute is, that the Apostles did not only make it the same, to

(w) Phil. ii. 9, 10, 11. (x) Heb. i. 1.—3. com. Acts ii. 36. Col. iii. 1, Matt. xxviii. 18. Rev. xi. 15. Eph. i. 10. with Acts iii. 13. John v. 23. Heb. iv. 14. (y) Rom. ii. 16. (z) John v. 22. com. Col. iii. 4. 2 Cor. v. 10. Acts x. 42. 2 Thess. i. 7. with 1 Thess. i. 10. Matt. xxv. 31, &c.

to *believe in Jesus Christ* and *the Son of God*; but they teach it as an express article of his religion, that JESUS CHRIST *is the* SON *of* GOD.—(a) *Whosoever shall confess that* JESUS *is the* SON OF GOD, GOD *dwelleth in him, and he in* GOD. (b) *Whosoever believeth that* JESUS *is the* CHRIST, *is born of* GOD. (c) *These are written, that ye might believe that* JESUS *is the* CHRIST, *the* SON OF GOD. (d) *Who is he that overcometh the world, but he that believeth that* JESUS CHRIST *is the* SON OF GOD? *This is* HE *that came by water and blood,* EVEN JESUS CHRIST. (e) *And to wait for his* SON *from heaven, whom he raised from the dead,* EVEN JESUS, *who delivered us from the wrath to come.*" Here is plain divine testimony in abundance, expressed in as strong terms as language will bear.

FROM these particulars, and many other that might be mentioned on this head, it plainly appears, that whatever is said of JESUS CHRIST, is also said of the SON OF GOD. The writers of the New Testament knew no such difference in the use of these terms, as writers after them have invented: And seeing all things concerning the oeconomy of salvation, are particularly attributed to the *Son of God*, we must either admit that he is called *Son* with reference to that oeconomy, or that the account the Apostles have given of him, is extremely dark and perplexed;—very unlike the plainness and simplicity of the men,—and more unworthy the wisdom and goodness of the divine Spirit that inspired them.

PERHAPS it will be said, (which is the last shift of such as love to deal in *mysteries*) that there
is a

(a) 1 John iv. 15. (b) ibid. v. 1. (c) John xx. 31. (d) 1 John v. 5, 6. (e) 1 Thess. i. 10.

is a *metonomy* in each of thefe texts, or one name put for another. If this is fo, then there is more than one-half of all the religion in the New Teftament, under the veil of tropes and figures: And fo we can underftand nothing concerning the *Son of God, our Redeemer,* and the way of falvation through him, but by the affiftance of *Antonomafia,* and other rhetorical figures. This at once deftroys that well-grounded maxim among chriftians: "*That all things neceffary to falvation, are fimple, plain, eafy to be underftood, and clearly revealed in the word of God.*" If this is denied, which it muft be if the other is maintained, then the *Bible* is no longer of univerfal ufe to mankind; the illiterate muft implicitly believe what the learned *critic* and *logician* are pleafed to fay is the fenfe of every text in revelation.

6. ANOTHER argument may be taken from the feveral parts of that character, in which the *Son of God* reprefents himfelf, when inditing the feven fhort epiftles which *John* wrote to the *Afian* churches. The whole, he challenges to himfelf as the *Son of God,* " *Thefe things write, faith the* SON OF GOD." If any unprejudiced reader will confult the firft three chapters of the revelation of JESUS CHRIST to *John,* [*] he will clearly fee from the other parts of his character there mentioned, in what fenfe he calls himfelf the SON OF GOD.

IT is the fame *Jefus Chrift,* " the faithful witnefs, the firft begotten of the dead, and the prince of

---

[*] This would be a more proper title to the book, than what it commonly bears, viz. " *The revelation of St John the divine.*" For the firft words of the book tell us, that it was " *the revelation of* JESUS CHRIST.

of the kings of the earth.—He that loved us, and waſhed us from our ſins in his blood, and hath made us kings and prieſts unto GOD and his Father;—behold he cometh with clouds, and every eye ſhall ſee him, and they who pierced him: And all kindreds of the earth ſhall wail becauſe of him." The ſame who *John* ſaw in the midſt of the candleſticks, of whom he gives ſuch a glorious deſcription, every part of which ſtrictly belongs to his oeconomical character. "I ſaw one like the *ſon of man* clothed with a garment down to the foot, and girt about the paps with a golden girdle: His head and his hair were white like wool, as white as ſnow; and his eyes were as a flame of fire; and his feet like unto fine braſs; as if they burned in a furnace; and his voice as the ſound of many waters.—Out of his mouth went a ſharp two edged ſword: And his countenance was as the ſun ſhining in his ſtrength." *John*'s deſcription being finiſhed, mark what he immediately ſays of himſelf.—" I am the firſt and the laſt: I am he that liveth, and was dead; and behold, I am alive for evermore, *Amen*; and have the keys of hell and of death."

To the *Philadelphian* church he ſays, " Behold, I come quickly,—him that overcometh, will I make a pillar in the temple of *my God*, and I will write upon him the name of *my God*, and the name of the city of *my God*, which is new *Jeruſalem*, which cometh down out of heaven from *my God*: And MY NEW NAME." To *Thyatira* he ſays, " That which ye have already, hold faſt till I come: And he that overcometh, and keepeth my works unto the end, to him will I give power over the nations,—*even as I received of my Father*." It is very

very evident from thefe, and many other expreffions, in what fenfe he calls himfelf the *fon of God* in thefe epiftles.

INDEED feveral parts of the defcriptions clearly point out his proper Deity, which tends to illuftrate my argument; for as they are connected with others, which muft be limited to his complex character and offices, and all faid of the fame perfon, the whole muft be taken as a defcription of *Emmanuel* the *Saviour*, or it is impoffible to form any juft ideas from this facred account of him, which, I conceive, is the moft ftriking of any we have in revelation, and reprefents him as *Emmanuel*, the *Son of God*, in the cleareft point of view.

7. ONE very clear argument may be taken from the *Son* being called the *image of the invifible God*. I confefs this is generally brought as an argument to prove that he is the SON, *as he is* GOD, the inconfiftency of which, I fhall confider afterwards. In the mean time, let us fee how far this part of his filial character is an argument for our prefent purpofe.

JESUS CHRIST may be called the *image of God*, in the three following refpects. (1.) As MAN, his human foul being the *holieft*, *wifeft*, *beft*, and *firft* of all created fpirits, made like GOD in the greateft perfection poffible for a creature. All the natural and moral perfections in the whole creation put together are not equal to what the human nature of the *Son of God* is poffeffed of: "*For in all things he muft have the pre-eminence.*" In this refpect, he may be called the *image of God*. But (2.) And more properly, as this glorious human nature is united to DEITY: In this refpect, the perfections

tions of GOD himself shine through his SON, in the most resplendent manner as EMMANUEL. In this sense, the Apostle says, with the utmost propriety, "He is the brightness of glory, and the express image of the invisible GOD: Thus, "the light of the knowledge of the glory of GOD, shines in the face of his SON JESUS CHRIST. (3.) He is the image of GOD, as he reveals GOD to men, in the character of his *ambassador* and *representative*: He represented GOD in the whole of the Old Testament oeconomy, and by his works shewed his power under the New: He is vested with sovereign dominion over all things in heaven and earth,—is appointed heir and LORD of all things,— the king of kings, and LORD of LORDS. As *Adam*, in his dominion over the creatures, was the *image of God*, much more is the *Son of God*, the glorious *image of God*, in his sovereign dominion over the upper and lower worlds.

ALL the moral perfections of GOD are manifested by him. "No man hath seen GOD at any time, the only begotten SON, which is in the bosom of the Father, he hath declared him.—All the treasures of wisdom and knowledge are in him. The fulness of Deity dwells in him bodily." His character is the brightest display of divine perfections. As the law of GOD in its utmost latitude was *in his heart*,—his life is an exact representation of its goodness and extent,—his death, a most striking image and declaration of the *strictness, holiness*, and *spiritual extent thereof*: His laws and government are a display of the *wisdom, power, equity*, and *goodness of God*: Out of *his* fulness the saints receive the abundant grace of GOD: To them, "he is made *of God, wisdom, righteousness, sanctification*, and *redemption*." The certain accomplishment

ment of all the promises of GOD,—and his threatnings upon his own and his people's enemies, is a clear manifestation of the *truth, justice,* and *unchangeableness of God.*—His appearing in the midst of the throne of GOD, as the slain lamb, is a *living, everlasting image* of the *infinite love* and *mercy of God,* in the *sending* and *sufferings* of his *beloved Son.*

UNDER these, and such like consideration, we may with propriety learn from the light of revelation, the divine beauty that shines in this part of *Christ's filial* character, the *image of God,* to our spiritual comfort and edification. But we come to another argument.

8. ALL the fundamental articles of faith necessary to salvation, are plain, familiar, easy to be understood, and clearly revealed in the word of GOD; but the *belief of Jesus Christ* being the *Son of God,* is made necessary to salvation: Therefore, it must be easy to be understood, and clearly revealed in the word of GOD. I need not stand to prove the *major* or first proposition, as it is granted by every *Protestant* who know his own principles. But with relation to the present subject, it may be observed, that as all true religion is practical, and is attained through knowledge of the object, it must therefore be necessary that we know in whom we believe: And as the only means of saving knowledge is divine revelation, it will follow, that the object of our faith must be clearly revealed therein. It cannot be supposed, that it is consistent with the wisdom and goodness of GOD, to leave that under the veil of *ineffable mystery,* the knowledge of which he hath made absolutely necessary to salvation.

AND

AND there is nothing more evident in the New Testament, than the necessity of believing that JESUS CHRIST *is the* SON *of* GOD, which the following texts, among many, put beyond doubt. (*a*) " Whosoever shall confess that JESUS *is the* SON *of* GOD, GOD dwelleth in him, and he in GOD. But these things are written, that ye might believe that JESUS is the *Christ*, the SON *of* GOD, and that believing, ye might have life through his name. He that believeth on *him*, is *not condemned:* But he that *believeth not*, is *condemned already*, because he hath not believed in the name of the only begotten SON *of* GOD. Whosoever *denieth the Son*, the same hath not the Father. And *Philip* said, if thou believest with all thine heart, thou mayest. And he answered, *I believe that* JESUS CHRIST *is the* SON *of* GOD : And he baptised him. These things have I written unto you that believe on the name of the SON *of* GOD ; *that ye may know* that ye have eternal life, and that ye may believe on the name of the SON *of* GOD. *He that believeth on the Son, hath everlasting life: And he that believeth not the Son, shall not see life*; but the *wrath of* GOD *abideth on him*.

Now from premises so evident, the conclusion may with safety be admitted, that the *sonship of Christ* must be easily understood, and clearly revealed in the word of GOD. Then the doctrine of his being *a Son, as he is* GOD, must be given up; because all the supporters thereof, acknowledge it to be an *ineffable mystery, so inconceivable, that no man can know it*. But as the *œconomical character* of our *Lord* and *Saviour* is every where clearly

(*a*) 1 John iv. 15. John xx. 31. ibid. iii. 18. 1 John ii. 23.
Acts viii. 37, 38. 1 John v. 13. John ii. 36.

clearly taught in revelation, yea, is the substance of both Old and New Testaments, we may without hesitation affirm, that it is in *that sense* the scripture makes the knowledge and belief of his character as the SON *of* GOD, *necessary to salvation*. This natively leads to another argument or reason why it must be so.

9. As the scriptures make *believing in the* SON *of* GOD *necessary to salvation*, of consequence there must be that in him *as a Son*, which is directly suitable to the sinful and miserable state of mankind,—which renders him a proper object of their *desire, dependence,* and *hope*. Now, this is not the *Deity abstractedly* considered; for we cannot suppose him under that consideration to have the least relation to creatures, much less to sinful apostate men: And tho' we suppose the relation of *creator* and *creatures* betwixt GOD and *sinful men*; yet, if we do not also take in the consideration of the *Son's complex character*, in which he stands related to them as their *kinsman*, and consequently their *surety* and *redeemer*, there is nothing in him, that we know of, that is more suitable to the miserable case of men, *as sinners*, than there is to the hopeless case of *Devils*, to whom he is under no such relation. All the *love, mercy,* and *grace* of GOD communicated to men, flow through *his Son*, in whom they are chosen: Nay, all that is known of GOD is in *Christ*, for OUT OF HIM † the scriptures do not reveal any GOD but heathen ones.

BUT

---

† "That GOD OUT OF CHRIST is a consuming fire," is a sentence that passes for sacred writ, I own; I was myself so far deceived through the prejudice of education, that I used it as a text in a former publication; but am now satisfied, that neither the

But consider the *Son of God* under the *relative* characters and *offices* he sustains, as the *glorious Emmanuel*, the *Saviour of men*, with his *all-sufficient capacity* to fulfil these *offices*, which he in *so great condescension* was clothed with; in this light, he is a comforting sight to a *poor, perishing, convinced sinner*, who is void of all hopes of salvation any other way. When the wretch, pursued with the curse, and stung with a sense of poignant guilt, beholds the *glorious* EMMANUEL, appointed a *Prophet* to enlighten his darkened soul,—a *Priest* to atone for his numberless sins, and manage his cause by appearing in the presence of GOD for him,—a *king* to rule, influence, and defend him against all the combined powers of sin and hell,—and *all-sufficient* for these sacred purposes; how happy must the poor soul be, who is thus through the power of his divine Spirit determined to trust in *him*, who is every way suitable for all he wants, or can desire in time and for ever?

10. THE ground of our *adoption*, and right to the *privileges of sons*, are laid in the *filiation* or *sonship of Christ*, taken in connexion with the *free love* of GOD, as the spring of his chusing us in him, to be heirs of GOD, and joint heirs with *Christ*. The scriptures prove this; but I can no ways agree with those, who make it an argument for a *natural* and *necessary sonship* in *Christ*; for the proposition if once admitted to be true, proves the contrary.

---

the words, nor the sentiments they convey, are in revelation, but like many other things, which custom only hath made canonical. I mention this, to shew the danger of taking things upon trust, and neglecting to examine the sentiments we have been nursed up in, many of which are not authenticated from scripture.

IF *believers sonship* is founded upon a *necessary sonship in Christ*, it will necessarily follow, that their sonship is *necessary* also: For a necessary cause, must produce a necessary effect. It must also follow, that the salvation of sinners was necessary in GOD. Where then will we find room for the least vestige of the *sovereign love*,—the *free will*, or even the *mercy* or *grace of God*? If the sonship of *Christ* was *natural* and *necessary*, it could in no wise depend upon the *will of God:* And if the sonship of believers is an *effect* of this *natural* sonship, then it must not depend on the *will of God*, more than the *cause* from which it doth flow. This makes our adoption, with the whole of redemption by *Christ Jesus*, to flow from *necessity*, not from the *good pleasure of the will of God.*

ALL GOD's children are made so by *disposition*, founded in *sovereign love* and grace; but is there, or can there be any connexion betwixt a *natural sonship of Christ*, and a sonship founded in *love* and *grace?* unless we can suppose that *Christ's* relation to his people, is *natural* and necessary to him, in the same way as his sonship is pretended to be. But in this case, it would unhappily follow, that it would no longer be a disposition of *grace*, but of *necessity*; which not only overthrows the whole plan of redeeming *love* and *grace*, but is a plain contradiction in terms.

JESUS CHRIST in the transaction which he *voluntarily* assumed, became the *kinsman* and *elder brother* of all who were chosen in him, as the objects of JEHOVAH's *love*,—sons and children by *immutable promise made to him*, and who in time should be actually adopted,—taken into the *family of God*, and made partakers of all the *privileges of sons,*

sons, by virtue of that infallible engagement of JEHOVAH (who had chosen them) to *his Son*, their head and representative; and through the divine efficacy of that redemption wrought for them, in shedding his precious blood, that they might *actually* enjoy the favour of GOD, and fellowship with him. Thus they are made partakers of a *divine nature*, and possessors of the inheritance they were chosen to in *Christ Jesus*, which they had incapacitated themselves for the enjoyment of, being alienated from the life of GOD, and by apostasy liable to the curse; all which, the *Son of God*, their *kinsman*, came down to redeem them from, by being made a curse for them.

IN this light there is a connexion supported by revelation, betwixt the *sonship of Christ, as the elder brother* in the family of GOD, and the saints *sonship, as younger brethren, heirs of God, and joint heirs with Christ*. This will appear still more obvious, by a little attention to the different characters and privileges of the saints, as *sons of God*, all which, have relation to some *name, appellation*, or *office* given to *Christ* in scripture. Are they called the *redeemed, ransomed, saved, purchased*? Or, is *redemption, salvation*, and *liberty* their privileges? He bears the names and offices of *Kinsman, Redeemer, Saviour, Goal*, &c. Are they called *bride, spouse, flock*, &c? He is the *Bridegroom, Husband, Shepherd*, &c. Are they *begotten of* GOD? He is the *only begotten Son of God*. Are they *sons* and *children*? He is the *holy child, Jesus, the beloved Son of God*.

Now if these, and all the other privileges of the saints refer to, or flow from some one part or other of the complex character of *Emmanuel*, as
they

they indisputably do, why should not this of their being *sons of* GOD, have a reference to him under the same consideration? There is a strict analogy betwixt the *sonship* of believers, and the *sonship* of *Christ* in his oeconomical character. They are in some measure *reciprocal* and *correlative*, as the existence of the one depends upon the existence of the other. They are *both* of the *same family*,—both *heirs* of the *same inheritance*: He is not ashamed to call *them brethren*,—and the *same* GOD *is the Father of both*. Hence he says, " I ascend to *my Father* and *your Father*, to *my* GOD and *your* GOD."

"BUT no one can have the least idea of any analogy or connexion betwixt the *sonship* of *saints*, and an *eternal, natural,* and *necessary sonship*. It is not because GOD is eternally, naturally, and necessarily holy, just, and good, that his people are made holy, just, and good; but because he hath of his sovereign love and good pleasure made them so in his *Son Jesus Christ*. All that the saints enjoy, flows from the *free will of* GOD, and not from *necessity* in his *nature*, which would be the consequence if their sonship depended upon a natural sonship in *Christ*.

I MUST now consider some texts, from which arguments are drawn against the doctrine I have been endeavouring to maintain: And, I presume the impartial reader will see, not only how little they are against *this sense* of *Christ*'s sonship; but how easily the texts may be accommodated to the support of it; and therefore may be considered as so many more arguments in its defence.

Object. THE objection that most weight seems to be laid on, is taken from what the Apostle says,

Moses

—(a) "*Moses* verily was faithful in all his house, as a *servant*. But *Christ*, as a *son*, over his own house: Whose house are we." From which it is thus argued, that to limit the sonship of *Christ* to his complex character as *Emmanuel*, must destroy the distinction betwixt *Christ* as a Son, and as a Servant, and spoil the beauty of the antithesis betwixt *Moses* and *Christ* in this passage."

Ans. It has been made manifest above, that to believe in *Jesus Christ*, and to believe in the Son *of* God, are of the same import; both must include his complex character. So to behold him as a *servant*, which we are commanded to do,—(b) "Behold, my *servant*, whom I uphold,"—must be of the same import with beholding him as the Lamb *of* God,—and hearing or believing in him as the Son *of* God in New Testament language.— (c) "Behold the Lamb of God, that taketh away the sins of the world.—This is my beloved Son, in whom I am well pleased: Hear ye him." In all these characters, he is the object of our faith; and the security of our salvation: For the consideration of faith in *Christ*, as it respects salvation, must include the consideration of his complex character, whether he be viewed as a *Son*, a *Servant*, a *Saviour*, or whatever other name the scriptures represent him under to us, as in that character he finished salvation for us, and also bestows it upon us.

His being called a *Servant*, points out the abased condition he humbled himself unto, in going through the work of our salvation; in which, tho' he as Emmanuel, was rich in the enjoyment

---

(a) Heb. iii. 5, 6. (b) Isa. xlii. 1. (c) John i. 29.

ment of all that is divine,—in him were hid all the treasures of wisdom and knowledge,—in him dwelt the fulness of *Deity* bodily,—he was the bright representation of JEHOVAH's glory;—yet for our sakes, he made himself of no reputation, —became so poor, as to be more destitute than the beasts of the earth,—calling himself a worm, and no man,—having no form or comeliness why he should be desired,—despised, and rejected of men, a man of sorrow, and acquainted with grief, —was wounded, bruised, oppressed, afflicted, and at last humbled to the dust of death. Thus EMMANUEL's glory, who was in the *form of* GOD, and thought it no robbery to assume the *names*, the *glory*, the *worship of* GOD, was veiled, and appeared in the form of a *servant*, *upheld* by the arm of GOD in the infinite work of man's salvation, who now (his servitude in suffering work being finished) " hath crowned him with glory and honour, far above all principality and power, might and dominion, &c. And hath put all things under his feet, and given him to be the head over all things to the church, which is his body, the fulness of him that filleth all in all."

To answer the objection, we need go no further than the text on which it is founded, which makes directly against it; and will be found one of the plainest arguments in favour of *Christ*'s oeconomical sonship. The text says, it is *as a Son* that *Christ* is over his *own house*. By the house here, must be meant the church, over which he is the governor and head. His right to rule, and the special relation he hath to the church *as a Son*, is expressed in its being called HIS OWN. The antithesis is not betwixt *Christ* as a *Son*, and a *servant*,

as

as the objection would infinuate: But betwixt *Mofes as a fervant*, and *Chrift as a Son*. The former is highly commended for his faithfulnefs as a *fervant*: But *Chrift Jefus*, fays the Apoftle, was counted worthy of more glory than *Mofes*, not only becaufe he was faithful to him that appointed him the *Apoftle* and *high-prieft* of our profeffion, but becaufe he had built the houfe, and being a SON, the *firft-born*, the right of rule and inheriting was his over his *own houfe*, which he had this double right unto.

Now, in whatever light we view *Chrift's* relation to the church, whether as their *head, goal, kinfman*, and *redeemer*: Or, as their *Prophet, Prieft, King*, &c. we muft include the confideration of his complex character. For the confideration of his being clothed with human nature, *actually* or *proleptically* by participation, is the foundation of his relation to the church, as the members of his body chofen in him, and his right as their *goal* to redeem them: Therefore, the fonfhip in the text, muft have a refpect to him as EMMANUEL, feeing it is in that character he is related to the church, and a SON over it as his OWN HOUSE.

But to fuppofe *Chrift's* fonfhip in the text to fignify (as the objectors would have it) his *Deity* abftractedly, makes the paffage wholly unintelligible to us. As a SON, he has a fpecial right and relation to the church, as his *own houfe*; but what relation can we fuppofe any of the *divine three* hath abftractedly, more than another? Hath abfolute Deity (which is what we know nothing about) any relation to creatures at all? Or, is it effential to the *Deity* of our *Lord Jefus Chrift* to be the *head* of the church? Once to fuppofe this (which yet

is

is an idea infeparable from their notion of fonfhip) would be to deftroy the *fovereignty* of JEHOVAH's *love*, in chufing the church in *Chrift* : And the *fovereign, voluntary condefcenfion* of EMMANUEL, in becoming the *head, hufband,* and *redeemer* of his church. Under that character, he is her *head,* and fhe his *members*. Abfolute Deity, for ought we know, is at an abfolute diftance from any connexion with, or relation to the creature, in any fenfe whatfoever.

As we ought not to conceive notions of GOD that are not revealed; neither fhould we too critically diftinguifh the revealed *names* and characters of the glorious EMMANUEL; but rather believe, and humbly admire his infinite condefcenfion, in becoming fo fuitably related to us in his complex character as EMMANUEL, in which he exhibits the divine glory and perfections,—executes all the divine purpofes concerning men,—and is the glorious medium through which the love, grace, and glory of JEHOVAH are, and fhall for ever be manifefted to his chofen. Thus he is revealed, and fo they believe, and fhall for ever behold the SON *of* GOD, in divine refulgence, having all things fubdued unto him, who himfelf, *as a* SON, "fhall be fubject or placed in order to him, that put all things under him, that GOD may be all in all."

Object. ANOTHER objection is taken from thefe texts, where *Chrift,* and *Son of God,* are both mentioned, particularly what *Peter* fays,——(d) "Thou art *Chrift,* the Son of the living GOD." From which it is inferred, "that as the term *Chrift* refers to his *office,* the term *Son* muft refer to his divine perfonality, or there would be a manifeft

(d) Matt. xvi. 16.

felt *tautology* in this, and such like texts, as if Peter should say, "thou art the *mediator*, the *mediator*." And this objection is reckoned unanswerable, if the text is read as some critics translate it, distinguishing the terms by what they call the Greek article THAT, "Thou art *that Christ*, *that* SON of the living GOD."

Anf. THAT the terms *Christ* and *Son*, present us with the same object of faith as they are used in the New Testament, is proved above: But to give the objection its full weight, we shall first consider how *Christ* is a term of *office*,—next, what is signified by the term *Son* in the text,—and then what strength the use of the Greek article affords the cause.

As to *Christ* being a term of *office*, let it be observed, that it is agreed on all hands, that *Christ* and *Messiah* are terms of the same import: *Messiah* in the Old Testament, is the same with *Christ* in the New. Now, should I ask the objector, whether he whom the *Jews* called the *Messiah*, was a *Person* or *office*? It would be reckoned of the same consequence, as if I should ask, whether a *Person* be a *Person* or not? Concerning the *Messiah* it is said,—(*e*) "The rulers took council against the *Lord*, and his *anointed*," (*Messiah* or *Christ*.) This passage would read, "They took council against the LORD, and his *office*." The same Person who is called his *Messiah or Christ*, in the beginning of this Psalm, is a little after called his *king*, and his *Son*, which is answer enough to the objection. But further, *Daniel* tells us, that the (*f*) "*Messiah*, the *prince*, should be cut off, but not for *himself*." This he could not say with propriety of an *office*.

Besides,

(*e*) Psa. ii. 1. (*f*) Dan. ix. 26.

Besides, when *Peter* says, " Thou art the *Christ*," it would mean no more in that sense, than if he had said, " Thou art the *office*."

But there is nothing more plain than that the names *King*, *Priest*, and *Prophet*, point at persons vested with these respective offices; in like manner, the name *Christ* points out the person authorized by office, for the discharge of the great work he was appointed to: And if it be granted, as common sense requires it should, that the term *Christ* is not confined to the *office*, but to the *Person* bearing the office, then the controversy is at an end, and the whole cause yielded, in as much as it has been proved above, that the same official characters are ascribed to the SON, as to CHRIST. The plain consequence is, that both terms point out the complex person of the glorious Redeemer, clothed with such offices, who is no other than the blessed EMMANUEL; for it is only as such, that he does, or can sustain any office in the business of man's redemption.

LET us next see what is most likely to be the meaning of the phrase, " SON OF GOD," in the text. This will appear exceeding plain, if the scope of the passage is attended to. Our blessed LORD had asked the disciples what the people's sentiments concerning him were. They having told him; he next requires their own; when *Peter*, in the name of the other disciples, answered, " Thou art CHRIST, the SON of the living GOD." Now, it must be at least supposed, that the answer which *Peter* gave, was direct to the question his master asked in such a plain manner: But the question was, with respect to the character of CHRIST *as come in the flesh*, " Whom say ye, that I the SON OF MAN am?"

am?" Therefore the terms in the anfwer, muft include his human nature, or they would be no direct reply to the queftion afked. But that the anfwer refpected his character as EMMANUEL, the ALL-SUFFICIENT SAVIOUR, is evident from our LORD's reply to *Peter*, and the fequel of the paffage. " Flefh and blood hath not revealed this unto thee, but my Father, which is in heaven." What was it that *Peter* had revealed unto him? Surely the character of the perfon who was fpeaking to him. The fame that all GOD's children hear and learn of their heavenly Father, " That he hath fent his SON, whofe name is EMMANUEL, to be the Saviour of the world." This is plain from what our LORD adds, " Upon this rock will I build my church: And the gates of hell fhall not prevail againft it." What is this rock on which the church is fo fecure? Surely the truth concerning the character of CHRIST, the SON of the living GOD, which the Father makes known to all his children, as well as to *Peter*, " For other *foundation* can no man lay, than that is laid, which is JESUS CHRIST. Brought unto the church, they " are built upon the foundation of the Apoftles and Prophets, (the doctrine they taught concerning) JESUS CHRIST himfelf, being the chief corner ftone; in whom (as a SON that builds his father's houfe) all the building fitly framed together, groweth into an holy temple in the LORD."

THE relative character and work of JESUS CHRIST, *the* SON *of* GOD, is the fum of the chriftian religion, and the foundation of the church's fecurity and privileges, againft which the powers of hell and earth are combined, but according to his promife, they fhall not prevail. He next acquaints the Apoftles, with a facred truft that
fhould

should afterwards be committed to them, which at that time, they very little underſtood, viz. the opening up and making known to the world the doctrines, laws, and ordinances, of his kingdom, both with reſpect to looſing the obligation to *Moſaic* rites and ceremonies, and the eſtabliſhing chriſtian ordinances, which ſhould never be altered. This our LORD calls *the keys of the kingdom of heaven*. Thus they ſhould *bind* and *looſe* by the doctrines which they ſhould infallibly be directed to teach. † But as the ſuitable time was not yet come, for ſuch an open declaration of his character, " he charged them, that they ſhould tell no man that he was JESUS, the CHRIST." This muſt have a direct reference to what they had confeſſed him to be; and ſhews that the ſum of their faith, as they expreſſed it, was, that they believed him to be the true *Meſſiah* or *Chriſt*, if we will allow their *maſter* to be a proper interpreter of their creed.

IF

† I know this way of difpoſing of the *keys*, will not pleaſe the kingdom of the *Clergy*, whoſe dominion over men is principally ſupported upon a notion, which they have in all ages taken great pains to cultivate, viz. That they are the Apoſtles *ſucceſſors*,—*Ambaſſadors* of *Chriſt* as the Apoſtles were,—have the *keys* of the *kingdom of heaven* committed to them, and ſo can open and ſhut at pleaſure; all which, are falſhoods impoſed upon the credulous multitude, to keep up that reverence and ſubjection expected from them, to ſuch as are more like *ſpiritual Lords*, than *ſpiritual leaders*.

If they are *ſucceſſors* to the Apoſtles, which of them was called, ſent, and ordained to this office immediately by *Jeſus Chriſt*. Which of them has the power of working miracles as a proof of his miſſion? If they are *Ambaſſadors*,—let them ſhew their commiſſion from heaven to make any *new laws*, or alter thoſe already made—what *new* revelation they have in truth to men.—And to ſay they have the *keys* of the *kingdom of heaven*, is manifeſtly to rob *Chriſt*,—uſurp his throne,—and intrude upon his kingly office, who *alone* " hath the *key* of *David*, he openeth, and *no man* ſhutteth, and ſhutteth, and *no man* openeth. Behold, I have ſet before thee an open door, and *no man can ſhut it*. I have the *keys* of hell and of death." Iſa. xxii. 22. Rev. iii. 7. and i. 18.

IF more proof were not superfluous, both *Mark* and *Luke* might be produced, as agreeing with their *master* in the meaning of *Peter's* words. *Mark* gives them thus, "*Peter* answering said, thou art the CHRIST." And *Luke* says, "*Peter* answering said, thou art the CHRIST of GOD." And adds, "And he straitly charged them and commanded to tell no man, that thing," viz. that he was the CHRIST. It is therefore evident from the whole, that our LORD, and the Evangelists, thought this expression, "the CHRIST OF GOD," sufficient to intimate the full sense of *Peter*'s confession; and we may safely conclude, that CHRIST OF GOD, and SON OF GOD, are still terms of the same import and meaning.

IT remains to be considered what force there is in the Greek *article*, to make such a wide difference betwixt the term CHRIST, and SON OF GOD, in the text.

THIS part of the objection might be very shortly dispatched, by denying that there is any occasion for the word *that* in the text, it being literally rendered in our *English* Bibles: But as the advocates for the distinction I am opposing, have the authority of some critics, and think the weight of their argument consists in admitting them, I shall not dispute the case, but rather shew how little they weaken my argument, or strengthen theirs.

AND *first*, I would observe, that it is paying a very uncomfortable compliment to the unlearned multitude, to tell them, that the grounds of their faith, on which the salvation of their souls depend, are only known by a critical acquaintance
with

with *Greek articles*, *untranslated* in our *Bibles*. Notable doctrine for *Papists*, whose faith must depend on what the learned say, but cannot judge for themselves, not having the scriptures in a language they know: Besides, it may seem strange, that the fidelity of the learned translators allowed them to with-hold words of such peculiar emphasis; this amounts at least to a strong presumption, that they did not judge them of such importance as *some now* would persuade us they are: But how far they are so, will appear by considering,

Secondly, The use and grammatical sense of the word THAT, which they would here supply. It sometimes signifies *the other*, as opposed to *this*. Sometimes it signifies WHO, when applied to a person mentioned before. When taken comparatively, it expresses the *eminence* of the *person spoken of*, above all others that bear the same name. In this last sense it must be taken, if added to the text; so THAT CHRIST, THAT SON, will point out the peculiar eminence of the person spoken of, above all others that were anointed to be Prophets, Priests, and Kings; and all that bare the title SON *of* GOD: Or, that he was the very person prophesied of, and described by these characters in the Old Testament. And I must also observe, if the word *that* is used here, it cannot properly be an *article*, but a *demonstrative* adjective or quality, pointing out our LORD to be *that* peculiar SON OF GOD, whom they so long expected, and who had a peculiar relation and likeness to GOD. But,

Thirdly, The critics are not agreed how often the word should be repeated in the text. *Goodwin* and others, think it should be read thus,
" *That*

"*That* CHRIST, *that* SON *of that* GOD, *that* living GOD." If this is so, and these articles (as they are called) have such influence upon the terms in the *first clause*, "*that* CHRIST, *that* SON," they must have the same in the *latter*, "*that* GOD, that *living* GOD," and so the term GOD, and *living* GOD, will not be of the same import; but as different in meaning, as they would have the terms CHRIST and SON to be. But as I hope none will presume to affirm, that they can make any difference in the sense of the terms in the *last clause*, we may safely affirm they make none in the *former*; and so this mighty argument, after so much weight has been laid upon it, makes against the contrivers of it, and tends to strengthen the cause it is brought against.

THO' the above objection is founded upon several other texts of the same import with that we have been considering, yet, it is unnecessary to take particular notice of each of them, as I have chosen that which the objectors reckon most for their purpose, and what is said on it equally shews the import of simliar texts where they occur. There are also some other passages of scripture which have been opposed to the above account of *Christ's* sonship: But as they are rather brought as arguments for *natural Sonship*, or that *he is a* SON, *as he is* GOD, I judged it more orderly to consider them among the other arguments produced for that doctrine. I shall then shew, that they are every one against the notion which they are brought to prove, and tend to confirm the truth of *Christ's œconomical Sonship*.

SECT.

SECT. IV.

HAVING given the scripture account of the character of CHRIST as a Son, it is necessary that something be said concerning the *name, title, appellation,* or *character* WORD, which is given him. As it is owing to the prejudice of education, that the term SON is so little understood, I suppose, it will be found, that on the same account, the term WORD is applied to CHRIST in a wrong sense: Whereby the significant ideas which are conveyed by the use of it in the sacred volumes, are in a great measure lost to such as are accustomed to take things of this kind upon trust, as handed down to them, without being at the pains to consult the scriptures impartially to find the true import thereof.

THE schoolmen's definitions of this term, as applied to CHRIST, are such as no man can have any ideas of, without first supposing him to be a mere creature; as they are inconsistent with any notions that revelation affords us of *Deity*. Even they themselves pretend not to know what is meant by the terms they use, and are therefore obliged to put this into the number of the *great mysteries* in religion, which cannot be understood, and so should not be inquired into. This is a fate which many of the plain truths in revelation have been subjected to. Many critics have attempted to reconcile the inferior characters of the WORD to true and eternal Deity, by supposing that both a real *derivation,* and some *natural* as well as oeconomical *inferiority* may be allowed to belong to the LOGOS, even in his *divine nature.* But this, with other

other things of the fame kind, I leave to thofe who can defend the doctrine of a *derived* GOD.

IT would be of fmall advantage to examine the fubtle diftinctions, which have been advanced on this point: Nor dare I depart fo far from the prefent purpofe. I fhall endeavour to make it appear, that the term WORD, is part of the *oeconomical character of* CHRIST in the New Teftament, and fo muft be of peculiar advantage for every chriftian to confider and know.

JOHN ufes this title of CHRIST oftener than the other writers of the New Teftament: But wherever it is mentioned, it is plainly meant of his oeconomical character. *Luke*, in the preface to his gofpel, fays, the difciples " were eye-witneffes, and minifters or fervants of the WORD." That by the WORD here, is meant JESUS CHRIST, and not the gofpel, as fome fuppofe, is evident from the words; for with the greateft propriety might the difciples be called *eye-witneffes* of CHRIST, as *Peter* alfo fpeaks of their being " *eye-witneffes* of his majefty." But it muft be a very forced conftruction, and in effect faying, that *Luke* did not write good fenfe, to call them *eye-witneffes* of the gofpel, which would rather been *ear-witneffes*, had that been the fenfe.

BESIDES, it would feem very ftrange in *Luke*, to write a preface to the hiftory of the life and actions of CHRIST, and not mention to *Theophilus*, (to whom he wrote it) any name or title of the perfon whofe hiftory he was about to write: But this muft be the cafe, if JESUS CHRIST is not intended by the term WORD in the preface,

B b   for

for there is not any other word that points him out in it.

Now, as the WORD here means JESUS CHRIST, (for I can see nothing of any consequence against it) this is one instance wherein he is called the WORD, in his *oeconomical character*; or the gospel of *Luke* is not a history of him under that consideration, which none will presume to say.

THE Apostle, in his epistle to the *Hebrews*, says, (*a*) "The WORD of GOD is quick and powerful, and sharper than any two-edged sword, piercing even to the dividing asunder of soul and spirit, and of joints and marrow; and is a discerner of the thoughts and intents of the heart." What is here predicated of the WORD, cannot with such propriety belong to the *written word*, as to JESUS CHRIST, the "*living* WORD *of* GOD." The last clause determines the whole, as it is the very character he challenges to himself, (*b*) "*I am he who searcheth the reins and the hearts.*" And the next verse connected with this shews, that it must be a *person*, not a *thing* that is meant, for the personal relatives are always used, which have no other antecedent than the WORD OF GOD mentioned before. "Neither, says the Apostle, is there any creature that is not manifest in HIS *sight:* But all things are naked, and open unto the eyes of HIM, with whom we have to do." Omniscience is here attributed to the WORD, which is not proper to the *written word:* And the scriptures certify us, that *Christ* shall judge the world, who must be the same with the WORD here spoken of, to whom, says the Apostle, we must give an account: Besides,

(*a*) Heb. iv. 12, 13. (*b*) Rev. ii. 23.

fides, it is added, this WORD is the " great *high-priest*, that is paſſed into the heavens, JESUS, the SON *of* GOD." This, with what the Apoſtle had formerly ſaid concerning the WORD, he makes an argument for the ſame thing, to encourage them in perſeverance and ſteadfaſtneſs. " Let us labour therefore to enter into that reſt, leſt any man fall after the ſame example of unbelief. For the WORD of GOD is quick and powerful, &c." Seeing the WORD is ſo powerful,—ſtrict in judgment,—irreſiſtable in operation,—critical in diſcerning the heart,—whoſe intelligence pervades over all,—whoſe eye beholds every ſecret thing,—to whom all ſhall give an account,—and who is paſſed into heaven in the character of the great high-prieſt of his people, JESUS *the* SON *of* GOD, " Let us hold faſt our profeſſion."

Now as it is pretty clear that it is JESUS CHRIST, who is here called the WORD, it cannot be denied that he bears that title with reſpect to his *oeconomical character*.

THE Apoſtle taking his leave of the *Epheſian* church, ſays,—(c) " Now, brethren, I commend you to GOD, and to the WORD of his grace, who is able to build you up, and to give you an inheritance among all them who are ſanctified." What is here ſaid, agrees much better with CHRIST, than the *written word* or the *goſpel*, which is only the means or inſtrument for the purpoſes mentioned. It is CHRIST who *builds* up his people by the Spirit: He builds this ſpiritual temple, and bears the glory. The goſpel is the glaſs in which
they

(c) Acts xx. 32.

they see their inheritance: But it is JESUS CHRIST that *gives* it, and puts them in possession thereof.

PAUL in all his salutations to the churches, joins GOD and the LORD JESUS CHRIST together, and therefore it is agreeable to his own phraseology, to consider JESUS CHRIST as intended, by the term WORD, in the text: And it is the more probable, as it argues his *equality*, which would not be agreeable with respect to the *written word*, to be put on a level with GOD, in so solemn a recommendation. To recommend the saints to CHRIST, is an honour which is due to him, and no diminution of the glory of GOD: But it would appear otherwise, if the gospel was here meant.

THE *Ephesians* are here *committed* to the care of GOD, and the WORD; but the saints are never committed to the care of the *written word*; for, from several other texts, we find *it* is committed to them. The saints are under the care of CHRIST their *shepherd*, *husband*, and *Saviour*, who shall at last present them to GOD without spot or wrinkle. None but one possessed of divine perfections is capable to take the charge of the saints. They never commit themselves or others to the care of any but *Christ*, and with the Apostle rest satisfied with their choice. " I know whom I have believed, and am persuaded that he is able to keep that I have *committed* to *him*, against that day." And at death, they are all of the same temper with *Stephen*, who with his last breath, and the greatest confidence, could *commit* his departing spirit to the care of *Jesus Christ*, saying, " Lord *Jesus, receive my spirit.*" From these considerations, we we may conclude that *Jesus Christ* bears the title WORD in the text; and that this is one instance more of his being called so in his *oeconomical character.*

As it would be tedious to be so particular on every instance, I shall only mention two or three more texts, in which I think the term WORD is used in the same sense. *Peter* says,—*(d)* " The saints are born of incorruptable seed, by the WORD OF GOD, who liveth and abideth for ever." Now *Jesus Christ* alone is the *living word of God*. He tells us, that the scoffers in his time were *(e)* " willingly ignorant, that by the WORD OF GOD the heavens were of old, and the earth standing out of the water, and in the water,—but the heavens and the earth which are now, by the same WORD are kept in store, reserved unto fire, &c." *Paul* says, *(f)* " Through faith we understand that the worlds were framed by the WORD OF GOD." The same WORD by whom *John* says,—*(g)* " All things were made, and without HIM was not any thing made that was made." *Paul* charges *Timothy* to *(h)* " preach the WORD." The words are, " preach the LOGOS," which must always be interpreted of *Christ*: And we may be very sure that *Paul* would charge *Timothy* to preach the same he did himself, but he says, " we preach *Christ* crucified."

IN these, and some other texts, this title of *Christ* is barely mentioned, and we can only learn in what sense it is applied to him from the scope and contexts, or comparing them with others of similar import. We shall now consider *John*'s account

---

(d) 1 Pet. i. 23. *(e)* 2 Pet. iii. 5, 7. *(f)* Heb. xi. 3. *(g)* John i. 3. *(h)* 2 Tim. iv. 2.

count of the Word, which in several places is more explicit.

It is a very needless inquiry which some have laboured much in, how *John* came by this term. If we believe the books which he wrote, to be part of the inspired writings, we need be in no doubt how he came by the whole, without the assistance of *Plato*, *Philo*, or any other whom he is supposed to borrow this term from. My present business is to shew in what sense he applies this title to *Jesus Christ*, which he does more frequently than in all the New Testament besides. If the passages are attended to, it will appear, that in every instance, the complex character of our Lord is included in the term Word.

About to prove the truth and excellency of the *Messiah*'s character, and that *Jesus of Nazareth* was he, *John* mentions several names applicable to him, whom he intended as the great subject of the gospel he wrote, which he begins with this title the Word or Logos. " In the beginning was the word, and the word was with God, and the word was God. The same was in the beginning with God." Here he declares three glorious facts. " In the beginning was the word." The scriptures copiously point out the ancient relation of *Christ* to the church, as the *medium* of communication betwixt God and men; in this capacity he was in the *beginning*, or the *beginning itself*, as some would render the text. " He was *set up from everlasting,—his goings forth were of old.*" And in this relative capacity, *John* says, " he was *with* God," and adds, " the word was God." By which he affirms the *Deity* of him he was speaking of. This divine, by a character of Em-

MANUEL,

Manuel, leads us to the knowledge of God. It had been well for the church, if thefe called *Divines* in all ages fince, had taught by the fame rule.

From the fcope of the whole chapter, it is evident that the character of *Emmanuel* is the fubject, whom he calls the Word. No other could be faid to be in the beginning with God, which expreffion the *Evangelift* repeats, to fhew the certainty of the truth I am now contending for. It was he who came to *his own*, and his *own* received him not,—gives the privilege of adoption to thofe that believe,—dwelt among the Apoftles, whofe glory they beheld,—who was full of grace and truth, of which they were made partakers.—He whom *John the Baptift* bare witnefs to, as coming after him and preferred before him, the latchet of whofe fhoes he was unworthy to loofe,—of whom he faid, behold the *Lamb of* God, that taketh away the fin of the world,—whom he faw the fpirit defcending upon,—and of whom he bare record, that this is the *Son of God*.—The fame *Son of God*, who declares and makes him known,—of whom *Andrew* faid to *Simon*, we have found the *Meffiah*, which is the *Chrift* ;—and the fame of whom *Philip* faid to *Nathaniel*, that *Mofes* and the *Prophets* did write. In fhort, he whom *John* calls the Word, fays himfelf, that they fhould fee the Angels of God afcending and defcending upon him, which can be no other than *Jefus Chrift*, the Saviour of men, to illuftrate whofe character as fuch, *John* declares he wrote his whole gofpel. " Thefe are written, fays he, that ye might believe that *Jefus* is the *Chrift*, the *Son of God*, and that believing ye might have life through his name."

That no doubt might remain concerning the
fenfe

sense of the term WORD, which *John* mentions in his gospel, he explains himself in the clearest manner in his first epistle.—(*i*) " That which was from the *beginning*, which we have *heard*, which we have *seen* with our *eyes*, which we have *looked upon*, and our hands have *handled* of the WORD *of life*; for *the life* was manifested, &c." He refers to the very *senses* for evidence, that the same *Jesus*, whom they had *heard*, *seen*, and *felt*, was the WORD *of life*, or the *living* WORD: And if we once admit that *John* is to be credited, sophistry itself cannot evade the force of his testimony. It is clear, and needs no comment.

ANOTHER passage of his is equally conspicuous.—(*k*) " I saw heaven opened, and behold, a white horse; and he that sat upon him was called faithful and true, and in righteousness he doth judge and make war: His eyes were as a flame of fire, and on his head were many crowns; and he had a name written, that no man knew but he himself: And he was clothed with a vesture dipt in blood: And his name is called, the WORD OF GOD." This description is applicable to no other than the once *humbled*,—now *exalted Jesus*, who is still called the WORD, and of whom *John* tells us, he bare record.—(*l*) " The revelation of *Jesus Christ*, which GOD gave to his servant *John*, who bare record of the WORD OF GOD."

I SHOULD also here consider that text in 1 John v. 7. where the *word* is mentioned, but as that text is made an argument for the names *Father*, *Word*, and *Holy Ghost*, being *natural* and *essential* to *Deity*, I shall refer the consideration the cof, 'till the arguments in favour of that opinion come to be answered,

(*i*) 1 John i. 1, 2. (*k*) Rev. xix. 11, 12, 13. (*l*) ibid. i. 1, 2.

answered, and shall very briefly add here, what I understand by the name, title, or appellation WORD, as given to *Jesus Christ.*

LOGOS, which is rendered WORD, is a scriptural name given to *Jesus Christ*, in both Old and New Testaments. The proper meaning of it is, *An outward declaration of God's wisdom and will to men:* And as applied to *Christ*, the *Messiah*, the *Jews* and Apostles both meant, that he was that glorious person by whom GOD was pleased fully and plainly to discover his will to men, as being acquainted with all his counsels, and impowered by him to give laws to the world in general, and the church in particular, and rule them accordingly.

AGREEABLE to this account of *Christ*, as the WORD OF GOD, the Apostle calls him, (*m*) "the *power of God, and the wisdom of God.*" And says, "that of God *he is made unto us wisdom.* In him are hid *all the treasures of wisdom* and *knowledge.*' (*n*) By him is *made known the manifold wisdom of God.*" With reference to this sense of his name, John says, he is the (*o*) "*light* of men,—the *light* that *lighteneth* every man that cometh into the world,—(*p*) He that believeth on him, no longer abideth in darkness.—(*q*) He is the *way*, the *truth*, and the *life*," as he affirms of himself. The *way* to the knowledge and enjoyment of GOD.—"No man cometh unto the Father but *by me.*" The *spirit* and *truth* of all the Old Testament promises, prophecies, declarations, &c. concerning the *Messiah.* Hence it is said, "The testimony of *Jesus*, is the spirit

(*m*) 1 Cor. i. 24, 30. (*n*) Eph. iii. 10. (*o*) John i. 4, 7. (*p*) ibid. xii. 46. (*q*) ibid. xiv. 6.

spirit of prophecy,"—the revealer, bestower, and exemplar of all divine truth,—the author and finisher of faith,—full of grace and truth.—The *life*, (*r*) " I am the resurrection and the *life:* He that believeth in me, tho' he were dead, yet shall he *live*. (*s*) I am that bread of *life*. (*t*) In him was *life*, and the *life* was the light of men. (*u*) The words I speak are *spirit* and *life*. (*v*) He that hath the Son, hath *life*. (*w*) The purpose and grace of GOD in *Christ* before the world began, is now made manifest by the appearing of our Saviour *Jesus Christ*, who hath abolished death, and brought *life* and *immortality* to *light*, through the gospel."

AND further, agreeable to this sense of the title WORD, being applied to *Christ*, he is called the *image* or *visible representation* of the *invisible God*.— (*x*) " The express *image* of his glory." He makes known the invisible GOD to men; hence he says, (*y*) " He that hath seen me, hath seen the Father. (*z*) I will *declare thy name* unto my brethren. (*a*) I have declared thy name unto them, and will declare it. No man hath seen GOD at any time; the only begotten *Son*, who is in the bosom of the Father, he hath declared him."

THUS it is evident from revelation, that *Jesus Christ* is called the WORD OF GOD, because by him GOD reveals himself to men. He is the great *medium* of all communication betwixt JEHOVAH and creatures.—In *him* all the gifts of GOD are bestowed.—By *him* the grateful services of his people are acceptable with GOD.—In *him* are all the counsels and purposes of GOD.—By *him* they are all executed

---

(*r*) John xi. 25. (*s*) vi. 35.—(*t*) i. 4. (*u*) vi. 63. (*v*) 1 John v. 12. (*w*) 2 Tim. i. 10. (*x*) Col. i. 15. Heb. i. 3. (*y*) John xiv. 9. (*z*) Heb. ii. 12. (*a*) John xvi. 26. ibid. i. 18.

executed with infinite wifdom and prudence.—*He is the fcope of the written word of* GOD.—*His character runs through the whole of revelation.*— All that we now know, or ever fhall learn of GOD, is in and by his *own Son Jefus Chrift*.—He may therefore with fuch propriety as only divine wifdom could dictate, be called the WORD, the LIVING WORD OF GOD.

WERE it of any advantage to this argument, it might be fhewn, that the *Jews* generally meant the *Meffiah*, when they wrote of the WORD or LOGOS. This is abundantly evident from their writings, tho' the paffages would be tedious to cite: And it is alfo evident, that *John* made ufe of the term WORD, from the common acceptation of it among the *Jews*, to exprefs him whom they expected as the promifed *Meffiah*. ‡ But I think a

'point

‡ The *Jews* had five different ideas of the *Logos*. (1) That it fignified GOD himfelf; hence they afcribe the words and actions of GOD to the *Memra*, or *word*. (2) It fignified fomething in, or of GOD, whereby he tranfacted his divine affairs. (3) It is taken for that *Angel* who appeared fo often, and affumed the names and titles of JEHOVAH, &c. and was worfhipped by the faints. (4) They frequently called him the *fon of God*. And (5) The *Meffiah*.—We might fairly collect all thefe ideas from the fcripture account of *Chrift*. *John* plainly calls him God. " The word was GOD." And the Apoftle as plainly calls him the *wifdom* and *power* of GOD. He is called the *Angel*, or meffenger of the covenant, by *Ifaiah* and *Malachi*: And in many places called the *Son of God* and *Meffiah*. From the whole, the *Logos* or *Word*, is the *revealer* of divine wifdom to men, the *medium* of divine manifeftations, and divine tranfactions: This he was before his appearing in flefh, and fhall continue to be till the oeconomy of GOD is finifhed.

It is remarkable in fcripture, that tho' the term *Father* often includes the divine three: And it is faid GOD is HOLY, and GOD is a SPIRIT, which are likewife inclufive terms: Yet the terms WORD and SON, never include any more than *one*, and are *peculiarly* applied to him only. This feems to point out, that the meaning of thefe names muft be fought in a certain refpect, wherein he that bears them is peculiarly diftinguifhed; and that is certainly

point of doctrine so very evident from revelation, needs no assistance from human authorities, either *Jewish* or *christian*.

tainly in his being EMMANUEL, and the offices he sustains in that character, to which, together with what he did in it, all such terms as *Word, Son, Jesus, Messiah,* &c. are properly applicable, as well as his being said to be *begotten, sent, glorified,* &c.

The names he assumed are all suited to the needs and wants of sinners, and have a relation to his character as OIKONOMOS, a steward or dispenser of grace,—OIKODOMOS, a builder of his church, the house of GOD,—or LOGOS, a revealer of the mind and will of GOD. All belonging to the oeconomy of saving sinners, setting them at liberty, and bestowing gracious gifts upon them.

SECT.

SECT. V.

HAVING shewed what the scriptures teach us concerning the oeconomical characters of *Father* and *Son*, the next inquiry should be into what we learn from them of the *Holy Ghost*. I have proved that he is GOD, from the *names*, *perfections*, and *works*, proper only to GOD, being ascribed to him: And shall now very briefly hint some things, to shew that his scripture character is *oeconomical*. As to the notion commonly received of a *natural*, *necessary*, and *eternal procession* of the *Holy Ghost*, from the *Father* and the *Son*, it is what I cannot find the least authority for in revelation.

THE only text alledged for proof of *eternal procession* is what our *Lord* says,—(b) "When the comforter is come, whom I will send unto you from the *Father*, even the *spirit* of *truth*, which *proceedeth* from the *Father*, he shall testify of me." The Spirit *proceeding from the Father* here, is manifestly spoken of his *mission*, not of his "*essence or divine personality*," as is supposed. Our LORD is there telling his disciples, how inexcusable the *Jews* were in continuing their hatred and resentment against him, after he had done so many great works before them, which were sufficient to convince them that he was sent of GOD, and the true *Messiah*, had not their inveterate prejudices so blinded them to every kind of evidence. At the same time he intimates to them, what *they* might expect from the *Jews*, for bearing testimony to the truth of his character: But for their comfort in
view

(b) John xv. 26.

view of such difficulties, he informs them, that he would " send the comforter as *another witness from the Father*, even the *Spirit of truth*, who proceeds or comes out from the *Father*, and *he should testify of him.*" The whole respects the greatness of the evidence, which he promises to add to what he had formerly given, concerning the truth of his being the *Messiah*.

It is very strange how so plain words should be *so far* mistaken, as to be applied to any other purpose: But it is still more strange to find a meaning imposed upon them, which neither they, nor any other text in revelation have the least relation to. But the text must be clouded with *mystery*, that those who deal in *mysteries* may find out the human *mystery* of *eternal procession* from it, or that doctrine would be without shadow of proof in scripture. It might be asked, how it comes to be imagined, that our Saviour, speaking of his *sending the spirit from the Father*, and the *spirit coming from the Father*, should not be understood in the same sense? The one must be oeconomical; why not the other?

The supporters of this doctrine will have the Spirit to proceed *naturally* and *eternally* from the Son, as well as from the Father, tho' there is not the least hint thereof in this text, nor any other. If they rest the *procession* from the *Father*, upon the word *proceedeth* in the text, the *procession* from the *Son* has not even this slender foundation; for the Spirit is no where said to proceed from the *Son*. A very learned divine proves the point by the following remarkable argument. " When God is said to send forth the Spirit of " his Son, it is evident that the Spirit is called the
" Spirit

" Spirit of the Son, not on the account of his
" miſſion, for that is aſcribed to the Father, but on
" ſome other account; and what can that be, but his
" proceeding from him as one in nature with him,
" and in order of nature, though not of time,
" being after the Son." This is all the evidence
he can give for the truth of an article which he
reckons neceſſary to ſalvation. But I ſuppoſe any
one of common ſenſe will ſee, that he ſays nothing
at all to prove it.

As the word *proceedeth* in the text is made
the ground of *eternal proceſſion*, I aſk why the *pro-*
ceſſion of the *Son* by *nature* and *neceſſity* from the
Father, is not made another article of religion?
For there is the ſame reaſon for the one, as for
the other, if our LORD is to be credited, who
ſaith, " I *proceeded* forth and came from GOD."
Now, this is never applied to the divine perſon of
Chriſt: No, nor (by any that I know) to what they
call his *eternal generation*: But is univerſally underſtood of his *miſſion*, and coming forth from GOD,
with commiſſion and authority as his *miniſter*:
And common ſenſe tells us, that to *come from* the
Father, and to be *ſent by him*, are terms of the
ſame import. Is it not then ſtrange! that the
proceeding and coming forth of the *Spirit* from the
Father, ſhould be ſcrewed up to an argument for his
eternal proceſſion, any more than the other. As the
proceeding and coming forth of *Chriſt*, ſignifies his
miſſion into the world: So that of the *Spirit*, muſt
refer to his *official character*, as a ſanctifier, and
comforter, which part he acts in conſummating
the great work of man's ſalvation. But it is impoſſible that one of the divine three can exiſt by
proceeding from another, conſiſtent with their *equality*
and *co-eternity*.

IT

IT is maintained, that the term *Holy Ghost* or *Spirit* is *natural*, and *peculiar* to one of the divine *three*; but such as do so, should inform us in what sense he is peculiarly *holy*, or a *Spirit*, that the other two are not. It is a pity that men should pretend to see so far beyond revelation, and yet can render no reason for what they so boldly affirm. The scriptures say that GOD is a *Spirit*, and that GOD is *holy*; which must include all that is called GOD. The name, *Holy Ghost*, can therefore be no definition of any distinguishing essential property of one in the divine plurality: And so can have no reference to the internal UNITY or DISTINCTION among the DIVINE THREE.

HOLY GHOST and *Spirit of God* are terms of the same signification in the New Testament; and are expressive of *that part he acts in the divine oeconomy revealed to us in scripture*. He is called HOLY SPIRIT, or INSPIRER, because sent by the *Father* and the *Son*, to sanctify and quicken the ▓ with a principle of *spiritual* and divine life, ▓▓ he enables to receive his testimony in the ▓▓▓. In ▓▓▓ sense, the *Father by office*, (or the part ▓▓▓stains in the great oeconomy) sends him as a *witness* and *comforter*.—In this sense, the *Son by office*, requests the *Father* to send him.—And in this sense, the *Holy Spirit by office, proceeds* or *comes from* the *Father*. The whole of this will appear manifest to the impartial reader, from a succinct view of the APPELLATIONS, MISSION, and WORKS attributed to the SPIRIT in scripture.

HE is called *Holy Spirit*, not to express the *manner* of his divine relation to the *Father* and *Son*, or his existence in *Deity*, as is commonly asserted; this we have no authority for in scripture:
But

But rather becaufe he is infallibly *holy in himfelf*, and has infpired *holy men* to write the word of GOD, full of *holy* and *fpiritual truth*, by which he works *holy* and *fpiritual principles, qualities,* and *affections* in his people, enabling them to perform the *holy* and *fpiritual exercifes,* or duties required therein.

―――― *The Spirit of God.*—Becaufe he is *fent* by *God* to carry on the fpiritual operations, which are neceffary for completing the great oeconomy pur-- pofed by him.—And the *Spirit of Chrift*, becaufe fent by him to execute the application of the *fpiritual work* of man's redemption.――――*The Spirit of truth.*—He is the author of all *fpiritual truth*, and the infallible teacher of it to others.―――― *Spirit of adoption.*—He brings finners into the *family of God,*—conforms them to the *image* of their *fpiritual Father,*—and witneffeth the truth of their *fpiritual adoption* to them.――――*Free Spirit.*—Sovereign and *free* in all his operations,—delivers his people from all *fpiritual bondage,*—gives them freedom in *fpiritual* exercifes, and accefs to their heavenly Father.――――*The Spirit of wifdom and revelation.* Infinite in wifdom himfelf, he beftows on his people eminent degrees of *wifdom* and underftanding in *fpiritual* things by means of *revelation,* which he is the author of.――――*Spirit of life in Jefus Chrift.*—His people dead in trefpaffes and fin, he quickens, gives them *fpiritual life* in union to *Chrift* the living head,—maintains, reftores, increafes, and at laft perfects their *fpiritual life* in glory with him.

HE is alfo called the Spirit of *Judgment,—Faith, —Love,—Holinefs,—a found mind,—of fupplication,— grace* and *glory.* All which appellations evidently refpect the oeconomy of redemption: So that we

D d   may

may conclude, that *these*, with all the other names the *Holy Ghost* gets in scripture are oeconomical. In the same sense are other words to be taken, which are predicated of the *Spirit* : Such as his being *sent, given, poured out, coming upon men*, or *falling upon them*. But as these fall under the next head, I only mention them here.

The scripture account of the Mission of the *Holy Ghost* will further prove his character to be oeconomical.—But it should be observed, that this *sending*, or what is commonly called the *Mission* of the *Holy Ghost*, does not include the many great works ascribed to the Spirit in the Old Testament, nor what is said of him with respect to the conception and life of *Jesus Christ*. Tho' these were great works, what is properly called the *Mission* or *sending* of the *Spirit* must be posterior to all these, for *Christ* always speaks of it as a *future* event, which should take place after his ascension.

Nor does the *Mission* of the Spirit imply that he is not God, as the enemies to his *Deity* would infer from it; for say they, " As he is sent by God, he is inferior to God, and consequently cannot be God in a proper sense." This argument would conclude equally against the *Deity* of the *Son* and *Holy Ghost* : And like most of the arguments from that quarter, is built upon a mistake concerning the oeconomical character of the *Son* and *Holy Ghost*. But I have made it evident from scripture, that *Jesus Christ* and the *Holy Ghost* are God, so that nothing can be inferred from his being *sent* to prove that the Spirit is not God. Besides, the argument is not universally true even among men, since by consent and agreement among equals, one may be delegated to a certain work for others,

who,

who, yet, are not superior by nature. Whatever may be in this, it is certainly unfair to argue against plain scripture evidence in favour of the Deity of either the *Son* or *Spirit*, because they are sent in that character to fulfil their part in the oeconomy of man's salvation, in which particular respect, it might be safely granted they are inferior, without infringing their right to the honour and glory of *Deity*.

MOREOVER, as the Spirit is GOD, his being *sent* cannot imply a *local mutation*, or change of place. This would make him a circumscribed being, and consequently not GOD : Nor can it imply the idea of *constraint* or necessary *servitude*, as the case is betwixt a master and servant. The Spirit is *free* in all his operations, and cannot be compelled. Neither does the sending of the Spirit infer his want of abilities with respect to the work, either in contriving, choosing the means, or accomplishing it, which is often the case with one who is employed to execute the designs of another. What *Christ* says of the Spirit makes nothing against this : " He shall not speak of himself, but whatsoever he shall hear, that shall he speak." From which some would infer, that he cannot speak the truth without being first taught it. Whereas the Apostle tells us, that " the Spirit searcheth all things, yea, the deep things of GOD." When it is said, " he shall not speak of *himself*," the meaning is, he shall not *forge* what he shall say,— or say any thing *contrary* to what *Christ* had spoken. That this is the idea conveyed in the words, might be proved from a critical consideration of the original : But we have a plainer proof for the unlearned reader at hand, for *John* says, " The anointing teacheth you all things, and is TRUTH, and is no LIE."

THO

THO' the Spirit had inspired the Prophets, witnessed to *Christ* at his baptism, and tho' *Christ* "breathed on his disciples, and said, Receive ye the *Holy Ghost*," yet none of these is meant by the *sending* or *mission* of the *Spirit*. "The *Holy Ghost* was not yet given, because *Christ* was not yet glorified." He was not given in that *visible, abundant, convincing,* and *glorious manner,* as after the ascension of *Christ*. Every previous sending, gift, or work of the Spirit, is as it were lost in scripture account, when compared with that at *Pentecost*; which was as *Peter* interprets it, the fulfilling of *Joel*'s prophecy, delivered in such amazing language.—(a) "And it shall come to pass afterwards, that I will pour out my Spirit upon all flesh, and your sons and your daughters shall prophesy, your old men shall dream dreams, your young men shall see visions: And also upon the servants, and upon the hand-maids in those days, will I pour out my Spirit: And I will shew wonders in the heavens, and in the earth, blood and fire, and pillars of smoke. The sun shall be turned into darkness, and the moon into blood, before that great and terrible day of the Lord, &c." It was *Christ*'s baptising his disciples with the *Holy Ghost*, and with fire,—a divine evidence to the truth of his character, and his being enthroned at GOD's right hand, and also of the Spirit's entrance, (so to speak) upon the actual ministration and management of all things necessary to the kingdom of our *Lord Jesus Christ*. For these and other weighty reasons, it is called *the* sending, *the* giving, or *the* coming of the *Holy Ghost*, by way of eminence. Tho' this pouring out of the Spirit, was more striking and visible in the effects at *Pentecost*, and in the Apostolic times than afterwards, yet, it extends to all the

churches

(a) Joel 2, 28.—31.

churches of *Chriſt* in all ages; for he was promiſed to abide for ever. He accompanies the word, and makes it effectual for the great ends for which it is ſent. The Spirit ſeparated from the word, renders it ineffectual to thoſe who uſe it.

We need not ſtay to prove the neceſſity of ſending the Spirit, ſince our LORD tells the diſciples, "It is *expedient* for you that I go away; for if I go not away, the comforter will not come; but if I depart, I will ſend him unto you." Notwithſtanding all the pains he had been at to teach the diſciples the nature of his kingdom, and what they had to do and ſuffer for him, yet they remained ſo remarkably ignorant of theſe things, through the reigning *Jewiſh* prejudices in favour of a temporal grandeur, which they expected by the *Meſſiah*, that when he was about to leave them, they ſaid, "LORD, wilt thou at this time reſtore the kingdom to *Iſrael*." But by the effuſion of the *Spirit*, their prejudices were removed;—they then underſtood what *Chriſt* had taught them,—and were prepared for the great work and ſufferings allotted them.

They were extremely fond of the *bodily preſence* of *Chriſt*, but as they were to be diſperſed abroad in the world, he could not be bodily preſent with each of them: But the Spirit was ſent to be with them at all times, and in all places. His preſence inſpired them with gifts ſuitable for them as witneſſes, to carry their teſtimony to the uttermoſt parts of the earth, enlightening their minds, and confirming them in the divine truth they taught,— endowing them with ſuch fortitude as they feared no kind of ſuffering;—they trampled upon torments,

ments, and the threats of kings and rulers of this world,—preached the gospel in the face of death, and were regardless of what men or Devils could do to them. Now, all that grace, and all the extraordinary gifts which the Spirit was sent to pour out upon the Apostles, and other instruments employed in propagating the gospel, taken together, make only one great link of the divine chain,—a part of the oeconomy of man's salvation, wherein the lustre of the love and grace of GOD appears to men : Which leads me next to observe,

THAT the *mission* of the Spirit is a blessing of the covenant of promise, and comes from *Christ*, as the head of the *church*, consequently it must belong to the oeconomy of redemption. As it is the *promise* of the *Father* to *Christ*, he claims the *power* to bestow it; accordingly he tells his disciples, that they should be witnesses of his death and resurrection, and in his name they should preach repentance and remission of sins unto all nations; and for their encouragement, he adds, (*b*) " Behold, *I send* upon you the *promise* of the Father : Tarry ye at *Jerusalem*, until ye be endowed with power from on high."

As all the promises are in *Christ*, yea, and in him, Amen; so must this great promise of sending the Spirit. Hence says the Apostle, " because ye are sons, GOD has sent forth the *Spirit of his Son* into your hearts.—According to his mercy he saved us by the washing of regeneration, and renewing of the *Holy Ghost, which he shed on us abundantly through Jesus Christ our Saviour*." Believers are " built an habitation of GOD through the Spirit.—And being
fitly

(*b*) Luke xxiv. 49.

fitly joined and compacted together, they grow up unto him in all things, who is their *head*, even *Chrift*." The promife of GOD is, " that he will put his Spirit within them." This *Chrift* accomplifhed when he afcended as head of the church, in fending the Spirit to apply the great bleffings he had promifed and purchafed. The order of this oeconomy is pointed out by the Apoftle.——(c) " Elect according to the fore-knowledge of GOD the FATHER, through the fanctification of the SPIRIT, and fprinkling of the blood of JESUS."

As I formerly hinted, the benefits of this *miffion* of the Spirit extend to the church in all ages. *Chrift* promifed that he fhould abide for ever, and it continues a diftinguifhing character of the world from the children of *Chrift*,—(d) " If any man has not the *Spirit of Chrift*, he is none of his." Thus the *miffion*, or *fending* of the *Holy Ghoft*, proves his character as fuch to be oeconomical.

BUT to make this ftill more evident, we fhall take a very fhort view of the works afcribed to the Spirit. It was proved above, that creation work is attributed to the SPIRIT JEHOVAH, and it muft neceffarily follow, that providence is another work in which he is intimately concerned. For it cannot be fuppofed, that any other carries on the fucceffion of individuals,—orders the various parts,—reftores their harmony and beauty,—and directs to the end they were defigned for, but him who at firft created them. Hence, fays the *Pfalmift*, " Thou fendeft forth thy *Spirit*, and they are *created*; thou reneweft the face of the earth."

THE

(c) 1 Pet. i. 2. (d) Rom. viii. 9.

THE conducting *Israel* in the wilderness, is a work attributed to the Spirit.—" The Spirit of the LORD (the SPIRIT JEHOVAH) caused him to rest: So didst thou lead thy people." He qualified the rulers to manage the affairs of that great assembly,—gave wisdom to those who did the work of the tabernacle, according to the pattern shewed on the mount,—and also those employed in making materials for the temple. In short, he conducted the Prophets, Judges, and Kings, under the whole *Jewish Theocracy*.

HE inspired the writers of the Old Testament. *David* says, " The SPIRIT JEHOVAH *spake by me.*" And *Peter* tells us, " That holy men of GOD spake as they were *moved by the Holy Ghost.*" The writings of the New Testament, were indited by the same unerring guide. " All scripture is given by inspiration of GOD,—able to make the man of GOD perfect,—wise to salvation,—and thoroughly furnished to every good work." Upon this foundation the church of *Christ* is built in all ages: And notwithstanding that fallible men were made use of in writing the scriptures, they were so conducted by the divine wisdom of the *Spirit*, as to be free of error or mistake, in what was intended for the sacred canon of revelation, which is the sure word of prophecy. " The things which we speak, says the Apostle, we speak in the words of the *Holy Ghost*."

ANOTHER work of the Spirit is, the giving to those whom he sent on extraordinary occasions the power of working miracles, as a testimony of their being sent of GOD. None can work miracles but by the power of the *Spirit*, therefore the Apostle puts miracles among the gifts of the *Holy Ghost*:

yea,

yea, with refpect to his human nature, *Chrift* fpeaks of himfelf as the *inftrument* of the *Holy Ghoft*, "I, fays he, caft out Devils by the *Spirit* of GOD." All the *figns*, *wonders*, and miracles done by *Stephen*, *Philip*, and the Apoftles are attributed to the Spirit. *Paul*, when telling the *Romans* what he had done, fays, all was wrought by the Spirit of GOD. GOD only, who governs the world, can turn the works of nature into an extraordinary channel,— do things above or contrary to the common courfe of nature.

A GREAT part of the Spirit's work mentioned in fcripture, has a particular relation to *Chrift* himfelf. Before his coming in flefh, the Spirit had given moft clear and glorious defcriptions of him. "To him gave all the Prophets witnefs." He tells his difciples, that the "things which were written in *Mofes*, the *Prophets*, and the *Pfalms* concerning him, muft be fulfilled.—And he expounded to them, in *all the fcriptures*, the things concerning himfelf. Search the fcriptures, faith he, for they are they which teftify of me." It would make a volume itfelf only to mention the defcriptions of *Chrift* in the Old Teftament: But I cannot help taking notice of one thing, which is too much over-looked, that the book of *Pfalms* is in general a defcription of *Chrift*; and if it were read in this point of light, it would be much more profitable than to apply the fubftance of it to *David*, *Solomon*, or *others*. See page 91.

As *Chrift fent* the Spirit when he afcended, it would feem that the Spirit *fent* him at his appearing in flefh; for when fpeaking of that time by *Ifaiah*, he fays, "The LORD GOD and his *Spirit* hath *fent* me." The HOLY GHOST framed the body of CHRIST, in the womb of the *virgin*. Hence fhe is said to be " with child of the HOLY GHOST. The HOLY GHOST shall come upon thee, and the power of the highest shall overshadow thee." When he was to enter upon his public ministry, the Spirit led him forth to begin the combat with the *Devil* in the wilderness.

IN the power of the Spirit, he returned from his victory over the *Devil*, and begun his ministry,—opening his commission with a solemn declaration, that the Spirit had *qualified* and *sent* him to the work.—(e) " The Spirit of the LORD is upon me, because he hath *anointed me* to preach the gospel to the poor; *he hath sent me* to heal the broken hearted, to preach deliverance to the captives, and recovering of sight to the blind, to set at liberty them that are bruised, to preach the acceptable year of the LORD." In all his ministrations on earth, he was assisted by the *Spirit*, from whom " he had an unction above all his fellows,—the Spirit above measure poured out upon him." The Apostle says, " GOD *anointed Jesus of Nazareth* with the HOLY GHOST, and with power; who went about doing good, and healing all that were oppressed with the *Devil*: For GOD was with him. He was declared to be the SON of GOD, by the *Spirit* of holiness." The Spirit raised the body of CHRIST from the dead.—" He was put to death in the flesh, but quickened (restored to life) by the Spirit." And the same Spirit that raised *Jesus* from the dead, the Apostle assures us, shall also quicken the mortal bodies of his members.

ANOTHER general part of the *Spirit's work* with reference to *Christ* is, his *bearing witness* or *testifying of him*. " When the comforter is come, (saith our

(e) Luke iv. 18, 19.

our LORD) the *Spirit of truth*, he shall *testify of me.*" The great contest betwixt the *Jews* and *christians* was, whether *Jesus* was the true *Messiah*, the SON *of* GOD. To this truth, *John* says, the *Spirit* was a witness.—" It is the *Spirit* that *beareth witness*, because the Spirit is truth." Our Saviour distinguisheth betwixt the *Spirit*'s *testimony* and the *Apostles*', " The Spirit of truth, *he* shall *witness* of me : And *ye also* shall bear *witness.*"

THE *matter* or substance of the Spirit's testimony, is all the truths concerning CHRIST. So says he to the Apostles, " He (the Spirit) shall guide you into *all truth."* A compendious abridgment of which we have in the Apostle's answer to the *Jewish* Sanhedrim, who reprimanded them for preaching in the name of *Jesus.* " Then *Peter* and the other Apostles answered and said, we ought to obey GOD rather than men. The GOD of our fathers raised up *Jesus*, whom ye slew and hanged on a tree : Him hath GOD exalted with his right-hand a prince and Saviour ; for to give repentance to *Israel*, and forgiveness of sin : And we are his *witnesses* of these things, and *so also is the Holy Ghost*, whom GOD hath given to them that obey him." After a similar account of the *mission, death, resurrection,* and *exaltation* of *Christ, Paul* tells the *Hebrews,* " whereof the *Holy Ghost also is a witness to us."*

THE *manner* and *time* of the Spirit's bearing witness to CHRIST, was either before his incarnation,—while he stayed on earth,—or after his ascension : Before he appeared in flesh, in all the prophesies, promises, and declarations concerning him in the Old Testament. So *Peter* tells us, " Of this
salvation

salvation the Prophets inquired; and searched diligently, who prophesied of the grace that should come,—searching what, or what manner of time the *Spirit of Christ*, which was in them did signify, when *it testified before-hand* the sufferings of *Christ*, and the glory that should follow."

BY the same *Spirit* that *John the Baptist* proclaimed his advent, and pointed him out as the Lamb of GOD,—*Zacharias, Simon, Elizabeth*, and *Mary* spake of him. But when CHRIST was to appear publickly, he was declared at his baptism by the Father to be his beloved Son, to which was added, the witness of the Spirit; for it was told *John the Baptist*, that on whom he saw the Spirit descending and remaining, the same should baptize with the HOLY GHOST. Now, *John* says, " I *saw* and bare record, that this is the SON *of* GOD." This descent of the *Spirit* in such a manner, was an extraordinary testimony to CHRIST, an honour never conferred upon any before, and shewed him to be the *holy one of* GOD, the *anointed* from above, the *king* of GOD's people, and the *heir of all things*.

BUT the special time of the Spirit's testifying of CHRIST, was after his ascension, when at *Pentecost* he appeared as cloven tongues of fire upon the Apostles, and caused them to bear witness for CHRIST in so extraordinary a manner, as to amaze all the spectators. No talents are competent to describe the wonderful effects of the effusion of the *Spirit*, in a more striking manner, than he hath done himself, by *Luke* and the Apostles in the New Testament; the whole of which, after the four gospels, is only an account of what he enabled them to teach, write, and suffer, as witnesses for CHRIST.

THIS

This pouring out of the Spirit, was a plain demonstration of the omniscience and divine veracity of CHRIST, in accomplishing his promise so punctually, and in a manner far beyond their expectations. It was likewise an ample fulfilling the Father's promise to send the HOLY GHOST. Both these are included in *Peter's* account of that solemn event to the wondering multitude, and must be a most glorious testimony given by the *Spirit*, to the truth of the *Messiah's* character.—*(f)* " This *Jesus* hath GOD raised up, whereof we are all witnesses. Wherefore being by the right-hand of GOD exalted, and having received of the Father the promise of the HOLY GHOST, he hath shed forth this, which ye now see and hear."

THE Spirit was further a witness to CHRIST, in bestowing extraordinary gifts upon the Apostles and others, whereby they were qualified to be peculiar witnesses for CHRIST. Now, they could speak the languages of the different nations intelligibly without learning them,—teach the truths concerning CHRIST with such power and energy, as *Peter* by a single discourse converted three thousand. This is one remarkable instance of the accomplishment of what CHRIST had told them, " That they should do greater works than they had seen him do." The converts to christianity were but few while he was among them, but now converts are made by thousands. The Spirit inspired them with such sound doctrine, as it should be worthy to complete the canon of revelation, and be called the *word of God*, which will in all ages be a glorious testimony to CHRIST, in converting and comforting his children, and confounding

(f) Acts ii. 32, 33.

founding all his and their enemies: And so absolutely sure, that if an *Angel from heaven* teach any other doctrine, the Apostle says, let him be accursed.

The effusion of the Spirit, at and after *Pentecost*,—the doctrines he taught,—the miracles he wrought,—the predictions he gave forth by the Apostles,—the gifts he bestowed,—and the infinite power he exerted in bringing thousands to the kingdom of CHRIST, make up such a testimony to the truth of our Saviour's character, as his combined enemies, the *Devil*, the *World*, and the *flesh*, can never prevail against. With respect to the extraordinary gifts which seemed necessary to the Spirit to bestow at that time, the Apostle gives a comprehensive view of them,—(g) " Now there are diversities of gifts, but the same Spirit,—to one is given by the same Spirit, the word of wisdom,—to another the word of knowledge by the same Spirit; to another faith; to another the gifts of healing; to another the working of miracles; to another prophecy; to another the discerning of spirits; to another divers kinds of tongues; to another the interpretation of tongues: But all these worketh that *one* and the *self-same Spirit*, dividing to every man severally *as he will*, &c."

I shall only add one particular testimony more which the Spirit gives to CHRIST, that is, his revealing CHRIST in the souls of his children. He takes the things of CHRIST and shews to the mind,—removes the habits of antipathy,—presents him in all his beauty, and allures the heart to love, honour,

(g) 1 Cor. xii. 4, 8,—11.

honour, and obey him: Hence, the Apoſtle tells us, that " no man can call JESUS, LORD, but by the HOLY GHOST."

ANOTHER great part of the *Spirit's work* with reference to CHRIST, is included in his *glorifying him*. When CHRIST was promiſing to ſend the Spirit, he ſays, " He ſhall *glorify me:* For he ſhall receive of mine, and ſhall ſhew it unto you."

THE coming of the Spirit as the *gift* of CHRIST, and by his *appointment*, glorified him. The greatneſs of the gift, ſhewed the height of glory and honour he was exalted to. It ſhews what divine power,—what unſpeakable favour he had in heaven, when he could ſend ſuch a meſſenger as the divine Spirit. It was the cleareſt demonſtration of his being the true *Meſſiah*, and the truth of what he had ſo often ſaid concerning the glory he was to be exalted to.

BUT further, the HOLY GHOST glorified CHRIST, by confirming the truth of his reſurrection from the dead. The Apoſtle makes the whole of the chriſtian religion turn upon the truth of CHRIST's reſurrection. It was the great conteſt betwixt the Apoſtles and the *Jews*, who held CHRIST to be an impoſtor, and his reſurrection fabulous: And it muſt be allowed, that if this truth is taken away, it is impoſſible to prove him the *Meſſiah*, or that the New Teſtament is any more than a deviſed fable: But the ſending of the HOLY GHOST put that matter beyond doubt. This was the uſe the Apoſtles made of it to the admiring multitude; the evidence of which was ſo powerful, as to convert ſome thouſands of them to the belief of it: And we find the Spirit directed ed the writers of the books contained in the New Teſtament, to be ſo careful on this point, that there is not one of them in which this truth is not aſſerted, or proved at large from inconteſtable evidence, as being the leading argument to prove that *Jeſus* of *Nazareth* was the SON *of* GOD, and the *Saviour of the world*, who was dead, and is alive, and lives for evermore. To doubt here, is to call the whole of the chriſtian religion in queſtion.

THE HOLY GHOST glorified CHRIST, by taking ſuch an effectual method to wipe off the ignominy and reproach he was ſubject to in his life, and at his death. This was done with ſuch divine wiſdom and power, that even many of the *Prieſts*, his inveterate enemies, were convicted,—ſuch as reſiſted the truth were amazed and confounded;—Satan fell as lightening from heaven,—his kingdom ſhook to the center, and his captives were led captive by the power of the truth.—" So mightily grew the word of the LORD and prevailed!" The HOLY GHOST, as an advocate for the glory of CHRIST, proved all the accuſations and reproaches of his enemies to be impotent malice; and vindicated the innocence, righteouſneſs, and honour of the divine Redeemer againſt all accuſers; making his friends to triumph, and praiſe the " Lamb who had been ſlain, as worthy of all power, and riches, and wiſdom, and ſtrength, and honour, and glory, and bleſſing."

THE Spirit glorifies CHRIST, in erecting a kingdom for him, and bringing ſubjects under his rule and government. This he does in oppoſition to all the power, malice, and craft of hell and earth,—in oppoſition to all the diſgrace he was under, and the popular prejudices which were ſo ſtrong againſt him—

him,—the natural or acquired enmity of the mind, and the disconformity of the powers, policy, laws, honours, customs, profits, and pleasures of this world, to the kingdom of CHRIST. Notwithstanding these, and other insuperable difficulties to all created power, the HOLY GHOST erects a kingdom for CHRIST, enthrones him in the hearts of men, whom he makes willing, loving, and obedient subjects, "built together a habitation for him through the *Spirit*, who inspires them with courage and honesty to propagate the glory of his kingdom, praise him as king of saints, and with holy submission say, "The LORD is our judge, the LORD is our lawgiver, the LORD is our *king*, and he will save us." To this we may add,

THAT the HOLY GHOST glorifies CHRIST, by conforming all his subjects to his image. He presents the glory and excellence of CHRIST in such a point of view, as the enmity of their hearts is melted down, and they allured through the preciousness of his character revealed in the gospel, where the knowledge of CHRIST is made manifest, which in them who are ready to perish, is the favour of life unto life; and to them who are saved from the reigning power of sin, is the favour of death unto death, or the mortification of remaining prejudices, evil affections, or corrupt passions in them. †

---

† Tho' the sense in which I take this expression of the Apostle, is directly contrary to the common interpretation of it, yet I humbly think it is the proper meaning thereof. He says, 2 Cor. ii. 14, 15, 16. "Now thanks be unto *God*, who always causeth us to triumph in *Christ*, and maketh manifest the favour of his knowledge by us in every place: For we are unto *God* a sweet favour of *Christ*, in them that are *saved*, and in them that perish (are *perishing* as it should be rendered) To the one, we are the favour of *death unto death*; and to the other, the favour of *life unto life*." According to the plain connexion of the passage, the manifestation

They " behold as in a glafs the glory of the LORD, are changed into the *same image*, from glory to glory, by the LORD the Spirit." As *Solomon* fays, " they are more excellent than their neighbours,"—all glorious within,—filled with his grace; they fulfil the good-pleafure of his will, and the name of the *Lord Jesus* is glorified by them. The former haughtinefs of their minds is brought low, and *Chrift* their LORD is alone exalted. Created for his praife, they increafe in holinefs, love, and good

manifeftation of the knowledge of *Chrift* was in the *saved*, the favour of *death unto death*, (not *death in the worft fenfe*, as the common opinion is, but) a *death unto fin of all kinds*, which the faved in *Chrift* die daily unto, and which the knowledge of *Chrift* in the gofpel is the powerful caufe of, agreeable to many fimilar expreffions of the Apoftles Rom. vi. 1, 2, 7, 8, 11. " Shall we (believers in *Chrift*) continue in fin, that grace may abound? God forbid; how fhall we that are *dead to fin*, live any longer therein? For he that is *dead*, is freed from fin. Now if we be *dead* with *Chrift*, we believe that we fhall alfo live with him: Likewife reckon ye alfo yourfelves to be *dead indeed unto fin*; but alive unto *God*, through *Jefus Chrift* our Lord. Chap. vii. 9. For I was alive without the law once; but when the commandment came, fin revived, and I *died*, Col. ii. 3. For ye are *dead*, and your life is hid with *Chrift* in God. 1 Pet. ii. 24.—Who his own felf bare our fins in his own body on the tree, that we being *dead to fin*, fhould live unto righteoufnefs." So that the *death* in the text, is the progreffive work of mortification of fin, which is the fpecial privilege of all who have the true knowledge of *Chrift*, and which is a *fweet favour to God through him*.

But this knowledge of *Chrift* in the gofpel, is alfo the favour of *life unto life* in them that are *perifhing*. The poor, deftitute, perifhing finner, ftung with guilt, purfued with the curfe, and void of all hopes of falvation from every other propofed remedy, has the knowledge of the all-fufficient Saviour in all his fulnefs prefented to him in the gofpel, which, by the power of the Spirit, is made a principle of new life in him,—deftroys all thofe vain hopes which wrought death in his foul, and makes him live a life of faith on the Son of God. This is the *death* and the *life* which are native fruits of the power of divine truth, manifefted in the gofpel of *Chrift*, and a particular part of the Spirit's work in the divine oeconomy, for which, the Apoftle *gives thanks unto God*, and which is a *fweat favour unto God of Chrift*. But how fhocking are the inferences which have been drawn from this paffage! As if the knowledge of *Chrift* in the gofpel, was the means

of

good works. The chief end of their actions is his glory; and their highest desire whether in life or in death, is, that *Christ* may be glorified in them. They have all the same sentiments concerning *Christ* and his kingdom: This is a work by which *Christ* is glorified, which neither the power nor policy of this world could ever bring about, by all the schemes established churches have been founded on. It could never be said of any of them, that all the members "were of one heart and mind,—that they with one mind, and one mouth glorified God."

This

of impenitency and unbelief, and consequently of death and damnation to them that perish. A thought every way unworthy of the goodness, mercy, and grace of God, manifested in the good tidings of salvation by *Christ Jesus*.

There is another text, which for want of due attention, has been misrepresented in the same manner, 2 Cor. iv. 3. "If our gospel be hid, it is hid to them that are lost. In whom the *god* of this world hath blinded the minds of them which believe not, &c." Not to speak of the abuse this passage hath met with from the corrupt use which has been made of it, the way it is rendered, is neither agreeable to the Apostle's scope, nor is it good sense: Whereas there is no passage of scripture plainer, if the scope is attended to. In the former chapter, the Apostle shews the excellency of the *gospel* dispensation above the *Mosaic*, and begins this with a declaration of the honesty, zeal, and freedom of the Apostles, in preaching the truths of the gospel. "But (says he) if our gospel be hid, it is hid *among the things that are abolished; by which,* (things) the God of this world hath blinded the minds of them who believe not, left the light of the glorious gospel of *Christ*,—should shine unto them." By the things which are abolished, it is plain, he means the *Jewish* ceremonies,—carnal commandments, the shadows and figures, together with the Levitical priesthood and laws concerning it, that were abolished and done away in *Christ*, which things being mixed with the truths of his gospel, made it dark, obscure, and of no effect, to such as had this veil remaining upon their hearts, as the Apostle tells us immediately before. In this light, the passage is clear, and free of these gross imputations upon the gospel of *Christ*, which have been founded upon this, and some other texts. Tho' the brevity of a note will not suffer me to set this matter in so full a view, as to convince such as are strongly prejudiced in favour of the common interpretation of such texts; yet, by this short hint, the candid inquiring reader, will at least, see the necessity of searching the scripture for himself, and the danger of taking religion upon trust without examination, which too many are disposed to do.

This unity is the peculiar privilege of the churches of *Chrift*, framed by the *Spirit*, upon the principles of truth in the word.

THE Spirit glorifies *Chrift*, by making known to his people the exceeding greatnefs of his merit, righteoufnefs, mercy, love, grace, and condefcenfion; through a fenfe of which, they magnify him who hath brought in an everlafting *righteoufnefs*, by which they are juftified and do glory. They fay with *Paul*, " I was a blafphemer, perfecutor, injurious; but I obtained *mercy*, and the *grace* of our LORD JESUS CHRIST was exceeding abundant towards me." They receive a fulnefs of grace that reigns through righteoufnefs to eternal life by JESUS CHRIST: And knowing all to be fovereign and free, it fweetens their eternal praife to him who *loved* them, and redeemed them unto GOD by his blood.

CHRIST is glorified by the Spirit, enabling his fervants to fuffer for his name. 'Tis the ftrongeft mark of loyalty in a fubject to give his life and all he has for his prince. By this method, through the Spirit's aid, the fubjects of *Chrift* have carried his praife to the ends of the earth. But to conclude this,

THE HOLY GHOST glorifies CHRIST, in perfecting all the members of his body, making them meet to be partakers with the faints in light,—all ready to attend their LORD at his coming, when he fhall be *glorified* in all his faints, whom the *Spirit* had taken from the depths of moral corruption and alienation from GOD,—deftroyed the Devil's image in them,—conformed them to the image of the
SON

Son of God,—washed them in his blood, and now they are before the throne without spot, praising him, world without end.

WERE it not that I will be thought too prolix on this subject already, many other things might be observed concerning the *work of the Spirit*; for the scriptures afford evidence sufficient to extend an account of this kind to many more particulars than are yet mentioned; particularly that great end of his *mission*, which our LORD mentions, " To reprove the world of sin, righteousness, and judgment," which, with the short comment he gives of these three parts of the Spirit's work, afford undeniable evidence to the oeconomical character of the *Holy Ghost*.

WE might also have noticed the convincing work of the Spirit upon the redeemed,—his uniting them to *Christ*,—his work in their justification, adoption, regeneration, and progressive sanctification,——in their consolation, perseverance, and growth in grace :—In his witnessing the truth of their adoption, sealing, leading, and guiding them, —in his giving them power to mortify evil habits, lusts, and passions,—resist the *Devil*, the world, and the flesh, and overcome temptations of every kind,—his strengthening their moral powers to understand and mind the truth, from which as a living principle, they bring forth the peaceable fruits of righteousness,—his assisting them in prayer, and other spiritual exercises of religion. These, together with what the Apostle mentions as fruits of the Spirit, " The fruits of the Spirit is love, joy, peace, long-suffering, gentleness, goodness, faith, meekness, temperance :" But to treat of all these particularly,

particularly, would be more like writing a treatife on the *works of the Spirit*, than defending a particular argument. I fhall therefore conclude this account by obferving,

From what has been briefly hinted concerning the *Appellations*, *Miſſion*, and *Works* of the *Spirit*, it is abundantly plain, that the character of the *Holy Ghoſt*, which we have in revelation, is wholly oeconomical: And that he is called *Holy Spirit*, and *Spirit of God*, from the nature of his work, which is all the internal and fpiritual part of the great oeconomy, which God hath purpofed to carry on in all ages, till the whole is confummated in the complete felicity of the chofen objects of his love, in the full enjoyment of himfelf. And I think it will be impoffible for the friends of a *natural*, *neceſſary*, and *eternal proceſſion* of the *Holy Ghoſt*, to find any thing faid of him in the Bible, that in the leaft favour *their* notion; or that is not applicable to the fcripture account of the oeconomy of God."

It may be further obferved, that the *Spirit* is the fovereign *agent*, Lord, and *adminiſtrator* of the whole gofpel oeconomy. The doctrines of the gofpel were immediately revealed by him,—preached by the gifts he beftowed, and accompanied in many by external miraculous works done by his power, and made effectual as a renewing, active principle by his divine energy. The Apoftle when comparing the gofpel difpenfation with the law, calls the whole of it the miniftration of the Spirit.—(*h*) " How fhall not the *miniſtration of the Spirit*, (compared

---

(*h*) 2 Cor. iii. 8.

pared with the *letter* under the ceremonial difpenfation) be rather glorious?" Which includes the whole of that fpiritual work the *Holy Ghoft* came to accomplifh in the oeconomy of man's falvation. The *Holy Ghoft* fpeaks of himfelf in the character of governor in the church, when he faid, (*i*) " Separate *me, Barnabas* and *Saul,* for the work whereunto I have called them." He carried on the work of *Chrift,* and perfects that falvation which he was promifed to be to the ends of the earth.—(*k*) " The comforter, the *Holy Ghoft,* whom the Father will fend in *my name,* he fhall teach you all things, and bring all things to your remembrance, whatfoever I have faid unto you." He had promifed to be with his people to the end of the world, but foon after left them; yet *Chrift's* promife is fully accomplifhed by the *Spirit,* who comes *in his name,* and " takes of the things of *Chrift,* and fhews them unto them."

(*i*) Acts xiii. 2. (*k*) John xiv. 26.

PART.

PART III.

HAVING in the two former parts given an account what the scriptures say concerning the Trinity; I shall in this part, as was promised, shew how little regard is due from christians, to the subtle distinctions invented among men concerning that subject; and the difficulties that have occurred to me, in the consideration of a pretended explication of that doctrine, which has been held pretty orthodox for many years past, and generally imposed as an article of faith.

It is manifest how copious and conclusive the scriptures are on this point, and sufficiently explain themselves by comparing one text with another, as far as is necessary for us mortals to know, without the least necessity for the stretches of human wit, to devise dark and perplexed explications of this doctrine; which human inventions, are so far from being clearly taught in scripture, that many of them are directly contrary thereto.

OF all the doctrines in revelation, there is the least room here for man's invention: For the most elevated strains of genius are utterly lost in profound darkness in attempting to wade beyond the line of revelation, there being nothing we can know of GOD, but what he is pleased to reveal of himself; which every christian should humbly, diligently, and devoutly learn from his own sacred word. While the strains of philosophical criticism are busied in defining a Deity, the mere product of proud imagination; which soaring spirit in some men, that will be wise above what is written, will not allow them to submit to the plain intelligible account GOD hath given of himself: And what notable discoveries do they make, who thus dive into the secrets of the most high? Why, they *change the glory of the incorruptable* GOD *into an image* of their own fancy, and the *truth of* GOD *into a lie, worshipping this creature of their own brain, instead of the creator, who is* GOD *over all, blessed for ever.*

MOST part of men have their minds fixed in certain notions, which in the early periods of their life they were taught by their tutors, or have received through the influence of a party, or out of respect to church authority, without examination; these they believe as undoubted truths; what is not agreeable thereto, they readily conclude to be false: And in every recourse to the divine word, these notions are the rules by which they explain it. Hence it is, that all parties appeal to scripture, and pretend to find their own notions there, by forcing it to speak agreeable to the opinions they hold. Thus, received opinions are the standard of the sense of scripture, which is divested of the honour of being the rule of faith. But as this is visibly

bly owing to prejudice, in favour of things received from men, which are believed to be unqueſtionably orthodox: If we would be right inquirers after truth, we ſhould come to revelation free and diſengaged,—read and meditate, as under the conduct of an unerring guide, the divine Spirit, without bias and partiality, without regard to human authority, parties, intereſt, or education, waiting upon the LORD for divine aid, who only can open our underſtandings to know the truth revealed in the ſcripture.

WITH reſpect to religion, I chuſe to reſt my faith upon the *divine teſtimony only*, which I am certain will never deceive: But dare not follow *human explications* through the maze of dark, ſubtle, and perplexing diſtinctions, in which ſo many of the contrivers of religious ſyſtems have bewildered themſelves; and much leſs dare I receive doctrines deviſed by ſhort-ſighted mortals as articles of faith. The word of GOD we may give an implicit aſſent unto, being confident that the dictates of heaven are abſolutely unerring: But devices of men in matters of faith, we ſhould approve and receive no further, than upon examination we find them agreeable to the *divine Oracles*.

IF any perſon be inclined to think that I treat thoſe things, which ſo many have received and admired, with too much freedom, (and perhaps what ſome will call contempt) let him conſider, that it is not a matter of divine revelation which is at preſent under conſideration; but an hypotheſis entirely human, only ſupported upon the tottering foundation of pretended antiquity, and the multitude of its votaries. I claim no more in this
caſe,

cafe, than the privilege of every chriſtian, which is to examine all ſuch ſyſtems by the word of GOD, and finding any part of them contrary thereto, is at liberty to reject the ſame as any part of his faith.

I AM far from ſaying that the inventors, or maintainers of this ſyſtem, a part of which I am to examine, are chargeable with all the conſequences that have, or may be drawn from it as principles of their's. Therefore, allow me once for all to ſay, that it is not men of any denomination I find fault with, but a HUMAN EXPLICATION of the Trinity, which, tho' rigouroufly impoſed as an article of faith, cannot be reconciled with the ſacred records: And for this reaſon, I ſhall in the following remarks, take the liberty to call it the HUMAN SCHEME.

THERE are ſo many parts of this human ſtructure, ſo many things ſaid to be *natural*, *neceſſary*, and *eſſential* to GOD, without authority from revelation, that 'tis nothing ſtrange for one to be at a loſs where to begin or end in the conſideration of them. As the human ſcheme ſeems to repreſent the characters of the *divine three* in contraſt, I ſhall follow it a little on the plan which the ſtretched imaginations of men have repreſented them in. But muſt firſt obſerve, that the following extract, is not taken from the ſentiments of any ſingle authors, who have wrote upon the ſubject, but from a ſyſtem as much in repute among Proteſtant eſtabliſhed churches, as any I know, in which it is aſſerted,

" THAT it is peculiarly proper to the divine perſonality of the FATHER to be *of none :* That he
alone

alone of the three divine perſons is the First : That he hath his being and perſonality of *himſelf*, being neither begotten by, nor proceeding *from another*.

But, that it is peculiarly proper to the divine perſonality of the Son to be *of another*, viz. the *Father* : That he *alone* is the Second : That he hath *not* his being, ſubſiſtence, and perſonality *of himſelf*; but as a *divine perſon* is *begotten* of the Father, by an act of Eternal Generation.

And, that it is peculiarly proper to the divine perſonality of the *Holy Ghoſt* to be *of the Father and the Son*,—That he *alone* is the Third.—That he hath not his being and perſonality *of himſelf*, but as a *divine perſon proceeds from the Father, and the Son, by an* Eternal Procession.

That it is the perſonal property of the Father, to beget a Son in his *own nature*.—That it is the perſonal property of the Son, to be begotten in the *Father's nature*.—That it is the perſonal property of the *Holy Ghoſt*, to proceed from both the *Father and the Son*.

That *paternity* is natural, and neceſſary to the ſubſiſtence of the Father *as a perſon in God-head* :. Or, that he is a Father, *as he is* God, and that theſe are ſynonimous convertable terms.—That *filiation* is natural, and neceſſary to the ſubſiſtence of the Son, *as a perſon in God-head* : Or, that he is a Son, *as he is* God, and that thoſe are ſynonimous convertable terms.—That the name *Holy Ghoſt* is natural, neceſſary, and peculiar to his ſubſiſtence *as a perſon in God-head* : Or, that this character is proper *only* to him, *as he is* God, excluſive of the other two perſons in the God-head.

That

THAT it is the peculiar property of the Father, to *communicate* the *whole* of the divine effence to the Son, by which communication he is *a Father in God-head*.—That it is the property of the *Son* to have the *whole* divine effence *communicated to him,* by which communication he is *a Son in God-head.*—That it is the property of the *Holy Ghoft,* to have the *whole* divine effence *communicated to him* from the *Father and the Son,* by which communication he is a *perfon in God-head.*

THESE, and many fuch, are the off-fpring of human invention, (except a particular or two concerning the Father) for which there is not the leaft countenance in the word of GOD; which will appear by comparing the particulars of this human fyftem, with the fcripture account of the Trinity, in the former parts of this work: And indeed, thefe are foft things, when compared with many other fubtle philofophical niceties, which fome have fpun from their own brains, and prefented to the world as explications of the Trinity. Out of many, I fhall only trouble the reader with one fhort note of an *orthodox* Divine. He fays, " The *firft* way of the *divine effence acting upon itfelf, produceth the firft perfon;* the *fecond* way of *its acting upon itfelf, produceth the fecond perfon;* and the *third* way *of its acting upon itfelf, produceth the third perfon."* This is a difcovery indeed! for which we are wholly indebted to the fchools: But I could not fay much in favour of his common fenfe, or knowledge of the fcriptures, that could admit it as a definition of the GOD he worfhipped.

I HAD no intention of taking any further notice in this place, of the fentiments of particular Divines

vines on this subject, had not the first volume of a work, now printing, come in my way, called "An illustration of the doctrines of the christian Religion, comprehending a complete Body of Divinity, by the late Reverend and Learned Mr Thomas Boston, minister of the gospel, at Ettrick." From which it was proper to give the reader this short extract, to shew the necessity there is of setting this subject in a scriptural light, and of exposing the absurdity of men's inventions thereon. It is evident from this extract, which is in the Author's own words, that the most admired writers among the systematics, even in the *present age*, do still on this subject follow the same unscriptural plan first contrived at the council of *Nice*, and further manufactured in the Popish schools, which the reformers from Popery adopted implicitly into their systems, and has been generally received as orthodox without examination.

He says, p. 189, "I am to explain the terms " *the God-head*, and a *Person*. By *the God-head*, is " meant the nature or essence of God, even as by " *manhood*, is understood the nature of man. A " divine person, or a person in the God-head, is " the God-head distinguished by personal proper- " ties: For consider the God-head, as the *fountain* " or *principle* of the *Deity*, *so it is the first person*; " consider *it* (the God-head) as *begotten of the Fa- " ther*, it is the *second*; and as *proceeding* from the " Father and the Son, *it* is the *third person*.—191. " They are distinguished by their order of subsist- " ing, and their incommunicable personal proper- " ties. In respect of the order of subsistence, the " Father is the *first* person, as the *fountain of the* " *Deity*, having the foundation of personal subsist- " ence in himself; the Son is the *second* person, and

" and hath the foundation of perfonal fubfiftence
" from the Father; and the Holy Ghoft is the
" *third* perfon, as having the foundation of per-
" fonal fubfiftence from the Father and the Son.—
" 192. This *generation* of the Son and Holy Ghoft
" was from all eternity,—and to deny it, would
" be to deny the fupreme and eternal God-head
" of all the glorious perfons.—They are not only
" of a like nature or fubftance, but one and the
" fame fubftance; and if fo, they are and muft be
" equal in all effential perfections.—Each of the
" three perfons hath the one whole God-head, or
" divine nature.—This myftery of the Trinity is
" fo interwoven with the whole of religion, that
" there can neither be true faith, right worfhip,
" or obedience without it.

" Pa. 522. U N L E S s *Chrift* had been the Son
" of God by eternal generation, he could not have
" been our mediator and redeemer, nor could he
" have obtained a throne and kingdom as fuch.
" —523. He is the Son of God, in a moft proper
" and fingular manner, viz. by the *Father's com-*
" *municating the divine effence to him by eternal gene-*
" *ration.*—524. The nature of this generation, our
" bleffed Lord himfelf doth explain to us, *John*
" v. 26. As the Father hath life in himfelf, fo
" hath he *given* to the Son to have life in himfelf.
" Which doth neceffarily import a communication
" of the fame individual effence. For to have life
" in himfelf, *was* an effential attribute of God;
" *i. e.* to have life independently, of and from
" himfelf, and to be the fource and fountain of life
" to all *creatures*, is a perfection proper to God,
" infeparable from his nature, yea, the very fame
" with his effence: And therefore, the Father cannot

" not give it, unlefs he give the effence itfelf, which
" he cannot give by way of alienation or partici-
" pation,—therefore it muft be by way of communi-
" cation. So that the generation of the Son is that
" *eternal action* of the Father, whereby he did *com-*
" *municate* to the Son the fame individual effence
" which he himfelf hath, that the Son might have
" it equal with himfelf;—in receiving whereof,
" the Son doth no more leffen or diminifh the ma-
" jefty or God-head of the Father, than the light
" of one candle doth the light of another from
" which it is taken. Wherefore the council of
" *Nice* faid well, that *Chrift* is GOD of GOD, light
" of light, very GOD of very GOD, not proceed-
" ing but begotten. Hence, it is clear, that he is
" the true GOD, and the moft high GOD, equal
" with the Father." A ftrange inference from
fuch premifes!

FEW men, perhaps, have been more popular in
the proteftant churches, than the author of this
work. His writings have been generally efteem-
ed by devout people, and his name reckoned a
fufficient recommendation to what has been printed
under that patronage: And no doubt the fyftematic doctrine of the Trinity will be received as
truth on the fame account, tho' evidently ridiculous and contradictory in itfelf. It is amazing
what weight men have laid upon doctrines, which
have not the leaft countenance from fcripture!—
So important, fo neceffary to falvation, that if in
the leaft doubted of, the whole of religion is ruined!
By this artifice, the bulk of mankind have been
frightened into a belief of the dreadful danger of
fo much as inquiring into the truth or falfehood of
fuch doctrines, as have been guarded by fanctions
of fo facred a nature. You might as foon perfuade

fuade many pious people to doubt of their own exiftence, as that this author, and others of equal repute among them, would lay fo much weight as he does in this cafe, upon a fcheme of doctrine which hath no foundation in revelation, reafon, or common fenfe. In many refpects he was juftly admired; but his authority, nor no man's elfe, can make that a part of the chriftian religion which GOD has not revealed.

THE ideas which this doctrine convey, feem to be more a-kin to the heathen mythology, than the revealed character of GOD in fcripture: And I cannot help thinking, that feveral parts of it are borrowed from that quarter, by the firft contrivers thereof, who ftill retained fome of the notions they had been bred up in, before converted to chriftianity. And like the reformers from popery, did not get clear of all the prejudices of their firft education, before they, in the heat of controverfy, compofed fyftems of doctrine, and forms of worfhip, which in many inftances, are rather what they formerly believed, the idolatries of the heathen, or the fuperftitions of popery, than what they afterwards profeffed, viz. an adherence to revelation, in oppofition to all the traditions of men. The terms (if there is any fenfe in them fo connected) convey ideas only fuitable to heathen deities, not to the one living and true GOD. To define the effence and nature of GOD, by the nature of man,—the communicating and receiving of deity by the lighting of one candle at another,— to tell us the God-head is diftinguifhed,—is the fountain of the deity,—is begotten of the father, —proceeds from the father and the fon, &c. &c. is wholly unintelligible,—fo confufed, that no man can know what is meant by God-head, effence, deity, father, fon, or any other term in the whole of the pretended definition.

I know not which is to be moft wondered at and lamented, how fo many great men could affume fuch a prerogative, as to load this doctrine with fo many unfuitable, unintelligible, and unmeaning diftinctions : Or, that fuch multitudes of people have without examination been difpofed to receive thefe diftinctions as undoubted truths, without feeing their difagreement with revelation. It is a pity the one fhould have fo much prefumption, and the other fo void of attention.

It would be too tedious a tafk to enter minutely into the particular parts of this human fcheme concerning the Trinity; I fhall only give fome hints of the moft glaring abfurdities and contradictions therein,—anfwer the moft plaufible arguments in favour of it ; and endeavour as I go along, to caft fome further light upon the oeconomical names or characters of Father, Son, and Holy Ghost.

SECT.

SECT. I.

I SHALL begin with the terms FIRST, SECOND, and THIRD, which are commonly applied to the *divine three*, as characters natural and essential to the manner of their subsistence in Deity: But upon what authority (tradition excepted) I know not. The scriptures no where teach that the Father is FIRST in subsistence in Deity, the SON SECOND, and the *Holy Ghost* THIRD. It is written " *there are three, and these three are one,*" and more we know not; for there is not one expression in the Bible which speaks of the Father, that calls him the FIRST. The *Lord Jesus Christ*, saith of himself, " I am *Alpha* and *Omega*, the *beginning* and the *end*, the *first* and the *last.*" No, say the supporters of this scheme, thou art the SECOND, the person of the Father is the FIRST: Is not this teaching him to speak, who gave a mouth to man? Or rather giving the lie to the GOD of truth?

THE only reason I ever heard advanced for this part of the scheme is, " that the persons are mentioned in that order in scripture." It must be granted, that in some places the Father is first mentioned, the Son next, and the Holy Ghost last, but not under the terms *first, second*, and *third:* And if the order of mentioning them so in some texts, had been to teach us in what manner they subsisted in Deity, then certainly the same order would always have been observed: But that order is frequently inverted, and in some texts the *Lord Jesus Christ* is mentioned *first,* in others, the *Holy Ghost*. (*l*) Therefore it may be justly concluded, that

(*l*) 2 Cor. 13, 14. 2 Thess. ii. 16, and iii. 5.

that this order of mentioning them in some texts, is not to teach us any thing concerning the manner of their subsistence in Deity.

Y E T this order of mentioning them may be improved to edification, if considered as expressive of the order of operation in the divine oeconomy of man's redemption, in which the Father is represented as sustaining the majesty of Deity, chusing and sending the Son; and exacting from him satisfaction for the sin of the elect company he was sent to redeem. The Son in undertaking, and giving that satisfaction: The Holy Ghost in applying the blessings, which *Christ*'s satisfaction hath made an egress for, to the chosen objects of divine love. I say, in the order of divine operation, the terms *first*, *second*, and *third* may have some meaning, but no way infer that they subsist in this manner in the divine nature.

I T is indeed pressed as an argument in favour of those terms, "That the order of operation among the divine persons, is intended to teach the internal order of their subsistence in Deity." But this is *gratis dictum*, for no such thing is revealed; how then came men by the knowledge of it? As GOD has not revealed the manner of his being and subsistence, it must be the most daring presumption for mortals to pretend to know, or attempt to explain it.

B E S I D E S, if this proposition could be granted, then those called *Arians*, have always been right in maintaining that *Christ* is an inferior, subordinate Deity; for they argue thus: "As the divine persons are represented in going through the work of man's salvation, so they are in the divine nature;

ture; but *Chrift* is reprefented in that work to be the Father's fervant, inferior to, and depending upon the will of the Father: Therefore, he is inferior and fubordinate to the Father in the divine nature." If the premifes are good, the confequence is undeniable. Let the fupporters of fuch a propofition anfwer for giving fuch an advantage to the adverfaries of the Deity of the SON and SPIRIT, for the fame confequence holds with refpect to both: And it is evident, if the propofition is maintained, the proper Deity of both muft be given up.

BUT in fact, the terms *firft*, *fecond*, and *third* will admit of no fenfe, but what import either *priority* and *pofteriority*, or *fuperiority* and *inferiority*. For I know no other fenfe the word FIRST will bear as applied to a perfon, but the following, viz. Him that is earlieft in exiftence: Him who is before all other in fome order: Him who is nobleft in dignity: Or, him who exceeds in excellency. And if the term FIRST be applied to any one in the Trinity, with refpect to the other two in any of thefe fenfes, it will neceffarily conclude againft their equality, or eternity, if not both. Tho' the *Lord Jefus Chrift* calls himfelf the FIRST, he is not then comparing himfelf with the Father or Holy Ghoft, and fo does not fuppofe any of them a SECOND, in that fenfe in which he calls himfelf the FIRST; for in the fame fenfe that he is the FIRST, fo are the other two; therefore, there can be no SECOND and THIRD, with refpect to the Deity of the *three who are one*.

THESE terms fo applied, lead even friends to the doctrine of the Trinity, into low and unfuitable conceptions of one in Deity being *before*, and another

another *after*, which are the natural ideas the terms convey: And at the same time, furnish enemies with arguments against the co-eternity and equality or sameness of the *divine three*. Were it not for these consequences, which natively flow from the use of the terms so applied, I should not hesitate to use them, were they intended merely for distinctions sake in speaking of the *divine three:* But yet, I think it is safest to speak of them under the distinguishing characters which the divine word hath given them, viz. FATHER, WORD, or SON, and HOLY GHOST, or SPIRIT.

2. AGAIN, I observe in general, that the supporters of this *scheme* allow, " That the three divine persons are one in the divine essence or nature; and that each divine person hath the whole of the divine essence." Yet in the same *scheme*, there is not only a distinction among the persons, (which must be admitted because the scripture calls them THREE) but there is a very *different manner* of subsisting in the same essence assigned to each person. Now, if this different manner of subsisting is *internal, natural,* or *necessary,* as is asserted, how then is it possible, that the same perfections in the same respect can be in each divine person?

IT is a truth, that the divine three exist *naturally, necessarily,* and *eternally*; but there are many things in the *human scheme* evidently contrary to this. " That one divine person is of none, neither begotten nor proceeding; but hath his being and subsistence of himself." All this is true; but are not the other two the same? No, saith the scheme; but the direct contrary." A first person communicates the divine essence, and a second and third receive the essence by communication." Can there

there be a more abſolute difference ſuppoſed, than is here affirmed among the *divine three*? What can differ more than *un-originated, ſelf-exiſtence,* and *derived, communicated exiſtence*? Is it not affirming in the plaineſt terms, that one perſon is ſelf-ſufficient for his own exiſtence and perfections; but the other two are not ſo; but depend upon the communication of them from another? Doth it not degrade them to the level of creatures, whoſe diſtinguiſhing character is, that have they all communicated to them; but cannot ſay they have their being, or any thing they enjoy of themſelves?— Does it not make the *divine three* differ as much as *mutability* and *time* differ from *immutability* and *eternity*? For he who is ſelf-exiſtent, and hath his being and perfections of himſelf, muſt be *eternal* and *immutable*: But on the contrary, he who hath his perſonality and perfections communicated to him, muſt be *mutable*; becauſe he is a dependent being in having that communicated to him, which is neceſſary to his exiſtence, and which he had not originally of himſelf: And as to *eternity*, he can have no claim to it conſiſtent with common ſenſe; for it is a contradiction in terms to ſay, a being is *eternal*, who hath his perſonality and perfections communicated to him from another.

It is the diſtinguiſhing characteriſtic betwixt ſupreme Deity and created exiſtence, that the one is ſelf-ſufficient for his own exiſtence and perfections, and the other is not, but depends upon the will of another for the communication of them. The communication of them from one to another, as I hinted juſt now, is a flat contradiction to the eternity and immutability of him to whom they are communicated: For as ſoon as the ſelf-exiſtent being

being did communicate any kind of perfection from himſelf, to another diſtinct from him, *time* commenced with that communication, and he to whom it was made, is declared *mutable*, in as much as that is communicated to him, which he had not originally of himſelf. A derived being, or perſon who is not ſelf-originated, is juſt, in other words, a *dependent creature*. Of this kind muſt our *Lord Jeſus Chriſt* be, if his eſſence or perſonality is communicated to him, which is plainly taught in the doctrine of the ſcheme we are conſidering.

To ſuppoſe the term begotten to ſignify that he derived his exiſtence or perſonality (as it is commonly called) from the Father, and in the mean time to ſay he is properly God, is directly contrary to the known principles of philoſophy and natural reaſon itſelf, which there is not one article of truth that contradicts; for it ſuppoſes ſomething derivative, and which is not ſelf-exiſtent in Deity; than which there can be nothing more repugnant to the ſelf-evident notion, which reaſon itſelf ſuggeſts to us of true and proper Deity; for if we exclude ſelf-exiſtence and independency out of our conceptions of Deity, (which muſt be the caſe with reſpect to the Deity of *Jeſus Chriſt* upon this plan) we leave nothing whereby it is diſtinguiſhed from created exiſtence: At leaſt, we exclude the chief thing which diſtinguiſhes the one from the other in our notions of them.

By this part of the ſcheme, the proper Deity of the *Lord Jeſus* and the *Holy Ghoſt*, is unavoidably betrayed or given up to the enemies of that doctrine. It is impoſſible to defend it upon ſuch a principle: And not only ſo, but there is the moſt glaring abſurdity and contradiction in it. For, firſt,

first, it is affirmed, that thefe fo very *different* properties are *natural* to the manner in which the *divine three exist* in the effence; and yet their famenefs in the effence is afferted;—that they are the SAME in fubftance, perfection, and glory. Which affirmations are as different as any two propofitions can be that contradict each other.

THERE can be no argument formed to prove that there are different properties in the divine three, whom revelation declares to be one. As far as we know thefe qualities, properties, and perfections afcribed to GOD in fcripture, which appear different to us, may be one and the fame in the view of GOD: And we are fure, that all perfections,—all that is afcribed to Deity, is afcribed to each of the divine three. Where then is either foundation for, or propriety in afcribing fuch different qualities or properties unknown in revelation to each of them, and then afferting in the ftrongeft terms, that thefe are as natural and neceffary to each, as to be GOD. This muft be fhocking, when we confider that among men, thefe qualities which are afcribed to them admit of degrees; but how is it poffible, that any thing of the kind can be afcribed in that manner to the *infinite* JEHOVAH? Who is abfolutely beyond all degrees of comparifon.

THO' the unfpeakable condefcenfion of GOD is manifeft, in revealing himfelf under relative characters; and expreffing what he defigned we fhould know of him by diftinct (and to the carnal conception very different) attributes.—Yet we muft not conceive, that thefe are in GOD, as qualities are in creatures, in whom power is different from wifdom, and fo of all other. In GOD there can

I i   not

not be *this* and *that* perfection, or different attritribute, who is a *simple, uncompounded, indivisible, divine Being.*

IT is said, these properties are only the *modes* of personal subsistence: 'Tis certain there are three in Deity; but these three are one in name, nature, and glory. What ground is there then to believe such a very different manner of subsistence, as evidently infers different degrees of personal perfections? Is not each of them all that GOD is? From whence then have we ground to believe such a difference of the divine nature in one more than in another? By a necessary consequence from the doctrine in the *scheme*, the divine nature primarily belongs to one person, and must be communicated to the other two. This not only introduceth a difference of personal glory among the divine three; but in effect says, there is none of them (at least the Son and Spirit) properly GOD; And if admitted, it must be at the expence of the equality or sameness, and co-eternity of the *three* who are *one*; which can never be supported upon the supposition of these so very different qualities, or properties mentioned in the human scheme, being applied to the divine nature of the *Father, Word,* and *Holy Ghost*; who are the *same* in substance, *equal* in name, *perfections,* and *glory.*

AND as there is no authority in revelation for any such *internal, natural,* or *necessary* distinctions, which are so very *different,* and yet *essential* to their personal subsistence as are alledged in the scheme; I cannot see how any man that has no other rule of faith than the scriptures, can obtain evidence sufficient to command his assent to such terms so applied.

IT

IT is abundantly evident from scripture, that with GOD there is neither *prior*, nor *posterior*; no *superior*, or *inferior*, when we speak of person or subsistence: But it will be difficult to determine, how this can be reconciled with the terms in the scheme, as *first, second,* and *third, communicating of the essence, - begetting in the essence,* &c. no part of which has the least countenance in revelation; but invented by men, to account for the distinction of the divine persons; while such terms restricted to Deity, (if they have any meaning at all so applied) destroy the proper Deity of each divine person. For such terms have not the least analogy to proper Deity, or what is commonly called self-existence, except we were to judge by the rule of contraries, and for *first, second,* and *third,*—read, *neither first, second,* nor *third*; for *communicated,* read, *uncommunicated,* &c. which conceptions are more agreeable to any account the Supreme Being hath given of himself in the sacred records, than these terms so much insisted on by the advocates for the divinity of the human scheme.

MUST it not be the highest presumption in men to say *positively* more concerning GOD, than he has been pleased to reveal of himself, by attempting to give definitions of his nature, or the manner of his existence? A subject confessed by all, to be infinite and inconceivable. " Surely it must be darkening wisdom with words without knowledge; and talking foolishly for GOD." Language itself must fail, in every attempt to express the sublimity of it. Would the unmeaning prattle of an infant, be sustained as a clear demonstration of the abstruse problems among astronomers? Infinitely less is the quintessence of all languages under heaven capable to demonstrate this inconceivable divine subject: And they certainly discredit the truth of its inconceiveableness, who begin to investigate or define it in terms of human invention: For that moment any one is capable to conceive it, *he* must either be endowed with infinite capacity; or *it* must cease to be an infinite mystery.

THE nature of GOD is not a subject of definition; nor can it be apprehended by one adequate conception or notion. All definitions limit the subject defined; but GOD is infinite, and cannot be limited by definition. Nor can the compound finite capacity of creatures apprehend the simple, infinite nature of GOD. Consequently to attempt a definition of the nature of GOD, must be a daring insult upon his infinite majesty,—an attempt to limit him within the bounds of finite comprehension,—and supposes him only a creature like ourselves. Can any one then imagine it equitable, for any number of men to compose an explication of this subject, independent on revelation, and impose it on the consciences of their fellow men, by requiring an implicit belief of it as a term of communion in the church of *Christ*?

SECT.

SECT. II.

I SHALL, now more particularly obferve fome things relating to that part of the fcheme, which concerns the fonfhip of the Lord *Jefus Chrift*. And *firſt*, I obferve, that the term GOD, when ufed in fcripture to denote the Supreme Being, generally includes the three fpecial denominations of his character, by which he difcovers himfelf to us in the work of our falvation; which are thefe of Father, Son, and Holy Ghoft; unlefs when one of thefe denominations is predicated to point out one of the facred three.

THE fcriptures intimate, that the divine plurality are as neceſſary, according to what they teach us concerning the Being and exiftence of GOD, as the divine nature which is but *one*: And as the word GOD points out to us, all that is in GOD; then it muft follow, that one perfon cannot be a caufe in any fenfe whatfoever of the perfonality or exiftence of another: And none of thefe perfons can be called the SON OF GOD, in that fenfe which it is neceffary for him to be GOD; feeing he muft be included in the term GOD. This does not hinder him from being SON OF GOD in another fenfe, viz. the relation he undertook in divine condefcenfion, to fulfil the purpofes of JEHOVAH concerning men, which was not abfolutely neceffary to the Being and exiftence of GOD.

Now, where *Chrift* is called *the Son of God*, if the term *God* be taken for the *Deity*, this will deftroy the *ſcheme*, for then he will be the Son of the effence: But according to it, he is the Son of

one

one perfon in the effence, by a communication of the effence. If this is so, it muſt follow, that wherefoever the *Son of God* is mentioned, the term *God* muſt be reſtricted to *one* perfon, viz. the Father, excluſive of the other *two*. Does not this plainly fuppofe, that the Father *only* is GOD? That is to fay, he is GOD in fuch a fenfe, as neither of the other two perfons are; which is the very foul of that doctrine commonly called *Arianifm*; for men of that denomination grant the *Word* and *Holy Ghoſt* to be GOD, not in the fame, but an inferior fenfe to that in which the Father is GOD; hence, agreeable to this fcheme, they reafon thus: "*Chriſt* is the Son of GOD as to his divine perfon; but the term GOD is to be reſtricted to the perfon of the Father: Therefore, he only is GOD in the higheſt fenfe of the word." Now, if thefe premifes hold, the inference is good; for if *Chriſt*, as to his *divine perfon*, is the Son of another perfon in Deity, he cannot be GOD in the fame fenfe *as a* SON, that the other who begat his *divine perfon* is *as a Father*.

THUS it is evident, that the *Arian* doctrine by neceffary confequence is countenanced in the pretended *orthodox fcheme*: But, I hope the fhame of thus yielding the glorious caufe of *Chriſt*'s proper divinity, by fuch incoherent notions fo far from fcripture, and beyond the fphere of human conception, as not to be made either good divinity or good fenfe, will roufe the lovers of his honour to the vindication of it from revelation *itſelf*, where it is abundantly evident to every unprejudiced inquirer.

2. IT is maintained in the fcheme, that it is peculiarly proper to the *Lord Jeſus*, to have his divine

vine perſonality *from another*. If this is ſo, it muſt be either from the divine *eſſence*, or from the *Perſon* of the *Father* : If the former, then he is the Son of the *eſſence*, and is no more from the Father, than the Father is from him: And if the divine eſſence is the Father of our *Lord Jeſus*, then he is as much the Son of himſelf, and the *Holy Ghoſt*, as of the Father : Since the eſſence or divine nature is common to all the three. But tho' this is allowed in one part of the ſcheme, it cannot be admitted conſiſtent with *this* part of it; for here the perſonality of the Son is limited to the communication of the eſſence from the Father, which not only contradicts ſome other parts of it, but manifeſtly veſts a ſupremacy in the Father, and appropriates a derived perſonality to the Son, which deſtroys his proper Deity.

IT cannot be denied, that every *effect* muſt in point of time be poſterior or after its cauſe. Conſequently every *effect* muſt have a beginning. *Filiation* or ſonſhip is an *effect*, and therefore muſt have had a beginning. Now, if one in Deity be naturally and neceſſarily a Son, it will as neceſſarily follow that his nature is *derived*; ſince that is affirmed to be *natural* to him which is an *effect*, and muſt be *derived*. Every kind of *derivation* ſuppoſeth the beginning of the thing *derived* : But *generation*, (according to all the ideas we can have of *generation*) is one kind of *derivation*, and muſt neceſſarily ſuppoſe a beginning of that which is generated. Conſequently to put *eternal* to *generation* with reference to time *paſt*, is a direct contradiction, and is the ſame as if we ſhould ſay, the *beginningleſs beginning* of any thing; which is no more a contradiction in terms than *eternal generation* is.

IF the *Lord Jesus Christ* had the divine nature communicated to him,—if he is naturally and necessarily a Son,—and was generated as a divine person, he must be derived, as he is not without an external cause of existence, and so cannot be self-existent: And if he is not without an external cause of existence, he must have had a beginning, —is posterior to some other being, and consequently is not eternal *à parte ante*.

THERE are but two ways any person can exist; either naturally, necessarily, and independently, which we call self-existence: Or, by some external cause, at the pleasure and will of another. It is an absolute truth that the *Lord Jesus Christ* self-exists, as I proved formerly. But a communicated personality, is the direct opposite of necessary existence: Hence, there is no tolerable sense the terms in the scheme will bear, but that the *Lord Jesus Christ* is a derived Being, who exists at the pleasure of GOD his Father; which is the most that ever any *Arian* did plead for.

3. THE argument mentioned, pa. 174, in favour of *Christ*'s oeconomical sonship, effectually destroys the notion of sonship by an eternal generation. All the fundamental articles of faith necessary to salvation, are plain, familiar, easy to be understood, and clearly revealed in the word of GOD; but the belief of *Christ* being the Son of GOD, is made necessary to salvation: Therefore, it must be easy to be understood, and clearly revealed in the word of GOD. Now, to take his sonship for an eternal generation of the divine person of the *Lord Jesus*, by the person of the Father, is what no man ever professed to understand any thing about: But even by all the supporters thereof, it is acknowledged to be

be an ineffable, unconceivable myftery: Which, neverthelefs, would not make it falfe, was it matter of divine revelation. Had GOD made known the truth of it, we were then bound to believe it, tho' we could not define the manner of it. But for my own part, I freely confefs, after many years fearch, I never could find, and I fuppofe it would puzzle the whole world to find, the leaft hint of any eternal generation in all the word of GOD. There is not one text, where the *Lord Jefus* is called the ETERNAL *Son of God*, or that he was begotten from *eternity*. That he is the ETERNAL GOD, is manifeft from abundance of fcriptures; but that he is an *eternal Son*, the divine Oracles no where infinuate. *Eternal generation* is merely the product of man's invention; for it cannot be gathered from revelation by the remoteft confequence.

'T I S true the doctrine of the Trinity,—the union of the nature of GOD and man, in the perfon of *Emmanuel*,—and the union of the Saints with *Chrift*, commonly called by the *fyftematics*, the *hypoftatic*, and *myftical* unions, are myfteries as to the manner of them, yet they are to be believed; but why? Not for their myfterioufnefs, but becaufe it is clearly revealed in the facred pages that they are; and tho' the manner of them remains a fecret to mortals; yet the teftimony of the LORD of hofts, is fufficient warrant for our believing the truth of them. There is nothing can be called a *myftery* that is *revealed* in any text of fcripture. A *revealed myftery* is no better fenfe than *eternal generation*. Had we one text for the eternal fonfhip of *Chrift*, we durft not hefitate a moment in receiving it as an article of faith, tho' we did not underftand the manner of his being begotten. We are bound to believe revealed truths on the veracity of the unerring

erring Spirit of God, without daring to bring them to the bar of our viciated reaſon, to judge of their *truth*, by what we can can learn of the *manner* of them.

If *eternal generation* be a truth, it requires exprefs revelation to ſupport it; nothing ſhort of a divine diſcovery could poſſibly make it known: Without this, every thing concerning the Trinity is beyond the reach of the moſt intelligent to inveſtigate by reaſoning and implication. Here created capacities are limited, and at their *neplus ultra*. This is one glory of divine revelation, that it diſcovers things otherwiſe unſearchable. But where is that text which teacheth us eternal ſonſhip? Or, that the divine perſon of the *Lord Jeſus* was begotten by *an act of eternal generation?* Now as this doctrine is not taught in the word of God, and even contrary to reaſon and common ſenſe; muſt it not be adulterating the precious truths of God,—abuſing the reaſon of mankind,—and doing violence to the rights of their conſciences, who will not be ruled in matters of faith by the dictates of men, to preſs upon them ſuch a notion as a fundamental article of the chriſtian faith?

4. I would obſerve, that there is nothing can be more evident, if the ſcope of the New Teſtament is conſidered, than that this was the great queſtion in that period: Whether *Jeſus Chriſt* was the promiſed, expected *Meſſiah*, the great Saviour propheſied of in the Old Teſtament? This was the criterion of the chriſtian religion, the teſt of diſcipleſhip, and term of communion in the church; the believing and confeſſing this, gave a title to the chriſtian character and communion. The moſt prejudiced in favour of any ſcheme, cannot well deny this:

this: And to recount the evidence particularly, would be to tranfcribe more than half of the New Teftament.

Our Saviour himfelf calls in the teftimony of his Father, his own preaching and miracles, the Old Teftament Prophets, with the voice of his forerunner, *John the Baptift*, to confirm this truth. The joint teftimony of the difciples, with thofe converted during *Chrift*'s abode here, efpecially the *Samaritan* woman, with her fellow citizens, are manifeft to this purpofe. The method which the Apoftles took to inftruct the infant churches, proves this point. As a fpecimen, the reader may confult *Peter*'s fermons, recorded in the 2d, 3d, and 10th ch. of the Acts, and *Paul*'s in the 17th. Thefe, with many other places in the Acts and Epiftles, put the matter paft doubt to the meaneft capacity. To which might be added, the manner of baptifing profelytes to the chriftian religion, efpecially from among the *Jews*, which was always in the name of JESUS CHRIST.

Now, tho' both the Apoftles and other converts freely and very frequently confeffed their faith in the *Son of God*, (which is proved above to be the fame with believing in *Jefus Chrift*, in New Teftament language) yet, it is ftrange, that neither *Chrift*, his Apoftles, nor any other, whofe fouls were filled with the Spirit and grace of GOD, ever gave the leaft hint of *eternal generation:* Or, that the divine perfon of *Chrift* was begotten; and that he had the *divine nature communicated to him from the Father*, &c. Is not the doctrines of *Chrift*, and the Apoftles, fufficient ground for our faith, without fo many different ideas as the wifdom of men have prefumptuoufly added thereto?

THOUGH

Though the divinity of *Christ* shines clearly in every page of the New Testament, and must be included in his character as the all-sufficient Saviour, by every one that believeth in him; yet, the wisdom of God directed the Apostles not to break in upon the prejudiced *Jews*, and blinded *Gentiles*, with the blaze of the Deity of *Christ:* But to lead them by degrees from the knowledge of *Jesus* of *Nazareth*, the son of man, to the knowledge of *Jesus* the *Messiah*, the *Son of God*, their *Prophet, Priest*, and *King:* From the revelation of *Christ*, the *Saviour*, to the revelation of *Christ*, the *true God* and eternal life: From the discovery of the presence of God with him, as sent for the salvation of men, to the doctrine of himself, being the true and eternal God. Thus *they* taught, and thus *they* believed; without limiting his character as a Son to his pure Deity; much less to an eternal generation, being begotten as he is a divine person, or having his divine nature communicated to him.

Eternal generations is an invention of men, who pretend to be ambassadors of *Christ*, that they may rank with the Apostles; and not content with this, they will assume the power of dictating articles of faith, and introducing *their mysteries* into religion, besides the mysteries and counsel of God, which the Apostle had in commission, to open up and declare to the churches. *Paul* tells the *Corinthians*, that the Apostles were (a) *stewards* of the mysteries of God: And in a very solemn manner declares to the elders of the church of *Ephesus*, (b) " That he had kept back nothing that was profitable to them—But had declared to them ALL the counsel of

---

(a) 1 Cor. iv. 1. (b) Acts xx. 20, 27.

of GOD." Now, as the Apoſtle never mentions *eternal generation,* nor any thing like it, in his epiſtles to thoſe or any other of the churches, it muſt be concluded by every one who is difpoſed to believe the Apoſtle, that *eternal generation* is none of the *myſteries of God,*—no part of *his counſel* made known to men,—nor any way *profitable* to them. The making it an article of faith, muſt therefore be a proud attempt to *add* to the counſel of GOD, —an impeachment of the Apoſtles, with the crimes of *faſehood* and *unfaithfulneſs*, in affirming that they had declared *all* the counſel of GOD, while they kept back that momentous point *eternal generation*. Their conduct is more than a bare inſinuation, that the ſcriptures are ſufficient for the purpoſes which the Apoſtles affirm they are.—(c) " All ſcripture is given by inſpiration of GOD, and is profitable for *doctrine*, for *reproof*, for *correction*, for *inſtruction,* in righteouſneſs,—*able* to make the man of GOD *perfect,—wiſe to ſalvation,—*and *thoroughly furniſhed* unto *all good works.*"

5. WE may further obſerve, that in theſe texts where *Chriſt* is called a SON, we cannot ſuppoſe his Deity abſtractedly is, or can be deſigned, according to the juſt and moſt natural interpretation of the texts. We ſhall mention only a few for example, and hint the inconſiſtency of applying the term SON, expreſſed or underſtood in them, to the pure Deity of our *Lord Jeſus Chriſt.*

He ſays,—(d) "As the Father gave me commandment, even ſo I do." To ſuppoſe one in the divine plurality commanding, another obeying, without relation to their oeconomical characters, is

(c) 2 Tim. iii. 15, 16, 17. *(d)* John xiv. 31.

is wholly inconfiftent with their equality or famenefs and felf-exiftence ; as the will, power, and glory of the *three* are *one* in the fame nature.

THE *will* of the facred *three* in Deity is *one* ; but we often find the SON as fuch, mentioning *his will* as diftinct from that of the Father.—(*e*) " Father, if thou be willing, remove this cup from me: Neverthelefs, not *my will*, but *thine* be done. I feek not *mine own will*, but the *will* of the *Father* who hath fent me." But the learned call this diftinct will of *Chrift* his *human will*, or the will of his *human nature* ONLY. This is diftinguifhing rather too nicely, and if it is juft, then he fuftained the character of our redeemer, as he was *man* ONLY. All things he fays of himfelf, or are faid of him, which imply fubordination and fubjection to the Father, are meant of his human nature ONLY. What then becomes of the value of his obedience and death,—of man's redemption,—or in fhort of the chriftian religion!

BUT there is a particular confequence infeparable from this notion of *Chrift*'s *human will*, which the profeffed orthodox will perhaps diflike as much as any, tho' far from having the fame danger attending it. It cannot be denied, that *Chrift* brought this diftinct will he fo often mentions from heaven with him ; for he fays,—(*f*) " I came down from heaven, not to do mine own *will*, but the *will* of him that *fent me*." Now, if this be the will of his human nature ONLY, then the *pre-exiftence* of his human foul, before he was manifefted in the flefh, muft be granted. There is no avoiding this confequence, without the affiftance

(*e*) Luke xxii. 42. John v. 30. (*f*) John vi. 38.

ance of some bold figure to explain those texts, which is the common refuge of the learned in cases of such distress. For my own part, I see no danger in admitting this last consequence; tho' I think the plain meaning of the texts, points out *Christ* in his oeconomical character, in which he was sent the Son of GOD, and Saviour of the world; in that respect he may have a distinct will from the Father.

(*g*) " FATHER, glorify me with thine own self, with the glory which I had with thee before the world began." To confine the sonship implied here to the divine person of *Christ*, would make one divine person pray to another, and that for the restoration of a glory which the same divine person once had, and is at that time divested of, all which is impossible in pure Deity; for,—(*h*) " He is without variableness, or shadow of turning."

(*i*) " THE *Father* loveth the *Son*, and hath given all things into his hand." As a Son, he receives all things from the Father, but *as he is God*, he can receive nothing; he hath an original right to every thing: Therefore, he is not a SON, as he is GOD.

WHEN the *Centurion*, and those who attended *Christ* on the cross, beheld the awful scene,—(*k*) " They said, truly this was the *Son of God*." Did they here mean they saw the eternal invisible GOD hanging dead upon the cross? Neither their words, nor the circumstances of the affair will admit of such a sense. By a deduction of what they saw

of

(*g*) John xvii. 5. (*h*) Ja. i. 17. (*i*) John iii. 35. (*k*) Matt. xxvii. 54.

of the man upon the cross, and the interposition of divine providence in so striking a manner on his behalf, they apprehended a relation betwixt him and GOD; that he was a favourite of heaven: And if we consider how the other Evangelists record this matter, it will be evident, that the meaning must be as above; and by no means, that they thought the *Son* they spoke of was GOD. *Mark* says,—(*l*) " When the *Centurion* saw that *he cried out*, and *gave up the Ghost*, he said, truly this *man* was the *Son of God.*" And *Luke* says,—(*m*) " Now when the *Centurion* saw what was done, *he glorified God*, saying, certainly this was a *righteous man.*"

IT is very plain the Evangelists had no such notion of the *Centurion*'s words, as many divines since have had, who would persuade the world, that they are a notable proof that *Christ* is *God*, as he is a *Son*: Whereas the direct contrary is not obscurely intimated, if we will admit the Evangelist *Luke* to interpret what is meant by the *Son of God* in the other two Evangelists. It is admirable, what pitiful shifts the advocates for that opinion have fled to. One of them on this subject, finds he cannot reconcile the Evangelists to his cause, and rather than yield to them, he boldly contradicts them, by alledging " that what some of them have said, is not the language of the *Centurion*, but of those who were with him," though all the three mention the *Centurion* particularly: And tho' it were even granted against the Evangelists, it would not in the least help that tottering cause.

I SHALL only mention one text more, as I think the matter is abundantly clear.—(*n*) " When all things

(*l*) Mark xv. 39. (*m*) Luke xxiii. 47. (*n*) 1 Cor. xv. 28.

things shall be subdued unto him (*Christ*); then shall the *Son* also himself be subject unto him that put all things under him, that GOD may be all in all." To take sonship here for the divine nature of our *Lord Jesus*, must infer, that he has no original right to the things which are put under him; for this is said to be done by another: But as he is GOD, he has the same underived claim to all things with the Father; if it be owned that he is of the same nature, power, and glory. 'Tis here said, "Then shall the SON *himself* be subject," (according to our translation of the text)—Which plainly shews, that as a SON he is subject; but as to his Deity, he is (*o*) " GOD over all, blessed for ever." Subjection is proper to his character as a SON; but sovereign and absolute dominion is natural to him as he is GOD: Therefore, as he is GOD, he cannot be a SON.

MANY more texts might be brought in here, to shew the weakness of confining the sonship of *Christ* to his pure Deity, or an act of eternal generation, whereby his divine person was begotten by the Father; the absurdity of which is evident from every text in the sacred records, that mention any thing concerning him as a SON. The reader may join these few with others mentioned, at p. 159, as equally clear in favour of oeconomical sonship, which will be still more conspicuous from the consideration of these texts, commonly advanced to prove that kind of sonship I am here disclaiming: But before I proceed to these, I shall observe further here,

6. THAT it is a sufficient reason to reject any human scheme introduced into religion, which hath

not

(*o*) Rom. ix. 5.

not the stamp of divine authority, when it is used with more advantage by adversaries against the truth; than it can be by friends in defence thereof. What countenance those of the *Arian* persuasion have in this scheme, is evident from the advantage they have taken from it to dishonour the *Lord* of life. To this is owing their success, since some of their modern advocates have refined the *Arian* hypothesis, by grafting on a stock so near of kin to this scheme, that they take occasion from it to insult the faith of christians, and reproach the doctrine of the Deity of our *Lord Jesus*, as if it had no better arguments to support it.

The affinity betwixt this scheme and the *Arian* hypothesis, shews it to be a very unnecessary opposition which the *Arians* have maintained for many years against it, which is only founded on the different ideas the contending parties affix to the same words. For there is very little in what is called the orthodox explanation of the Trinity, to hinder the strictest *Arian* in the world to subscribe it. The words used in it, cannot by the unprejudiced be understood in any other sense than what the *Arians* contend for: And perhaps the most intelligent among them, would find some difficulty to express their own sentiments in stronger terms than the pretended orthodox have done for them, which incoherent, unscriptural notions, have contributed more to the growth of *Arianism*, than all other means besides.

There are indeed some phrases thrust into the scheme, merely in opposition to the *Arians*, without any regard to scripture, or their connection and agreement with the other parts of it; which only make the whole appear the more inconsistent, and

and tend to confirm the enemies to the Deity of the *Lord Jefus* and the *Holy Ghoft*, in their oppofition to a truth maintained in a manner fo void of fcripture ideas, and fo contradictory in itfelf, as to render the whole fcheme unintelligible to any *impartial inquirer*.

IN fuch a mind it begets a mighty prejudice againft the belief of the Deity of *Chrift*, when he finds it maintained that he is a SON, as he is GOD :— That his *divine perfonality* is *begotten* :—That his Deity depends upon his *Sonfhip* :—That his *divine nature* is *communicated to him*. Which is all of a kind; not a word of truth in the whole; and amounts to no more than that his Deity depends upon his derived, dependent character. For the notion of a *Son* in all languages among mankind, imports derivation and dependence; and the fcheme infinuates in the ftrongeft terms, that *Chrift*'s divinity is of this kind, fince he receives it by communication. Whereas the notion of proper Deity imports independence, inorigination, and felf-exiftence, which to the impartial inquirer, carries a contradiction in the very terms: And there is the greateft probability, if fuch a perfon had no other means of learning the Deity of *Chrift*, than by this human fcheme of doctrine, he would either prove an *Arian*, or conclude it beyond his conceptions, from the contradictions fo manifeft in every part of it: And that it may appear, I do not fay this out of any ill-grounded prejudice againft this *fcheme*, I fhall conclude the reflections in this fection, with a fhort account of a few of the *felf-evident contradictions* therein.

THE firft leading contradiction, which I take to be the foundation of all others, is, That tho' 'tis

acknow-

acknowledged, that revelation only teacheth us the true knowledge of God: That nothing is matter of divine faith, but what hath a divine teftimony: That we are to believe nothing concerning the Trinity, but what is clearly revealed in fcripture: That God alone is author of all the knowledge we can have of himfelf; and that this is contained in his word of revelation. Thefe propofitions are ſtrictly true, and confeffed to be fo by the profeffed orthodox, who, yet, are fond of a fcheme in which there are many things faid of God not revealed by him, but deviſed, and impofed by men; who take it upon them to correct the divine eloquence, as if he who holds the fabric of nature in his hand, did not know how to accommodate his doctrines to the capacities of his creatures: And will teach him to fpeak who gave a mouth to man.

But what notable difcovery do *they* make, who are thus wife above what is written, in their additions to the divine Oracles? Why, they are fo honeft as to tell us, that the words they ufe, are not to be taken in any fenfe that mankind is capable of underftanding them in. Now, what prefumption is this, for mortals to clothe divine truth with modes of expreffion which they themfelves are ignorant of, and know not how they are applicable to the fubject which they pretend to explain by them! This is juft to form a fcheme, and then tell the world it muſt be believed: But the words it is compofed of, are void of fenfe and meaning when fo applied! How difmal had the cafe of mankind been, had God dealt thus in inditing his facred revelation?——

But

BUT further, they tell us that the *nature of God* is an *ineffable myftery*, beyond the comprehenfion of all creatures: Yet in this fcheme, there is a *demonftration* of it, a *definition* of the *internal modes* of fubfiftence of all the perfons in Deity.

HERE we are alfo taught, that the divine perfon of the FATHER is FIRST, the SON SECOND, and the HOLY GHOST THIRD :—Yet none of the perfons are either AFORE or AFTER another.——— That the Father *communicates* the *whole* of his *effence* to the Son, and Holy Ghoft :—Yet, it is impoffible that the divine effence can be *communicated* at all, either in *whole*, or in part: For GOD is a *fimple, infinite, indivifible Being*.————He *communicates* his whole ESSENCE :—Yet, his effence is HIMSELF; his very indivifible felf: So that to communicate his ESSENCE, muft be to communicate or give HIMSELF.

——HE communicates his effence, whereby he BECOMES A FATHER :—Yet was always the SAME.—By the communication of the effence to another, HE BECOMES A SON :—Yet from all eternity the SAME. The one perfon *communicates*; the other *receives* by *communication* the divine effence: Yet all the perfons are the *fame* in the effence; and impoffible that there can be any *change* in either *perfons* or *effence*.

THOSE among the fupporters of the fcheme who fpeak plainly, fay, that *Chrift* in *becoming a Son, became God:* But others reckon themfelves more modeft in faying, that his *divine perfon was begotten*. But in fact, the laft fentiment is the fame with the other, which is plain from the following fhort argument. As *Chrift* is a divine perfon, he

is

is God; but as a divine person, he is begotten: Therefore, he is begotten, as he is God. This is the language of the scheme, which compared with other sentiments in the same well contrived system, is pregnant with contradictions.

―――― C H R I S T, by being begotten a Son, he *becomes God :*—Yet he is God over all, *eternally the same* with the *Father.*―――――The Son as a distinct person thus generated, is God of God :—(that must be, one would think, *another God* distinct from the *God* he is *of*) Yet, there is but one God.

―――― T H E *divine person* of *Christ* was begotten : —Yet, not his *Deity* begotten.―――――*Jesus Christ* is the *Son of God,* according to his *divine nature :*— Yet, the *divine nature* of the *Son,* is no more begotten, than the *divine nature* of the *Father.*―――― One of the persons is begotten, in the divine *nature* of *another person,* and not begotten in his *own nature :*—Yet, the divine *nature* is but *one,* and *common* to all the persons.

―――― J E S U S C H R I S T is the *Son of God* by eternal generation of the substance of the Father :—Yet, he is not the *Son* of the essence; nor is the Father's substance the matter out of which he is begotten.―――――The *persons* are begotten in the essence :—Yet, but *one* person is said to be begotten.

―――― T H E Son is a second person in Deity, the Holy Ghost a third :—The Son was *begotten* in the Father's essence,—*received* his personal subsistence by *generation* and *communication*; and the Holy Ghost, by *procession* and *communication* from the *Father* and the *Son* :—Yet all the persons in Deity *are*, and *will be*, what they *always were, eternally, unchangeably the same*.

────── T H E Father is *of none*; he hath the essence *of himself*; the Son is *from* the *Father's essence*; and the Holy Ghost *from both* :──Yet, no *essential* difference among the persons; they are the *same* in *substance* or *essence*; no *superior* or *inferior*; no *prior* or *posterior*.

────── T H E divine *personalities* of the *Son* and *Holy Ghost*, are *derived* by *communication*; the one by *generation*, the other by *procession* :──Yet all the persons in Deity are self-existent. (All that is in Deity must necessarily and eternally exist.)

T H E Son is all that the Father is :──Yet, he is not of himself, which the Father is.──Not unbegotten, which the Father is.──The Son can do all that the Father does :──Yet cannot beget a Son in his own nature, which the Father does. There is no end of absurdities here; however, I shall only mention one more.──

J E S U S C H R I S T was a Son previous to, or before he was a mediator :──Yet *Jesus Christ* was anointed as mediator from all eternity.

M A N Y such contradictions might be collected from this human system; and still more from the works of such as have appeared in defence of it. These few are sufficient to shew how contrary it is to itself, and also to the revelation GOD hath given us. Self-contradiction is a sure evidence of a false hypothesis, whether philosophical or divine. Such are the improvements made upon the doctrine of

the

Trinity, by the profound stretches of their wit, who have been prying into this sacred doctrine beyond what is revealed by GOD, who knows best what measure of knowledge therein was necessary for our imperfect state.

SUCH philosophical demonstrations of this doctrine are the effects of proud, corrupt nature: And a confounding of reason by a misapplication of it. Yet, these human inventions are fathered upon divine revelation; which is charging the GOD of consummate wisdom with folly,—and a most notorious reproach upon the christian religion in general.

SECT.

SECT. III.

Arguments in favour of the natural and necessary Sonship of Christ, or, what is commonly called eternal generation, considered.

AFTER all, it is but fair to give an impartial hearing to what the advocates for this scheme, which they pretend is of such consequence, have advanced in defence of it : And as they sometimes endeavour to prove it by general propositions, and sometimes from scripture texts, I shall consider these separately, lest I should do their cause injustice, by allowing any evidence they produce for it to escape unnoticed.

FIRST, it is alledged, "That if the *son of man* denotes the human nature of *Christ*, or that he is really man; so the name *Son of God* must signify his divine nature, or that he is truly and properly GOD."

Ans. THE case differs very widely; for the name *Son of man* is never applied to any person who is not true and real man; but the name *Son of God* is often applied to both Angels and men, yet they are not truly and properly GOD. So that the argument proves nothing to the purpose for which it is brought; and only infers, that as his being called *the son of man*, shews him to be the chief of the sons of men; so his being called *Son of God*, points him out to be the most eminent of all who are so called, both in character and office. Besides, I know not one text where he is called *son of man*, to shew that he is real man, or where the sense is to be restricted to his human nature without including

cluding his office; * nor do I know one where he is called *Son of God*, to denote his pure Deity: And as he is called *son of man*, without including the idea of his human nature being BEGOTTEN BY MAN; why may he not be called *Son of God*, without the confideration of his divine perfon being BEGOTTEN BY GOD?

ANOTHER argument is, "That the word *Son* among men, properly fignifies one of the fame nature with the Father; therefore *Son of God*, when applied to *Chrift*, muft fignify one of the fame nature with GOD the Father.

Anf. THE word *Son* among men has feveral ideas; as, derivation from the Father, fubordination, or inferior relation to the father;—Likenefs to, or imitation of the father;—A Being of the fame fpecies or kind with the father;—An individual being diftinct from the father. There are none of thefe ideas can with propriety be applied to the divine perfon of *Chrift* in relation of nature with the Father: But feveral of them may be applied to him in his fubordinate character, as *Meffiah*, his being appointed, and fent by the Father, his being vicegerant in the kingdom, &c. Befides, Angels and men are called *Sons of God*, (*p*) yea, men are faid to be begotten of GOD, (*q*) yet neither of thefe are of the fame nature with GOD their Father in that fenfe they would have *Chrift*, becaufe he is called the *Son of God*; nor is it poffible it can be fo.

2. WHERE *Son* among men denotes famenefs of nature, it fignifies the fame *fpecific nature*

(*p*) Job xxxviii. 7. Hof. i. 10. (*q*) Phil. ii. 15. 1 John iii. 1, 2, and v. 1.

* See p. 141. for the fenfe of the term *fon of man* as applied to *Chrift*.

ture, or one of the same kind and species; but never means the same *individual nature*. It constantly denotes a *distinct, individual being*. So if the parallel in the argument must be supported; 'tis time for christians to look to the necessary consequence thereof, *i. e.* that *Christ* in his divine person is a *distinct, individual being*, of the same kind with the Father, which necessarily makes them TWO GODS.

3. THERE is also another consequence that attends this argument if it hold, which I hope the friends of *Christ*'s proper Deity will be very unwilling to grant, viz. As the term *Son*, in all languages among mankind, carries in it the idea of *derivation* and *dependence*; to insist on a parallel here, gives the cause wholly to the *Arians*; who say, that as he is GOD, he is a *derived, dependent Being*.

THE philosophical gentlemen, who presume to account for the manner of the existence of GOD, having got eternal generation and procession into their scheme, are so confident of their orthodoxy on that head, that one of them tells us, " There " is one consideration, which, when thoroughly " pursued, will obviate all objections against it,— " that is, that as time is a mode of all creature " existence, so eternity is a mode of uncreated " existence."

Anf. THE more I pursue this proposition, the more I find it an imaginary phantom. Some modes are very precarious and uncertain, some are invariable: but it will perhaps suit the philosopher better to distinguish them into accidental, and essential,—or into accidents and qualities. Now, if eter-

nity

nity is a mode in the same sense to the Almighty, that time is to creatures, then it is merely accidental to him; for creatures, as Angels and men, shall exist when there is no time, when days, years, and all manner of duration by measure shall come to an end: And as time will cease to be a mode of creature existence, being thus accidental, if eternity be the same to uncreated existence, (which must be the sense of the proposition, if it has any) then the Almighty will (at least may) cease to exist, when creatures enter upon an endless stage of existence, and time is no more a mode of existence to them.

But if we consider time and eternity as *essential* modes of human and divine existence, the natural consequence is, that man will never get out of time; and eternity to them will never commence. Thus, if we consider these modes as *accidental*, the proposition lands us in *Atheism*; and if *essential*, we must give up *immortality*.

Again, if a mode be considered under the notion of an *accident*, then it cannot with any propriety be applied to the Deity; for there is nothing accidental in God, or to him: And if it is considered as a *quality*, then it supposes some *substratum*, and so we are just as far from the nature in which it adheres as we were.

In the sense this philosopher seems to understand modes, time is a mode of present existence to both God and man; for both exist in time; and eternity must be a mode of human existence, in as much as it shall exist in eternity, when time is no more. So that the proposition proves nothing to the purpose for which it was brought: And take it it even in its utmoſt latitude, the terms have no regard to the *nature* of either GOD or man abſtractedly conſidered. In time and eternity beings exiſt, and if eternity be a mode of the divine *nature*, as time is of the human, then it is no more than continual exiſtence. Eternity is not a property of *nature*, more than *time* is of the human *nature*.

BUT the difpute is not at all concerning the meaſure of duration; but the internal operations of the divine nature, which are two very different things. Tho' we ſhould grant that eternity is a mode of divine exiſtence, will it follow, that generation and proceſſion are other two modes of it? Is there any connection neceſſary betwixt theſe ideas? Tho' the ſcriptures affirm that GOD is eternal, they do not ſay he begat a Son from eternity. When eternity is called a mode of divine exiſtence, it ſtill fuppoſes a nature that exiſts, and the queſtion is not about modes, but operations of the divine nature. It might be aſked, whether there are three modes, or three natures that exiſted from eternity? And whether every one of theſe modes equally partake of the divine nature: Or, whether every nature hath not diſtinct modes of ſubſiſtence? However, if theſe modes exiſted from eternity, by *paternity*, *generation*, and *proceſſion*, we may conclude according to any ideas our language affords, or words to expreſs the ſubject, that the *Son* and *Holy Ghoſt* are eternally dependent upon, and inferior to the Father.

WHEN our philoſophical thoughts enter into eternity, either before or after time, they, like a drop of water in the ocean, are loſt. Our ideas of eternity are relative, and reſpect ſome meaſure of duration. When we apply them to exiſtence be-

fore

fore time, we cannot tell what it is. Our views can reach no further than some beginning of operation. We may go so far back as the creation of dependent beings, when GOD is said to have begun his works, but *then* we are within the limits of time or measurable duration. A step further we cannot go, without losing ourselves in conjecture. The modes of divine existence we can know no farther than they are displayed in that plan, where the designs of his government are exposed to our view, even the holy scriptures, which are the unerring guide concerning the knowledge of GOD.

BUT I must follow this gentleman one step further. He says, "That in the existence of GOD, "as well as in his essence, there is a *non-successivity*, "whether succession be applied to time or space; "and in respect of this non-successivity, eternal "generation can never imply or infer ground for "any of the objections made against it."

Ans. I CANNOT stay to examine this proposition critically, any further than it respects the present purpose: And tho' it is produced for an argument in favour of eternal generation, I think it makes directly against it. For where there is no *succession*, there can be no generation, so far as we have any ideas thereof; and where there is generation, it indisputably implies succession. By all the supporters of eternal generation, it is maintained that it is by *communication of essence*; now does not communication imply succession? Surely. —As there is no *succession in the divine essence* or nature, there can be no *communication of* the divine nature. Wherever there is a communication of the same nature, there must be a succession. There

may

may be a creation, without a succession in the creator; for the creature does not partake of the nature of the creator: But in begetting, the Son partakes of the same nature; yea, in the present case, it is maintained that the whole nature is communicated to the Son, by or from the Father; and if so, succession must be a necessary consequence thereof. How can that person be self-existent or non-successive, who derives his very *person* from another?! 'Tis no presumption to ask this of a philosopher, who dares investigate the unsearchable things of God.

PHILOSOPHY could not afford a better argument against eternal generation. Language does not afford us any idea of generation to a being, where there is not succession: And unless the scriptures inform us expressly of its being attributed to God, no arguments beside can prove it. There is no warrant from scripture to apply generation to Deity, but inferences taken from the words *begotten*, *Father*, and *Son*, which terms in scripture language do not imply generation; but do rather express acts of power, goodness, &c. and are applied to several persons beside *Christ*. "Is he not thy Father that bought thee? Have we not all one Father? I have begotten thee by the gospel. Onesimus, whom I have begotten in my bonds. Who hath begotten us again to a lively hope, by the resurrection of *Christ* from the dead, &c." But the phrase eternal generation or eternally begotten, is no where in revelation, nor any terms that in the least imply it.

WHEN the supporters of this scheme are pressed with certain difficulties that attend it, they frequently

quently tell us, that " Effence doth not beget effence, but the perfons in the effence." Tho' I have often both read and heard this, yet I could never learn the meaning of it, or in what refpect it favoured their caufe. " Effence doth not beget effence," that is, I fuppofe, one Deity doth not beget another Deity, which is an abfolute truth; here we are agreed.—" But the perfons in the effence." This paffeth my underftanding. If they mean by it, that the effence begets the divine perfons, then all the divine perfons muft be begotten; but this will wholly deftroy the fcheme, for according to it, only one perfon is begotten: Nay, the Father is exprefsly faid to be of none, neither begotten nor proceeding. To make this tally, we muft fuppofe only two perfons begotten in the effence: Still this will infer, that the *Holy Ghoft* has a two-fold manner of fubfiftence.—That the divine effence exifted prior to the divine perfons:—That there is a difference betwixt the perfons and the effence in Deity.: With many other fhocking confequences too grating to chriftian ears to mention!

But as confidering it in this light is fo very inconfiftent, let us view it in a glafs of their polifhing, who are the fupporters of the fcheme. " But the perfons in the effence?" That is, fay they, " The divine effence felf-exifts in the perfon of the Father, and the divine perfon of *Chrift* is begotten by the Father." Not to mention how ill the explication agrees with the propofition in terms; the one fays the *perfons* are begotten, the other that only one perfon is begotten, which makes it neceffary to provide another noftrum to account for the fubfiftence of the *Holy Ghoft*; but eternal proceffion is at hand for this purpofe. Then,

1. I must

1. I MUST obferve, 'tis marvellous! that fuch a demonftrative account can be given of the manner the Son and Holy Ghoft fubfift in Deity; but none of the Father's fubfiftence, further than that he hath it of himfelf, which is denied of the other two divine perfons; this certainly carries the direct idea of inorigination in the Father, and a derived perfonal fubfiftence in the other two perfons in Deity.

2. I OBSERVE, that it is impoffible upon this foundation, that the perfonal glory of the *Lord Jefus* can be equal with the Father's. For if the divine effence felf-exifts in the perfon of the Father, neceffarily his perfonal glory muft be *effential*, and felf-exiftent: But if the divine perfon of the *Lord Jefus* is begotten of the Father, his perfonal glory can neither be *effential*, nor felf-exiftent, but *communicated*, *derived* glory from another; which may be called *relative*; but not felf-exiftent glory. When there is fuch an *effential* difference in the manner the divine perfons fubfift in Deity, it is impoffible the *fame identical* glory can belong to all the perfons. The Father muft have a fupreme glory in Deity, which neither the Word nor Holy Ghoft have; how then can they be equal or the fame in perfection and glory? This leads me further to obferve,

3. THAT here the maintainers of the fcheme, and the *Arians* are almoft at one. The *Arians* fay, the divine perfon of the *Lord Jefus* was created; the others fay, he is begotten: Now, let the honeft inquirer fearch the fcriptures and try, if he can find fuch a difference betwixt a created and a begotten being, as we are bound to believe there is betwixt the higheft created or begotten glory

and the self-existent, unoriginated glory of the *Lord Jesus*. There is a near analogy betwixt what is said of the acts of GOD in creating and begetting; but none between any thing created or begotten, and self-existence. In this case, the *Arians* are the more consistent of the two, in denying the self-existence of the *Lord Jesus*, while they hold that he was created: But the others, while they hold that he was begotten, and had his personality communicated to him, at the same time say, that he is self-existent; which is a manifest contradiction in terms.

I MUST acknowledge here, that I have met with a modern author, an advocate for the scheme, more consistent than the rest. He wrote against the *Arian* hypothesis, and finding it impossible to reconcile the terms in the scheme with *self-existence*, which the *Arians* object, he very complaisantly (or rather blasphemously) yields the self-existence of both WORD and HOLY GHOST, and writes a chapter, intituled, " *The divine person of the Father* ONLY SELF-EXISTENT."—Astonishing! That men to support their darling notions of the *Lord Jesus* being a *Son, as he is God*, or that his divine person was begotten, which they can never prove from revelation, should thus give up his divine and self-existent glories into the hands of adversaries to his proper divinity! Tell it not in christian churches, lest *Arians, Socinians*, yea, *Atheists*, rejoice!

THERE are some other things said in favour of eternal generation, but they are so trifling, and so little to the purpose, that I shall not detain the reader with them, but come to the consideration of the only argument that can be produced in favour

vour of that doctrine, viz. " The ANTIQUITY of it, and the MULTITUDE of its efpoufers," which I fhall confider together.

Anf. IT fhould be well obferved, that revelation is the true antiquity: And what GOD hath revealed and prefcribed therein, has more authority for binding the confcience, than the dictates and traditions of multitudes in every age. There is a wide difference betwixt the primary antiquity and authority of the fcriptures, and that which is traditional, flowing only from the cuftom and obfervation of men. There is often too great regard paid to traditional antiquity, human authority, and the practice of multitudes, to the difhonour of the *facred word*.

ANTIQUITY, fimply confidered, can never add ftrength to a caufe, nor honour to any profeffion. *Sin* deferves not applaufe, becaufe committed in *paradife*, and bears date with the ancient records of *Mofes*. Nor fhould the *Romifh beaft* be held in repute, becaufe the myftery of iniquity began to work in the Apoftolic age. Human authority, if it has any weight, it is owing to the word of GOD; confequently the divine teftimony, which is more ancient than any other, is fufficient without it. The celebrated *Hervey* hath a very notable remark to the prefent purpofe. " Human autho-
" rity," fays he, " compared with the oracle of
" revelation, is like a range of cyphers connected
" with the initial figure, which, were they de-
" tached, would be infignificant; but in fuch fub-
" ordination are confiderable." A multitude of votaries cannot dignify a caufe, nor prove any doctrine to be true. If it could, *Chrift's* little flock
muft

must have been wrong in all ages, for they were always the fewest.

ANTIQUITY, a great number of espousers, and the sentiments of great, learned, and good men, have, like pilgrims' staves leaning against the walls of the noble structure of divine revelation, been too often, by unthinking multitudes, mistaken for the pillars that supported the magnificent fabric. It shews a cause to be weak indeed, when no better arguments can be brought to support it. Every argument of this kind will serve the *Popish* cause against reformation, as well as eternal generation: But the reformers despised the weapons of antiquity, learning, and multitudes of votaries, and betook themselves to the " *Sword of the Spirit, which is the word of God.*" Had they observed the same rule in forming their own *systems*, as in opposing *Popery*, Protestants at this time would have known less about eternal generation, than they know of transubstantiation: Such as were disposed to support the one, would have found it as difficult as *Papist's* did to maintain the other. The sum of all that can be said for either is, that it is old, and has been countenanced by all those who are best pleased with that in religion, which costs them least trouble to examine. I think a striking parallel may be drawn betwixt these sister mysteries, *transubstantiation* and *eternal generation:* But I must return to my argument of *antiquity* in favour of the latter.

I CONFESS it is a very ancient method of pleading, but always in favour of error and delusion. The *Jews* resolved to (*r*) " bake cakes, and burn incense

(*r*) Jer. vii. 18. and xliv. 17.

incenfe to the queen of heaven, as their *princes* and *fathers* had done, &c." (s) The *Samaritans* could plead the cuftom of their fathers, worfhipping in that mountain, for the ground of their own practice:—And how evident is it, that the *Jews* moft fatally preferred the (t) traditions of their *Rabbies*, to the doctrine of the bleffed JESUS. They thought it a fufficient reafon to reject him, becaufe none of the rulers and *Pharifees* believed in him.

BUT if we inquire into the antiquity of this hypothefis, and find it fall fhort of the period in which revelation was compiled and completed, it muft be of *human invention*, and with refpect to religion, deferves to be *antiquated*.

BESIDES the fcriptures, in the firft two centuries, there were no fettled forms of this doctrine of the Trinity. Every one had his own fpeculations, which were very different, and fome particularly odd. As Dr *Cave* fays, " Things were not defined then as they are now, by explicit articles, and nice propofitions." They not only differed from one another in their explications; but their beft writers cannot be made orthodox, according to what we *now* call *ftandard fyftems*, without forced and unnatural comments. To believe and agree in the fcripture account of the Trinity was thought fufficient, without differing about philofophical diftinctions concerning the *manner* of it: Till the *Sabellian* notion broke out, which feemed to explain the doctrine quite away; the fupporters thereof fuppofing the Father, Son, and Holy Ghoft, to be only three modes of operation: Or rather, one *Being*, under two modes of operation: Making the *Son* and *Spirit* mere attributes, or emanations from

(s) John iv. 20. (t) Matt. xv. 15. 2, 3. John vii. 48.

from the Supreme Being; the *Son* the wifdom or reafon of the Father, by which he made the world, &c. The *Spirit* a mere operation. This fcheme was fet up by *Praxeas*, about the end of the fecond century, at *Rome*: Afterwards by *Noetus*, at *Ephefus*. And about the year 257, it was fpread by *Sabellius*, at *Pentapolis* : From him it takes the name of *Sabellianifm*. The rife of this fect gave occafion for the church to be more exact in their terms and explications.—Notwithftanding, even in the middle of the third century, there feems not to be any fyftematic notion of the Trinity agreed upon in the church, which is evident from *Dionyfius* of *Alexandria*, who fell into herefy in writing againft *Sabellianifm*, not knowing what to fet up againft it, till better informed by *Dionyfius* of *Rome*.

The general opinion of thefe ancients, concerning the Son, was, " That he exifted in the Father from eternity, and at the creation, the Father put him without him, to create the world ; which they called *a bringing him forth*, *prolation*, or *generation*. Whilft he was in the Father, he was God from eternity, as every thing that is in God, is God ; but by his coming out from the Father, as *he became the Son of God*, fo from thence they ftiled him *God of God*." If they had any notion of his exifting as a perfon from eternity with the Father, it was either *potentially*, as *Eufebius* reprefents it in his account of the *Nicene* faith ; or, according to *Tertullian's* diftinction, as the *ratio* or *reafon* of the Father from eternity, 'till brought forth into *fermo* or *word*, and fo became diftinct from the Father, and as fuch a Son. That this was the general doctrine of the three firft centuries, is allowed by Dr *Waterland*, who cannot be fufpected any ways

inclinable

inclinable to betray the caufe of *eternal generation*. In this doctrine, the reader will obferve, we have nothing of an *eternal*, but a *temporary generation* only.

T H A T this was the notion which prevailed at the council of *Nice* is manifeft, in that they *anathematifed* all who fhould fay, " That he did not exift before he was *begotten*." The word *begotten* here, is not to be underftood of his generation of the *Virgin*, for this decree was made againft the *Arians*, who never denied his exifting before that; but it refers to the generation defcribed above. *Arius* and his followers, having explained this temporary generation into a real creation, maintaining *Chrift* to be a mere creature; the *fynod*, in oppofition to this, brought in the word *confubftantial*, to fhew, that tho' they thought the Son generated, yet he was not created as other creatures; but that he was God from eternity in the Father; tho' as a Son, he was generated and brought forth as above. This was the faith of the *Nicene* council in the fourth century; fo that no fuch notion of *eternal generation* was in the church for 300 years, as it is now explained.

A s to the original of the doctrine of *eternal generation*, I will not pofitively determine, but if we may depend upon the authority of fome, well acquainted with the antiquities of thofe periods, it was the invention of apoftate *Jews*; " which felf-contradictory notions, (faith a very eminent author) with other things of their production, have more confounded the chriftian faith, than any other pofitions :" And further fays, " that *Peter Galatine* cites the perfon whofe manufacture this doctrine was."

However

However, it is certain, that the doctrines of the primitive fathers are not the rule of our faith. I suppose very few of the greatest advocates for antiquity will acquiesce in that notion of theirs, " Of the Father bringing forth the Son of himself at the creation, and putting him without him ;" tho' it was general among them.

But if the antiquity of this doctrine should still be thought worthy of regard; and that it should have a place in our *credenda*, for its goodly age of 1400 years ; hen we are no more to judge of doctrines by their evidence, and agreeableness to scripture; but by their age; and if so, it would have been much to the advantage of this, that it had been 373 years older. Indeed 1400 years is a great age ; but if it began no sooner, it is not the true antiquity, and no more true for being of that age, than if it had been only 14 days old.

Still, say its friends, it is venerable for its age.—But should this be granted, some grey-headed errors, will for the same reason, claim the same respect. *Sabellianism* prevailed both in the *eastern* and *western* churches, 100 years before the council of *Nice* ; 'till *Arianism* took up the ball, and turned the waters of contention into another channel ; this was confirmed in several councils, and kept the seat of *orthodoxy* for many years. Now, 'tis certain these errors have a better right to the antique title, as the latter was the very occasion of inventing this hypothesis.—I do not know what is meant by the stream of antiquity, so much boasted of in favour of this scheme, if it be not that it has been favoured by the strongest party, and continued long; and if this be the rule to measure truth, the ancient errors should be naturalized among

among our fyftems : This is a fine argument in favour of *popery*, which, it feems, the longer it lafts, will be the better.

HAVING anfwered the arguments in favour of *eternal generation*, before I proceed to confider the texts produced for proof of it, I muft remove a prejudice which fome are ready to be overtaken with. It perhaps will be alledged, that tho' I have been finding fault with this *fcheme*, becaufe the terms therein are unfcriptural: Yet, in treating of the fame doctrine, I ufe terms not to be found in fcripture. To this I anfwer,

THAT tho' it would be highly commendable, in fuch fublime doctrines, if every one would both fpeak and write in the language of revelation as near as poffible, fince the truth is in danger, in a number of human confequences ; yet, it fhould be carefully obferved, that there is a great difference betwixt one bringing forth all the evidence he can for the illuftration of any particular truth, that others may be invited to embrace it, upon the evidence offered which hath perfuaded himfelf :— And another perfon or more, forming a fcheme of human deductions for a rule of faith to be impofed on others, upon the pain of damnation, whether they have any evidence to believe them or not. A miftake in the firft cafe remains with the author ; none is defired to believe further than they fee evidence to fupport the truth :—But an error in the latter cafe is fundamental, and of the moft dangerous confequence.

BESIDES, I do not altogether reject the terms in the fcheme, becaufe they are not in fcripture ; but for their being fuch as will bear no tolerable

rable meaning confiftent with what is revealed of that doctrine. For the fame reafon, I diflike fome explications of fcriptural phrafes, becaufe they have not the leaft degree of analogy with the texts they are pretended explications of: And tho' I have ufed fome terms not expreffed in fcripture, yet the fenfe is included therein by neceffary confequence. As for example, the words *plurality* and *Trinity*, tho' not in fcripture, yet the plain and undeniable meaning of them is—"Thefe THREE are one." The fame may be faid of the terms BEING, ESSENCE, EXISTENCE, &c. As to the terms SUBSISTENCE, and PERSON, which I have fometimes ufed, not becaufe I think in a ftrict fenfe they are properly applicable to the fubject, but for want of other words more proper in their ftead; and becaufe they will be beft underftood, long cuftom having eftablifhed the ufe of them. It might give uneafinefs to the minds of fome chriftians to introduce any new terms into this doctrine, and fo lofe that advantage propofed from any clearer ideas included in them.

I CONCEIVE it will be acceptable to moft of my readers, to be informed on what occafion thofe terms came to be applied to this fubject. For this purpofe let it be obferved, that about the fecond century, the prevailing part of the leaders in the church, in oppofition to the Sabellian doctrine, adopted the word *Hypoftafis* to exprefs the doctrine of the Trinity by, which was not till then ufed in that doctrine: And to appear as far contrary to Sabellianifm as poffible, they made it to fignify *fubftance*, which is the direct oppofite to that opinion they wanted to deftroy. But the difficulty which this arbitrary definition involved the caufe in foon appeared, from the neceffity of guarding againft againſt the other extreme: For the term *ſubſtance* led immediately into the notion of *three Beings* or *Gods*. In the heat of oppoſition, a general council was called, where it was determined, that the term *ſubſtance*, as applied to the Trinity, ſhould not ſignify a *diſtinct being*, or *ſeparate ſubſtance*, but ſomething more than a name; that is, ſomething *real* or *ſubſtantial*, which afterwards was called *ſubſiſtence*. This was ſtill defining without authority from revelation: But the *Latin* church, not ſatisfied with the word *Hypoſtaſis* being applied to the Trinity, brought in the word *Perſona* or *Perſon*, which continues to this day, tho' as little countenanced from ſcripture, in this application of it, as the other. † The word indeed is in our tranſlation of Heb. i. 3. No doubt in conformity to ſeveral hundred years cuſtom before. But that *Hypoſtaſis*, the word from which *Perſon* is taken, has no relation to that ſubject; and that *perſon* is not a proper tranſlation of it, I ſhall ſhew when we come to conſider that text.

ONLY allow me to obſerve here, that the word *perſon*, is not applied to any of the *divine three* in any place of ſcripture: But for as much as the properties

† If the word *perſon* is applied to the Trinity in that ſenſe which it is underſtood, and applied to finite beings, among whom it always implies a diſtinct underſtanding and will, as well as a diſtinct individual Being, and as the perſons are multipled, ſo are the diſtinct Beings: To aſſert three perſons in Deity in this ſenſe, and yet but one GOD, would be a groſs contradiction. *Arians* take the advantage of this difficulty in the uſe of the word *perſon*, againſt the orthodox; and the method they take to extricate themſelves, only involves them in more difficulties, being liable to the ſame, and other exceptions. They ſay, that the divine eſſence, ſubſiſts in a different manner in each of the three perſons, which is the foundation of their diſtinct perſonality: Or thus, the different manner that each perſon poſſeſſes the divine eſſence, the one as a *Father*, the other as a *Son*, and a third as *Holy Ghoſt*, is the foundation of their diſtinct perſonality. This certainly implies a difference of perſonal glory, and can never be maintained, but at the expence of the proper Deity of both the *Son* and *Holy Ghoſt*.

properties of real being and existence is attributed to each of them, the ancients no doubt thought they might safely use the word *hypostasis* with the above limitation, and the moderns the word *subsistence*, which they reckon the import of it so limited: And the sum of all that can be said for the use of the word *person* is, that real personal properties, powers, attributes, and works, are affirmed of *each* of them, and nothing said that is inconsistent with personality. Tho' all this should be granted oeconomically; yet it will by no means favour the use that is commonly made of the term; nor make it necessary that it should be used at all, since it is not so used in revelation. God hath revealed terms sufficient to express all he designed we should know of him: But if others will add to these the inventions of men, we must leave them to take their own way.

And observe further, that such terms as have been sanctified by men,—received upon their authority, and held sacred in religion, (tho' only the product of unguarded zeal, and opposition among parties, in which every one adopted such terms as seemed most contrary to the opinions they would have condemned) have been of ill consequence, both to such as have believed them, and those who have zealously opposed them. By the former, these terms have been received implicitly, without knowing how they were applicable to the subject; and yet so zealously defended, as often to issue in persecuting to death such as would not follow them in the dark. On the other hand, many of those who opposed the use of those terms, from the wrong application of them, have carried their opposition too far, not distinguishing betwixt the truth as made known in revelation, and as cloathed

with

with dark and unmeaning phrases by men. Consequently, the truth being abused by the one, have occasioned the denial of it by the other. To this cause, I refer all the opposition which has been made to the proper divinity of *Jesus Christ* by those called *Arians*, and others, which took its rise upon the first application of such terms to the doctrine of the Trinity. Had they restricted their opposition to such innovations, it had been laudable; but the history of 1400 years shews the case to be otherwise.

THOSE who have been called the orthodox, have also occasioned endless controversies concerning the Deity of *Jesus Christ*, by not properly distinguishing betwixt what is said of him in scripture, with relation to his inferior oeconomical character, and the proofs which support his proper Deity. Having accustomed themselves to confound these, *Arius*, and his followers, took the advantage of their applying the terms which belonged to the official oeconomical character of *Christ*, to the proof of his Deity; and from these, as premises, very justly concluded the arguments of the orthodox weak; and the consequence they drew was, that *Jesus Christ* was not properly GOD. The orthodox, instead of mending the fault in their own hypothesis, invented a *generation*, or *begetting of his divine person from all eternity*, which rather strengthened than answered the objections of the *Arians*, since that *filiation* plainly implied the *derivation of his person*. For tho' the generation or begetting be carried into eternity, (which is without authority from scripture) the terms themselves still prove it to have had a beginning.

THE premises the *Arians* build upon are granted
ed

ed by the orthodox: Here both are miftaken. The former are right in their conclufion from fuch premifes; but inconfiftent with fcripture by the miftake in the choice of their premifes. The latter are right in maintaining the proper Deity of *Chrift*; but inconfiftent with *themfelves* in the manner they pretend to fupport their caufe. The error of both lies, in not attending to the diftinction betwixt what relates to the inferior oeconomical character of *Chrift*, and the paffages from which his Deity may be more directly proved. The *Arians* commonly argue from the former, and thence conclude his inferior Deity to the Supreme God, which their premifes will very well bear; and which the orthodox might, and fhould grant without any danger to the truth, while there are other inconteftable evidences of his proper Deity, which is not liable to the exceptions commonly brought againft it. All the advantage the *Arians* have gained, is from the orthodox pretending to prove their caufe from arguments which have not the leaft relation to it: And the Deity of the Spirit has been denied and oppofed from the fame principles. Such are the woeful effects of the ancients, adding their own inventions to religion, and impofing them on the confciences of others!

SECT.

SECT. IV.

THE next thing to be confidered, is the paffages of fcripture generally brought to prove the *eternal generation* of the *Son of God*, and that the terms *Father*, *Son*, and *Holy Ghoſt*, are *natural, neceſſary,* and *internal* characters of *Deity*.

HERE the advocates for this doctrine are ſtrangely divided in their ſentiments. There are ſome texts applied as clear proofs of it, which others of them ſay have not the leaſt relation to the ſubject. Yea, ſome of them are ſo ſelf-denied, as plainly to contradict themſelves in different parts of their own works.—" A kingdom divided againſt itſelf cannot ſtand."—As there is no need to ſay much about ſuch texts as themſelves doubt of,— I ſhall endeavour to make it evident, that ſuch as are generally ſuſtained proofs of that doctrine, are nothing to the purpoſe; but rather favour that oeconomical ſenſe, which the ſcriptures repreſent theſe terms in.

THE firſt that ſhould claim our attention is that in the ſecond Pſalm: But as I have fairly demonſtrated, that it refers to *Chriſt*'s oeconomical fonſhip, in p. 155. I ſhall only deſire the reader to read what is there ſaid over again.

I MUST here notice, how ſtrangely a learned critic has tortured a paſſage in the 110th Pſalm, to make it favour the cauſe of *eternal generation*. The text ſays, " From (or *of*) the womb of the (early) morning, thou haſt (to thee, or thou ſhalt have, *marg.*) the due of thy youth." But he makes it read thus,—" *Of mine own eſſence before* the early morning,

morning, or *before the world was*, thou hadſt the due of thy youth, or birth; as noting his eternal generation before all worlds." Here the words " *mine own eſſence*, before the early morning," or as he interprets it, " before all worlds," are thruſt into the text, contrary to the very ſenſe and ſcope of the paſſage, that it might appear a proof of that doctrine which hath no better foundation in revelation to ſupport it. This is one text which our modern advocates for eternal generation acknowledge has no relation to it.

ANOTHER we have in the Proverbs, (*x*) " I was *ſet up* from everlaſting, from the beginning, or ever the earth was. When there were no depths, I was *brought forth*:—Before the mountains were ſettled; before the hills, was I *brought forth*." A learned modern Doctor affirms in one part of his writings, that this " is to be underſtood
" of the *eternal generation* and ſonſhip of *Chriſt*;
" and the repetition of the phraſe *brought forth*,
" partly ſhews the importance of it; it being a
" matter of *infinite* moment and concern, and de-
" ſerving the *ſtricteſt attention* and obſervation:
" And partly ſhews the certainty of it; the eter-
" nal generation of *Chriſt* being an *article of faith*
" *moſt ſurely to be believed*." But in another part of his works, the ſame author ſays, " This paſſage
" is a glorious proof of *Chriſt*'s *eternal exiſtence*,
" tho' not ſo clear a one of his *eternal Sonſhip*.
" The phraſes of *ſetting up, poſſeſſing, bringing forth*,
" and *bringing up*, ſeem rather to refer to his *media-*
" *torial office*." The Doctor's candor is very commendable, in making ſo fair a retreat. In great humility he would rather contradict himſelf, than
expoſe

(*x*) Prov. viii. 23, 24, 25.

expofe an article of faith moſt furely to be believed,—a matter of infinite moment,—to the charge of felf-contradiction. The terms in the paſſage fuit fo ill with his leading fentiment, " *That Chriſt is a Son, as he is God,*—that he was begotten as GOD, &c." if applied to it would wholly deſtroy the *important truth.* It was neceſſary either to apply them another way, or call in the affiſtance of figures, (or myſteries, the only remedies in fuch cafes of diſtreſs) which can never be accommodated or explained on fuch a principle, and muſt only involve the author in endleſs criticifms and debates, about words that have no meaning at all when fo applied.

WE have another fuppofed proof of eternal generation in the *Proverbs, (y)* " What is his name, and what is his Son's name, if thou canſt tell?" Which the fame Doctor paraphrafes thus, " *What* " *is his name?* That is his nature and perfections, " which are incomprehenfible and ineffable: And " feeing he is a Son of the fame nature with him, " fay what is his nature and perfections ? Declare " *his generation,* and the manner of it, his divine " *filiation,* and in what *claſs* it is."

THE *Doctor* makes a very unfuitable fupplement to the text, that it may feem to favour his caufe. It fays nothing about *generation* or *filiation.* Nor has it any relation to GOD, or *Jeſus Chriſt,* his Son, at all. † But tho' we ſhould grant they are intended here, and by *name* is meant *nature,* the queſtion will only refer to his nature and perfections, not his *generation,* and the *manner of it,*—not his *filiation,* and in what *claſs* it is? Befides, if generation

(y) Prov. xxx. 4.   † See p. 154.

neration muſt be forced into the text, the queſtion relates as much to the generation of the one, as the other. I ſay, if *name* here ſignify *generation*, as the *Doctor* ſays, it muſt refer to the generation of the *Father*, as well as the generation of the *Son*; which effectually deſtroys all his fine paraphraſe.

WHAT *Iſaiah* faith, is held as another proof of *eternal generation.*—(z) " He was taken from priſon and from judgment: and who ſhall declare his generation? For he was cut off out of the land of the living." This middle clauſe is very differently applied by commentators. Some to the incarnation of *Chriſt:*—Some to the eternal duration of his life after his reſurrection:—And others, both ancient and modern, apply it to his numberleſs offſpring, or ſpiritual ſeed. Any one of theſe is more conſiſtent, than to ſcrew up the meaning of the expreſſion to an eternal begetting of the divine perſon of the *Lord Jeſus*, as many inſinuate; which neither the words themſelves, nor theſe going before or following them, will by any means allow. The verſe before, and this, are a ſtriking deſcription of our Redeemer's ſurpaſſing humility, under the ſeveral ſteps of the *Jews* ſtubborn cruelty towards him.

THEREFORE, taking the words in connection, I think the following ſentiment is clearly pointed out: " Who ſhall declare his generation?" Who ſhall declare the perverſe obſtinacy, the wickedneſs, and injuſtice of that generation in which he lived?—So cruel as thus to oppreſs the innocent Lamb of GOD; againſt whom their ſtretched invention, tho' aſſiſted with diabolical malice, could
find

(z) Iſa. liii. 8.

find no charge worthy of puniſhment, or death. The Prophet therefore adds, "He was cut off out of the land of the living, (yet not for himſelf, as *Daniel* ſpeaks, for no crime of his own, but) for the tranſgreſſion of my people was he ſmitten." Which is a plain reaſon for both the depth of his humility in his voluntary ſufferings and death for his people, and the unaccountable cruelty of that crooked and perverſe generation the *Jews*, and *Roman* governors, who conſpired to crucify an innocent perſon, in whom they could find no fault. This ſenſe of the text is highly favoured by the character *Moſes* gives *Iſrael* in his time, whom he calls a (*a*) "crooked and perverſe generation." The language is almoſt the ſame in both texts.

But what will put this ſenſe of the text beyond all exception, and fix it as the only meaning thereof, is, that the ſame word Dor, which is here tranſlated *generation*, is through all the Old Teſtament put for a certain period of time; and the people that lived in that age or period,—a certain race or claſs of people, living at the ſame time, as in the laſt cited text; and alſo in theſe, (*b*) "One generation paſſeth away, and another generation cometh.—The Lord will have war with *Amalek* from generation to generation. Lord thou haſt been our dwelling place in all generations." In generation and generation. *marg.* Now, as the word Dor in theſe, and many other places, invariably ſignifies the ſame thing, and never the *act* or *manner* of *generation*, it is certainly ſufficient to ſettle the meaning of it in this text, eſpecially as the ſcope ſo evidently favours it: And

it

(*a*) Deut. xxxii. 5. (*b*) Eccl. i. 4. Exo. xvii. 16. Pſa. xc. 1.

it must be a base prejudice, that makes people impose a sense upon the text, which neither it, nor any similar one hath the least relation to.

As to *Nebuchadnezzar* saying, the (*c*) " form of the fourth, (whom he saw in the furnace) is like the *Son of God*," I have shewed, p. 154, that he could not mean *Christ* by what he said, and shall only add here, that it is very difficult to account for *Nebuchadnezzar*'s obtaining such knowledge of *Christ*; but more so, how his words can be made a proof of eternal generation. But should his knowledge of *Christ* be admitted; he that is mentioned as the *Son of God*, *Nebuchadnezzar* calls a *man*, which is very inconsistent with the notion of his being *God*, as he is a *Son*. The words would rather infer, that his manhood is included in the notion of sonship, which belongs to his inferior character, as he is called " the *Angel of the God* of *Shadrach*, &c." But I wish them much good of all the help they can get from *Nebuchadnezzar* to their weak cause; for I chuse not that any should imagine the cause I contend for stands in need of any such assistance.

The next text is in *Micah*,—(*d*) ". Out of thee (*Bethlehem*) shall he come forth into me, that is to be ruler in *Israel:* Whose *goings forth* have been from of *old, from everlasting*." I own this is spoken of *Christ* the *Messiah*; but to apply it to the manner of his existence, or an act of eternal generation, is doing the greatest injustice to the text, which mentions his GOINGS FORTH in the plural, and not any *one act:* Besides, it cannot be meant

(*c*) Dan. iii. 25. (*d*) Micah v. 2.

meant of the *Father's begetting* the *Son*, since the *goings forth* are spoken as acts of CHRIST, and not of the FATHER.

It may refer to the egress of his wisdom and love, concerning the future salvation of his people, who were chosen in him. (*e*) " For verily, he was fore-ordained before the foundation of the world, but was manifest in these last times." Or to the exercise of his wisdom and power, in making and governing all things.—(*f*) " For by him were all things created, that are in heaven, and that are in earth." If we understand the Prophet *Micah* in this sense, the Apostle *John* will be the best commentator in the beginning of his gospel.

These *goings forth* may also include the great works he performed, and remarkable appearances he made to *Adam*, *Noah*, *Abraham*, &c. And this sense of his goings forth, is no way contrary to the other clause, " from everlasting;" for there seems plainly to be a gradation in the two parts of the sentence. So that these appearances he made, with his works of creation and government, may be pointed out in his " goings forth of old," which agree well with an expression of the Psalmist on the same subject.—(*g*) " O GOD, when thou *wentest forth* before thy people," &c. and also with the scripture use of the word *of old*: And the other idea of his councils of love, wisdom, and grace, concerning his people, will be meant in his " *goings forth from everlasting.*" Now, instead of that text being a proof of *eternal generation*, it rather exhibits his occonomical character, set up from everlasting as the mediator, guide, and governor

(*e*) 1 Pet. i. 20. (*f*) Col. i. 16. (*g*) Psa. lxviii, 7.

vernor of his church; together with the difpenfations of his grace and goodnefs to them, in ancient ages of the world.—It is the fame whom *Micah* fays fhould be born in *Bethlehem*, and be ruler in *Ifrael*, which is none other than *Jefus Chrift*, the Son of God.

I have now done with the texts in the Old Teftament, which are brought to fupport eternal generation, and I think he will be very wife that can find it in any one of them. The firft text in the New Teftament that claims our confideration, is the anfwer of *Peter* to his mafter's queftion, "whom fay ye that I am? *Peter* anfwered, thou art *Chrift*, the Son of the living God." The reader will remember, that this text was confidered at fome length, as an objection againft that fenfe of *Chrift*'s fonfhip, which I formerly proved. To what was faid thereon, beginning at p. 184, I beg leave to add in this place:

That it increafes my aftonifhment, to find fo many who profefs the higheft regard for the divine glory of *Chrift*, and the *Holy Ghoft*, and feem to abhor the conceits of fuch as are for accounting them no more than inferior Deities: Yet agreeing with them in the very principles on which they build their fcheme, particularly in limiting the term living God, to the perfon of the *Father*, exclufive of the *Word* and *Holy Ghoft*. This is the certain confequence of all they fay for their caufe, from this and feveral other fimilar texts. Indeed the *Arian* fcheme, and that called the *Orthodox*, both require it fhould be fo; and without this be fuppofed, they muft both fall. The *Arian* fays, he is God, but inferior to, and created by the *living* God:—The *Orthodox* fay, he is a *Son*, as he is *God*, and was begotten

gotten by the *living* GOD. In both, the term *living God* is suppofed to be peculiar to the *Father*, exclufive of *Chrift* and the Spirit. Dr *Clark*, the modern champion for the *Arian* caufe, lays it down as a maxim, " that the word GOD in fcripture, " never fignifies a complex notion of more perfons " than one; but always means one perfon only, viz. " The perfon of the Father fingly, or the perfon " of the Son fingly."

Now, if this is granted them, all other difficulties they reckon eafily furmountable in proving the inferior Deity of *Chrift*; for, fay they, "all thefe terms, *living God, only wife God, one God, great God*, &c. muft be limited to the Father only, confequently all that is faid of *Chrift* as GOD, is in an inferior fenfe, as the Father's fervant, inftrument, &c. And the fupporters of the other fcheme alfo, muft in confiftency with their own terms, explain every text where the *Son of God* is mentioned in favour of the *Arian* hypothefis. For if the divine perfon of *Chrift* be included in the term *living God*, or in the term *God*, where he is mentioned as the *Son of God*, then their whole fcheme is deftroyed; and all I have been contending for granted, viz. That it is under another confideration that he is called *Son*, than that wherein he is called *God*.

THE *Holy Ghoft* by this hypothefis, muft be alfo excluded from the glory of this title *living God*. Peremptorily to exclude him, is the fame as to fay, he is not the *living God*. Yet for the honour and fafety of this fcheme, excluded he muft be, let the confequence be ever fo dangerous to truth; for to include the *Holy Ghoft* in this term, makes the

divine

divine person of the *Lord Jesus*, to be the Son of the *Holy Ghost*, which will wound this *human scheme* in a very tender part, viz. that of his being begotten only by the person of the Father. Now, let the admirers of this scheme, chuse whether they will degrade the divine persons of the *Word* and *Spirit*, by denying them the honour of this title the *living God*, which is the same with saying they are not God; or expose their human hypothesis to the charge of self-contradiction, which, if maintained, sets revelation at variance with itself. Every impartial reader must account it an amazing infatuation in favour of that darling notion, which has not the least countenance in scripture; that to support it, they will give up the glory of *Christ* into the hands of such as affirm that he is not properly God. As for my own part, in all the 25 texts where this term living God is mentioned, I see no reason why the *divine three* may not be included, without doing violence to the analogy of faith, or the scope of the passages.

There are two passages in *John*,—(*h*) which a great deal of weight is laid upon, in support of *Christ* being a Son, as he is God. Our *Lord*, in the course of his teaching had asserted, that God was his Father. The *Jews*, through their malice and prejudice, charge him with blasphemy; for according as they drew the inference, by saying that God was his father, he made himself equal with God: And taking it for granted, that their inference was just, the advocates for eternal generation conclude, that *Christ* is God, as he is a *Son*.

Ans. I f

(*h*) John v. 18, 19. and x. 30,—39.

Anf. IF our *Lord's* answers to the *Jews* in both places be carefully attended to, especially the first, which serves to explain the other, it will appear quite different from what either the *Jews* or their modern friends do suppose. As to the first, we are told that *Jesus* said, "my Father worketh hitherto, and I work." For this the *Jews* sought to kill him, because he said GOD was his father, making himself equal with GOD. Now, hear his defence, "Then answered *Jesus*, and said unto them, verily, verily, I say unto you, the Son can do nothing of himself, but what he seeth the father do.—For the Father loveth the Son, and sheweth him all things that himself doth: And he will shew him greater works than these, that ye may marvel.—I can do nothing of myself, I seek not mine own will, but the will of the father that sent me." In this reply of our *Lord*, it is very plain that he contradicts their inference, by declaring in the strongest terms his inferior character, *as a Son.* As GOD, he knows all things of himself,—can do all things by his own power and will,—is supreme and independent,—and his knowledge, will, and power are the same, not different from, much less subordinate to the Father's: But all this he expresly denies of himself *as a Son;* therefore, if we will believe JESUS, rather than the malicious *Jews*, he is not *God*, as he is a *Son:* Or he must be such a GOD as some think he is, subordinate, inferior, and dependent, for these are plain in his character of himself, as a Son. So that this passage is a direct proof of his sonship belonging to his inferior character, and therefore may be added to the other arguments to that purpose above.

As to the other passage, it must be of the same import, if one place may be allowed to explain another.

another. Here alſo they accuſe him for calling himſelf the Son of GOD; and he had certainly the ſame notion of his own ſonſhip now as formerly, ſo that we might here ſhew his ſenſe of ſonſhip, from his former anſwer to a ſimilar charge againſt him; but as he replies in other terms, we ſhall conſider how far they favour the cauſe they are brought to ſupport.

IT is obſervable, that tho' the character of the *Meſſiah* be ſo exhibited in the Old Teſtament, that ſome among the *Jews* might probably know he was GOD, as well as man: Yet they were in general ſhamefully ignorant of his true character. For had they thought of his Deity, that queſtion of our *Lord*, would not have ſilenced them, " If the *Meſſiah* be *David*'s Son, how could *David* call him LORD?" Or, " If *David* calls him LORD, how is he his Son?" The leaſt thought of his Deity, would have eaſily reſolved this difficulty; but it is evident they had no ſuch notion of the *Meſſiah*. The deſign of theſe wicked *Jews*, was to bring the higheſt accuſations againſt our Saviour, and to load him with the groſſeſt calumnies that their wit or malice could draw from his words or actions, " Laying wait for him, and ſeeking to catch ſomething out of his mouth, that they might accuſe him." If he ſpake of his kingdom, it is ſedition and rebellion, he is an enemy to *Cæſar*:—If he calls GOD his Father, their malice conſtrues it blaſphemy, in making himſelf equal with GOD: And ſhall a conſequence ſtrained from our Saviour's words by malicious *Jews*, be ſuſtained an only warrant for a " doctrine of the *utmoſt conſequence*, an article of faith moſt *ſurely to be believed*, on which the ſalvation of our ſouls depends?"

AND

AND that the consequence was strained, is evident from our LORD's reply, "*Jesus'* answered them, is it not written in your law; I said, ye are GODS? If he called *them* GODS, unto whom the word of GOD came; and the scriptures cannot be broken: Say ye of him, whom the Father hath *sanctified*, and *sent* into the world, thou blasphemest, because I said, I am the SON OF GOD?" Where we may observe, (1) That he doth neither plainly own nor deny himself to be the true GOD.—. Yet, (2) If he had not been the true GOD, he would have renounced their conclusion of equality with GOD; but he only denies the justness of their inference, that his calling himself the *Son of God*, was in consequence making himself GOD. Since he admits the one, we may safely conclude he is GOD; and seeing he denies the other, we may fairly infer that his *sonship* does not denote his Deity. For (3) it is plain, his design in the answer he gave, was to refute the calumny of the *Jews*, and shew the weakness of their inference, that the name *Son of God* does necessarily signify one *equal with God*. The argument our LORD uses here, is what is called *á minori ad majus*; putting the reason of his more unquestionable right to this title, upon the superiority of his character and mission, or his more immediate commission from the Father, than those Prophets, Kings, and Judges, who were called GODS, from the word of GOD coming to them. The argument plainly runs thus, They who were originally in and of this world, were made Prophets, Teachers, and Kings, merely by the word of GOD coming to them, receiving their commission by some voice, vision, divine message or inspiration, and they were called GODS: Therefore the Messiah, who was not originally of this world,

but

but was sanctified, or anointed, set apart, and sent immediately by God himself into this world for such incomparable purposes, may surely be called the *Son of God*, without danger of blasphemy. In short, if they were called *Gods*, the Messiah may well be called the *Son of God*. (4) It is very remarkable, that tho' the *Jews* built part of their accusation upon his saying, "I and my Father are one," yet our Lord does not directly answer to these words, because they bear an intimation of his Deity: But applies himself to answer that part of it, taken from his calling *God his father*, and himself the *Son of God*; denying the charge, and refuting their inference, no doubt, to teach them and us both, that the term *Son of God*, does not prove *equality with God*.

Indeed, if the character *Son of God* here, means his Deity, it must infer his equality with God, as the *Jews* inferred: But besides the difficulty, or rather impossibility of the divine nature of *Christ* being *sanctified*, or *anointed*, and *sent*; which he says he was, *as a Son*; it plainly destroys the whole force of our blessed Saviour's argument, and concludes his defence trifling; and consequently, leaves the accusation of the malicious *Jews* in full force against the *Lord Jesus Christ!*

To illustrate this a little further, it should be observed, that the question betwixt our Lord and the *Jews*, was not whether the Messiah was a *divine person* or not; but whether he to whom they were speaking, was the *Messiah* or not. Therefore, when he assumed an epithet, which, as used in the Old Testament, was characteristical of the *Messiah*, they charge him with blasphemy; for, he as they supposed, being only a mere man, had assumed a

title

title which the scriptures appropriated to the promised *Messiah*, whom the same scriptures call the *mighty* GOD. " The GOD of the whole earth shall he be called." To be the *Messiah*, and to be the *Son of God*, was reckoned by the *Jews*, and may be by us christians, the same. The Psalmist applies them both to the same person in the second Psalm; and in the New Testament, the same arguments are used to prove the one as the other. The Old Testament pointed forth; and the Apostles preached the *Messiah*, the power and the wisdom of GOD. As in the former, *Son of God* was a known character of the *Messiah*, so the Angel intimated under that term to the *virgin*, that she was to be the mother of the *Messiah*. " The holy thing which shall be born of thee, shall be called the SON OF GOD." This she understood to be the promised *Messiah*, and therefore says in her song, " He hath holpen his servant *Israel*, in remembrance of his mercy, as he spake to our fathers, to *Abraham*, and to his seed for ever."

Now, tho' the *Jews*, through their traditions, and hopes of a *Messiah*, that would bring them temporal glory, had not so clear views of the divinity of the promised *Messiah*, nor the spiritual nature of his kingdom, as the Old Testament pointed out: Yet, from the known characters of the *Messiah*, in these oracles; and the special application of the term *Son* to him, when they find our LORD assuming those to himself, whose appearance was so unlike the *Messiah* they expected, might charge him with blasphemy through the violence of their prejudice. To be *the Son of God* by way of eminence, was to be the *Messiah*, and *vice versa* in the *Jews* sense. " Thou art the *Son of God*; thou art the *King of Israel*. Art thou the *Christ*,

Chrift, or *Meffiah*, the *Son of the bleffed?* Thou fhalt call his name *Jefus*,—and he fhall be called the Son of the higheft." This, one would think, is more evidently the fenfe of the *Jews*, in their difpute with our LORD, than that they drew a logical inference from the nature and quality of *generation*, confidered abfolutely in GOD.

THE 3d and 4th verfes of *Paul*'s introduction to his epiftle to the *Romans*, is another paffage that has been tortured by all the art of criticifm, to make it prove natural fonfhip. It is fcarcely credible, what different terms of interpretation the words have got to make them anfwer that purpofe; whereas if the fcope be attended to, it is both plain in itfelf, and evidently points forth another meaning than is commonly put upon it. The whole paragraph reads thus : " *Paul*, a fervant of *Jefus Chrift*, called to be an Apoftle, feparated unto the gofpel of GOD, (which he had promifed afore by his Prophets in the holy fcriptures) concerning his Son *Jefus Chrift* our LORD, who was made of the feed of *David*, according to the flefh, and declared (determined) to be the Son of GOD with power, according to (by) the Spirit of holinefs, (and) by the refurrection from the dead : By whom we have received grace and Apoftlefhip, for (to the) obedience to (of) the faith among all nations for his name : Among whom, are ye alfo the called of *Jefus Chrift*."

IN this introduction, the Apoftle calls himfelf a *fervant* of *Jefus Chrift* ; and to invite the faints at *Rome* to give proper attention to what he was about to write to them, he points forth in feveral diftinct particulars, the truth and importance of his mafter's character,

character, and concludes with their particular interest therein. He proves and illustrates the authenticity of the gospel he was appointed to preach concerning *Jesus Christ*, the *Son of* GOD, (1) From the authority of GOD, who had sent the Prophets under the Old Testament, to proclaim by promise the advent of his Son. (2) From the accomplishment of these promises, in raising up *Jesus* of the seed of *David*, according to the flesh, which was so often foretold: And as the great dispute at that time, was, whether that same *Jesus* was the *Messiah*, the *Son of* GOD and *Saviour*, that GOD promised by the Prophets, he proceeds to put that matter beyond doubt.

FIRST, he says, it was *determined by the Spirit of holiness*. (1) It is manifest that an extraordinary measure of the Spirit attended him in all the great things he did, which are just so many attestations from GOD of the truth of his character, as both himself and his Apostles frequently alledge. (*n*) " For he whom GOD hath sent, speaketh the words of GOD: For GOD giveth not the Spirit by measure unto him. (*o*) But if I cast out Devils by the Spirit of GOD, then the kingdom of GOD is come unto you. (*p*) GOD *anointed Jesus* of *Nazareth* with the Holy Ghost, and with power; who went about doing good, and healing all that were oppressed of the Devil: For GOD was with him. Until the day in which he was taken up, after that he, through the Holy Ghost, had given commandments unto the Apostles whom he had chosen." (2) He was determined to be the SON OF GOD, by that divine effusion of the Spirit upon the Apostles at *Pentecost*, which their now ascended master

(*n*) John iii. 34. (*o*) Matt. xii. 28. (*p*) Acts x. 38. and i. 2.

master had promised to send when he went away. This in the most eminent manner confirmed the truth of his character as the Sent of GOD; because it had been promised by GOD in the Old Testament, and expected by the *Jews* as a part of the glory of the *Messiah*'s kingdom. *Peter* tells the astonished spectators, that what they saw and heard was the same that *Joel* foretold. *Jesus* himself commanded his disciples to tarry at *Jerusalem*, until they were endowed with the Spirit: And the event happening so soon after his ascension, in so striking and visible a manner, must be the clearest demonstration of his being the sent and chosen of GOD: Or, as the Apostle hath it in the text, it "determined him to be the SON OF GOD with power." See more of this, Part 2. sect. 5.

SECONDLY, another proof which he says determines him to be the SON OF GOD, is his *resurrection from the dead.* The Old Testament Prophets had said a great deal about the glory and perspicuity of the kingdom and reign of the *Messiah*, who was to be the seed of *David*;—*Christ* himself frequently affirmed that he would rise from the dead.—(*q*) "The son of man shall be betrayed to the chief Priests,—and they shall condemn him to death,—and the third day he shall rise again." Yea, when the *Jews* tempted him to give a proof of his being the *Messiah*, he puts the whole upon his *resurrection*, saying, (*r*) "destroy this temple, and in three days I will raise it up: But he spake of the temple of his body." Now, as the whole was without dispute exactly accomplished, it amounts to the clearest evidence of his being the true *Messiah*, that can possibly be supposed. The Apostle

---

(*q*) Matt. xx. 18, 19. (*r*) John ii. 19, 21. Matt. xii. 38,—41.

Apoſtle ſaw the great importance of it, when he puts the truth of the whole chriſtian religion upon it. (*s*) " If *Chriſt* be not riſen, then is our preaching vain, and your faith is alſo vain." And here he ſays, by this he was " *determined to be the Son of* God."

THIRDLY, as a further demonſtration of the power and precious effects of this truth, that he is the Son of God, he had beſtowed the grace of Apoſtleſhip upon *Paul*, and others, that they might ſpread the goſpel among the nations, to bring many into the obedience of faith in his name ; among which converts, the ſaints at *Rome*, to whom he wrote the epiſtle, were living inſtances of the power of the truth ; as he ſays, " *Among whom are ye alſo the called of Jeſus Chriſt.*"

As the above is the plain ſcope of this paſſage, it muſt be a clear demonſtration that the ſonſhip of *Chriſt* refers to the oeconomy of redemption, as the execution of that plan in its ſeveral parts, are here brought to prove the truth of his *ſonſhip*, otherwiſe the reaſoning of the Apoſtle appears very trifling. For what analogy can be ſuppoſed betwixt the proofs here alledged by *Paul*, and a *natural ſonſhip*, or *Chriſt* being *a Son, as he is God*? What relation have his riſing from the dead,—ſending the Holy Ghoſt,—giving commiſſion to Apoſtles,—and converting the *Gentile* nations, to his *being eternally begotten as a perſon in Deity*? This notion, tho' it were true, could have no manner of relation to any part of redemption, without ſuppoſing it neceſſary in the nature of God to redeem mankind : But as this is abſurd, it follows,

R r that

(*s*) 1 Cor. xv. 14.

that this text is a manifest proof of *Christ*'s *oeconomical sonship*, and can have no relation to a *natural sonship*, or *eternal generation*, for which it hath been so often alledged as a proof.

There is another text in this epistle frequently pressed into the same service.—(*t*) "He that spared not his own Son, but delivered him up for us all, how shall he not with him also freely give us all things." Here we are told, that the word *proper* should be added to *Son*, which they affirm is the same with *natural Son*. It would be needless to expose the weakness of this way of reasoning, since it is so evident in the text itself, that the sonship supposed, must be taken in a sense consistent with what is predicated of the Son, which is that great work he was given by God to finish, for the redemption of his people; this limits the sense to an oeconomical sonship. But his being *given,—delivered up by God,*—his *sufferings* and *death* for his people, are ideas not very consistent with *pure Deity*.

Where the *Lord Jesus* is called the *image of* God, it is imagined the character belongs to him as a divine person, and consequently favours the doctrine of natural sonship; but I must be allowed to differ from this opinion. The phrase is but thrice used in our translation, (*u*) "*Christ*, who is the *image of* God—Who is the *image* of the *invisible* God, the first born of every creature.—The brighness of glory, and the express *image* of his person." (*Hypostasis*.)

Now, the *Lord Jesus* cannot be the *image of* God, either in his divine nature, or *divine personality*.

(*t*) Rom. viii. 32.   (*u*) 2 Cor. iv. 4.   Col. i. 15.   Heb. i. 3.

ality. ‡ Not the firſt, for the ſelf-ſame numerical nature or eſſence, is one and the ſame in all the divine perſons, and ſo he would be as much the *image* of *himſelf*, as of the *Father* : And is there any propriety in ſaying a thing is the *image of itſelf ?* It amounts to no more in the preſent caſe, than ſaying the *divine nature* is the *image* of the *divine nature*.

AND according to the ſcheme itſelf, the *divine perſonality* of the Son, cannot be the *image* of the *Father's perſonality*; for it maintains *Chriſt* to be a divine perſon, as he is a SON; which, if true, makes it impoſſible that *as ſuch*, he can be the *image* of the FATHER; for *filiation* is by no means an *image* of *paternity*. Nay, *ſonſhip* is the very reverſe or contrary to *fatherhood* ; and it is not to be imagined, how contrary characters can be the *image* or reſemblance of each other. Beſides, his ſonſhip or divine perſonality is ſaid to be communicated by, or derived from the Father ; now, it is a contradiction in terms, to ſay that a *communicated* or *derived* manner of ſubſiſtence, is the *image* or reſemblance of an *underived*, *unoriginated* manner of ſubſiſtence. This the Father's muſt be, as he is of *none:* That the Son's muſt be, as he is *of the Father*, as to his divine perſon, if the human ſcheme be true.

BUT again, the text ſays, *Chriſt* is the image of the *inviſible* GOD, which term muſt include the three in Deity,—all that is called GOD. Now, as the perſons in Deity, and the divine eſſence in each

perſon,

‡ The reader will ſee, I hope, the neceſſity I am under to uſe the language of the human ſcheme in this third part, tho' I do not otherwiſe approve of many of the terms ſo applied.

person, must be *alike invisible*; he who is the image of the *invisible God*, cannot be so abstractedly, but as he manifests, exhibits, represents, or makes known the *invisible God* to men; this is none other than the LORD JESUS in his complex character as EMMANUEL, GOD in our nature, as I shewed above.

As for the phrase *essential image*, so frequent in systems, it is void of meaning,—there is no countenance in scripture for it; and among men there can be no rational ideas affixed to it. Therefore to talk of an *essential image*, must be as good sense as to tell us of *substantial forms*, another unmeaning phrase used in treating this subject, both are absurd in *Ontology*, or the doctrine of the properties of being in the abstract. It seems very strange, that the abstruse, self-contradictory, and unintelligible phrases among mankind, should be chosen to clothe divine mysteries, (or rather to make mysteries of plain truths) and the people commanded to believe them under that dress, as articles of faith, at the peril of their souls! Does the adopting such phrases into schemes of divinity make them good sense? Or, must the people's faith be so implicit as to receive for truth what their leaders are pleased to dictate; tho' they can neither reconcile their notions with scripture, reason, nor good sense? But to return:

CHRIST, as he is GOD, cannot be the *image of GOD*: Because the image is different from, and inferior to the original: But the LORD JESUS, neither in his divine nature, nor divine person, is different from, nor inferior to the Father. He hath the same divine nature, and in his person he is equal in all
divine

divine glory and perfection.—Moreover, to say *Chrift*, as a divine perſon, is the *image of* God, is too low a character of him as God, when it is conſidered, that every man is called the *image of* God. There is no way of making this opinion conſiſtent with any ideas we can have, but by ſuppoſing *two* Gods, the one the *image* and repreſentation of the other, and inferior to him, which is the ſum of the *Arian* hypotheſis.

The reader will remember that I ſhewed, at p. 172, in what reſpects *Chriſt* may be called the *image of* God, agreeable to his œconomical, ſubordinate character, and no ways inconſiſtent with his divine glory and perfections. To which I ſhall here add, that he is the image of God as he reveals, makes known, or repreſents God, to men, " Who (the Apoſtle ſays) dwelleth in light, which no man can approach into, whom no man hath ſeen, or can ſee." This he doth as Emmanuel, the medium or mirror of all we know or enjoy of God. It is very plainly expreſſed in Col. i. 13.— " That God's dear Son (Son of his love, *marg.*) is the image of the inviſible God." The ſame into whoſe kingdom the ſaints are tranſlated,—with whom they are fellow heirs,—in whom they have redemption through his blood,—who is the head of the body, the church, the firſt-born from the dead,—in whom all fulneſs dwells,—and who made peace through the blood of his croſs. He, ſays the Apoſtle " is the image of the inviſible God." But to reaſon that he is the image of God, as a Son, and as a Son he is God, is to deſtroy this part of his character altogether, and ſay, " as God he is the *image of* God," that is, either God is the image of himſelf,—or, one God

is

is the image of another—or in the most favourable acceptation, one in Deity is visible, another is invisible.

WE now come to the first chaper of the *Hebrews*, where it is said of the SON, that he is "Heir of all things—the brightness of glory, and the express image of his person,—that he made the worlds, and upholds all things,—that he was made so much better than the Angels, as he hath by inheritance obtained a more excellent name than they—Angels are commanded to worship him,—and he is called GOD: Thy throne, O GOD, is for ever and ever." All these expressions are supposed proofs of natural sonship, or that *Jesus Christ* is GOD, as he is a SON. It is argued that the things said of the SON, are proper only to GOD; therefore he is GOD, as he is a SON. But it is evident by a little consideration, that this conclusion has no countenance, either from the scope of the Epistle in general,—this first chapter in particular,—or the several particulars here attributed to the *Son*; all which I shall consider very concisely.

THE Apostle wrote this epistle to the *Hebrews*, who had embraced christianity; yet were so far prejudiced in favour of *Mosaic* rites and ceremonies, as to think them necessary to be joined to the gospel of *Christ*. On account of their professing christianity, they suffered a kind of persecution from their gainsaying brethren, which, with their own prejudices, were ready to weaken their attachment to, and endanger their apostatizing from the profession of the christian religion. To prevent this, and remove their prejudices, the Apostle introduces a variety of arguments to prove the christian dispensation to be transcendently more excellent

excellent than that under the Old Teſtament. He gives them a glorious deſcription of *Chriſt* in his complex character as EMMANUEL,—in his *offices* as the great *Legiſlator* and *Adminiſtrator* of the oeconomy of GOD in creation, providence, and redemption; and particularly in his offices of *Prophet*, *Prieſt*, and *King*. He proves at large that *Chriſt* was greater than *Angels* :—A greater lawgiver than *Moſes* :—A greater Prieſt than *Aaron* :— A greater prince than *Melchiſedec*. He points out to them the fatal conſequences of Apoſtacy, the bleſſings of perſeverance in the faith, and concludes the whole with a pathetic exhortation to ſteadfaſtneſs.

IN this firſt chapter he proſecutes a part of this great plan, and mentions ſeveral things concerning *Chriſt*, who is the great ſubject of the epiſtle, which infer moſt evidently that he is truly and properly GOD, as well as man : But as the Apoſtle's ſcope is to ſhew the excellency of EMMANUEL above *Angels*, *Moſes*, &c. the whole of his reaſoning muſt be viewed as deſcriptive of him in that character, *as God manifeſt in fleſh*, with a connotation of his offices, and the term *Son of God*, muſt be limited to that ſenſe, conſiſtent with the ſcope of the epiſtle.

SHOULD it be aſked, what is the Apoſtle's ſcope in this firſt chapter ? The anſwer is briefly given in the contents of our *Engliſh* common Bibles, " CHRIST *preferred to Angels*." *Chriſt*, the *Son of God*, is the ſubject, the whole is a deſcription of him. But if he is ſpoken of as *God* under the title *Son*, then the whole is a deſcription of Deity abſolutely conſidered. Now can any one ever

ever imagine, that the Apoſtle would write two whole chapters to prove that the *eternal God* was greater than *Angels*, and a third to prove that he was greater than *Moſes ?* What occaſion was there for it? Who ever denied that GOD was ſuperior to all thoſe the *Son of God* is contraſted with in this epiſtle? The queſtion with the unconverted *Hebrews* was not about what GOD was; but who *Jeſus* of *Nazareth* was? Whom they ſuppoſed only a *mere man*, and none of the beſt neither; not the promiſed *Meſſiah*, but an impoſtor: And if we will not grant that the Apoſtle is here vindicating the character of the *Meſſiah* from the falſe charges of the *Jews*, but will confine the term *Son* to his *Deity*, we plainly affirm, that he took all this pains to prove what no body denied, and what had not the leaſt relation to his purpoſe; except we abſurdly ſuppoſe, that he deſigned to inculcate the notion of TWO GODS.

WE ſhall now more particularly conſider the phraſes uſed here by the Apoſtle, which have been commonly ſo rendered and interpreted, as to make his meaning included in them quite obſcure; and like the dark ſide of the cloud which was turned towards the Egyptians, the character of *Chriſt* given from them, has been rather *confounding* than *edifying*. They have been generally forced in as proofs of his *eternal generation*, whereas if they are carefully conſidered, they will be found to prove a very different doctrine: For our ideas are confined to the character of *Chriſt* as Emmanuel, concerned in the work of our ſalvation, from the conſideration of theſe very expreſſions being applied to him, which have been ſo inadvertently perverted to other purpoſes.

IN verses 1st, and 2d, the Apostle tells the *Hebrews*, that "GOD who spake in times past to their fathers by the Prophets, hath in these last days spoken by his SON, *whom he hath appointed heir of all things.*"—It was surely JESUS CHRIST, *as come in the flesh*, who is here said to speak to them, who could not be *appointed heir purely as* GOD, for it was GOD who appointed him as *his* SON; and *delegation* must imply inferiority; for tho' the person appointed or delegated, may be in other respects equal to him or any of them who send, impower, or communicate authority to him; yet, in that particular respect in which he is *appointed, authorized, sent,* or *deputed,* he is certainly inferior. Therefore the SON being *appointed* as heir, must refer to that part of his character in which he is *inferior,* and *subject* to the *paternal* authority of GOD, displayed in the divine occonomy, and evidently implied in the act of *appointing or communicating* the power, right, or privilege of heirship. Hence, *Christ* himself says, " My *father* who gave them me, is *greater* than all." But this I shall consider a little further, when we come to the 4th verse.

AND before we enter upon the 3d, I must observe, that there are many who with regard to receiving sentiments in religion, act with more indifference than they would do in purchasing the meanest trifles in the world. In the latter case, they chuse to go if possible to the first hand, and careful to have their goods pure and unsophisticated, without adulteration; but they are far from being so circumspect with regard to religion, which they can receive adulterated with the inventions of men,—admit the meaning of passages from interpolations and comments, which rather shew the sentiments of the translator

translator or interpreter, than the mind of God revealed in them. Thus the scriptures are forced to speak the language of systematics. Among many passages that have suffered by such methods, this text is a most glaring example, which commonly runs thus when cited, "Who is the brightness of *his father's* glory, and the express image of his person."—And according to this reading, has been sustained an undoubted proof of eternal generation; or *Christ* being a *Son*, as he is *God*. But if the reader will please to take his Bible, he will see that the words *father* and *his*, are not even in the English version. The translators have supplied the word *his*, and custom only has added *father* to it, which is a gross corruption of the text, and tends to obscure the obvious meaning of it.

The first clause reads thus, "Who being the brightness, splendor, or refulgence of that glory." The *glory* here refers to the *divers manners* in which God spake to the fathers at sundry times, mentioned in the first verse: And the plain easy meaning is, that the Son, by whom God had spoken in the last days, was the brightness or resplendence of all the glory exhibited, promised, or prophesied of in the Old Testament dispensation. The glory that was then revealed, was but like the dawn of the morning in comparison of the noon-day splendor of the sun of righteousness: Such morning rays only announced the approach of the refulgent sun, who spread abroad the glorious light of divine truth through the world, in the most open, clear, and conspicuous manner. *Jesus Christ* was the spirit and substance of all the glory manifested in the declarations, appearances, tabernacle, temple, priest-hood, and pompous services. They all center in him whose character and work is the meri-

dian

dian luftre, the excelling glory of what was more darkly faid and fhadowed of him under the Old Teftament. The glorious appearances which were made, the glory of the tabernacle, temple, and prieft-hood, and efpecially that glory which appeared from off the mercy-feat, (to which this phrafe in the text may perhaps particularly allude) was externally ftriking to the fenfes, and often furprized the beholders: But not to be compared with that permanent, fpiritual, and divine glory, which fhone fo confpicuoufly in the whole character of JESUS CHRIST.

THO' the latter *Jewifh* temple wanted many things that tended to enhance the glory of the firft, as we are told by *Haggai*,—(*v*) " Who is among you that faw this houfe in her *firft glory?* and how do ye fee it *now?* Is it not in your eyes in *comparifon of it as nothing?* Notwithftanding this preference with refpect to *external glory*, and feveral valuable privileges fuited to that difpenfation, which were wanting in the latter temple; the fame Prophet tells us,—(*w*) " I will fhake all nations, and the defire of all nations fhall come, and I will fill this houfe with *glory*, faith the LORD of hofts. The *glory* of this latter houfe *fhall be greater* than the former, faith the LORD of hofts." The prefence of GOD manifefted in flefh, did more than make up all defects in the latter temple, and made it exceedingly excel the former in glory: Yea, with refpect to all the glory of the *Jewifh* œconomy, the Apoftle fays,—(*x*) " That which was made glorious, had no glory in this refpect, by reafon of the *glory that excelleth*. For if that which was

done

(*v*) Hag. ii. 3. (*w*) ver. 7, 9. (*x*) 2 Cor. iii. 10, 11.

done away was glorious, *much more that which remaineth*."—The life of *Christ* here, was a most glorious exhibition of the moral perfections of *God*,—his death an amazing declaration of the love, mercy, and condescension of *God*,—his resurrection the clearest display of the omnipotent power and unerring faithfulness of *God*,—his exaltation at *God's* right hand,—kingly dignity, universal dominion and government, and giving such holy and divine laws and ordinances for the perpetual order, comfort, and establishment of his church, make up such a refulgence of glory, as made *Isaiah*, under a prophetic view thereof, cry out to the church with admiration,—*(y)* " Arise, shine, for thy light is come, and the *glory* of JEHOVAH is risen upon thee.—JEHOVAH shall arise upon thee, and his *glory* shall be seen upon thee.—Rejoice ye with *Jerusalem*, and be glad with her, all ye that love her, rejoice for joy with her,—and be delighted with the *abundance of her glory*." Not the boasted glory of *Sharon*, *Carmel*, and *Lebanon*, which the *Jews* delighted so much in : But the quintessence and excellence of *all glory*. " The glory of JEHOVAH, the excellency of ELOHIM." HE, who is the medium or mirror of all the divine *perfections*,—who exhibits all the glorious *relations* which JEHOVAH stands in to his church. Hence, says *John*,— *(z)* " The WORD was made flesh, and dwelt among us, (and we beheld his *glory*, the *glory* as of the only begotten of the father) full of grace and truth." *Paul* tells us, *(a)* " In him dwelleth all the fulness of Deity bodily." Therefore he says here with the utmost propriety, " WHO IS THE BRIGHTNESS OR REFULGENCE OF GLORY."

THE

(y) Isa. lx. 1, 2. ibid. lxvi. 10, 11. *(z)* John i. 14. *(a)* Col. ii. 9.

THE next clause in this verse is rendered, "The express image of his person." The ordinary sense imposed upon these words so translated is, "That *Christ* as a *Son*, is the *essential image* of the *father's person.*" The inconsistency of this sentiment I considered above.

I SHALL here shew that neither such words nor ideas are in the text. The *Greek* word χαρακτηρ *character*, which is not that I know of in the New Testament, except in this verse, signifies literally a *distinguishing mark :* And ὑποστασις is a word compounded of *hypo*, *under*, and *stasis*, a *station*, and so literally signifies an *under station*, or *foundation :* And according to the use of it in this place, may be justly expressed by the English word *condescension*. So the text will read, "*Who is the brightness or splendor of glory, and the distinguishing mark of his condescension.*" This can have no relation to *person* at all. The word *hypostasis*, here translated *person*, is other four times in the New Testament, in three of which, it is rendered *confidence*, and in the other *substance* ; neither of these can have any relation to *person* ; nor is any of them the proper meaning of the word. But what makes it pretty evident that *foundation* would be a better translation of it is, that this word agrees better with the scope of the Apostle, in every place where it is used, than any other word it is rendered by. As for example, (*b*) "Faith is the *firm foundation* of things not seen, &c." In the other three texts, (*c*) it is *confidence*, but *foundation* would read much better, as the reader may see by consulting the passages.

WHATEVER way ecclesiastical writers may render this word, there is no classical author that
makes

(*b*) Heb. xi. 1. (*c*) 2 Cor. ix . 4 and xi. 17. Heb. iii. 14.

makes ufe of it to fignify *perfon*. Revelation would have appeared more clear, if Divines had taken words in their neareft fignification; and not borrowed for them a remote fenfe, that they might be eafier adapted to fyftems compofed by themfelves or others, as the meaning of Revelation. In this inftance, it is plain the text is wrefted to favour fome fuch purpofe, whereas the obvious meaning of it is agreeable to the fcope of Revelation in general, a glorious difplay of the character of *Chrift* our Saviour, and conveys the ftrongeft idea of the great love and condefcenfion of God, expreffed in *Chrift* coming to fave finners. This is here fet forth as a moft interefting part of his character. That he who was heir of all things,—by whom the worlds were made,—who upholds all things,—who was the brightnefs of glory, fhould humble himfelf to that *low ftation* he was in here, fubmit to a fhameful and ignominious death for *finners*, out of voluntary and matchlefs condefcenfion! And that this is the idea included in the phrafe, is evident from what immediately follows, which is another branch of his character as the Saviour of men: "When he had by himfelf purged our fins, fat down on the right hand of the majefty on high."

In this view of the paffage, the ideas are connected, and quite agreeable to the fcope of the Apoftle, in prefenting to the *Hebrews* a defcription of the Son of God, as the fubftance and fplendor of all that difpenfation, in which they gloried fo much,—his coming to fave finners, the *moft diftinguifhed mark of divine condefcenfion*: And having finifhed his humiliation work, was advanced at God's right hand, "being made (as in the 4th verfe) fo much better than the Angels, as he had

by

by inheritance obtained a more excellent name than they." Whatever *myſteries* others may *think* they ſee in this paſſage, as *eternal generation,—natural ſonſhip,—Chriſt the eſſential image of the father's perſon,* &c. according to the plain meaning of the words, and the deſign of the Apoſtle's argument in this part of the epiſtle, the impartial examiner will ſay with him,—*(d)* " We ſee JESUS, who was made a little lower than the Angels, for the ſuffering of death, crowned with glory and honour." This is the beſt comment on the paſſage, given by the Apoſtle himſelf. *

IN

(d) Heb. ii. 9.

* I hope the impartial reader is fully convinced of the propriety of theſe obſervations, and that we have now attained to a clear and determined ſenſe of this paſſage, which hath been not a little excruciating to interpreters. The embarraſſment they have been under, was owing to their departure from the ſenſe of ſcripture terms, which are clearly diſcovered, and impoſing a meaning upon them to favour doctrines, which could not otherwiſe find any countenance in ſcripture: And in this inſtance, as well as ſome others, which we have had occaſion to notice before, it is eaſy to ſee, how far they have departed from the plain ſenſe of the terms: And alſo how eaſily the inattentive may be miſled by traditions and ſyſtems. When once words acquire a meaning, which the writer did not intend they ſhould convey, it is nothing ſtrange, if the paſſages where ſuch words occur, appear dark and perplexed. In ſuch caſes, the reader generally brings ideas to the paſſages, which the writer was a ſtranger to, and no wonder, if they are then intricate, and perhaps contradictory to him. There have been many complaints about the darkneſs of ſcripture, which the readers have occaſioned to themſelves, by ſtriving to reconcile them to their own pre-conceived notions, which never were in the ſcriptures; but learned from ſyſtems compoſed by men, who ſeem to have paid more regard to the traditions of their fathers as a rule, than the ſpirit and ſcope of the ſcriptures. The veil that has been upon many paſſages for centuries paſt, is a moſt glaring proof of this lamentable fact: And, 'tis no way ſurpriſing, that the veil of error hath ſo long remained over texts, which have been once miſconſtrued in favour of doctrines invented by men: For the falſe interpretation being once received,—error ſubſtituted and eſtabliſhed for truth, it is afterwards taken for granted, and continues a received doctrine without examination. Hence tranſubſtantiation, purgatory, &c. continue among Papiſts, and other ſiſter myſteries in the reformed churches,—gloſſed over by interpreters, and inculcated

IN the 4th verse, the Apostle tells us, that "he was made much better than the Angels, as he hath *by inheritance obtained* a more excellent name than they. For unto which of the Angels said he at any time, thou art my SON, this day have I begotten thee? And again, *I will* be to him a father, and he *shall* be to me a Son." It is here said, that he OBTAINED the name SON OF GOD by *inheritance*, which is directly contrary to an *eternal sonship, by an act of generation.* Were he naturally, and eternally a *Son*, it could not be said with any propriety that he *obtained* this name by inheritance; but this the Apostle says he did, while others in effect say, he did not, but it was natural to him as he is GOD. The inquiring christian may determine for himself, which of these sentiments he should hold for truth; both he cannot, as they are directly opposite.

IT is manifest on the face of the text, that by his *obtaining* this excellent *name* by inheritance, he was *made so much better than Angels*. Now, this must be something *not eternal*, for then it were not *obtained*, nor he made thereby better than Angels, who were not in being.—And how ridiculous is it to suppose, that GOD *obtained* a name *by inheritance, to make him better than Angels?* which is the plain language of the Apostle, if it is true, that

CHRIST

cated as necessary truths by leaders in religion, they have been swallowed for ages with very little ceremony, and held equally sacred with the abused texts, which they are supposed to be taken from.

But when this, or any other text, is rescued from the perplexed, incoherent ideas commonly prefixed to it; and presented to the reader in that simplicity and plainness so peculiar to the scriptures, clearly connected with the writer's scope, and the character of *Christ* in revelation, it must stamp a value on the discovery to all who love the truths of GOD, exhibited in their own original beauty and divine purity.

CHRIST is a *Son*, as he is GOD. But it is evident from this text, that his sonship belongs to his oeconomical character, in which the Apostle is treating of him here, and with the utmost propriety says, " *He was made so much better than the Angels, as he hath by inheritance obtained a more excellent name than they.*"

IT should here be remarked, that what the scriptures say concerning *Christ* as an *Heir*, or *First-born*, which are terms of the same import when applied to him, mostly refer to some part of his exalted character after his death. This is pretty clear from the Apostle's reasoning, in this chapter. " GOD,—hath in these last days spoken by his *Son*, whom he *hath appointed heir of all things*,—who is the brightness of glory, and the distinguishing mark of his condescension, when he had by himself purged our sins, sat down on the right-hand of the majesty on high: Being made so much better than Angels, *as he hath by inheritance obtained* a more excellent name than they.— Thou hast loved righteousness, and hated iniquity; therefore GOD, thy GOD *hath anointed* thee with the oil of gladness *above thy fellows.*" He told his disciples after his resurrection, " That all power in heaven and earth was given unto him," which was the accomplishment of the promise made concerning him in the Psalms,—(e) " Also I will make him my first-born, higher than the kings of the earth." †

(e) Psa. lxxxix. 27.

† The translators have thought fit to supply the word *my* in this text, but it evidently mars the sense, as it makes it contain only one promise,—and supposes the *first-born* to be the person concerning whom this promise is given, of being " made higher than the kings of the earth." Whereas it is plain that the text, without this supplement, includes two promises; the one, " I will make him

The next verse of this chapter I had occasion to consider before, and shall not detain the reader any longer on a subject so clear:

But come to another text in this epistle, which is made an argument for eternal sonship,—*f*) " The law maketh men high priests which have infirmities; but the word of the oath which was since the law, maketh the Son, who is consecrated (or as in the margin, *perfected*) for evermore." From this text they reason, " that as those who " had infirmity were MEN before they were Priests; " so *Christ* was a Son before his investiture in the " priestly office; consequently his sonship did not " arise from his priesthood."

Ans.

(f) Heb. vii. 28.

him *first-born*; the other explanatory of the former: I will make him such a *first-born*, as to be higher than the kings of the earth. This is clear from the scope of the whole passage, beginning at the 20th verse, where we have the designation of *Christ* to his work of mediator, which is followed by several promises of aid and support, in going through the arduous work of humiliation, with the faith and confidence he should express in God, as his father, and the rock of his salvation; then follow several promises that respect his exaltation, " *Also*, saith God, will I make *him first-born.*" What him? The phraseology points it out as another promise made to the same person mentioned before: And this primogeniture was to be of such a sort, as to admit of no equal. He should be heir to an inheritance of such glory, extent, and duration, as every way to excel the kings of the earth. Hence, it is said, " I will set him on high, because he hath made my name known." To the same purpose are the other texts, where he is called *first-born*, " *Jesus Christ* the *first begotten* of the dead, and the prince of the kings of the earth.—He is the head of the body, the church: Who is the beginning, the *first-born* from the dead; that in all things he might have the pre-eminence." Now, if this primogenial right conferred on *Jesus Christ*, refers to his exaltation after he had finished the work of man's redemption, as revelation plainly declares it does, how can it have any relation to a *natural* and *necessary primogeniture*, or to his being a *Son*, as he is *God*? This by no means destroys the idea of priority included in that text, " He is the first-born of every creature." The ideas are very distinct: The one re-

fers

Anf. THE argument here is merely specious, it may amuse the unwary, but has no relation to the point it is brought to prove. For the question is not, whether he was a *Son* before he actually entered upon the office of priesthood? But whether his divine person was eternally begotten, and so an *eternal Son*? I not only grant, but hold it as a principle, that the consideration of his sonship, as *Emmanuel*, was necessary in order of nature (to speak as men) before even his ordination to his office as mediator, ‡ much more his actual investiture in the office of priesthood; which is more than can be drawn from the text: But what does even this say for *eternal generation*, which the text is brought to prove? The most that can be alledged from it is, that he was a *Son* before his investiture in that office, by the word of the oath, which was *since the law*, this might be even after his incarnation. As to what the Psalmist says of his priest-

fers to his early existence: The other to his being put in possession of the power and privileges of GOD's first-born, after he had finished the work the father gave him to do.

There is a most emphatical idea of the *extent* of the *Messiah*'s kingly power and government, expressed in an ancient prophecy by *Baalam*. Num. xxiv. 17. "I shall see him, but not now; I shall behold him, but not nigh: There shall proceed a star out of *Jacob*, and a sceptre shall rise out of *Israel*, and shall smite the corners of *Moab*, and *destroy all the children of Seth*." *Seth* was the son of *Adam*, whom GOD gave him, instead of *Abel*, whom *Cain* slew. As all *Cain*'s posterity was destroyed by the flood, it was the race of *Seth* only, that was saved in the Ark. Therefore the whole world is now the children of *Seth*. The idea then, that is conveyed by the last clause of the verse, as we have it translated, is, that the *Messiah should destroy the whole world of mankind!* But it reads, he shall UN-WALL, or have *uninterrupted dominion* and power over all the children of *Seth*, which respects his universal rule and government over the whole world, and is agreeable to many other prophesies and and promises concerning him. Psa. lxxii. 8. "He shall have dominion from sea to sea, and from the river to the ends of the earth. Psa. ii. 8. Ask of me, and I shall give thee the heathen for thine inheritance, and the uttermost parts of the earth for thy possession." All which refer to that exalted state of government he was raised to, after his sufferings here, and resurrection from the dead.

‡ See p. 183.

priesthood, it may be to point out his excellency above figurative priests; and exhibit his character that he might be known when manifested in flesh, as the end and substance of *Melchizedecian* and *Aaronical* priesthoods: And tho' spoken in the present tense, yet refers to things future: But will as natively prove *Melchizedec* to be an *eternal man*, as that *Christ* was *eternally begotten*.

THE text says, the Son was *consecrated* to be a Priest; but will any say his pure Deity could be consecrated or perfected? Or that he could be our Priest, without the consideration of his human nature, which must be included in every idea of his appointment to, or undertaking and assumption of this office of priesthood. So that instead of the text proving *eternal generation*, (like all the rest, as I hope the reader plainly sees) it is an evident proof of his being a SON, in his complex character as the glorious EMMANUEL.

THERE yet remain two texts, which are not only reckoned proofs of *Christ*'s natural sonship, but are supposed sufficient to prove the terms *Father, Son, Word,* and *Holy Ghost*, natural, necessary, and essential in Deity. One is our LORD's command to his Apostles,—(*y*) " Go ye therefore and teach all nations, baptising them in the name of the Father, and of the Son, and of the Holy Ghost." From which it is argued in favour of *Christ* being a Son, as he is GOD, " That as baptism is a solemn "act of divine worship, it must be administered in "the name of a divine person, therefore Son "in the text must express his divine nature. "Whereas if the term Son refers to one, as he is
" mediator,

(*y*) Matt. xxviii. 19.

" mediator, then we are baptifed in the name of two divine perfons in their higheft titles; and in the name of the other, in his lower and inferior title and character."

Anf. THIS reafoning is extremely weak, for it takes for granted that the terms Father and Holy Ghoft, are titles that exprefs the divine nature of two perfons; but thefe I have fhewed to be oeconomical, confequently the argument is without any foundation, and can conclude nothing in favour of natural fonfhip: And I think by confidering the fubject a little, it will appear a fair evidence of the names Father, Son, and Holy Ghoft being oeconomical. As this was the way our LORD commanded his Apoftles to initiate the *Gentile* nations into the chriftian religion, in or *into* the name of the *Father, Son,* and *Holy Ghoft,* thefe names muft have a fpecial relation to the religion they were to take on the badge of, or the ufe of them would be infignificant in that ordinance, efpecially to heathens, who had no notion of *three* confiftent with the unity of Deity, nor the religion *they* under thefe characters were difplayed in.

To fay they were baptifed into the belief of a Trinity abftractedly confidered, is faying they were baptifed into what neither they nor the Apoftles knew any thing about, feeing there is no fuch revelation in Deity. Befides, this would not have been baptifing into the chriftian religion; as it is moft certain, that abfolute Deity is equally related to *Jewifh* and *chriftian* religion, that is, has no manner of relation to either. The knowledge we have of GOD, is in what he hath revealed; faith in GOD is founded upon that knowledge we attain from revelation, which is a difplay of his perfections

tions in creation, providence, and redemption; in the laſt of which, he hath made himſelf known as three diſtinct agents, under the names of Father, Son, and Holy Ghoſt, each repreſented as having peculiar work in that divine tranſaction. So that the whole of redemption is contained in the *work* of the Father, the *work* of the Son, and the *work* of the Holy Ghoſt; confequently being baptiſed into their names, is profeſſing to believe the whole of the chriſtian religion, which theſe names are ſo neceſſarily connected with in every part, as to be the ſum of the whole, and in ſuch manner, as every chriſtian may ſay, take theſe names from my religion, and what have I more?

The other text is,—(z) "There are three that bear record in heaven, the Father, the Word, and the Holy Ghoſt: And theſe three are one." As I have proved the terms Father, Word, and Holy Ghoſt, to be œconomically applied to God, it might here ſuffice; for if it is a truth, there is no text in revelation that will contradict it. But left the friends of the other opinion ſhould imagine they are left in full poſſeſſion of this text, I ſhall very briefly ſhew how little it is to their purpoſe.

Here again I meet with the philoſophical gentleman formerly mentioned, who deduces ſeveral arguments from this text, to prove his beloved tenet *eternal generation*: and as he reduces his reaſoning into the form of ſyllogiſms, I ſhall lay them before the reader, who may judge how much they are to his purpoſe.

"The Father, the Word, and the Holy Ghoſt,
"are

(z) 1 John v. 7.

" are the three subjects spoken of in the text, 1 John
" v. 7.—But the three subjects spoken of in the text,
" are spoken of as persons in God-head.—*Ergo*,
" The Father, the Word, and the Holy Ghost, are
" spoken of in the text, as persons in the God-
" head: That is, one as a divine person is called
" the Father, another as a divine person is called
" the Word, and a third as a divine person is cal-
" led the Holy Ghost."

" THE subjects or divine persons spoken of in
" the text, 1 John v. 7. are spoken of *as they are*.—
" But the subjects or divine persons spoken of in
" the text, are the Father, Word, and Holy Ghost.
" —*Ergo*, the subjects or divine persons spoken of
" in the text, are spoken of *as they are* the Father,
" the Word, and the Holy Ghost."

HERE, reader, is a brace of syllogisms for you.
—Carefully view the two great pillars on which a
fundamental article of religion stands,—so absolutely necessary in this gentleman's account, that
to deny it, he says, is to " make faith vain,—sal-
" vation void,—a chimera,—all christianity a mere
" phantom,—to sap the foundation of all christian
" religion, and enervate the hope of eternal hap-
" piness."

BUT one would think as the whole of religion
depends upon this article, it would be so clearly
revealed in the word of GOD, that every one, the
clown as well as the philosopher, might know and
understand it. Is it then mentioned in express words?
No. Can it be found by comparing texts together?
No, not without forced interpretations. Is there
any other revelation than the Bible, to certify us of its truth and importance? No, without
we

we take the dictates of men for a revelation. What evidence then is it attended with to merit our credit; and how shall we come by that evidence? We must become Logicians, and learn to reason metaphysically: Consequently the best Logicians are the best christians: Or, it is Logic that makes the christian. This cardinal point must then (as I dare say it does) remain unintelligible to the generality of mankind, since it requires a train of syllogistical reasoning to bring the evidence on which it rests to their view: Or they must (which is a much shorter way) believe it upon the authority of the learned; but still this will not be their faith, but the Logician's: And if they pretend to judge for themselves, they lie open to imposition, as 19 of 20 among professed christians do not know the difference betwixt a well formed syllogism upon rules of ratiocination, and a sophism artfully composed; so that they are still at the mercy of the *Rabbies*.

How miserably has religion been tortured by learned contenders for the *faith delivered to systematics*, who have mustered great numbers of syllogisms *pro & con*, adorned with all the trappings of mood and figure; and by all appearance, rather contending who should appear the most acute reasoner or best Logician, than who should most elucidate the truth, which has been left buried under the rubbish of scholastic subtilties? What advantage has religion received from all the dialectical subtilties of *Tho. Aquinas, Duns Scotus*, and other modern critics, who have attempted to reduce it to a system of scholastic niceties, fitter to be the sport of school-boys, than the study of sober minds? Thanks be to GOD that all necessary truths in religion are clearly revealed in his own word. On

this

this all our hopes and comfort depend. The evidence arising from such abstruse reasoning in favour of religion, which not one in a hundred knows any thing about, will give the immortal soul very little satisfaction, upon a serious consideration in view of death and judgement.

As I write not for the *Literati*, but to further the instruction of such as can and do read their *Bible*, and chuse *it* for their guide, it would be entirely beside my plan, to enter into a course of intricate reasoning; I only beg their leave to step aside for a moment to speak with this gentleman in his own stile.

Sir, your syllogisms cannot be admitted as fair arguments to prove the point you maintain. The first, you found upon there being *three* subjects in the text, whereas according to your own method of reasoning there are *four*. A Logical subject is that of which something is predicated. Now *Unity* is as capable of predication as *Trinity*: For it is as true that the *unity* in the text is *three*, as that the *three* are *one*. Now, as there are four subjects in the text, your syllogism, Sir, should have run thus, " The Father, the Word, the Holy Ghost, and the Unity, are the four subjects spoken of in the text, 1 John v. 7. But the four subjects spoken of in the text, are spoken of as persons in the God-head.— *Ergo*, the Father, the Word, the Holy Ghost, and the Unity, are spoken of as persons in the Godhead"—These premises are full as good as the former, and consequently the conclusion. This makes void your argument in its first form.

But should both your major and minor be denied, the conclusion must fall of course. The major, upon the authority of the text itself, which says, "These three are one." So that there is but one subject in the text. The minor, I have shewed to be false, by proving at large from scripture evidence, that the terms Father, Word, and Holy Ghost, are oeconomically applied to the divine three, and so are not natural and essential to them as persons in Deity. With equal propriety, Sir, you may draw such conclusions from every text, where any of the covenant characters of the sacred three are mentioned; but would it not be absurd to infer from thence, that all the names they bear in scripture, are essential to their nature as persons in Deity?

But seeing this inconveniency, I suppose, and to avoid it as much as your cause would allow, you formed the syllogism in a different dress, in which the weight of the argument depends upon the words *as they are*. But pray, Sir, who denies that the sacred three are spoken of *as they are?* The text says they are Father, Word, and Holy Ghost, but what is that to *eternal generation*, or *natural* and *eternal procession*, which you were to prove from the text? Therefore, to speak in the dialectical stile, your argument, Sir, is *Ignoratio Elenchi*; for it has no connection with the matter in dispute: And as in both forms of the argument, you chuse for premises what is not granted, and what you have not proved to be true; I may, agreeable to the rules of *Logic*, reject your conclusion, and tell you the argument is only a sophism, commonly called *Petitio Principii*, or what goes by the name of *begging the question*. If better arguments cannot be found to

sup-

support your cause, it must soon be very low in the esteem of all who impartially search the scriptures.

Now, Reader, I dare say you are not much wiser either by this gentleman's syllogisms, or my remarks upon them. Such has been too often the effect of the scholastic manner of disputing about religion *from* texts, that is, never coming near them: And that we don't err in the same manner, let us return to the text. Interpreters have commonly detached this verse from the Apostle's scope, and considered it as "a definition of Deity, and the manner how the divine persons exist in the divine nature." If there is any thing of this kind in the text, it must be in the last clause, "these three are one," which is a fact divinely attested; but how the *one* is *three*, or the *three one*, or how either exists can be collected from the words, is far beyond my comprehension, and must be referred to curious wits, who are fond of knowing what no man can know; and subjecting that to a definition, which is infinitely beyond all definition. Poor clods of dust, that will presume to define the GOD that made them! Deity is not the subject of definition. All definitions limit things, but Deity is unlimited, and cannot come within the laws or limits of definition.

IF the Apostle's scope is attended to, it will appear evident that he is proving the truth of the character of the *Messiah*, and the religion which he established: Or, as he says himself, (*a*) "*That Jesus is the Son of God.*" He produces six witnesses, three of which are in the text, "There are three that

(*a*) ver. 5.

that bear record."—To what? That JESUS was the SON OF GOD, the *Saviour* of the world. Who are the witnesses? "The Father, the Word, and the Holy Ghost" The same who are mentioned in other texts, as bearing witness that JESUS was the true MESSIAH.— *b*) "The Father himself, which hath sent me, hath born witness of me." This he did with an audible voice from heaven, both at his baptism and transfiguration.—(*c*) "JESUS answered,—though I bear witness of myself, yet my record is true. For this cause came I into the world, that I should bear witness to the *truth*.—I am the way, the *truth*, and the life." He bore witness to his own character, to *Paul* at his conversion, and to *John* in the isle of *Patmos*.—(*d*) "And we are his witnesses, and so also is the Holy Ghost." Who in a conspicuous manner bore witness to his being the *Messiah*, the *Son of God*, in his visible resting upon him at his baptism,—in all the miracles he wrought, which he says were done through the power of the Spirit,—and in that plentiful effusion at *Pentecost*, whereby his disciples were qualified to spread his name and doctrine through the world: And *John* tells us in the verse immediately preceding the text, "It is the Spirit that beareth witness."—Thus the three witnesses bare record, and gave testimony to the incarnate *Jesus*, the SON OF GOD. To the same purpose are other evidences upon record, The scriptures of the Old Testament—*John the Baptist*—his own divine works,—the water and the blood,—his resurrection and ascension,—with the evidence of the twelve Apostles, all which testify the same truth that JESUS was the true *Messiah*, the *sent of God*, who came to die and rise

---

(*b*) John v. 37.   (*c*) ibid. viii. 14. and xviii. 37.   (*d*) Acts v. 32.

rise again, according to the scriptures. This was the test of discipleship, as *John* in this passage expresses it, " Who is he that overcometh the world, but he that believeth that JESUS is the SON OF GOD ?"

BUT it is very strange that there is never among all these testimonies, the least hint concerning this *essential* article *eternal generation*, which they would screw out of this and many other texts, contrary to the spirit and design of the truths conveyed in them !

C O N-

CONCLUSION.

NOW, reader, as I am done with these texts, and have not to my knowledge overlooked any one that is commonly taken to favour *eternal generation:* So I hope it appears evident, that none of these have any relation to it. It is matter of wonder how any considerate person should lay such weight upon this as an essential article of religion, while it hath no countenance at all in revelation: Whereas were it of such consequence as some would have the world believe, it might be expected to be clearly revealed, as all articles of religion necessary to salvation really are.

FROM the whole, it is abundantly clear, that the appellations or titles so frequently given our Lord and *Saviour* in revelation, *Word,—Son of God,—Son of man,—Messiah,—Christ Jesus,—Lamb of God,—only begotten,—first-born,—Heir,* &c. are synonimous in the general idea which they convey of the person spoken of, all relating to him as *Emmanuel* the *Saviour:* And if any unprejudiced person shall keep this in his eye in reading the scripture, especially the New Testament, where they most frequently occur, I may venture to promise a more easy, plain, and satisfactory account of the character of *Christ*, than he ever saw before, when falsely conceiving some of these terms to have a respect to pure Deity, or what is commonly called *eternal generation.*

THIS

THIS matter concerning the character of *Chriſt* being ſet in a fair light, and eſtabliſhed upon ſcripture arguments, takes off the force of many pretences againſt his proper Deity, ariſing from the ſuppoſed derivation of one divine perſon from another in Deity, and a ſuppoſed act of *eternal generation* producing a co-eſſential, eternal ſon; which things are not expreſſed or implied in any part of revelation, and are acknowledged on all ſides to be great and incomprehenſible difficulties.

A GREAT part of what is objected againſt the Deity of *Chriſt*, is founded upon the human definitions of GOD. Some haughty mortals have undertaken to tell what GOD is, and becauſe the complex character which we have of him in ſcripture, does not anſwer their definitions, they cannot apprehend how he can be GOD. By confounding of things they confuſe their own ideas, and loſe the truth. If ſimilitude of attributes argues a ſameneſs of moral rectitude and character, the ſcriptures have fairly determined *Jeſus Chriſt* to be GOD; for there is not any revealed attribute or perfection of GOD, but what is in the plaineſt terms aſcribed to him. But what the phyſical eſſence of GOD is, the Books of revelation have no where declared.

ALL attempts are vain to define the manner of the exiſtence of a ſupreme cauſe. This far in general we may argue with certainty, that a cauſe or being, that has in nature no ſuperior cauſe, and therefore is alſo unproduced, and independent, muſt be ſelf-exiſtent: That is, exiſtence muſt be eſſential to him; or, ſuch is his nature, that he cannot but be. Every being muſt either exiſt *of itſelf*, or not *of itſelf*: That which exiſts not of itſelf,

felf, muft derive its existence from some other, and so be dependent: But the Being mentioned above is independent, and uncaused. The root of his existence is no where but in his own nature: To suppose it any where else, is to suppose a superior cause to the supreme, which is a contradiction.

Such a Being must be eternal and infinite. Eternal, because there is no way by which such a being can begin, existence being of his nature. Infinite, because his existence cannot be limited by any other.

Such a Being is above all things that come under our cognizance; and therefore the manner of his existence must be above all our conceptions. He necessarily exists. But there is nothing falls within our comprehension of that kind. We know of no being, but what we can *imagine it not to be* without any contradiction to nature, but this Supreme Being himself. With respect to him, we know by reasoning, that there *must be one* Being, who cannot be supposed *not to be*, as certainly as we know any thing at all: Tho' at the same time we cannot know him, and *how he exists*. Adequate ideas of eternity and infinity are above us, who are *Finites*. What relation or analogy there is betwixt time, which is a succession of moments, and *eternal*, unchangeable existence;—how any being should be no older *now*, than he was five thousand years ago, &c. are speculations which involve finite minds in insuperable difficulties.

As our minds are *finite*, they cannot without a contradiction comprehend what is *infinite*. What tho' they were enlarged to ever so great a capacity, yet so long as
they

they retain their general nature, and continue to be of the same *kind*, they would by that be only rendered capable to apprehend *more* and *more finite ideas*; out of which, however increased or exalted, no positive ideas of the perfection of GOD can ever be framed. In the nature of a perfect infinite being, there can be nothing *finite*, nor any composition of *finites*. Tho' we cannot comprehend his essence and manner of being; yet we may say with certainty, that he is free from all defects.

IT is extremely inconsistent for us to talk about how the supreme incorporeal Being exists, as if we comprehended his nature, while we do not comprehend the nature of the most *inferior spirits*; nor have any conceptions even of matter itself divested of its accidents: When we cannot turn ourselves any way, but we are accosted with something above our understandings, besides the numberless undescried regions, with their several states and circumstances, which our philosophy has never yet frequented.—If we cannot penetrate so far as to discover the nature and effects of *them*, is it to be expected that we should, that we *can*, see the mysteries of *his nature*, who is the supreme cause of all?

WE may and ought in our conceptions of GOD, to remove from him what are defects in ourselves, as want of life, ignorance, impotence, acting inconsistently with truth, and the like; these are defects in us, and would be much more so in him, therefore cannot in any sense be ascribed to him. For as ignorance is the same in every subject, we understand what it is, and may literally deny that it belongs to GOD: The like may be said of his power, &c. Tho' we do not understand how he knows things, and his manner of operation. *Thus* we may speak, without pretending to comprehend his nature.

In like manner we may draw conclusions from the confideration of his works, in the production and government of the world, without pretending to comprehend the manner of his exiftence. So far from this, that a juft contemplation of his works, will lead to the necefity of acknowledging, that there muft be an incomprehenfible Being at the head of them: And tho' we do not comprehend the *mode* or manner in which the world depends upon him, and he influences and difpofes things, becaufe this enters into the knowledge of his nature, the one cannot be underftood without the other: Yet when we fee things, which are not felf-exiftent, and plainly obferve an oeconomy and defign in the difpofition of them, we may conclude there is *fome Being*, upon whom their exiftence depends, and by whom they are modelled and managed.

But great care fhould be taken in all our behaviour towards God, that we make no falfe reprefentation of him. We muft take care not to reprefent him by any picture or image, either mental or material, for this is to deny at once his incorporiety, and incomprehenfible nature, &c. So far from this, the language we ufe when we fpeak of him ought not only to be well chofen, but alfo underftood in the moft fublime fenfe poffible: And the fame care is neceffary with refpect to our thoughts. For tho' our terms be the moft reverent and proper that we can conceive, he is ftill fomething above all our conceptions. For as the mode of his exiftence and effential attributes are

incom-

incomprehenfible by us, our words and phrafes, and the objects of our faculties, muft be inadequate expreflions of them.

A s for example, when we fpeak of his *mercy*, we muft not by mercy underftand what is called cómpaffion in us, which is attended with a certain uneafinefs, and therefore cannot be afcribed to God in that fenfe we afcribe it to ourfelves, whofe *affections* are moved by pathetic arts of rhetoric, or tears of importunity ; but there can be no alteration fuppofed in the Deity, tho' from the weaknefs of our underftanding, we denominate the perfections of God varioufly, as he exerts himfelf on this or that occafion.

Perhaps it may be affirmed upon good grounds, that among men there is nothing that refembles the *mercy* of God. So different are the ideas we have of what is called *mercy* among men, as to the objects, extent, caufes, and manner of fhewing it, that there is not any example which feems to have the leaft relation to the true idea we ought to have of *God*'s *mercy* revealed in his word. Among *criminals* they are pardoned who appear to be *leaft guilty*;—in fhewing mercy, the preference is given on account of fome circumftances in the crimes, or in the perfons who commit them. Men fhew mercy in pardoning fuch as injure them, when the offender repents, and perhaps muft crave forgivenefs. Mercy is fhewed to the miferable, from the impreflions the nature and degree of the mifery hath upon men's feelings, which depends upon the art of reprefenting the cafe, or the difpofition the perfons are in to be affected with it.

But

" BUT the *mercy of God* is extended to the chief of sinners, the *most guilty*,—not because they repent, nor on account of any good qualities in them more than others; but the mercy contained in his promise, all *sovereign*, and *free*, being shewed them in forgiving their offences, moves them to repentance; Or, rather (to speak more agreeable to the gospel) is the cause of that gracious change in them, and these new dispositions to love GOD and hate sin, which is an effect peculiar to the divine cause, the *mercy of God*.—Nor is this mercy shewed, because of any feelings their misery can excite in GOD from any form of representation; (which I doubt we too often imagine); this were to bring GOD on a level with men, whose weakness and imperfections are the causes of their partiality in such cases.

WHEN we speak of the knowledge of GOD, we must not mean, that he knows things *as we do*, that intention or operation of mind must produce it,—that he apprehends by impressions made upon him,—that he reasons by the help of ideas,—or that even what we call *intuitive* and immediate knowledge in us, comes up to the mode in which he knows things, as some have supposed; who, not capable to bring the creature up to GOD, have attempted to bring him down to them, rather than be thought not to know what GOD is. The most we can say is, that there is nothing of which he is, or can be ignorant, and that is all we can safely say.

THO' men have accustomed themselves to speak of GOD, in terms taken from such things as they in their weakness admired, and have incorporated such ideas into their language as *divines*; and tho' considering what defects there are in our way of speaking and thinking, we cannot well part with
them

them all: Yet we should remember in the use of these terms, to take them in the most exalted sense possible, and annex a *mental* qualification to the use of such epithets and ways of speaking, as are introduced by custom, antiquity, or by necessity, from the narrowness of either the *minds* of men or their *language*.

But when God reveals any thing concerning himself, it becomes us creatures to give credit to what he says, tho' we cannot comprehend the manner of it. It is easy to conceive, that there maybe perfections in the divine nature, which finite creatures cannot comprehend, as to the manner of their existence: And it must be the highest pitch of arrogance in any creature of the most perfect kind, to call in question the truths revealed by God concerning himself, because he cannot comprehend the manner of them. Does God say these things are so? There is no further question as to the certainty of them, however dark they may be as to the manner *how* they are. God is the supreme truth,—his word alone is the infallible rule, the unerring oracle to guide and instruct us in the knowledge of every thing that is suitable for us, or possible to be known with certainty concerning himself. † "*The secret things belong unto the* Lord *our* God : *But those things which are revealed belong unto us, and to our children for ever.*"

† Deut. xxix. 19.

ADDEN-

ADDENDA.

THERE is a particular sentiment which I have frequently hinted in the foregoing work, being willing the reader should always keep it in view, viz. That the character we have of GOD in revelation is relative, or œconomical:—That we have no definition of the simple or abstract nature of Deity in all the scriptures: And notwithstanding I differ in this from the *Jewish Rabbies*, and *christian critics*, I can see no cause to retract; as I know no name or designation ascribed to GOD, but what is some way or other a characteristic appellation of him, under some relation to his creatures: Nor can I conceive of what use any name or title of GOD could be to them, or what ideas they could have of such name or title that had no relation to them.

BUT I find it necessary here to remove an objection to this, which I was not formerly aware of, " That the name JEHOVAH is directly and immediately descriptive of the divine essence and nature, without any proper relation to us—a *name of essence*," as it is called by *Jews* and christian critics. But if it is so, this name must define his essence, which of consequence must be limited; for every definition sets bounds to the thing defined: But

GOD

GOD cannot be limited, and therefore there can be no definition of his essence. As we cannot know his *essence*, it is presumption to enquire after the name of it, which is beyond the capacity of finite intellects. He does but confound himself, that presumes to know more of GOD than he reveals of himself; but he has revealed no name that defines his essence; such revelation would be of no use to creatures, as they could have no understanding of such names, consequently they would be unnecessary in a religion suited to their capacities.

I OWN the name JEHOVAH is peculiar to the divine Being, and is not applicable to any creature; but wherever it is used, there is something predicated of the Supreme Being under that name, which has some relation in particular to his church and people. Even the sense which both *Jews* and christians imagine is imported in the *letters*, which the word is composed of, viz. the *time past, present,* and *future,* have a relation to creatures; for with respect to GOD, strictly speaking, these terms can have no existence, further than they respect his revealed relations to men. With GOD there is no change of times. "He is without variableness or shadow of turning:" And the *times past, present,* and *future,* are but a poor definition of GOD's *eternal* existence, which they are supposed to be in this case, for none of the terms, nor any measure of duration can be applicable to *eternity*.

BUT if these terms (if they are pointed out in the name JEHOVAH) are viewed with respect to his power, faithfulness, mercy, and care, exercised about his church,—that in every revolving generation, he is to them *present*, what he has been to

those

" those *past*, and will be the same to those that *shall*
" *succeed*. This tends to their edification and comfort; and is a constant ground of praise to JEHOVAH, whose mighty acts done for his people, and gracious promises upon record, certify them what he *is*, and *will be to them*, JEHOVAH, a sure dwelling place in all generations.

" THAT the name JEHOVAH respects his revealed relation to his church, is plain from its being joined in those sacred inscriptions, which were designed to strengthen the faith, hope, and confidence of his people, as JEHOVAH-JIREH, the LORD will *see*, or *provide*;—JEHOVAH-NISI, the LORD is *my Banner*;—JEHOVAH-ROPHI, the LORD *healeth*;— JEHOVAH-SHALLOM, the LORD will *perfect*, or send *peace*;—JEHOVAH-SHAMMAH, the LORD *is there*; all which have an immediate relation to what he *has been, is*, and *will be to his people*.

THE intimation JEHOVAH himself gives, why he would be called by that name, is sufficient to limit our curiosity, and instruct us in the use and meaning thereof to the church. He had made himself known by the name of *God-Almighty* to the ancient *Patriarchs*, making promises which sustained their faith in his *Almighty power*, without receiving the thing promised: But to their children, he says, he would be known by the name JEHOVAH, in efficaciously *giving being to*, and *fulfilling* his promises made to their fathers: So that they should not only experience his *power*; but also his divine *veracity*, *goodness*, and *mercy*. Accordingly we find them celebrating the praises of JEHOVAH, and attributing their deliverance from the *Egyptians* to him; * " Then sang *Moses* and the children of
Israel

* EXO. XV. 1, 2, 3.

Ifrael this fong unto JEHOVAH,—faying, I will fing unto JEHOVAH.—JEHOVAH is my ftrength and fong, and he is become my falvation. † —JEHOVAH is a man of war: JEHOVAH is his name."

AND it is very remarkable to this purpofe, that when he promifed any fpecial favour or bleffing to the church, or threatened any diftinguifhing judgment to their enemies on their behalf, which was the fame as promifes to them, he gave this as a reafon, " *That they might know his name to be* JEHOVAH," which expreffion is very frequent in the Old Teftament, and certainly fhews that the name itfelf, has a relation to what he promifes to do for them; when by the mighty works he would perform on their behalf, they fhould learn the relation he ftood in to them as JEHOVAH, their faviour, fulfilling his promifes to them.

IN like manner when he gave them ordinances and laws, he always put them in mind of their obligation to obferve them, from the confideration of his name, JEHOVAH. Accordingly, when any particular commandment is enjoined them, he commonly adds, " I AM JEHOVAH," or, " I AM JEHOVAH THY GOD." And it is very obfervable, that the ten commandments which were given them with fo great external folemnity, are prefaced with thefe remarkable works, ‡ " I AM JEHOVAH THY ELOHIM, who brought thee out of the land of *Egypt*, out of the houfe of bondage." This expreffion being fo often repeated, muft have been of the greateft importance to that people, and if rightly underftood, is full of inftruction to us.

At

---

† In the fame words *Ifaiah* triumphs in JEHOVAH, who, he fays, was become his, JESUS. See p. 92.

‡ EXO. xx. 2.

At the same time, that every repetition thereof put them in mind of the power and prerogative of JEHOVAH, to give out what laws, statutes, and ordinances he pleased, and require their obedience and conformity to them in the manner he directed.—It gave them the strongest assurance of the infallible performance of all the promises he had made. It secured to them the enjoyment of such blessings as he in sovereignty had added to their dutiful obedience to the laws he had given them,—and was a divine certification, that the comminations he prefixed to the violation of these statutes, should be as certainly executed.

WHEN he says, "*I am* JEHOVAH *your* GOD," it must certainly denote the relation he stood in to them; and that he would aid and protect them in the exercise of their duty, and amply reward them for it. This was not like *Egyptian* bondage, of making brick without straw; for at the same time that he imposes the duties, he intimates the gracious relation he was come under to them, in names every way significant and expressive of that divine aid necessary to their right performance of the duties required. Thus, the same gospel was preached to them as to us, in whom the power of divine truth, expressed in the names and relations in which GOD in his sovereign mercy and grace has revealed himself to us, is the all-powerful cause of that love and conformity we shew to the commandments of the LORD *our* GOD.

TRUE believers were then, as well as now, distinguished from such as only professed to believe, by the power of truth contained in these declarations made by JEHOVAH, of what he was to them, and what he would do for them, included in significant

nificant names, promises, prophesies, signs, sacrifices, &c. the spirit and intent of which being known and believed by them, was a principle and cause of that love and filial obedience they expressed for the honour and glory of him, who had conferred such valuable privileges upon them. The truly righteous in all periods, have viewed the duties required of them, in the light of privileges conferred upon them. But the other, who saw no further than the *letter*, was void of that knowledge on which belief is founded, consequently, their obedience was without principle, and had no higher end than *self* under some consideration or other: And the great reason is frequently given, " *They knew not the name of* JEHOVAH, *and therefore they did not regard the words of his mouth.—But they that knew his name, put their trust in him.*"

THIS subject is capable of exemplification from a variety of passages, but I shall only notice one in *Isaiah*,† where JEHOVAH declares several things concerning *Christ*, the saviour, and the great work he should perform, especially the extent of the privileges of the gospel to the blinded Gentile nations; and to command credit to these sovereign declarations, he says, ‡ " *I am* JEHOVAH, *that is my name, and my glory will I not give to another.*"—The glory of bringing to pass these great events, which were as certain as to their accomplishment, as other promises made formerly, which were already fulfilled, therefore he adds, " Behold, the former things are come to pass, and new things do I declare, before they spring forth I tell you of them." His glory as JEHOVAH is pledged for the performance; and the Gentile nations are invited to rejoice

† Isa. xlii.   ‡ ver. 8.

joice in JEHOVAH, who had thus engaged himself for their salvation: And to confirm their hopes, he declares the divine cause and method of bringing to pass the grand event. * " JEHOVAH is pleased for his righteousness sake, for he *shall magnify the law, and make it honourable*," by bringing into being, and actually accomplishing what JEHOVAH had engaged the honour of his name for.

THE word TORAH here rendered *Law*, might as well be *Doctrine, Institution*, or *Disposition*. The word ADAR signifies *Illustrious, Eminent, Magnificent*. The verbs, as in many other declarations of *Jehovah*, are in the *Hiphil* conjugation, which is always expressive of the *cause*,—is the same as if he had said, " *I will cause to be*;" and with respect to his promises, points out the absolute certainty of their accomplishment. The verse reads, " JEHOVAH is pleased to manifest his faithfulness: He will cause his institutions to be magnified: He will cause his law or doctrine to be illustrious." JEHOVAH is represented as the *efficient cause* of the promises made respecting the salvation of men being accomplished, which plainly shews the connexion betwixt the name, and the salvation promised.

WHEN Divines speak of *Christ* fulfilling the *Law*, it is generally restricted to what is called the *moral law*, or ten commandments, which he perfectly obeyed in his life, and is commonly called his *active obedience*. But the *law* here must be taken in a larger sense, including what gives instruction, as well as what implies obligation, and extends to every thing in the Old Testament concerning him, whether *doctrines, promises, prophesies, types, signs, shadows*,

shadows, &c. all which are fulfilled with unerring exactness in him.—Every circumstance concerning him in the New Testament, (many of which perhaps seem very trifling to a carnal conception) was a fulfilling something that referred to him in the Old. Hence it is so often said,—" *As it is written— That the Scriptures might be fulfilled.*" In this manner JEHOVAH manifested his faithfulness, and made his institutions, doctrine, or law, magnificent and illustrious, every tittle whereof being fulfilled in JESUS CHRIST: And of so great importance was it to the glory of JEHOVAH, that JESUS CHRIST could not dispense with the least circumstance, without the strictest conformity and most perfect obedience thereto, not only in the *letter*, but the *spirit* and *intent* of it: And his mind being capacious enough to investigate the extensive subject in every necessary point of view,—the principles of obedience and springs of action in him, being commensurate to the *extent* of the law in its utmost latitude, and adequate to the divine *spirituality* thereof, gave such worth to his obedience, as when viewed by the impartial eye of JEHOVAH, who sent him to fulfil all righteousness, the sentence of approbation is proclaimed from heaven in his favour, " *This is my beloved Son, in whom I am well pleased.*"

BUT to make this point still more evident, let it be considered, that the name JEHOVAH is given to JESUS CHRIST in the Old Testament, joined with the common names of Saviour, Redeemer, &c. which certainly belong to the oeconomy of redemption: And to confirm the faith of the church, it is promised, that he should be called by this name, joined with another peculiar to him as our redeemer, and which is declared by JEHOVAH in

the

the before cited text, to be the capital ground of his being pleased with us.—* " *This is the name whereby he shall be called*, JEHOVAH-TSIDKENU, *the Lord our righteousness.*" † This refers to the time he should appear in flesh. Accordingly, as JEHOVAH cannot be rightly pronounced in the *Greek* tongue, it is commonly rendered LORD in the New Testament, and by way of speciality given to JESUS CHRIST. ‖ " This day is born unto you a Saviour, who is CHRIST the LORD: Or the LORD CHRIST. The word which GOD sent to the children of *Israel*, preaching peace by *Jesus Christ*, he is LORD of all. To this end *Christ* both died and rose, that he might be LORD both of the dead and living: And he hath on his vesture, and on his thigh, a name written, *King of Kings*, and LORD *of* LORDS."

THE attentive reader will mind that it was proved at large, part I. sect. 5th. That what is said of JEHOVAH in the Old Testament, is applied to JESUS CHRIST in the New: To which I shall only

---

* Jer. xxiii. 6.

† We have a strange translation of a similar text, Jer. xxxiii. 16. " In those days shall *Judah* be saved, and *Jerusalem* shall dwell safely: And this is the name whereby she shall be called, the LORD our righteousness." Not to expose the glaring incongruity of the terms, " SHE shall be called the LORD," the sentiment conveyed by them destroys the foundation of our acceptance with GOD, by attributing that to the church, which is the peculiar prerogative of *Christ* our Redeemer, who is " made unto us *righteousness*,—who brought in an *everlasting righteousness.*—with which JEHOVAH is said to be well pleased."—The idea in the text, as it is translated, suits that church well in which there is a stock of merit supposed to be lodged, which may be purchased on conditions, to recommend her members to the favour of GOD : But the scriptures know no such church. The glory of being our righteousness, is every where given to *Christ*, and so does this text, which should read thus,—" And he who shall call her, or, he shall be called by her JEHOVAH, *our righteousness*," which is the same with the other text, and agreeable to the scope of revelation.

‖ Luke ii. 11. Acts x. 36. Rom. xiv. 9. Rev xix. 16.

only add one idea here. It was JEHOVAH that guided and governed the *Jewish* church under the Old Testament,—that exercised his divine paternal care about her in such variety of compassionate and tender expressions, and indulgent methods, declaring his concern for their frequent contempt of duty and privilege,—raising up Prophets in every age, who came in the name of JEHOVAH to testify against their defections, warn them of their danger, and endeavour to reclaim them: But all this JESUS CHRIST declares HE had done, when he sat down on the mount over against *Jerusalem*; and with the same sympathetic tenderness, he had often before lamented their impending fate, (which now must take place, the measure of their wickedness being filled up in shedding his innocent blood, which crowned the guilt of killing the Prophets he had from time to time sent unto them, which blood should be required of that generation;) he says, † " O *Jerusalem, Jerusalem*, thou that killest the Prophets, and stonest them who were sent unto you, *how often would I have* gathered thy children together, as a hen gathereth her chickens under her wings, and ye would not! Behold, your house is left unto you desolate, &c."

DIVINE wisdom is conspicuous in giving the relative name LORD, which JEHOVAH is rendered by, to JESUS CHRIST in the New Testament, WHEN, he *really gave being* to his promises he had made under the Old Testament; this being the very reason for which, as he told *Moses*, he would make himself known by the name JEHOVAH;— and WHEN, he performed those great works he had promised in behalf of his people, by which they should know his name to be JEHOVAH. He *now* appears as the spirit and design of all 'the sacred inscrip-

---

† Matt. xxiii. 37.

inscriptions to which JEHOVAH is joined, which are just so many parts of the character of *Christ*,— the sum of all the mercy and truth promised to the fathers by JEHOVAH.* And in his instructions to the churches, he assumes the same title under the name LORD, which he did under the name JEHOVAH.‡ "I am *Alpha and Omega*, the *beginning and the end*, saith the LORD, *who is*, and *who was, and who is to come, the Almighty.*"

AND agreeable to his inferior character as a Son, the Saviour, and Redeemer of men, the name LORD is joined with others, expressive of the salvation he in so great condescension came to procure. Hence he is called the LORD JESUS CHRIST,—JESUS *the* LORD,—CHRIST *the* LORD,—SAVIOUR *the* LORD,—SPIRIT *the* LORD. And this phraseology is not confined to the New Testament, for *Isaiah* expresses this connexion in very plain terms. § " I will trust, and not be afraid; for the LORD JEHOVAH is my strength and song; he also is become my salvation." JESUS, as in the original.

AND

* *Eve* seems to have thought that JEHOVAH, who proclaimed the glad tidings of salvation by the seed of the woman, should be that seed himself: Or, that he who was the promised seed might be called JEHOVAH. For, she supposing that her first child was the seed promised, said with exultation,—" I have gotten the MAN, the JEHOVAH,' as Gen iv. 1. reads. Tho' she was mistaken in thinking that *Cain*, her first-born, was the promised seed; yet she cannot be supposed to have misunderstood the promise itself so far, as to apply the name JEHOVAH to the seed promised, if it had no relation to it. She seems to have rather understood this divine connexion better than many since, notwithstanding their having the whole of revelation to learn it from, which shews plainly, that he who made this and all other promises respecting the salvation of of men, under the character of JEHOVAH, was the efficient himself,—and in the fulness of time appeared in infinite condescension as the *son of man*,—the promised seed of the woman, compleatly fulfilling every thing that pointed at him in that humble character and related to that salvation which he as JEHOVAH had promised to the church.

‡ Com. Rev. i. 8. iv. 8. xi. 17. with Isa. xli. 4. xliv. 6. xlviii. 12. See p. 96.

§ Isa. xii. 2. See p. 92.

AND according to every notion and acceptation of the word, he bears the name LORD in the moſt proper ſenſe poſſible, whether we conſider the appellations which imply or expreſs LORDSHIP, or the right and foundation thereof. With regard to the firſt, he is called King, Prince, Maſter, Captain, Ruler, Lawgiver, Leader, &c. And with reſpect to the other,—if uncontroulable power and ability to govern, be a ground of LORDSHIP, he moſt juſtly claims the title LORD in the higheſt reſpect: And alſo, as he created, preſerves, upholds, maintains, and provides for all. If conqueſt gives any title to dominion, he has every right this way.— If purchaſe or primogeniture gives a right to rule and government among men, how much more is it due to CHRIST? He planned and erected the church, inſtituted laws and ordinances for her government, —guards her from all enemies,—brings members into her by his power,—he is the LORD, head, huſband, ſupreme teacher, director, governor, and ſource of endleſs happineſs to all her members.

THIS is a ſubject too copious and extenſive to be properly diſcuſſed in a ſhort excurſion of this kind; yet from theſe few ſhort hints, it is plain, that the name JEHOVAH in the Old Teſtament, and the name which anſwers to it in the New, are deſigned to inſtruct us in the knowledge of ſome relation he that bears them ſtands in to his church: And as I have ſhewed above, that the other names aſſumed by the divine Being, refer to the great oeconomy he is carrying on with reſpect to his church; we may ſafely conclude, that there is no abſtract name or definition of the Supreme Being in revelation: And conſequently that all the fine ſpeculations on that head, are without foundation in ſcripture.

By the TABLE *here subjoined, I doubt not but I shall oblige many of my readers, especially such as have their minds formed to relish the beauty of divine truth, so plainly revealed in the sacred records. Besides the great number of texts barely cited, the following either differ from our common translation, and is marked* * : *Or, are more or less explained, and marked* † . *If the same text is some way illustrated, and differently translated, it is marked* § ‡.

	chap.	ver.	page.		chap.	ver.	page.
		GEN.				2 SAM.	
*	i.	1.	17.	†	vii.	13, 14.	147.
*	—	2.	55, 56.	*	—	23.	18.
*	—	26.	19.			JOB	
†	iii.	15.	150.	*	v.	7.	130.
§‡	—	22.	19, 20.	*	xix.	25.	75.
§‡	iv.	1.	360.	*	xxxiii.	4.	34.
*	xx.	13.	17.	*	xxxv.	10.	18.
*	xxxv.	7.				PSA.	
*	xli.	38.	55.	§‡	ii.	6, 7.	86, 155.
†	lxviii.	15, 16.	68, 75.	*	lviii.	11.	18.
		EXO.		*	lxxix.	11.	131.
†	iii.	2, 4, 6.	67.	†	lxxx.	17.	150.
†	—	14.	5.	§‡	lxxxix.	26, 27.	136, 152, 329
†	vi.	3.	352.	§‡	xci.	14.	148.
†	—	7.	353.	†	xcvii.	1---7.	85.
†	xxiii.	20, 21.	70.	*	cx.	3.	295.
		NUM.		*	cxlix.	2.	18.
§‡	xxiv.	17.	331.			PRO.	
		DEUT.		†	viii.	23, 24, 25.	296.
*	iv.	7.	18.	§‡	xxx.	3, 4.	18, 154, 297.
*	v.	26.				ECCL.	
§‡	vi.	4.	12, 109	*	xii.	1.	18.
		JOS.				ISA.	
*	xxiv.	19.	18.	†	vi.	3.	20.
		JUDG.		†	vii.	14.	152.
*	xiii.	18.	81.	*	ix.	6.	35.
*	xv.	14.	28.	†	—	7.	153.
		1 SAM.		*	xi.	2.	55.
*	xx.	31.	131.	†	—	10.	88.
				*	xii.	1, 2.	360.

A TABLE of TEXTS.

	chap.	ver.	page.
*	xxvi.	1.	92.
§‡	xxxv.	2.	107.
†	xlii.	1.	161, 181.
§‡	—	8, 27.	355, 356.
*	xliv.	6.	40.
†	xlv.	3, 6.	353.
§‡	liii.	8.	296.
*	liv.	5.	18.
†	lx.	1, 2.	324.
*	lxi.	1.	28, 55.
*	lxiii.	9.	78.
*	—	14.	216.

JER.

*	x.	10.	18.
‡	xxiii.	6.	28, 358.
*	—	26.	18.
*	xxxiii.	16.	358.

EZEK.

†	xliii.	10--12.	105.

DAN.

†	iii.	25.	154, 300.

HOS.

†	v.	11, 12.	9. Addrefs.

JOEL.

†	ii.	27--32.	84.

MICAH.

†	v.	2.	300.

HAGGAI.

†	ii.	3, 7, 9.	323.

MAL.

*	i.	6.	18.
†	—	11.	77.
†	iii.	1.	87.

MATT.

†	vi.	9.	77, 115.
†	xvi.	16, 17, 18.	184, 302.
†	xvii.	5.	159.
†	xxiii.	37	359.
†	xxvii.	54.	263.
†	xxviii.	19.	332.

LUKE.

	chap.	ver.	page.
†	i.	2.	193.
†	xxii.	42.	262.

JOHN.

†	i.	1, 2.	198.
†	—	14.	97.
†	iii.	35.	263.
†	iv.	24.	127.
†	v.	18, 19.	304.
†	—	30.	147.
†	vi.	38.	262.
†	viii.	58.	93.
†	ix.	35, 36, 37.	162.
†	x.	30--39.	304.
†	xii.	34.	151.
†	xiv.	12.	221.
†	—	31.	261.
†	xv.	26.	205.
†	xvi.	3.	211.
†	xvii.	5.	263.
‡	xx.	17.	164.

ACTS.

†	i.	24.	100.
†	ii.	1.	212.
†	v.	3, 4.	33.
*	vii.	59, 60.	99.
†	viii.	37.	163.
†	xiii.	32, 33.	157.
†	xiv.	11.	62.
†	xx.	32.	195.

ROM.

§‡	i.	1---6.	310.
*	—	20.	1.
†	viii.	32.	314.
§‡	ix.	5.	30.

1 COR.

†	i.	24.	95.
§‡	xv.	28.	125, 264.

2 COR.

§‡	ii.	14, 15, 16.	225.
†	iii.	8.	230.

A TABLE of TEXTS.

chap.	ver.	page.
† iii.	10, 11.	323.
§‡ —	17, 18.	29.
§‡ iv.	3.	227.
* ix.	4.	325.
* xi.	17.	

EPH.

† ii.	20.	138.

COL.

* i.	13.	121, 317.
† —	15.	172.

2 THESS.

† iii.	5.	21.

1 TIM.

* i.	1.	31.

2 TIM.

* iv.	2.	197.

TITUS.

§‡ ii.	13.	31.

HEB.

§‡ i.	1, 2, 3, 4.	321.
† iii.	5, 6.	181.
* —	14.	325.
† iv.	12, 13.	194.

chap.	ver.	page.
† v.	4, 5.	156.
† vii.	28.	330.
* xi.	1.	325.
† —	26.	94.
† xii.	25, 26.	76.
† xiii.	8.	48.

1 PET.

* iii.	18.	218.

2 PET.

* i.	1.	31.
† —	17.	160.

1 JOHN.

† i.	1, 2.	200.
† v.	7.	334.
§‡ —	10.	9. Addreſs

JUDE.

* ver.	4.	31.

REV.

† ii.	18.	170.
† iv.	8.	20.
† xix.	10.	128.
† ---	11, 12, 13.	200.
† xxii.	20, 21.	101.

ERRATA.

Beſides a very few literal errors of no great moment, the reader will pleaſe to correct the following:—P. 29, l. 4, from the bottom, put *a* before *more*.—P. 56. for Gen. ii. 2. r. Gen. i. 2—P. 103, l. 6, dele *and*.—P. 142, l. 16, dele *the*, before ſon of man.—P. 155. l. 5, for *Aſtoples* r. *Apoſtles*.—P. 161. l. 16, for the period after elect, ſubſtitute a comma.—P. 174. l. 22, for *know*, r. *knows*.—P. 247, l. 10, for *have they*, r. *they have*.——P. 261. l. 13. for *ſufficient*, r. *inſufficient*.—P. 279, l. 15, put *applied* after generation.—P. 297, l. 21, for *is*, r. *has*.—P. 310, l. 42, for *terms*, r. *turns*.——The firſt ſentence of the laſt paragraph in p. 256, read interrogatively, "Is it truth, that the divine three exiſt *naturally, neceſſarily,* and *eternally?*"

A

Vindication of the FACTS

IN THE

FREE ENQUIRER'S LETTER,

AND THE

Misrepresentations in the *Reply* thereto considered.

Addressed to the AUTHOR of the REPLY.

ALSO, AN

EXAMINATION

OF THE

Disguised Quaker's DREAM;

IN WHICH

His CRITICISMS are detected; and his Reasoning in Favour of *Human Systems*, to the Discredit of the Authority and Use of *Divine Revelation*, exposed.

By A. M. Author of a *View of the Trinity in the Glass of Divine Revelation*, &c.

NEWCASTLE:

Printed for the Author: And sold by the Booksellers in Town and Country. M DCC LXVII.

[Price SIX-PENCE.]

READER.

I Humbly conceive, that the occasion of so many different and dishonourable opinions concerning the LORD JESUS, *is the want of due attention to the scope of the Divine Oracles, in which* HE *is the leading subject. Hence some violently contend, out of pretended zeal to the honour of* CHRIST, *that the relative names He bears, are proper and peculiar properties of his person, as he is God abstractedly; and that such are as natural and necessary to him as to be God. These persons do not remember how little countenance the scriptures give to such an opinion, nor what improvement the enemies of* CHRIST'S *Deity and Self-existent glories make upon such concessions, as thus at once deliver into their hands the whole cause.—And as the* Arian *gains advantage on the one hand, the* Socinian *triumphs on the other, while they see the pretended orthodox stripping the* LORD JESUS *of the titles and names he bears as* EMMANUEL, *the Sent of God, and Saviour of sinners, to support a scheme which never was revealed by God to men, viz. How the three Divine persons subsist in the Divine nature, or God-head, while the terms they use are for ever incompatable with Deity abstractedly considered.**

I am also afraid, that thro' the same inattention to Divine revelation, there are many who consider the LORD JESUS *in no other view than that of a Saviour, as the Father's servant, fulfilling the work he had given him to do. But the contemplation of what is revealed of him, will lead us to something of a higher consideration concerning the* LORD JESUS, *than merely that of his being a* SAVIOUR : *For tho' considered purely in his relation to sinners, as clothed with his saving office in its several branches, he is worthy of our grateful acknowledgments, and most ardent gratitude : Yet the consideration of his saving office, will lead us up to the transcendent dignity of his glorious* PERSON, *by which he was able to procure and confer so great salvation. In his Person we contemplate the mysterious constitution of it, as the God-man, the incomparable* EMMANUEL ; *in him, as such, created and uncreated glories shine ; he is the product of eternal council and prudence ; the glass of Divine perfections ; the object of the Divine, immense complacency and delight ; the final cause of the glorified creation ; yea, of that*

---

* This is evident from the method a modern author takes to confute the *Arian* hypothesis, which objects against the consistency of such terms with self-existence : he sees it impossible to reconcile them, and therefore daringly (I had almost said blasphemously) endeavours to prove, that the Divine person of the Father is ONLY SELF-EXISTENT.—Astonishing! that men to support their darling notion of the LORD JESUS being a son as he is GOD, or that his Divine person was begotten, which they can never prove from revelation, should thus give up his Divine and self-existent glories into the hands of adversaries to this important truth! Tell it not in the churches, lest blaspheming *Arians* rejoice!

that *saving office*, with which he is *vested.*—*In such predominant regards, he receives the zealous adoration and applause of (those that are least related to him as a Saviour) the august arch-angelical spirits that surround the throne.* In this *respect the united assemblies of angels and redeemed, eternally behold and admire the face of the* DIVINE EMMANUEL, *the* glorious, well-beloved, *and* only begotten Son of God, *in whom shines all the perfections of Deity*; yea, *in him* " dwells " all the fullness of the God-head bodily."

BUT as this is not the subject I intend to pursue in the following pages, any who inclines to see it more fully discussed may peruse what I formerly published,† *which I thought sufficient to answer Mr* Nimmo's *Reply, without taking notice of the author; and also to shew how false these reports were which have been industriously circulated to my prejudice. But after keeping them from the press several months, I found that not only what respects my principles required regard, but the matters of fact also. Which, upon the bare authority of the author, have (much to my disadvantage) passed for truths with the obsequious multitude, as if the clerical character endued persons with that virtue, which the poets feign of a* Lydian *king, of turning all things by their touch, not into gold, but into truth, which is more precious.*—*It became therefore necessary, either to shew the weakness of alledging such things against me and others by a direct Reply; or lie under the reproach of being guilty wherein we knew ourselves innocent. And how little ground the author had to charge us with many things, will be found from the short remarks following.*

BUT notwithstanding so many gross misrepresentations as appear in the Reply, I could not be prevailed upon (for the author's sake) directly to detect them, had not another performance appeared, which is so contrived as to homologate the Replier's relation of facts;—*defame us;*—*and strike at the foundation of christianity, by a subtle endeavour to supplant the authority and use of revelation, in favour of systems composed by men. And tho' not directly written against me; yet as the gentleman it is intended to reproach, was innocently, without any cause on his part, involved, and as the stroke of calumny, aimed at him, is for our sake, it is no more than gratitude, and in effect self-defence, to endeavour to ward it off. Tho' the contemptibleness of that performance, so far as it concerns him, makes it unworthy of his notice; yet, as its specious reasoning to the dishonour of the sacred oracles may ensnare the inattentive, I have added a few remarks upon it, which I acknowledge are far short of the manner it deserves to be exposed: As all such subtle attacks upon the credit of revelation, merit only the utmost scorn and contempt of every christian, who has a regard to the truth as revealed in the word of God.*

† A pamphlet, intitled *A View of the Trinity in the Glass of Divine Revelation: With some Reflections on human Explications concerning that Subject. And a defence of private judgment in Opposition to blind Obedience, in three Dissertations.* Price 1 s.

A
VINDICATION, &c.

Rev. Sir,

WE were pleased to find your first sentiments so favourable concerning the letter to you and your session, as that you were no ways apprehensive that either religion or your character could suffer by it. We wish you had either kept in the same opinion, or given us no reason to judge otherways concerning your reply; which, we must be so free as to say, is not much to the credit of either religion, or any person's character concerned in it.

As whatever relates to the doctrines of religion in your's is fully answered in the dissertations: What follows, is intended only as short remarks on some matters of fact, wherein we differ widely from you in the account you give in your *true reply*. And indeed, Sir, we for your sake blush to write freely, what we certainly know; yet the truth, and our own characters, will not allow us to be altogether silent.

These several charges we lay against your reply, (1.) It is far from answering the character the author has assumed, *the true replier*; there being several falshoods therein. (2.) There are many things misrepresented. (3.) Many remarks foreign to the point, merely to amuse the inconsiderate reader, and throw a gloom upon our conduct or principles. (4.) Several very in.ecent remarks not only upon us, but some others no ways interested in the affair. We shall only mention a few of these things there are no foundation for in truth. Page 2d, That the affair (viz. our heresy, as you call it) was published by us, long before your public declaration complained of.—That it was before others beside your Rev. brother, that two of us vented and defended it in your own house.—That it was not known that any of us entertained these principles 'till after the middle of summer 1765.—Page 3d, That you mentioned that text, *John* ii. 23. or any other in your declaration.—That all you cite from Mr *Erskine* in the Reply, (or the third part of it) or any of

A   the

the texts you include there, were mentioned in your public declaration.—Page 5th, That we impugn thefe truths the Martyrs fealed with their blood, and avouch thefe principles they bore a teftimony againft.—That we took brow-beating, infolent, and overbearing meafures with you.—Page 6th, That we brought forth the old exploded arguments of *Socinians* to fupport our caufe.—That it was upon the point of difference that we by a letter craved a converfation with you.—That you fent for one of *us* to your houfe, *who* brought another along with him: And that you converfed *fome hours* with *us* on that occafion.—Page 7th, That you converfed on *that point* with the *moft of us* more than once or *twice* before it came to the feffion.—Page 8th, That we wanted liberty to fpeak all ourfelves, and the feffion fhould take all for truth we fhould advance. —That it was to us who were fuftained panels at that feffion, that text *Heb.* vii. 28. and the reafoning from it was mentioned.—Page 10th, That we craved a copy of your minutes, and not of our charge or libel.—Page 11th, That the things contained in the copy we got was *marked in our own words.*—Page 12th, That *J. G*—'s minute was read without thefe paragraphs from the Confeffion of Faith, which he and the feffion did not differ about; and which was the alteration he craved to be made in it.—That hundreds knew it was read with the required alteration.—That fome of us appeared that day to have fury and fcorn filling our breafts.— That we condemn your intention.—That you held a conference in your own houfe with *J. G*— upon the difference, before *G. S*—*y.*—Page 14th, That we fet up confcience, not the word of GOD, as the infallible rule of our duty.—Page 17th, That we are guilty of rejecting Divine truths, and of imbibing and venting grievous errors.—Page 21ft, That there are *few* things in the letter you reply to, but what are indifputably falfe.

Now, Sir, Thefe with many other of the kind you affirm as *truths*, but we humbly conceive they would more properly bear another name.—It is eafy to fee the importance you affume as a hiftorian in your reply; no doubt expecting your authority was fufficient to authenticate every thing advanced by you. Whilft a thoufand fuch as us *reclaiming*, muft pafs for nothing. Efpecially as you have taken care not only to affirm roundly; but alfo to offer the fanction of your oath as a fence to your afleverations; and folemnly protefted againft taking ours. What is left for us? Nothing, but by filence to fay Amen: Tho' we fhould give the lie to our confciences, and even our fenfes in doing fo. To deny is ufelefs.—To recriminate is to accufe you; but not exculpate ourfelves.—To give our oath you have told us will be perjury.—What remains? Guilty we muft be; merely becaufe you have faid fo. But as your evidence is incompetent for our conviction, we muft be allowed to diffent, and fhall propofe an appeal, which certainly will

will be agreeable to *you*.—We offer to produce the evidence of other persons beside ourselves, for proof of *some* particulars in question.—Undeniable circumstances in support of *others*.—And, as for what comes not under these heads, we shall refer it to you, whether you will give your own oath, or be satisfied with some of your own session, whom we shall name to you, giving their's. But if you reject this proposal, we have but another, viz. That we are willing to abide by the truth of what is advanced in the letter you reply to upon oath. So that you have your choice either to submit to the above, or be content to bear the just reproach of what is alledged against you in the letter, and of propagating things in print which have no foundation in truth. For we know no other way of deciding the difference concerning these matters of fact.

WE shall next consider, and very briefly, some of the things you have misrepresented. And tho' we put not these among the things you have advanced without any foundation, yet we reckon them as contrary to your assumed character of a *true replier*.

As an instance of our venting and publishing that heresy (as you term it) before your declaration, you say, page 2d, " That one " of us vented and endeavoured to defend it, before a company in " his own house." Here you would insinuate that the person defended it as a principle of his own; but unhappily for you, we can produce the witnesses present to prove, that before he would speak on that point, he told them, that they were not to consider what he said as his own principles; but as there were so many Divines present, he thought Mr *Allan*'s doctrine might be tried how far it was agreeable to the word of GOD. Accordingly, a divine present and him took one side of the question: And we are persuaded none present had any other view of the conference; tho' now made a *venting grievous errors*. But this reproach will equally affect the other Rev. Gentleman, who has often declared he had not the remotest thought of speaking on that subject as a principle of his own.—Thus, Sir, you stumble at the threshold, which in some cases would be held ominous, especially as this misrepresentation lies in the same womb (or sentence) with three f—f—ds, which of necessity must make an im———l birth.

YOU say one of us put a restriction upon your ministerial freedom, in saying the congregation would not be rent, " in case you " did not teach that doctrine that was contrary to our opinions." If the matter will look a little worse by interpolations, we find you are not restricted there. The person's words were these, " In case " you did not rent the congregation with your preaching, he " should never do it with his opinions." The plain import of which is, that he intended to keep his opinions to himself; this was no restriction of your ministry; but perhaps too much so of his own christian liberty. However, rather than you would not

have

have a ftroke at thefe opinions where none in prudence could reply, you would rifk the fate of the congregation in bringing it to the public by your declaration: Which you fpend feveral pages feeking an excufe for: Accordingly in page 3d,

You fay, by your lecturing on *Rom.* viii. 32. " New trouble was brought upon you, by converfations, reading of papers, and requiring a fight of your notes."—If you converfed fo often, it was with none of us.—As for papers there were never any read to you but *one* on the fubject, which was *after* your declaration, tho' by a kind of fatality you make it a *caufe thereof*: Forgetting the ufe of that paper, which was to reprefent the bad effects your declaration was like to have upon the congregation, and characters of thofe fo traduced therein. Had we chofen to give you trouble, Sir, you gave us fufficient ground to do it otherways than in the humbleft manner to let you know we were injured by the reports which you were the fole occafion of raifing.

The perfon who wrote and prefented the above-mentioned paper, alfo fignified, that if you would give him out of your notes the arguments you had ufed for eternal Sonfhip, he would either give you anfwers to them, or own the doctrine. We humbly conceive this was no great infolence in him; and not below the importance of a fervant of JESUS CHRIST to grant; at leaft the Apoftle thought it not grievous to write the fame things for the edification of church members.—It is evident how hard you have been pinched to find *reafons* for that warning, (as you call it) when every trifle muft be made fo; especially when *effects* muft be turned into *caufes*, as you have done here.

You go on to tell the world, that " all this was extinguifhed " in a little time, and two of thefe had children baptized, and " came under folemn engagements to bring them up in an agree- " ablenefs to the word of God, and to the doctrines laid down in " our Confeffion of Faith and Catechifms." Were there no more in all your reply that required an anfwer, this could not be omitted. The fcope is to inform your readers that we had now given up thefe principles formerly maintained, and come under engagements to the Confeffion of Faith and Catechifms *as you hold them*. But you will not deny, we hope, that both thefe perfons made exceptions againft coming under thefe engagements as you ordinarily lay them on, viz. To be bound to the Confeffion, Catechifms, and other human compofitions (commonly mentioned by you on fuch occafions) without any difference made betwixt them, and the word of God. And without you would grant to put all thefe human compofitions in fubordination to the fcriptures, (which you never do in laying on baptifmal vows) they both declared they had no freedom to prefent their children to baptifm.—This you granted to do, and actually did fo to them both. Where then is the ftrength of

this

this mighty argument againſt us? But tho' you have maſk'd this relation with all your art to make it bear upon us, your readers have not been ſo blind as not to ſee that it recoils upon yourſelf. How came you (who are ſo very regular in diſcipline and government) to admit perſons to ſealing ordinances whom you knew had been *venting, defending,* and *ſupporting grievous, unſcriptural hereſies*; re*ſtricting your miniſterial freedom*; *traducing the doctrines of the Confeſſion of faith as traditional, and not ſupported by Divine revelation:* Yea, and guilty of *ſpreading this infection in the congregation?*—All which were, according to your own account, prior to the baptizing theſe children, which was done without ſo much as a queſtion concerning the matter in diſpute. Beſides, one of theſe two was ordained an *Elder,* who not only to yourſelf in private, but in the face of the congregation, reclaimed againſt being bound to human compoſitions as expreſſed in the queſtions of the formula, any further than he ſaw they bore evidence from the word of GOD. Why ſo lax, Sir. as admit ſuch a nonconformiſt? Was our hereſy ſo groſs as to deſerve excommunication a little after, and ſo innocent now as *with it* to be admitted to ſpecial privileges and offices in the church? We muſt think, Sir, that ſilence on this part of the affair would have been more prudent in you, as well as on that part of your warning in which you charged us with adopting ſuch horrid principles *to pleaſe ourſelves;* which, we ſuppoſe, was too glaring an encroachment upon Divine omniſcience to admit of any excuſe, and therefore you offer none for it.

WE cannot underſtand what you mean by a new outbreaking, if it be not your unexpected declaration. And now you ſay, we " uſed means to impoſe on the weak, ſpread the infection through the congregation, and trouble others." This is a great part of the charge againſt us, and what you make the leading motive for bringing the affair to the public. Indeed you charged us with it before the ſeſſion; but did we not refuſe the juſtneſs thereof? You were not then capable to prove it; and as an evidence that you relinquiſhed this part of the charge, it is not ſo much as mentioned in the copy of the minute we got, which ſhould certainly contain the whole of the charge againſt us. If it was juſt, why was it not minuted? If groundleſs, why were we charged with it at all? And why now expoſe that to the world as our crime, which you could not prove at our trial? Nevertheleſs, of your induſtry† to find us culpable herein, we challenge you to produce the perſons in the congregation whom we perſuaded to embrace, or impoſed our opinions

† One inſtance of this, was your aſſerting that A-*ch-d* E—*s* told *you,* it was thro' our influence and perſuaſion that he ſigned the declinature: But he is ſo honeſt as to deny that ever he ſaid ſo. We are ſorry you engaged your own credit for the truth of it; and that you did not rather report it among other hearſays.

nions upon. If you find none, be content to bear the blame of bringing it unnecessarily to the public in your warning: And now exposing us to the world for faults that never had existence, that your unaccountable treatment of us may have some shadow of excuse.

PAGE 5th, you first interpolate the words of the letter, and then triumphs: You make the author say, "That for nine or ten " Sabbaths running, he never touched the point." Such a sentence is not in all the letter. He says, page 3d, " It is none of " my business to consider how you acquitted yourself on that sub- " ject.—And that you produced the monstrous doctrines of *Soci-* " *nus*, &c. and answered them, without touching the *points wherein* " *they differed from you*." What need you then ask what point he meant? Did you not know wherein we differed from you? We own it was likely you did not, in substituting things so very remote or rather contrary to our opinions in their room, as *Arianism*, &c. But we think you should have been better informed, before you spent so many Sabbaths in endeavouring to reconcile things as different as light and darkness are.

THE first sentence in page 6th, we know not whether you intend it as the words of the letter or your own: They are not in the former, and if your own, they are against you. However, we shall adopt this orphan clause, viz. Nor could you tell in all your discourses upon that subject, that the principles which we held, did —land in *Arianism, Sabellianism*, or *Socinianism*; nor have yet seen cause to change our opinions herein, *i. e.* you cannot tell yet in your reply, except the world take your word for the whole.

BUT to come to the promised conference, in which we are more likely to agree, as you have been so fair in relating it from the making of the promise, to the charging us as delinquents instead of performing it: However, we shall here insert both accounts. The free enquirer says, " In extraordinary complaisance, you were plea- " sed to promise them a conference with your brethren who came " to assist you at the sacrament; this promise you so far kept as to " invite them to it, and appointed the time and place, which by " them was viewed as uncommonly lenitive, and readily complied " with.—How were their hopes with your fidelity wrecked at " once, when instead of so much as offering an excuse for denying " them the privilege of this promised conference, you constituted " the court, and called them as panels to the bar."

THE true Replier says, page 7th, " Being loth to do any thing " rashly, I was willing to defer the affair until some brethren came " to assist me in sacramental-work, and *promised them* a *conference* " about the matter at that time. This was agreed unto with ap- " parent satisfaction by all parties.—The session met on Thursday " evening before the sacrament, and was constituted."

Now

Now, wherein lies the difference betwixt these accounts? Both own the conference was promised, and agreed to by all parties. Both acknowledge the session was constituted, and we charged as panels without giving us the conference. And this is the very thing complained of by the free enquirer. As the replier's relation of it is the same, what fairer light has he represented it in? How can you complain of being falsly accused in this matter? We with you shall submit it to the impartial, whether the promised conference should have come before making us panels, or after? Could that be a free conference when one party was first made delinquent, and the other in the capacity of judges? We must still conclude according to your concession, Sir, that this was a more ridiculous conduct than all the former; and that the free enquirer has but done you justice in charging you with a breach of faith. .

To create matter of triumph to yourself, you bring in the enquirer, alledging, that for us to " defire this conference would have " betrayed a baseness of mind." He says no such thing, but affirms that on the condition you proposed, viz. That we would declare we were uncertain of the truth of these principles maintained by us, which we had learned from the word of GOD, and undertaking to prove them from it. To comply with this would have betrayed a baseness of mind. But let us ask you, Sir, was this condition, or any other, mentioned, when you first proposed the conference? No, it was to be a free conference. Why then would you at the session affix such a condition to it? Which, we affirm with the enquirer, bore the face of a snare in the session to require: And was much like that cruel and reproachful condition of agreement that *Nahash*, the *Ammonite*, proposed to the men of *Jabish-Gilead*, 1 Sam. xi. 2.— " On this condition will I make a covenant with you, that I may " *thrust out all your right eyes*, and lay it for a reproach upon all " *Israel*." You might as well have told us we should have no conference, as add a condition to it which no honest man that knew his principles could accept of. Besides, the condition was inconsistent with the nature of the conference: That one party must renounce their evidence for, and certainty in, the truth of these principles they are about to defend. This is manifestly giving up the cause before they begin to plead it.

" STRANGE! say you, they did not desire a conversation, yet " were undertaking to prove, that their opinion was agreeable to " the word of GOD! This must be a palpable contradiction, or " that they wanted to force their principles upon us."—This, Sir, like many other extatic admirations flows from the force of imagination. You first imagine we did not desire the conference, then begin to wonder, and draw consequences. But is it not more strange, Sir, that you should infer from our rejecting the conversation embarrassed with your entangling condition, that we did not

desire

(8)

desire it at all? When we not only craved it as was promised: But put you upon performing your promise in the face of the session. Or does it infer the forcing our opinions upon you, that we were willing to shew scripture evidence for what we believe? And where is the contradiction, in a panel to give evidence for the truth of things he is charged with as as errors?

Your design at that meeting was not to confer with us from scripture: But to sit judges of our sentiments and condemn them judicially. Which is evident, (1.) From you constituting the session, and proposing that matter as the end of its being constituted. (2.) From denying us the conference, if we would not accept of the unreasonable condition annexed to it. (3.) From your hasty determinations.* (4.) From your refusing to hear what scripture evidence we had to offer for our sentiments. And (5.) From your producing the Confession of Faith to try our faith by, and refusing to read the scripture proofs for the articles we differed about.

Page 7th, You reckon it defamation to call the Confession of Faith a *human system*. Pray, Sir, do you call it a Divine system? It is likely, when you put it in the place of GOD's word to try people's faith; and call it a test of orthodoxy:—A form of sound words; as if the same which *Timothy* was enjoined to hold fast. These are characters only proper to the unerring word of GOD, which it is a greater pity to discard than all human systems upon earth. But more of this afterwards.

In page 10th, you say, "Had we required a copy of our *libel* you "could not have refused it, but we were the first ever sought a "copy of *minutes*."

The person you mean, as soon as called before the session, required a copy of the *charge* against him, (not your minutes). The Rev. Mr *Nimmo* replied, "There was no libel formed against him, "he was called there to see if he would adhere to the doctrines in "the Confession of Faith formerly read to the three elders," who had been at the bar before him. How can you say "you could not have refused," when you must be sensible now readily we can prove that you obstinately refused the copy of a charge which lay before your session for three years.—But here the replier tells the truth, tho' to the discredit of the session!—" In *ecclesiastical courts* "nothing is more ordinary, than to serve the party *summoned* with "a copy of the *charge* laid against them, unto which they are to "answer." This you acknowledge is just, as no doubt it is. Why then, Sir, guilty of such injustice to us, as neither to give us

a

* An elder, who was not known to be of our sentiments, owned it in the session, and was that moment sisted as a panel, and without further examination, was in three minutes found guilty and condemned. Other two were cited, examined, concluded guilty, and excluded from communion in about five minutes Amazing expedition!

a summons, nor a copy of charge? By your own confession, your seffion is either not an ecclesiastical court, or it manifestly deviated from the just rules of such courts. What a degree of sympathy you make the granting that copy!† A mighty favour indeed, to let a man

† You make it an act of the greatest sympathy and indulgence to give a copy of your minutes, lest our civil interest should suffer from what the seffion had done; thereby intimating, how tender you were in that point.—Saying and not doing differs widely, Sir; but doing contrary to what we say, still more —What regard you, and some of your very zealous disciples have lately shewed for the safety (rather destruction) of our civil interest, some of us know by experience: And it is evident from your answer to the following letter, sent to you by one of us, to make trial if you really would do as you said on that head.
"REV. SIR,
I AM not willing to detain you, by giving an account how far our difference affects my spirits. But as an additional weight, it is like to affect my *civil interest* nearly. And as I have heard you with pleasure often declare that you would be sorry if it was so: Then, Sir, you will be glad when I present you with an occasion to shew, that you do not want to confound the things of this world, with the kingdom of CHRIST. And evidencing you abhor that *persecution* should attend the execution of the office of a minister of CHRIST. Which you will do by writing a short line, importing, that tho' different sentiments take place betwixt A. M. and you in *things religious*, yet it is neither your opinion nor inclination, that others should take occasion from thence to deprive him of the means of gaining his livelihood; or hinder him from being connected with civil society, in a way of getting his livelihood in the world, &c."
The Answer.
"SIR,
I HAVE nothing to do with your civil privileges, and as I have been no way active in suppressing them, neither can I support them.
This from yours, ALEX. NIMMO."
Now, Sir, as the granting this line would have manifested you abhorred these *Erastian* principles; so your refusing it, declares you are well enough satisfied with such adulterations, when a party cause is to serve. And so have renounced the Seceders' Testimony particularly designed against *Erastian* tenets.
BUT what is of more consequence, it is rejecting what is required in both the sixth and eighth commandments, viz. To use all lawful means to preserve the life, and procure, and further the wealth and outward estate of others.
THIS you say, "*you have nothing to do with*." But, Sir, if the person had been even your enemy, the law of GOD demanded your assistance not only to himself but his very beast. " If thine *enemy* hunger, *give* him bread to eat; and if he be " thirsty, *give* him water to drink.* If thou meet thine *enemy's ox* or his *ass* going " astray, thou shalt surely bring it back to him again. If thou see the *ass* of him " that *hateth thee* lying under his burden,—thou *shalt surely help him*."§ The difference in religious sentiments was very great betwixt the *Jews* and *Samaritans*; yet one of the latter has the character of *neighbour* for his tenderness and humanity towards the other in distress. And tho' you give up this name, (as our Lord defines it) there are others in the parable this part of your conduct gives you a very just claim to; for having wounded our reputation by your inconsiderate declaration, which tends to strip us of the means of life; like the Priest and Levite, you say you " have nothing to do with our *civil privileges*;" and refuse to preserve them when evidently in your power. These are not christian principles that lead people to unchristian practices. To deny our assistance to any creature in distress, while the Almighty by his bounty supports it in being, is a violation of his will, who commands us to do good unto all;

* *Prov.* xxv. 21. § *Exod.* xxiii. 4, 5.

man know what he is condemned as a heretic and denied communion for! But you say, "you were under no obligation." What, not obliged to do what you own to be right, and the ordinary practice of courts. Not the copy of their minutes you will say. But, Sir, had you given us a copy of charge, we had no occasion for your minutes. Turn this affair which way you please, your fault is conspicuous in it.

You take a strange method, Sir, to exculpate yourself concerning the reading of the minute that was altered. Subtract your strong affirmations, appeals to GOD, the world, &c. the evidence amounts to no more, than " that some hundreds know it to " be false. And by comparing the original, the alteration, and " extract together, it will convince any that it is false." Now, Sir, as you have put the merit of this accusation upon such a footing, " if true, *you* should justly be accounted the vilest of mankind, " and utterly unfit for any society, but that of the infernal regions." We say, to pass such a sentence upon yourself, in case what the *Free Enquirer* hath said be true, and then to produce such slender evidence to the contrary, really gives us pain. You say, " Some hundreds know it to be false." It may be called millions with equal propriety. You mean the congregation who heard it read. But can you suppose any one so stupid, as to imagine, that all these could know if it was the altered minute that was read, when they knew nothing about whether it was altered or not. How then can they be evidences either for, or against it? If we suppose a proclamation from the court, read publickly in this town, would any be so senseless as say, that all the croud that heard it, could tell what alterations it underwent in the committee that drew it? The case is parallel, for the minute was altered in the session, which you certainly do not mean by the some hundreds, seeing they are not half a score. But your other evidence is still weaker. For tho' the original alteration and extract were compared, the question still remains, Which was read? And if put to the whole congregation, perhaps not one could say with a safe conscience, that either this,

or all; and in effect saying, the government of the Most High is exceptionable in maintaining such creatures in being.—Therefore, Sir, tell us no more of your sympathy and tenderness about the civil interests of any but your own party, since you have given it under your hand you have nothing to do with any other.

We had taken no notice of the above letters, had not the person been so traduced for making that request, which he needed not expect to be favoured by you, who in page 4th, glories in the honourable employment of laying a grave stone on the christian characters of these who are so unhappy as to differ in sentiments from you; which you call slaying, and burying their own characters; as if all that differed from you were not only without characters as christians, but themselves the murderers of their own characters. And were it even so, they are more the objects of pity, than to complete the tragedy by laying grave-stones upon them.

or that was read; much less risk an eternal society in the infernal regions. It would have been safer, Sir, to have given your word for evidence, and left it so.

You say, page 13th, " All of them had a free conference with " a Rev. brother and me, in the presence of the elders."—Not all, only three of us; and on your part it was far from being free, except upbraiding us for setting ourselves up to preach and teach our betters, be free conferring. As to the Rev. Mr *Hunter*, (to his praise we mention his name) he reasoned with a spirit of mildness becoming a christian: The sum of his arguments is considered, page 30th of the Dissertations. This could not be a free conference, since the session had found us guilty long before. It was kind in the gentleman to use means to convice us wherein he supposed us wrong: But this converse with Mr *Hunter*, *Aug.* 10, could not perform your promise, *May* 22, when instead of conferring, sustained us delinquents, and proceeded with us accordingly.

There are sundry other misrepresentations in your *Reply*; but as we chuse not to detain you, Sir, with a particular review of them, so we could not clear ourselves of the charge of prolixity, were we to enumerate all the things entirely foreign to the point, tending only to amuse the inconsiderate: This would be to transcribe more than half your *Reply*, and so be faulty in the same respect.

You certainly supposed your readers endued with very weak memories, especially the impartial public, &c. to whom you make about as many appeals as you have pages.—Nevertheless of your promise to take no notice of sarcasms, that subject is often resumed.—That our opinions have not, nor cannot be proved agreeable to scripture, you tell us *only* eight times. And that your principles and terms of communion are so, you make a whole dozen repetitions of.— Our errors, misconduct, or antiscriptural principles, is but about *seventeen* times mentioned.——And the Free Enquirer as often traduced for favouring them or us. Had these particulars been *seven*, instead of *seventy*, your reply had been shorter, and the strength (or rather weakness) of your reasoning appeared less in disguise. But in this we suppose, you have assumed the office of a schoolmaster that lay so near your mind, who is obliged by frequent repetitions, to draw his pupils into the habit of knowing and believing some things to be true upon his authority, because not capable to demonstrate them to their capacities.

Under this head we cannot escape that very rich period, page 1st, " Free Enquirers will be free thinkers, and free writers too, " who can hinder them?" A notable discovery! But where's the crime? To enquire freely, is the duty of all, and the glory of protestants. To think freely, is an innate principle in every individual of mankind, which they cannot be divested of more than

their

their being. To write freely, is the privilege of *British* subjects. And did you lay aside any of these in writing your Reply? Can it be a crime, what you as a man, and a christian, must daily exercise?

Nor should we neglect what you say you were *necessitated* to mention, viz. the authority of Mr *Ralph Erskine*, page 3, 4. Which was wholly superfluous, after human authorities were all set aside; even that of the venerable *Westminster* assembly, as incompetent evidence, and the matter submitted only to the Divine testimony; what *necessity* then for producing the sentiments of one Divine? Especially one whose reputation as a christian, and divine, you in connexion with the synod you belong to had endeavoured to blast, in passing the greater sentence of excommunication upon him. He must be delivered over to Satan for his unsoundness, yet his sentiments composed since that sentence made the standard to try people's faith. Tho' to us, Mr *Erskine*'s memory and works are very dear; yet we humbly conceive, another human testimony (since you are so fond of them) would have suited *you* better.

Page 6th, You call it a plain truth, "That our opinions were so " near a-kin to the *Socinians*, that we could not abide to hear them " confuted, &c." This must be of the same consequence with our opinions having a *tendency* to *Arianism*, *Sabellianism*,&c. you have equally proved both, *i. e.* proved neither.

Could you ever have a fairer opportunity to prove these things than when writing against our opinions? But this you have never so much as attempted to do in all your Reply. Your saying so is sufficient, and no doubt you expected your words would carry a determined signification to your readers, viz. that we were *Arians*, &c. This you teach them from experience, page 15th, "Whenever " I hear *Arianism* or *Socinianism* mentioned, I conceive of them to " be nothing but the principles which *Arians* and *Socinians* hold." Now they must have dull conceptions indeed, that will not conceive us to be of these denominations when you have mentioned them so often: And added such cogent proofs, as, " I freely declare " that I will never decline from calling an *Arian* an *Arian*, a *Sa-* " *bellian* a *Sabellian*, nor from saying that opinions tending to " these have such a tendency.—These men's opinions are a-kin to " the *Socinians*, &c." Here is *ipse dixit* for the whole. This is the concisest method of proving things imaginable: And a short way of making heretics. But we must be allowed to say, that such weakness makes evident your incapacity to prove our opinions heretical. It is not your saying so, and another going as far as you do, that will prove it: But that is the sum of your evidence to that purpose through the whole of your Reply.

The Free Enquirer puts this question, " Has not every person " a power of leaving the communion of any society, as well as a
" power

"power to join it, when the terms of communion the fociety pro"pofes to him, are fuch as in confcience he cannot agree with?" You were aware how much of your caufe depended upon a fair anfwer to this queftion, therefore you neither anfwer pofitively, nor negatively, which were both dangerous for you. The firft was fo, for then by your own confent, page 13th, you had no right from GOD to excommunicate us, and fo would have confirmed every thing the Free Enquirer alledges againft you : The laft was equally dangerous, by giving a thruft at chriftian liberty, confcience, reafon, and feceders' principles avowed in their act and teftimony. What fuits you better than either of thefe, is to fpend two pages turning the queftion into an argument of your own devifing, then branding it as moft abominable, a fetting up of confcience as the infallible rule. Thus you evade the queftion by a multitude of words which have not the leaft reference to it. You always fuppofe that your terms of communion are unerringly fixed on fcripture, therefore finful in us to forfake communion with you. But the matter comes to this, Who is to judge for a perfon whether terms of communion be agreeable to GOD's word or not? If he take the impofer's word for it, and fo approves of them, his faith is implicit, he that moment commences *Papift*, fubmitting his confcience blindly to the dictates of the church. If he does not this, what then muft he do? Why, judge for himfelf whether thefe terms are agreeable to fcripture. And if his confcience, informed from fcripture, concludes thefe terms difagreeable thereto, it is his duty to decline that communion from a principle of confcience. Is this fetting up confcience as the unerring rule? Or muft the man continue in that communion, and fo declare war againft the GOD of heaven, whofe deputy confcience is ; and live under the conftant accufations of that monitor and judge he perpetually carries in his own breaft. " For " if our heart condemn us, GOD is greater than our heart.—Be" loved, if our heart condemn us not, then have we confidence " towards GOD."†

BUT the fault in the queftion is, that the word of GOD is not mentioned inftead of confcience. The Free Enquirer lays no more on confcience than the apoftle did.§ And tho' the word of GOD had been put in, the Replier's ordinary refuge was ready, " That it was only our conceptions of their terms being difagree" able to fcripture, but our thinking fo did not make it fo." But, Sir, our thinking fo from fcripture evidence will make it fo to us. And what do you think the feceders had more for ground of feparation from the church of *Scotland?* Did that church acknowledge their terms of communion were unlawful? No, they maintained that

† 1 *John* iii 20, 21.
§ 1 *Tim.* i. 5. *Acts* xxiv. 16. *Rom.* ix. 1.—ii. 15.—xiii. 5. *Titus* i. 15. 1 *Cor.* viii. 12. 2 *Cor.* i. 12.—iv. 2. 1 *Pet.* iii. 16, &c.

that their terms were agreeable to the word of God. Was not this sufficient to make the seceders heretics, in separating from them upon the supposition that their terms of communion were not such as they in conscience could agree with ? We would know what peculiar privilege the seceders had of judging for themselves in that case, which other christians have not in judging of their terms of communion ? But say you, " They are granted all the liberty the " word of God allows them." What liberty is it, so long as they are restricted to your opinion, or some other fallible men's, concerning the meaning of scripture ? The church of *Rome* gives a liberty as extensive ; some judge of the meaning of scripture, and the vulgar must be satisfied with their judgment as the true sense ; and so every one must believe as the church doth. This liberty depends not on revelation, but the good-will of the church. So that the difference betwixt them and us is only this ; they have their teachers' interpretation without the scriptures ; and we have the scriptures with our teachers' interpretation, which last we are obliged to believe. This is a change of popes, but not of popery. The Free Enquirer alledges, it is most like a christian " to believe and " profess what he sees evidences in the word of God to support."— This you say, " makes as much for any *Arian* in the world as for " him." Now since conscience, and evidences from the word of God are both excluded ; what remains, but to give up all to the judgment and discretion of our teachers ?—But what must poor souls do who cannot see the propriety of their interpretations ; and in the mean time are assured by the great God, that they must be accountable to him themselves as individuals, for every thing they believe or profess ? One would think they ought to be satisfied in their own judgments before they assent to these interpretations.— But alas! if they search the scriptures to see if these things are so, and find evidences to the contrary, they are brought to this woeful dilemma, either to be pronounced heretics in dissenting from the opinions of their leaders ; or profess and believe contrary to their consciences and the evidences of revelation.—This, Sir, is the case betwixt you and us. And let your Reply be rightly attended to, it will not obscurely point out this doctrine of implicit faith.

There is another point you labour much in these pages, viz. That we were in communion with you when you excommunicated us. It may be asked, Sir, if it be possible for a person to leave your communion when once he is in it ? Your reasoning would infer it was not. Our declinature was given in writing, subscribed by us, and the causes mentioned ; tho' not sufficient to you, they were so to us ; it was received in a constituted session, read, and kept without any answers returned. By your own consent then, we were no longer under your jurisdiction when you accepted the declinature, in which we explicitly renounced your authority over us. Had
you

you thought it unjuſt, it ſhould have been rejected or anſwered. You could not but know after reading, that it was intended to diſſolve our connexion as members of your ſociety; and in as much as you accepted thereof, the ſeparation was mutual on both ſides. We could expect no further privilege in communion with your congregation 'till we had withdrawn our declinature: How could you pretend to have ſtill authority over us as if in full communion with you?—Sir, as to expoſe this, and the way you take to defend it as they eaſily might, would be too like a deſign to expoſe you and your ſeſſion; we ſhall only add this reflection:

THAT when any degree of perſecution is recommended to the world in print, it is the duty of every friend of chriſtian liberty to appear againſt it. And as the principles couched in your Reply, make it evident there is only the want of countenance from civil power, (which we may thank GOD runs in another channel) to deſtroy the chriſtian liberty which GOD hath made the privilege of every individual that comes not up to your ſtandard, or meaning, impoſed upon the ſcriptures. We ſhould think it ſtrange if men were ſo infatuated, as not to hold ſuch principles in deteſtation. In vain have proteſtants caſt off the yoke of *Romiſh* ſlavery, if they are obliged to take on another equally ſevere. Every chriſtian muſt certainly think himſelf free in his choice of what doctrines he is to believe beſide the ſcriptures. He cannot be diveſted of that power the Almighty GOD hath endowed him with, of judging for himſelf in things of the laſt conſequence to him, and for which he himſelf, and not another for him, muſt be judged, according to the uſe and improvement he makes of the rights and privileges beſtowed upon him: Therefore, ſhould beware of giving up his judgment and conſcience to be governed by any man or ſociety, 'till he can find ſecurity from them, that they ſhall anſwer at the bar of GOD for what errors may be in his faith; and for his affronting the Majeſty of heaven, in rejecting his Divine command of judging for himſelf; and ſetting up fallible mortals in the throne of GOD, as lords over his conſcience.

WE muſt now diſpatch the Reply, and ſupercede what was further intended upon it, to give place for ſome remarks upon a later performance. Therefore ſhall only remark on the 4th general fault we find to your Reply: That it was certainly indecent in you, Sir, to treat the gentleman ſo, whom you ſuppoſed to be the author of the letter: And particularly ſo, when it is conſidered, that you had all the certainty which any perſon could require that he was not the author of it, previous to your writing the Reply. Did you not deſire a Rev. gentleman, to enquire at the ſuppoſed author whether he was ſo or not? This he did, and was certified in the ſtrongeſt terms, from his own mouth, that he was not. Did not this gentleman return you an anſwer, aſſuring you the other he enquired

enquired at was not the author? Was not this sufficient to satisfy any reasonable person? But you would still sustain him the author, in spite of the clearest evidence to the contrary; and so sport yourself with the gentleman's evidence, and your own incredulity: For it seems you did not intend to credit his information, tho' you sent him to obtain it for you.

But if you ask why the true author concealed his proper name? We answer, it was to save you the labour of throwing out personal reflections, and that you might have only the subject itself to consider. And you have given evidence that his jealousy was well founded, since rather than you would not be dissecting characters, you would substitute an author which you were assured had not the least hand in writing the letter.

But lest you should repeat your error, we certainly inform you, that the real author is the same with the author of the dissertations.*—And now perhaps you have sufficient matter for another reply, containing all the hearsays concerning him. And indeed we are sorry to hear so many say, that this is a department among the *literati* which you seem peculiarly qualified for. As hearsays make but lame arguments, had you in place of them, and other disparaging characteristics, substituted some better arguments in defence of your own and sessions' conduct towards us; your candor would have been more conspicuous, and your Reply perhaps had more admirers.

Being now to conclude, permit us, Sir, to express how deeply we lament, the many unhappy and unchristian-like consequences that have attended this difference betwixt you and us! What occasion enemies to religion take to insult it, with the professors thereof in general, when they find the strictest of them, in constant strife, who shall be most active in destroying the reputations and interests of others: Making detraction and defamation the business of their lives; and all under colour of zeal for religion, as if it were now become a sanctuary for the grossest immoralities, and an excuse for the destruction of all that is dear to their fellow christians.

Suffer us also, to lament our own fate, in the very hard treatment measured out to us: Who for embracing truths, which appeared so to us, not from any principles of prejudice, education, or party; but from evidences drawn immediately from the word of God; which we could not recede from, without offering violence to our understandings, consciences, and duty to God; and manifestly betraying the privilege he hath granted us, of believing for ourselves what we see the strongest evidences from revelation to support. For this, as it were the greatest crime, we must be brought under the dismal necessity of either renouncing what we were persuaded in our own judgments were the truths of God: Or in refusing

to

---

* A Pamphlet, entitled *a View of the Trinity*, &c.

to renounce them, be denied communion, pointed out as the vileſt of heretics, expoſed to all the ridicule and reproach which wit or malice could invent, and be ſubjected to all the infamy thoſe could caſt upon us, who would have acted more like chriſtians, had they mourned over our fall (as they ſuppoſed); and uſed means for our recovery; than with all the vehemence of declared enemies, to go about and traduce and calumniate us as the vileſt of men. This practice muſt be ſurpriſing to every perſon of candor; and a diſhonour to chriſtianity itſelf: That the religion of the meek and lowly JESUS, ſhould be uſed as an incitement to the paſſions of men, ſo viſible in the acrimonious party quarrels, which have been ſubſtituted in the place of chriſtian piety and brotherly love, which are eſſential ingredients in the heaven-born religion of the prince of peace. How inconſiderate a part do they act, who proclaim how little themſelves deſerve the name of chriſtians, by their forwardneſs and diligence to ruin the chriſtian characters, and even civil intereſts of others? Manifold are the examples we could produce; but as we chuſe rather to lament their weakneſs, and wiſh their reformation, than recriminate: So we take this opportunity to declare our real ſorrow, that you, Sir, whom we always perſuaded ourſelves, were far otherways inclined, ſhould in ſo many inſtances have been ſo nearly connected.——But as far as we know our own hearts, and theſe things concern us, we ſincerely forgive you, and others who have ſo manifeſtly injured us. And deſire to pray that GOD may grant forgiveneſs; and grace to preſerve you all from ſin, and every ſnare of the devil: And that at laſt you may be made poſſeſſors of the peaceful regions of immortal bliſs. When all the jarring ſentiments of CHRIST's diſciples ſhall be for ever loſt in oblivion, and they eternally united in harmonious concord, celebrating the praiſes of GOD and the LAMB:—That we may all live here as expectants of that pure inheritance, into which nothing can enter that defileth or maketh a lie, and be ready for the enjoyment thereof, when time with us ſhall be no more; is the prayer of us, who remain. Rev. SIR,

YOURS, &c.

Note, *The above is expreſſed in the plural, becauſe ſome others are concerned, who approved of publiſhing it; and knowing moſt of the facts here vindicated, are ready on any proper occaſion to atteſt the truth of them.*

A N
EXAMINATION, &c.

Dreams are but interludes, which fancy makes;
When monarch reason sleeps, this mimic wakes,
Compounds a medley of disjointed things,
A court of coblers, and a mob of kings.   DRYDEN.

When apparitions fill the mind,
The soul's unnerv'd, and reason's blind.   R——.

AS dreams are but fictions, the effects of a disturbed brain or imagination, it might be reckoned as profuse in me to be particular in replying to such visionary fables, as it was in the pretended quaker to publish his dreams: But as " his waking thoughts" are added, which are as fictitious, at least specious, as what he calls " the visions of his head" upon his bed, allow me to make the following short remarks upon the whole.

THE character of a quaker is so ill supported through the whole of the performance, that he must be wilfully blind, or very little acquainted with quaker principles, who does not see it to be counterfeit: In this respect the author has not only exposed his own weakness; but most grosly abused the people of that party; who universally hold these things in the greatest detestation, which this metamorphosed quaker is here made to defend. This impotency is not only obvious in every page; but any ordinary reader will see, what signals of distress, like a ship in a storm, this dreamer shews, and like the Psalmist's destitute mariner, staggers to and fro, and is at his wits end, for want of matter in Mr *M——y*'s letter to find fault with. This makes me think he had better consigned three-fourths of it to oblivion, with what was culled from it after his manuscript was shewn to his friends, owing to a tenderness in some of them to the characters of other men, which it would seem this Dreamer has got a very small share of.

As

(19)

As the dreamer says he had read Mr *M—y's* letter before he "dropped fast asleep," let me ask him, why he did not detect that lying demon which appeared to him, while he utters with such demonian rage so many things that are not in the letter, and so demon like, throws such a reproach upon the sacred word of God, and the inspired *Solomon*, a penman thereof, in calling his words, "a list of the very opprobrious names given by Mr *M—y?*" It would appear that either the dreamer acts in concert with this lying spirit, which here exhibited the true character of satan the father of lies: Or that he intended to expose this apparition, by publishing his lies and abuse of revelation to the world.

If *Solomon* had affronted Mr *N—o*, why does he not take him to task for it? And not with impudence, peculiar to demons, cal *Solomon's* language the words of Mr *M—y*. By this rule of his, every text that is used in either the Reply or this performance of the dreamer, are not the words of God, but the words of the Replier and Dreamer.

But let me not accuse the demon for what he is not guilty of; when I read again, I find they are not the apparition's words, but a comment of the fictitious quaker, or rather Mr *N—o*, who it seems challenges the honour of writing the notes.

Now, I cannot help expressing my sorrow, that any of his character and profession should have in the least countenanced, much less corrected, printed, and written notes of approbation to such a heterogenious jumble of incoherent and indecent reveries, as are contained in this performance of the Dreamer. How ludicrous must it be among the scoffers at religion and every thing serious? How grating to the christian ear, to find the sacred word of God, and the privileges of christians so shamefully treated? Who could ever imagine how it could enter the heart of any christian to compare the right of private judgment, to a right of *pissing* in another's face! Which plainly insinuates there is no right of private judgment at all, seeing none can be so void of common sense as to pretend a right for the other. Such language could hardly be expected from professed enemies to religion, who must certainly conclude, that whatever is preached and professed about religion and piety is all a solemn mockery, when they find the greatest devotees thereto, who, by a blazing profession, say stand by for we are holier than you; yet sporting themselves wantonly with the institutions of heaven, which are so plainly taught in the word of God, so often sealed with the blood of martyrs, and the very distinguishing characteristics of protestants!

But this part of the dream is not only ludicrous and profane, but it is nonsense. What comparison can we suppose betwixt the right a man has to think for himself in matters of religion, and a brutal and more than impertinent action, which for any one to do

to

to another, offers violence to common sense? Is there no difference betwixt a man thinking he hath a right from the word of GOD to judge what he should receive from men as matter of faith; and doing that to his neighbour which would expose his own shame, be rude, unmannerly, and indecent in the highest degree? He who would attempt such an action, only deserves to have *Horace*'s rule applied to him, *Testes laud amique salacem demeteret ferrum.*

THERE are so many lineaments of the Replier in this Dreamer, that one would be ready to think it is the same person: But the Dreamer's declared connections with familiar spirits, forbid me in charity to think it is so.

HOWEVER, there is an uncommon agreement of sentiment prevails through both performances. The Replier, page 4, concludes some that differed from him to be self-murderers of their own characters, and glories in his own humanity in laying a grave-stone upon them. And this Dreamer brings Mr *M—y* in guilty of *felo de se*, or self-murder, (pretty language for pious professors indeed)! and no doubt accounts it an act of charity to bury his character also. But with their leave, the verdict of the coroner's inquest was necessary for both, before they had found them guilty, much less buried them. This perhaps may be sufficiently supplied by the authority of the Replier and his session, who upon the same principle, may bring in all the people of *Britain* that differ in opinion from them guilty of *felo de se*; but this will be so far from proving any man guilty, that every one of common sense must laugh at their folly.

BUT what makes Mr *M—y* a self-murderer? Why, it was his being so credulous as to believe that the Replier pointed him out as the author of the letter he replied to. This he had very good ground for, not only from the scope of the Reply, and citing and misconstructing a passage from the preface to his sermons: But from the united voice of the Replier's congregation, who were fond of certifying all they had access to, that he was the very person intended. But if all are self-murderers that thought Mr *M—y* pointed at in the Reply, there will be work enough for both Replier and Dreamer in burying and laying on grave-stones: But unhappily for the Replier, he must do this good office for the most of his own congregation who are under the same predicament.

MR *M—y* needs not be much offended with the character which this se———ng quaker hath given him, while there have been so many that have shined in the church much longer than he, with fair and unblemished characters, yet being so unhappy as to differ from that party, must go down to the grave with all the odium they could cast upon them. It seems to be held as a peculiar right, to which se—ers are only intitled, to abuse and reproach those that differ from them, who yet have no right to defend themselves; but must remain content with the characters of liars, *Arians*, &c. or

what

what the godly prelates of that party shall please to impose upon them; which leads me to observe,

THAT both Replier and Dreamer make a mighty noise about *Arianism, Socinianism,* &c. being called words of course and without meaning, when applied to persons they have no relation to. Tho' the meaning of words are generally settled by custom, yet when persons use words they neither know the meaning of, nor why they apply them to such persons, certainly these must be words of course to them.—Suppose some of the Replier's congregation should call the men that lately differed from them *Arians, Sabellians,* &c. and being asked, as some of them were, what these names meant, should answer they did not know; would not these be words of course and void of meaning to them?

If a seceder should be asked the meaning of the word *Latitudinarian*? If he could not tell, pray what was it more to him than a word of course in his swearing against it in the bond of the covenant?

BUT the Dreamer goes on with his witless criticisms, and is so fond of reproaching, that even the printer's boy cannot escape him, who now must be blamed for the ungrammatical citation from Mr M—y's preface, and no doubt for changing the *Latin* participle *crambe recocta* also. But the Dreamer did not mind, I suppose, that Mr M—y has the Replier's angry letter, vindicating *recoxta* to be the proper construction, and withal desires him to go to his Dictionary again, or borrow one of his friends if he had none of his own. This wholly clears the printer of the charge; and so the trifling criticisms of menacing pedagogue, man of the rod, &c. might have been spared: Which last, I suppose, will be as singular phraseology as *crambe recoxta:* But I hope this disguised quaker will find us examples the next time he dreams.

As for groundless surmises being incapable of sufficient evidence, it may be observed, that many things may have no truth in themselves, which to us have the highest probability. Thus many judges have been imposed upon by evidence which they could not reject, being brought to prove things which in themselves were without real existence, and so must be groundless. I suppose had two or three persons whom the Replier could credit, told him they saw Mr M—y write the Free Enquirer's letter, he would have reckoned this sufficient evidence, tho' in fact it was a groundless surmise.

THE Dreamer enquires, how Mr M—y will " account for his " supposing that either a weak man or a strong man can believe " without evidence?" But he lays no such thing, only supposes that the Replier had believed without *sufficient* evidence. Which is too common among many in matters of much greater concern than the character of Mr M—y; as for instance, there are many who

who believe that the DIVINE PERSON of the LORD JESUS was BEGOTTEN, and that his PERSONALITY with all his DIVINE PERFECTIONS were COMMUNICATED to him from the FATHER. I would be obliged to the Dreamer, would he produce sufficient evidence for this doctrine from the scripture. But to go on.

Mr *M—y* hath these words, "I am ashamed to think that any "person, who assumes the name of a teacher of righteousness, "should publish a report of *persons, they are not acquainted with*, "from *hearsay*, and the uncertain *voice of fame*, which have so often "been found at fault."

ON this sentence the Dreamer learnedly observes, that it is like a crooked Ram's horn; why, (1.) Mr *M—y* stumbles by joining a single person to a plural verb. (2.) He defileth his conscience by vain repetitions, a sin against the precepts of both the gospel and grammar. (3.) He writes found at fault. Grievous crimes indeed! But as to the first, the quaker is so intoxicated with the spirit of criticism, that he cannot see an antecedent standing immediately before a relative, but brings a false one from the beginning of the sentence. The sentence is intended to shew how uncharitable it is, to publish reports upon persons without first acquainting them, that they may have opportunity to disallow them if false, or confess them if true. So that it is only a dream that " a " single person is married to a plural verb :" And the second is like unto it: For none can suppose that writing to Mr *N—o*, and praying to GOD are of the same consequence; in the latter we are in danger of defiling our consciences by vain repetitions; but I think not in the former. Besides, the act concerning the doctrine of grace (a *seceding standard*) tells us there are no precepts in the gospel at all: How then can Mr *M—y* sin against them? And he is the first certainly that has found this new way of sinning against grammar. But with those that can make sins and duties at pleasure, it is easy to make it an aggravated offence, to mention *hearsay* and the *voice of fame* in one sentence. And were it not for fear of sinning against grammar, I would say they are very often different; for I have *heard it said*, that a quaker wrote the Dream; but the *voice of common fame* says a seceding minister wrote it: Now is there no difference betwixt a seceding minister and a quaker?

THE Dreamer betrays his own ignorance in saying he knows no warrant for writing " found at fault." For besides many other unexceptionable grammarians, he will find it in *Johnson's* and *Rider's* Dictionaries, and in Dr *Swift's* works, such idioms are oftener than once. And no less does his folly appear in putting the question, " Were ever the names of heresies applied to persons?" Surely, or how came *Clark, Whiston*, &c. to get the name of *Arians* otherways; their names were *Samuel Clark*, and *John Whiston*; but
when

when they are called *Arians* and *Socinians*, this muſt be an application of heretical names to perſons.

BUT let us ſee how he vindicates the Replier in applying heretical names to perſons not tainted with the hereſies. Well, it's by ſetting up the Replier as equal with the apoſtle *John* in the propriety of applying hereſies to men: Or rather brings down the apoſtle to the Replier. For he ſays, that *John* had no knowledge of any perſon in *Pergamos* that could be accuſed with holding *Balaam*'s hereſy. But tho' this ſhould be granted, will it infer that JESUS CHRIST did not know who in *Pergamos* this hereſy was applicable to, for it was him that ſent *John* to deliver the meſſage to that church? Now, if the Replier be as certain that the perſons he applies theſe heretical names to are *Arians*, and *Socinians*, as CHRIST was in the other caſe, then the Dreamer gains his point, otherways he muſt be dreaming ſtill. But it is likely he imagined it was ſomething Divine that inſpired him in his ſleep, for he ſpeaks with equal certainty concerning his revelation, as *John* did of his; ſaying, we may with *equal propriety* interrogate the *Apoſtle* as the *Replier*.—Amazing!

IN page 6th, we have the Dreamer's vindication of the Replier's vow or covenant. And ſure *Egyptian* bondage, nor gally ſlavery were not ſo unnatural, as the forcing this quaker to vindicate that which deſtroys the whole of his own principles, and apologize for that oath in which quakeriſm is renounced. But how is he recompenced? With the character of a malicious ſlanderer by him whom he ſo aukwardly is attempting to excuſe. The Dreamer ſays twice that the Replier had vowed to *extirpate* error. No, faith the Replier in his note, the word *extirpate* is not to be found in it, and therefore is a *malicious ſlander*. A poor reward indeed! But as humanity obliges to protect the injured, I muſt let the Replier know that the quaker is in the right, for he will find the word *extirpation* in the 2d par. of the Solemn League and Covenant, and the words *root out* in the National Covenant, with many other of ſtronger emphaſis. Therefore it is a ſlander both upon quaker and covenants to ſay the words are not to be found in them.

BUT to come to the Dreamer's defence. He gives us a definition of perſecution, which I find no fault with; but he entirely fails in clearing the management of theſe covenants from perſecution, which was his principal purpoſe. For it is well known that theſe covenants were enforced by the higheſt pains in law when the civil power happened to be on that ſide: And no ſeceder will deny, that the manner theſe covenants were impoſed was the occaſion of much perjury and profanation, eſpecially from 1638 to 1650, when many thouſands were forced to ſwear, who had no knowledge or faith about what they were ſwearing. Then both church and ſtate conſpired to force every one under the obligation of theſe covenants:

Which

Which is evident from the acts of the Affembly at *Edinburgh, Aug.* 3^, 1639, Seff. 23. By which they not only by their authority order all to fubfcribe the Confeffion of Faith and Covenants under pain of the higheft church cenfures; but petition the Privy Council to add their authority: And alfo petition the Parliament to enjoin the fubfcription under *all civil pains.* Accordingly the Privy Council ordained the fubfcription of them, *Aug.* 30, 1639. And the Parliament, *June* 11, 1640, ordains and commands all his Majefty's fubjects, of what rank and quality foever, to fubfcribe the Confeffion of Faith and Covenant, *under all civil pains.* Char. I. Parl. 2, Act 5. Could this be called a voluntary fubfcription when people were obliged to fwear, however different their private fentiments were, and in fwearing fay as the covenant begins, " We proteft, " that after long and due examination of our own confciences in " matters of true and falfe religion, we are now thoroughly refol- " ved in the truth by the word and Spirit of God; therefore we " believe with our hearts, confefs with our mouths, fubfcribe with " our hands, and affirm before God and the whole world, that this " *only* is the true chriftian faith, &c." Was not this perfecution, to force fubjects to fwear in the moft folemn manner to what they were ignorant of, or very much difinclined to, and that under the higheft cenfures and punifhments?

But the Dreamer will perhaps fay, what is all this to the Replier? The feceders do not enforce them by civil penalties; and they have changed the obligation to the Covenants, therefore cannot be chargeable with fuch perfecution.

As to the firft, there is good reafon for it, the civil powers are not of their party. But were circumftances to fuit, as the note writer fays, page 11th, they would act the fame tragedy; which is plain from the prefbytery lamenting in their anfwers to Mr *Nairn*'s diffent, page 39, " Nor are we fo fituated as our reformers, in having the concurrence of the civil powers, for managing neceffary and lawful procefs againft malignants." In the fame anfwer, they efpoufe that act of Parliament whereby princes were obliged to fwear, " That they fhould be careful *to root out* of their lands and empire all heretics, that fhould be convicted by the kirk." They alfo fay, " that it was not fuitable to their prefent circumftances, to blend civil and ecclefiaftical matters in the oath of God in renewing the Covenants." From all which 'tis plain, there requires no more than a change of circumftances to renew the old fcene of *commanding, enforcing, ordaining,* and *compelling* all to fubfcribe, as the zealous reformers had done before.

But they have altered the covenants and the obligation to them. This no doubt is a *ftep of reformation!* The Dreamer defines the covenant to be a " promife to obey all the commands of God," fo muft be of the fame import with that of *Ifrael, Exod.* xix. 8. " All that

that the LORD hath spoken, we will do." The laws of GOD none will deny, are of perpetual obligation; and seceders constantly teach that the Covenants are of moral, and so of perpetual obligation upon posterity, whether they swear to them or not, and this certainly the laws of GOD are:—Yet they have changed the articles of the Covenants; and the note writer says, "they are to be suited to times, places, and circumstances." But where got they an authority to alter the laws of GOD, or change the obligation to that which is morally binding?—It must be either the substance, or manner of expressing the Covenants that is binding. If the first, that is the laws of GOD and CHRIST, as the Dreamer says, which were morally binding, antecedent to either making or mending the Covenants, and could not be subject to alteration. If the latter, it must follow, that the moral obligation of the Covenants in their former form of expression must cease when it is altered, they cannot be both binding at the same time when so different. How shall we then know whether it is the Covenants made by the Assembly, or those mended by seceders, that is binding upon the succeeding generations? If a church judicature hath power to make one alteration in *perpetual obligations*, they may make a thousand, and go on *ad infinitum*; and so we shall be for ever uncertain what is binding, and what not.

M R *M—y* says, the Replier had sworn to root out all opinions but his own. The Dreamer says, he is sworn to extirpate all error. Now we cannot doubt that the Replier thinks every opinion erroneous but his own; and therefore is sworn to extirpate all that do not agree with him. So that Mr *M—y* says no more of the Replier than the Dreamer does.

WHAT I have said is not directly against Covenants; but the abuse of them: And shews how fictitious the Dreamer's account is of the Replier's vow; which by an unjustifiable use of it, hath been the occasion of more persecution than ever was in *Britain* besides.

M R *M—y* says, "the word of GOD, without the consideration of conscience, has no more fitness to direct men than other animals." The Dreamer says, "The word of GOD is the infallible rule among rational and moral agents." Which plainly supposeth it can be no rule to any other. Here they are agreed. For without a principle of conscientiousness, no being can be called rational or moral. Wherein men agree with animals, the word of GOD can be of no use to them, without we suppose some other consideration, viz. understanding and conscience, by which men are capable of using it. This is plain from the Dreamer's own sentiments: But he is so fond of differing, as to fix a contrary meaning to the words, viz. "That conscience must fix a meaning to the word of GOD before it can be fit to direct men more than beasts."

D   And

And this he proves to be the true meaning, by quoting a golden sentence, as he calls it, from Mr *M—y*'s letter, which was never in it; and so makes him say, that a "man may judge and receive what he thinks fit from the word of GOD." Mr *M—y* is speaking of human doctrines, and inferences held forth by men to be believed, of which every man has a right to receive as much and no more than he thinks right or agreeable to the word of GOD; but the Dreamer will have the word of GOD itself intended here. Is not this a gross perversion? It was not possible any person awake and in his senses could so mistake without design.

The same justice he does to this sentence, page 14th, where having cited this clause from the letter, " every man hath un- " doubtedly a right to judge for himself concerning the meaning of " scripture, and cannot receive it but by an assent of his own " judgment." Which the Dreamer says no man in his senses will deny. But what way will he find it faulty? He takes a part of this sentence, and a part of another, transposeth both parts, points it to answer his purpose, and then barefacedly cites them as words of the letter, and the meaning of the other sentence. Is this justice, Mr Dreamer? To put a bad sense upon a person's words when they will bear a more favourable one, is base: But to transpose, interpolate, and change the pointing, to make an author speak nonsense or error, is an affront to religion, reason, and common sense. By the use of this method the Dreamer's best sentences might be made blasphemy; and the most elegant composition, unintelligible jargon.

I would ask the Dreamer, how he came to approve of the Confession of Faith? Was it not because he was persuaded in his own conscience that it was agreeable to scripture? Or how came the Replier's society to fix the meaning of scripture? Did not their consciences tell them that their inferences were justly drawn from scripture? If they did so, how come others to be guilty in using the same privilege? If they did not, then they have believed implicitly without any judgment of their own.

But I must not omit that marvelous definition of conscience given by the Replier in his note: He says, it is " an intellectual power, by which an assent is given unto the principles of moral operations." Which is right in genus, but wrong in species and use. That it is an intellectual power is right. But that it always assents to the principles of moral action is false. These principles are either external, or internal; the word of GOD is the external principle of moral operation; but this many consciences have not yet assented to. If motives of action in the mind are internal principles, the conscience often dissents from these; for the Apostle tells us that our hearts or consciences condemn us.

Besides, it is not the work of conscience to assent, but to judge
of

of motives and actions. When the mind assents, it is called the understanding or will; when it judgeth, it is the conscience. To assent is to believe, not to judge. This definition belongs to the understanding, if the Replier still holds by the school definition of faculties in the soul; but perhaps he has forgot, and so substituted the conscience in room of another power of the soul, as he seems to have done with the *Greek* word συντηρησις he uses, which is not in the language. The printer's boy has perhaps been found at fault again. It would be needful either to use a *Lexicon*, or never trouble *Greek* or *Latin* languages.

PAGE 8th begins with some terms extremely delicate, and very decently applied to Mr *M—y*; such as fire, frying-pan, pope, popery, devil, bottomless depths, scepticism, &c. From his culinary phrases some might imagine he had been cook; however, such kitchen stuff is tolerably innocent: But such a circle of frightful words together, from one who was so lately conversing with demons, looks so conjuration like, that I must say, from pope, devil, and bottomless pit, *Libera nos Domine*.

AT the bottom of this sensible page, the Dreamer quotes a passage from Mr *M—y*'s letter, and roundly tells us that no protestant will differ from what he saith: Yet immediately calls it a *noisy parade* of words, an *invidiously designed* sentence. From whence we infer the Dreamer is no protestant. He blames Mr *M—y* for judging Mr *N—o* upon evidence. But here he repays him with interest, without evidence. He cannot find fault with the passage itself, therefore falls upon the author's design. This must be uncharitable presumption indeed! Who boldly steps into the throne of GOD, now, Mr Dreamer? From whence were you endued with such penetration, as to dissect the intention of the speaker, when his words are without exception?

HE says, "the Replier and his session never set up for dictators for every individual upon earth." This is fine *Logic*; every individual upon earth, are not in the Replier's congregation; therefore there are no individuals in it. But if they dictate to any one individual, it is the same presumption as to kind, with pretending to dictate for the whole.

BUT I must pass over many things in these pages, to come to the particular purpose intended in writing these remarks, which was to shew the weakness of the Dreamer's subtle and specious reasoning in favour of human systems, to the prejudice of christian liberty, and the Divine authority and use of the sacred word of GOD.

BUT before I proceed, it must be observed how apt the similitude is which the Dreamer produces, to prove that men are accountable to others than the Almighty, for what their consciences receive from the word of GOD. It is no less than that of *King Charles*

Charles the first, who, becaufe he ftretched the prerogative, impofed upon his fubjects, and fubverted their facred and civil rights and privileges, was therefore by the laws of the land, accountable for thefe depredations to his fubjects whom he had thus fo manifeftly injured.—So that becaufe one man is accountable to another for the injuries he does to him, contrary to religion, reafon, and common fenfe; therefore he is accountable to him for his inward fentiments, and what his confcience receives from the word of GOD. Can any one poffibly find the leaft connection here? What, no difference betwixt the fentiments of a man's mind which he gathers from the word of GOD for himfelf, and his actions with refpect to fociety! If his reafoning hold, GOD is not *alone* LORD of the confcience. But to keep to the fimile, which is admirably fuited to the author's purpofe! And I cannot help thinking that the hand of the Replier is therein, from its likenefs to thefe of the fchoolmafter and fcholar, &c. in the Reply, which were as ingenioufly applied in a fimilar cafe. I am perfuaded, if King *Charles* had made no more of the prerogative and liberties of his fubjects than a cafe of confcience or matter of fentiment, he might have gone to his fathers in peace for them. He was condemned for what he did, not for what he believed. In all King *Charles*'s fentence before me, I find not a word of his confcience. A man's confcience lies without the reach of human laws. Pray, Mr Dreamer, what could his Majefty's fubjects do with his confcience; do you imagine they beheaded it with his body? You confefs yourfelf, laft page, to be the unfitteft man in the world to pafs judgment on the Replier's fimilies, you fhould have been better qualified before you had fo expofed your own weaknefs in drawing any.

IN that dull parenthefis immediately before this memorable account of King *Charles*, he fays, a man and his confcience cannot be parted: But here he puts a fpecial difference betwixt the King and his confcience, telling us in *Italics*, left we fhould not obferve it, that *him*, and *his confcience both were* called to an account for his depredations. Unhappy Dreamer, thus to contradict yourfelf fo exprefly in the fame paragraph!

BUT as there are fome very fevere things confidently afferted concerning thefe that diffented from the Replier's congregation; I cannot help correcting a little, the Dreamer's miftake. He calls the Free Enquirer an anonymous libeller, and unknown buffoon; this would have been more to the purpofe, had he not appeared in fuch difguife himfelf: But I think the author of the letter will be as readily known by the name of a Free Enquirer, as the Dreamer will by his titles Quaker, and Benjamin Broadbrim. Befides, the Free Enquirer faid nothing inconfiftent with the character he took; but this Dreamer is fo unhappy as to fay nothing confiftent with the principles of a Quaker. As for the term Buffoon, (or *Merry-Andrew*)

Andrew) if his performance has not merited him this title, it is none of his fault, for his nonsense, witless criticisms, and contradictions; together with his blending things sacred, civil, and profane, cannot miss to be ground of contempt among the serious, and matter of sport with *Deists* and profligates.

But to come to the charge against these men, page 11th, he says, " They swerved from it (viz. the Replier's society) in the " most fundamental doctrines of christianity." But does not tell what they were till page 14th, where he says the " congregation agreed to the sense of Scripture as in the words of the Confession of Faith;" he should have added the Act and Testimony, and Doctrine of Grace, which are standards as well as the other. But " a " few men took it into their heads to differ from the congregation." —How knows he but it was in their hearts also? This is the same as the Replier's saying it was to *please themselves*. Who judgeth now, Mr Dreamer? But " they differed from their former selves." —There is no dishonour in changing *sentiments* (which I suppose he means by *selves*) if it be for better: But take his word for it, 'tis far otherways; why, 'tis from the received sense of Scripture he means, to be sure, as it is in the above standards, which he says " respects the *original basis* of christianity." This intimates there are others; but if he keeps to the sense as in the Confession of Faith, we have a notable discovery, viz. That christianity commenced when the Assembly summed up the sense of Scripture in their Confession! I have heard of christianity as old as the creation; but never that it was no older than since 1648.

But let us come to the charge, What do the men assert? Hear his own words, they " assert things which appeared to thee; thy " session and congregation, to remove all the *revealed* grounds of ," the personal distinction among the three persons of the God- " Head, to overturn the eternal generation of the Son, and to in- " validate the Mediator's right of redemption." An awful charge indeed! But they may comfort themselves a little, that they only " appeared to be so to the Replier and his session," who are not infallible judges of other men's faith. The parts of this charge are, first, they " remove all the *revealed grounds* of the personal dis- " tinctions among the three persons of the God-Head." I am at no small strait to know what he means by *revealed grounds*. If by grounds he means the fundamental causes or reasons of this personal distinction, it is more than stupid to express himself so; for there are no such thing revealed, nor can all the divines that exist shew from revelation the causes or reasons of this distinction. God never did, and perhaps never will, reveal the cause of his being three persons in one God-Head. If this be what he intends by the word grounds here, it has no meaning but a blasphemous one; to suppose any cause of the being of God, is to suppose him no God. And

And as the persons in JEHOVAH are as natural and necessary in their existence as the being of GOD, they must be absolutely beyond all cause.

BUT I would favourably judge, that by grounds here he means these principles upon which we found our faith of the personal distinction, which are only revealed in the word of GOD. Why then does he call them so emphatically *revealed* grounds, as if there were *unrevealed* grounds for our faith in this point? And why does he say these persons removed these revealed grounds? Will the Replier, or any of his session and congregation, say that they refused any thing revealed concerning the Trinity? No. Here is the ground of the dispute, they constantly affirmed that revelation alone was the foundation of all we could know or should believe concerning GOD. Had he said they were for removing some human inventions concerning that mystery, it would have been truth: But that they believe a distinction of persons in the GOD-HEAD any one may be fully satisfied by looking into the first Dissertation of a work entitled, *a View of the Trinity in the Glass of Divine Revelation*. So that this part of the charge is visionary, and a gross slander.

THE second is, they " took it into their heads to overturn the " eternal generation of the Son." If the phrase *revealed grounds* be connected with this, it would have been a special favour had he intimated the place in revelation where this doctrine is taught. But as I never could find it, the Dreamer will excuse me if I say, that its appearing true to the Replier and his session is not sufficient ground of my faith: For as he grants, every man hath undoubtedly a right to judge of the meaning of Scripture for himself.

BUT thirdly, they " took it into their heads to invalidate the " Mediator's right of redemption." He adduces nothing for proof, but asserts strongly. I suppose he dreamed this with the Replier's letter before him, where 'tis said these men were a-kin to *Socinians*; the one asserts without proof, and the other follows; but this is no reason why any of them should be believed, when asserting things that never entered either into the heads or hearts of these they are so traducing. But the hand of the Replier is visible in every part of this charge, only a change of words. The supposed denial of a distinction of persons, is the same with the Replier's *Sabellianism*: To deny eternal generation makes an *Arian* with him: And having supposed them a-kin to *Socinians*, it was easy to infer they denied the Mediator's right of redemption. But the next time any of these gentlemen writes, they will please to lay aside bare assertions, and take to proving these men guilty from the word of GOD, not from what they are pleased to impute to them.

BUT the Dreamer having got into the way of telling falshoods, he gives us a bundle of them together. " When these men were " required by thee and thy session, with the concurrence of thy so-
" ciety,

" ciety, either to shew that their new tenets were more agreeable
" to the tenor of Scripture than those which they opposed, or else
" return from that opposition; they could not do the first, nor
" would they do the last." I cannot but observe how nearly related the Replier and Dreamer are as historians, none of them scruples at turning matters of fact into the contrary, when it will best suit them in that dress. The Dreamer could not have told any thing more contrary to truth than this; for these men at the session, *May* 22, 1766, often proposed to shew that their principles were agreeable to Scripture; and requested the session to prove what they read of the Confession from Scripture. The Free Enquirer hath told the answer they got, viz. " That they had no time to read any proofs." This the Replier hath not thought fit to deny: Why then should the very fault of the session be imputed to them? These men might have been set at liberty had they not appealed to Scripture for determination of the matter in dispute. But this is vindicated against the Replier above.

THE Dreamer imagines he hath set all things in order, and confidently puts the question, " Where is there, in all this, the least " foundation for the charge of imposition." I shall briefly tell you, Mr Dreamer: It was in the session insisting on these men renouncing their opinions, without giving them leave to shew what evidence they had from scripture to support them :—And imposing the terms of a human composition upon them, refusing to prove the terms to be agreeable to scripture. And then denying these persons communion for not renouncing the one, and embracing the other, without scripture evidence. And your own imposition is no less conspicuous, in imposing upon the world a scheme of these men's principles they never held.—In transmitting the very fault of the session upon them, and from thence concluding it was right in the session to exclude them. But it shews you had little to accuse them of, when their guilt must be inferred from other people's faults.

I SHALL not further detain the reader with the weakness of his reasoning against Mr *M—y*, or them that differed from the Replier; as the controversy in his remaining pages is not so much betwixt him and them, as betwixt *revelation* and *human systems*. And here the Dreamer will excuse me in changing my address to those, who, *Berean* like, search the scriptures to see if these things are so. Such cannot but observe what a preference this author gives the latter, to the prejudice of the authority, honour, and use of the former, by his weak endeavours to prove that they are " the only " credible profession of christianity, the only preservative against " error, the rule to conduct social worship and spiritual harmony,
" and

" and which christian churches ought in duty, and may with safety,
" rest satisfied with."

I HOPE you will agree with me, that the scriptures were calculated by GOD for these noble ends. This he refuses, by maintaining that every society may and ought to compose a confession, or agree to one already composed by others to answer all these purposes, by which that society, and every member thereof, is to be directed in matters of faith and worship. At what bar shall we try this controversy? We would incline the scriptures should be judge. But he no doubt will then think the favourite system of his society dishonoured. Here I shall not differ with him; but shall admit the system he pleads for, and his own sentiments too into the evidence. Only with his leave, I must be allowed to make revelation the leading evidence in its own favour.

HENCE it is said, " To the law and to the testimony: if they " speak not according to this word, it is because there is no light " in them."* Here the scriptures are made the unalterable standard of whatever is said concerning GOD or our duty: The least variation from them is an evidence of darkness. Only that which is taught in scripture can be sure, edifying, and profitable to make us wise unto salvation; and lead to eternal life. Thus our Saviour answered the lawyer.—" What is written in the law, how " readest thou?"† And thus *Paul* to *Timothy*,—" From a child " thou hast known the holy scriptures, which are able to make " thee wise unto salvation."‡ Ignorance of the scriptures is the road to error, as our LORD saith,—" Ye do err, not knowing the " scriptures."‖ But let us hear how comprehensively the Apostle *Paul* sums up the authority and use of the scriptures. " All scrip- " ture is given by inspiration of GOD, and is profitable for doctrine, " for reproof, for correction, for instruction in righteousness: that " the man of GOD may be perfect, thoroughly furnished unto all " good works."§ Do we chuse an unerring guide? Here is one indited by Divine inspiration. Do we want rules sufficient to constitute a credible profession of christianity? The scriptures are profitable for doctrine and instruction. Are social worship and spiritual harmony christian duties? This Divine system thoroughly furnishes the man of GOD for these good works. Are any in error? This word of GOD is for reproof and correction. Is it a duty to be guarded against error, and defend the truth? On this sacred ground we may safely stand, and be completely furnished for this, and all other good works. Is it the church's duty to cut off errors? Lo, here is the " sword of the spirit, which is the word of GOD."*

As it is impossible to collect all the evident testimonies JEHOVAH gives in favour of his word, let it suffice, to hear its character

---

* *Isa.* viii. 20. † *Luke* x. 25, 26. ‡ 2 *Tim.* iii. 15. ‖ *Matth.* xxii. 29. § 2 *Tim.* iii. 16, 17. * *Eph.* vi. 17.

ter from the seraphic *Psalmist*. "The law (or as in the margin, the doctrine) of the LORD is perfect, converting, or restoring the soul: The testimony of the LORD is sure, making wise the simple. The statutes of the LORD are right, rejoicing the heart: The commandment of the LORD is pure, enlightening the eyes. More to be desired are they than gold, Yea than much fine gold *(or all human systems)*: Sweeter also than honey, and the honey comb. Moreover, by them is thy servant warned: And in keeping of them, there is great reward, &c."† Can any such characters be given to the best composed system on earth besides the scriptures? May not the wit of men and devils be challenged to produce a single instance, wherein the scriptures are defective for answering all the purposes GOD hath revealed, as to the duty, interest, or privileges of the church, and every individual member of the body of CHRIST in their militant ·state. And to shew where GOD hath given the least hint that his mind was to be known any other way: Or, that any other rule was necessary for trying doctrines, and guarding his people from errors.

BUT let us hear what the *Westminster* Confession saith, which by this author is so grosly abused in his setting it up to rival the scriptures. "The authority of the Holy Scripture, for which it ought to be believed and obeyed, dependeth not upon the testimony of any man, or church; but wholly upon GOD (who is truth itself) the author thereof; and therefore it is to be received, because it is the word of GOD.—The whole council of GOD concerning all things necessary for his glory, man's salvation, faith and life, is either expresly set down in scripture, or by good and necessary consequence may be deduced from scripture: Unto which nothing at any time is to be added, whether by new revelations of the Spirit, or traditions of men.—All scriptures are not alike plain in themselves, nor alike clear unto all: Yet those things which are necessary to be known, believed, and observed for salvation, are so clearly propounded and opened in some place of scripture or other, that not only the learned, but the unlearned, in a due use of the ordinary means, may attain unto a sufficient understanding of them. The infallible rule of interpretation of scripture, is scripture itself; and therefore when there is a question about the true and full sense of scripture (which is not manifold but one) it must be searched and known by other places that speak more clearly. The Supreme Judge, by which all controversies of religion are to be determined, and all decrees of councils, opinions of ancient writers, doctrines of men, and private spirits are to be examined; and in whose sentence we are to rest; can be no other but the Holy Spirit speaking in the scripture."‡

† *Psal.* xix. 7, 8, 10, 11. ‡ Chap. i. Par. 4, 6, 7 9, 10.

Much more to the same purpose might be cited from the *Westminster* Conf. But let us hear what this author says himself, P. 8. "Is not the word of God itself the *infallible rule* of all religious "sentiments; and, at the same time, the infallible and catholic "INTERPRETER of its own meaning *(Isa.* viii. 20.) among "rational and moral agents? Is not the word of God sufficiently "determinate in its meaning; else, where is the perspicuity of the "scriptures? Yea, where is there any revelation at all? An *unre-* "*vealed revelation* is a contradiction.—The word of God hath "sufficiently determined its own sense; and the Almighty author "thereof hath bound every man's conscience to submit unto that "meaning, without bringing his own sense unto it. God hath "not mocked us with an indeterminate or unrevealed reve-"lation."

Now, when the Spirit of God, the *Westminster* Assembly, and even the author himself, hath given their verdict so explicitly in favour of the scriptures; who could have imagined he would have spent so many pages, endeavouring to prove that the Confession of Faith, not the scriptures, is the *only credible profession* of *christianity?* Which is in the plainest terms to say, that it is not he that professeth christianity as taught in the scripture, but he that professeth it as taught in the Confession of Faith, that is the christian. And that christianity is better taught in the latter, than in the former. His words will bear no other meaning, or I should be glad to give it. To profess christianity, is to profess the truths or doctrines of Christ laid down in his word. The word *credible* signifies that which is worthy of credit, assent, or belief. The word *only* taken as an adjective, signifies *this above all other:* As an adverb it signifies, *singly,* or *this and no other.* So that the natural construction of his words is, that the Confession of Faith is that book and *no other,* that contains the doctrines of christianity. It *only* is worthy to be believed and credited. It *only* can preserve from error: And it *only* the churches *may,* and *ought* to rest satisfied with, as the *only form of sound words,* and *rule,* to conduct them in worship and spiritual harmony.

Now, could we be so infidel as to credit this author, there is no further use for the Bible; seeing this system is *only* fit to answer all the purposes that concern christians; which it seems foolish men have dreamed the scriptures were *only* sufficient for. But let me tell this author, that in thus exalting any system under heaven, tho' the whole fund of wisdom that men and angels are endued with was included in it, into the place of the sacred word of God, is *only* blasphemous; and tends to divert unthinking men from a due attention unto, and regard for the oracles of the living God!

I am not here condemning the Confession of Faith and other useful

useful syſtems, which may tend to elucidate the meaning of ſcripture, and have no doubt been bleſſed by GOD as means of inſtruction concerning the knowledge of his will revealed in his word: But diſapproving the conduct of men who ſet them up as competitors for prerogative with the Divine word, from which they ought all to be framed, and kept in due ſubordination thereto: Since the difference muſt always remain ſo great, as betwixt the unerring dictates of the infinitely wiſe JEHOVAH, and the words of finite, frail, and worm man.

THIS I deſire the reader to keep always in view.—If the doctrines of chriſtianity be ſimple, plain, and eaſy to be underſtood, which the author grants: Whether does it moſt honour GOD, to hold forth the eaſy and plain words of his ſon JESUS CHRIST and his apoſtles, as the *only credible* profeſſion of chriſtianity, teſt of orthodoxy, and term of communion, which are ſure, unerring, and cannot deceive? Or, to hold forth for theſe purpoſes the manufactured explications of men, who are not only liable to error, but are conſtantly divided in their opinions concerning the ſenſe of ſcripture; and many of them deſtroying in one period of their lives, what themſelves have laboured hard to build up in another. I ſay, whether are the words of CHRIST himſelf, or thoſe of fallible men moſt worthy of credit and belief? Can any be at a loſs to know whether the words of GOD or men merit our aſſent?

SHOULD it be ſaid, by clothing the doctrines of revelation in words of man's deviſing, they become more familiar to the unlearned. But is it not granted that the ſcriptures are ſo plain, that even the unlearned through a due uſe of the means may attain the knowledge of all that is neceſſary to ſalvation?† Beſides, this is a groſs reflection upon the wiſdom of GOD in inditing the ſcriptures, and impoſing them as a rule of faith and practice, while they needed the aſſiſtance of the creatures who were to be ruled by them, to render them intelligible. It reflects on the goodneſs of GOD, to command conformity to a rule on the peril of damnation which was not in itſelf ſo plain as to be underſtood. It ſtrongly inſinuates, that chriſtianity was never properly profeſſed or underſtood till the *Weſtminſter* Confeſſion was compiled; and that ſuch as had no other means than the Bible to teach them chriſtianity, could not know or profeſs it aright. Certainly then, ſuch as are called chriſtians in the New Teſtament did not deſerve the name, ſeeing in their time, not only the canon of ſcripture was incomplete, but they wanted that which *only* can be a credible profeſſion of chriſtianity, viz. ſyſtems compoſed by particular ſocieties.

SHOULD it be ſaid, every ſociety muſt agree in what they judge the ſenſe of ſcripture, to be a rule for admiſſion of members, and ground of cenſuring delinquents. I grant that as every man, ſo every

† Chap. i. par. 7. Conf. Faith.

every fociety have a right to judge for themfelves what is the fenfe of fcripture: But this no way infers that their fenfe of fcripture is the only credible teft of chriftianity, and the only term of communion in the church of CHRIST. This determination is either *neceffary* to the church's edification, or it is not. If it is not, then there is no need to lay fuch weight upon it. But if it be neceffary, then either the fcriptures have provided for it, or they are not a perfect rule, and fufficient for all things *neceffary* to the edification of the church.

IF this fociety fuppofed be a part of the church of CHRIST, it certainly ought to have no other terms of admiffion than CHRIST hath made, could terms of CHRIST's making be reckoned *credible*. And I would be glad to know, what fcripture authority can be produced for any fociety fo far to new model the government of CHRIST's church, as to fuit times, places, and circumftances, which power this author fays every fociety hath. Are the inftitutions of CHRIST the lawgiver fo defective as they need to be fupplied? Or are they fo intricate as not to be underftood? If the firft, then CHRIST has not been faithful in all things over his own houfe, and it muft be falfe, that the *fcriptures are fufficient to make us wife unto falvation, and furnifh thoroughly for every good work*. If the laft, then there could be no chriftian church without other directories than the fcriptures; and fo the faith of the church depends not upon the word of GOD, but upon the fenfe every particular fociety is pleafed to affix to it, which may be right, but cannot unerringly be fo, without fuppofing infallibility in that fociety.

BUT I would rather think fuch a fociety did not belong to the church which hath one head or lawgiver, and one law; but it feems this fociety may and ought to make laws for itfelf, to entitle to, and exclude from, the privileges thereof: Therefore, when it cafts out a member, it is but mocking of CHRIST to do it in his name, they ought to do it in the name of the fociety whofe laws the perfon hath offended againft. Tho' we read in fcripture of the Royal law, the law of CHRIST, and the law of liberty, yet we do not read of any particular laws made by particular focieties for their own government. No, they all continued ftedfaftly in the apoftles doctrine, which it feems is not fo fufficient now; times, places, and circumftances being changed, the doctrines of the gofpel muft be dreffed in another form, before they can be the *only credible profeffion of chriftianity.*

THE perfon who receives this fenfe of fcripture, thus framed, and held out by the fociety, either fees it to be authorized by GOD from his word, or he does not. If the firft, what does it add to his faith, that this fociety or all the fons of *Adam* fhould fay it is the true fenfe, when he only receives it upon the evidence the fcriptures afford of their own fenfe? It may add to his comfort

that

that many embrace it; but his faith would be the same tho' none entertained that sense; as it is not the wisdom of man, but the authority of GOD that is the foundation of his faith. But if he does not see evidence in scripture for that sense, and yet receives it, his faith is but human, not divine; seeing it is only the authority of the society that is the foundation thereof; for tho' it may be the true sense, yet as he receives it not upon Divine authority and evidence, it cannot be to him a Divine faith. Both the society, in imposing it as the only sense of scripture, because they judge so, and the person who receives it upon such grounds, plainly refuse that the word of GOD is the only and infallible interpreter of its own meaning, and the rule of religious sentiments. For if it hath sufficiently determined its own sense, why should not every one apply directly unto it for that purpose?—Should it be plead that it is to prevent heresies: This argues that the scriptures are not sufficiently provided for that end: But as was hinted, if this be a *good work*, *they furnish thoroughly for it*. And the apostle *Paul* lets *Titus* know, that the way *to convince gainsayers, was, to " hold fast the faithful " word, as he had been taught."*†

WHAT can give greater advantage to the enemies of truth, than give them ground to think we suspect the sufficiency of the scriptures, by having recourse to human forms as tests of our faith? Where the words of scripture are plain, there is no need for explications or tests of our understanding of, and adhering to them. And if in any thing the Spirit of GOD hath thought fit to leave it not so plain, it must be presumption in men to make their explications of such points a test of faith. To put doctrines necessary to salvation upon any other foundation than the scriptures, is to betray them into the hands of enemies; and prejudice pious christians against the best compositions of men, when they find them thrust into the place of GOD's sacred word. The gracious design of GOD in committing revelation to writing by inspired men is, that we may have the knowledge of all things necessary to salvation in such words as were most fit to express them, and so most proper for us to keep to: And that we might be delivered from the uncertainty of tradition, and from the attempts of enemies to draw us off from the true foundation, to build our faith upon human authority, and words of men's invention. We ought therefore, to regard the advice which *Eliphaz* gives, " Receive, I pray thee, the law from " *his mouth*, and lay up *his words* in thine heart."§ The scriptures were indited by GOD, and given to men as the standing rule of their faith, and that upon the view of all the heresies which were to take place, by men's perverting the words, and corrupting or misconstructing the sense; yet he hath provided no other rule or standard but his own word; no where hinted that other systems

should

† *Titus* i. 9. § *Job* xxii. 22.

should be composed to prevent errors. And must it not be strange then, to say men have no other way to testify that they do not wrong the scripture sense, than by adhering to a system of words not in the scriptures! If the scriptures have a determinate sense of their own, as this author grants, then they are every way sufficient as a test of faith, and no other is to be preferred to them: But if it be necessary that explications determine the sense for them, then they have not a determinate sense of their own, and their sufficiency is entirely given up.

It must be mighty obliging, to put an addenda to the rule of faith, and finish the work of GOD, as if imperfect; to fortify revelation with bulwarks, without which it could not be saved from error! It must be a prodigious favour done the church, to provide her with means to catch these foxes that spoil her vines; to secure her from, or enable her to destroy these enemies to truth, her peace and safety, yea, secure a seed to the church in succeeding generations! "No doubt but ye are the people, and wisdom shall die with you."‡ GOD hath said, "there must be heresies."‖ No, saith this society, we will agree upon the sense of scripture, fence it with church authority; and to make it impregnable against all enemies, it shall be fortified by civil laws, enforced by the highest penalties, which shall be executed on the guilty wretch that will not believe it to be the sense of scripture; yea, and swear too never to think or speak otherways: But he who is capable of such insolence as to refuse his assent, or speak unbecomingly of this system, shall see the demerit of his crime in the confiscation of his effects, the imprisonment of himself, and may be thankful a gibbet does not finish him with his heresy. This is a part of the plan for preventing heresy! But where have we in the word of GOD either precept or example of forcing men into religion, and employing the arm of the magistrate to punish such as will not comply? What have we from CHRIST or his apostles to favour the modelling the church so much after the fashion of the kingdoms of this world? The apostle saith, "The wisdom that is from above, is first pure, then peace-
"able, gentle, and easy to be entreated, full of mercy and good
"fruits, without partiality, and without hypocrisy. The servant
"of the LORD must not strive; but be gentle unto all men, apt
"to teach, patient, or forbearing, in meekness instructing those
"that oppose themselves, if GOD peradventure will give them
"repentance to the acknowledging of the truth; and that they
"may recover themselves out of the snare of the devil, who are
"taken captive by him at his will."*

It is needless to say, that this compulsive method is not intended here by preventing of heresies. What is then intended? This was the method taken to crush heresy when the civil power favoured the
system

‡ Job xii. 2. ‖ 1 Cor. xi. 19. * James iii. 17. 2 Tim. ii. 24, 25, 26.

syſtem plead for; and if this is not uſed, how ſhall it anſwer the end? If every one is left to his own choice, what influence can the ſenſe ſo agreed on, have to prevent error among thoſe who are diſpoſed to embrace it?

It is agreed that the true ſenſe of ſcripture is but one; yet almoſt every ſociety hath a different ſenſe; and as they cannot all be the true ſenſe, what is the beſt method a perſon ſhould take who is for finding the true ſenſe? To conſult the parties, each accounts their own the only one. To compare them, is an endleſs taſk; beſides the danger of being prejudiced thro' the ſuperior talents of the compilers, who have uſed their whole art to undo all others, and render their own moſt acceptable. Would it not then be ſafeſt to ſearch the ſcriptures, and chuſe his religion upon their own evidence, and the authority of their Author, who has ſuited the revelation of His will to the capacities of his creatures that are moral agents: And take juſt ſo much of human ſyſtems, as he found agreable to this unerring rule?

Does not binding the members of a ſociety to that particular ſenſe of ſcripture they have once agreed upon, limit the Spirit of God in his teachings; and diſcourage the induſtry of chriſtians in ſearching after ſpiritual knowledge? For whatever any perſon may be privileged with through the bleſſing of God upon his ſearching the ſcriptures, tho' perſuaded of the perſpicuity of the evidence, yet, if it be not agreeable to the ſenſe already admitted by the ſociety, he muſt neither believe nor profeſs it: For the full ſenſe is ſettled, the matter of his faith is limited, ſo his enquiries are needleſs, and wherein he believes more, or otherways, he is a heretic. He has all in the ſyſtem needful; to learn more is dangerous.

But the ſociety hath a right to judge of the ſenſe of ſcripture for themſelves. This is granted. But has not every individual the ſame right after uſing diligent and conſcientious enquiries? The author grants this, but will not allow the profeſſing the words of ſcripture to be a credible profeſſion.—Let me aſk, if the lovers of the ſcripture can imagine, how the ſenſe of ſcripture is to be conveyed in human ſyſtems without words? If it cannot, as muſt be granted, how then comes it to paſs that the ſenſe as contained in words of men's deviſing is ſo profitable, which it cannot be in the words that God hath choſen? The Holy Ghost hath held forth the ſenſe in words calculated by his infinite wiſdom and goodneſs. Men put the ſenſe in other words, and call that the *only credible* profeſſion of truth. Why? The author ſays, the words of God may be taken without the ſenſe; true, but may not the words of men be taken without the ſenſe alſo? None can ſuppoſe but the words of men are more liable to miſconſtruction and different interpretations than the words of God; and certainly every one will think himſelf more at liberty, to impoſe his own ſenſe upon the words of

men

men than those of the HOLY GHOST. Can it be supposed, that every individual among the thousands who have founded their profession upon systems, is thoroughly acquainted with the sense the compilers held forth or intended by these words? Nay, how can it be, when they seldom and perhaps never read them? Yet a professed adherence to them constitutes such a profession of christianity, as the greatest knowledge in, and conformity to the scriptures are incapable of!

Is not this a direct attack upon the perfection of revelation, yea, on the perfections of GOD himself? 'Tis plainly saying, JEHOVAH is not so capable to teach his creatures as they are to teach one another: A discrediting his authority in the intelligence he hath given in his sacred word: A setting up human systems to rival revelation. For that must certainly be the most preferable which is most capable to teach us the mind of GOD in the scriptures; this they are not sufficient for in themselves, because the words and sense may be parted; this human systems are capable of, for in them the sense is fixed; therefore they should be called the *Divine Books*, since they have a perfection which the word of GOD is not endued with! What advantage hath the scriptures in having GOD for their author, when compositions of men are more to the purpose?

It is strange these men do not say that CHRIST shall judge the world by such systems! One would think it naturally follows, that what is the only test and standard of his faith and profession here, would be that by which he shall be judged. *" Shall not the Judge of all the earth do right?"** I know not whether to call such doctrine *Deism* or *Atheism*. If GOD has not displayed his Divine perfections in his word, he has no where done it; for *he hath magnified his word above all his name*.† If we cannot depend upon the scriptures themselves, we are yet without any certain guide of GOD's giving: And for human systems, the most perfect of them are every period changing; so in fact we have no sure rule of religion at all.—Amazing!

If heretics will make a bad use of revelation, who can help it? But as *Solomon* understood the true mother by her tenderness towards the child, so the true children of the church, are best known by their tender regard for the scriptures, and practical conformity to them. Such are not for dividing the authority of scripture betwixt GOD and men; giving God the honour of speaking to the church; and men the honour of fixing the meaning of JEHOVAH's words for the church. This cannot in any respect agree with the scriptures having in themselves a determinate sense: And that they sufficiently explain their own meaning, which is granted even by this author.

BUT

* *Gen.* xviii. 25. † *Psal.* cxxxviii. 2.

BUT perhaps this may be thought to militate against the office of ministers preaching the gospel, and explaining the scriptures: A discouragement to people to attend the preaching of the word; and a rejecting scripture consequences: Though this is none of the Dreamer's objections, nothing of his bears so much the face of an argument, yet it may occur to others.

I SHALL therefore observe, that none of these can follow from keeping the word of GOD, and the works of men in their proper places. For tho' it be the duty of ministers to bring forth the truths revealed in scripture, and by all means discover the sense, and elucidate the same with all the perspicuity they are capable of, and endeavour by all the arguments in their power to convince the people that such is the true sense: Yet the consequences they draw, however clear to themselves, are not the standard of the people's faith; much less is their seeing them to be just consequences, a sufficient reason for any to receive them with equal credit as express revelation. The limiting the sense of scripture by a society as a test of orthodoxy, plainly lays a restraint upon ministers that belong to it; for then they must preach nothing as the sense of scripture, however clear it appears to them, but what is agreeable to that sense already fixed. Being thus confined, they must either crush what fresh discoveries they obtain from scripture; or in bringing them forth, be declared heretics for deviating from the received faith of the society.

IT is also the duty of every christian to use all the helps he can, as serious reading, comparing spiritual things with spiritual, earnest prayer to GOD for direction by his spirit in searching the scriptures, and using other means that he may " grow in grace, and in the knowledge of our Lord and Saviour JESUS CHRIST." That he may " be nourished in the words of faith, and of good doctrine." That his " love may abound yet more and more in knowledge, and in all judgment." That he " may approve things that are excellent." And that he may have his " spiritual senses exercised to discern both good and evil."† But whether the christian using his liberty of searching the scriptures, and receiving the truth from its own evidence, and the authority of GOD; Or, his taking all things as settled by the society he happens to be connected with, and submitting his judgment thereto, without further enquiry; be the method to attain these noble ends, let every impartial person judge.

As to scripture consequences, there are two kinds of persons I think they are binding upon. First, Such as see them to be necessarily connected with scripture; to such they are the sense of scripture, and nothing can excuse such persons from an obligation to believe them. They are also obligatory on such as have had sufficient means to see

and

† 2 Pet. iii. 18. 1 Tim. iv. 6. Phil. i. 9, 10. Heb. v. 14.

and know this connexion, but have either thro' carelesness, or obstinacy, neglected the use of these means. For none can be innocent who have the means of attaining knowledge, and yet continue ignorant.—But such a person as useth all the means in his power conscienciously, yet cannot see consequences drawn by a course of reasoning from scripture to be necessarily connected with revelation; I cannot think such consequences are obligatory upon him.

I APPREHEND nothing of any seeming strength can be brought against this, except what follows: That if a person be not bound to believe scripture consequences, because he does not see them; it follows, if a person does not see evidence for Divine revelation, it will discharge his obligation to believe the scriptures themselves.

THIS objection certainly includes a conscientious enquiry by the person supposed, or it is merely specious: For he that sinfully indulges a neglect of searching the scriptures, cannot be expected to know either the one or the other, as the scriptures carry their own evidence. But when the person does make diligent and impartial enquiries, there may be many consequences he cannot come to the knowledge of: But 'tis more than probable, that an instance cannot happen in the other case. As the scriptures are so full, and every way so well accommodated by Divine wisdom to all capacities, and containing such indisputable attestations to the truth of the gospel, if the person's enquiries were fair and conscientious, he could not reject the evidence revelation contains in favour of itself. So that the one case does not follow necessarily upon the other.

BUT if a person must be cast out of church communion for not seeing some consequences that are evident to others, and yet is using all the means in his power to understand the mind of GOD in scripture, and in other respects appears conscientious: It must be either because something more than a credible profession of christianity is necessary to church communion; or because he is not a credible professor of christianity. The first, even this author does not pretend to affirm; but the last is what he so faintly has attempted to prove: But then one of these three things must follow, either they who refuse him communion, must put themselves in place of GOD, and assume the prerogative to judge of the man's sincerity: Or, that there is more required to make a christian, than is expresly declared in scripture: Or, the doctrine of the scripture being a perfect rule, must be disclaimed. All which are glaring and manifest errors.

THOUGH these consequences were as certain in themselves as mathematical deductions; yet, the abstruseness which attends the reasonings to weak capacities, intimates that consequences which require a course of reasoning to deduce them, were not designed by GOD to be of equal necessity to all with the plain and easy truths which are clear to the meanest. Besides, the reasoning of fallible

men,

men, being mixed in such deductions with the declarations of GOD, must in some measure weaken the force of them in comparison with the primary truths they are deduced from.

THOUGH the sense of scripture in such a consequence be manifest to us, and so necessarily depending on scripture in our judgment, as to be believed by us, with the principles from which it is deduced: Yet as it is not so to others (who are as diligent in their enquiries as we can pretend to be) they cannot believe it. Nor can it be esteemed as strictly a part of revelation to christians in general, as the words of scripture are. The importance of consequences ought to be measured by the plainness and easiness of their deduction from revelation, for it is a perfection of it to be universally useful, being designed for the benefit of mankind. But it must militate against this perfection of revelation, to say there is any truth necessary to salvation not expresly taught in it; or not so clearly deduceable as to be manifest to every honest mind. The scriptures were not intended for the learned only; what was hid from them with all their reasoning, was revealed to the unlearned, as fit to make them wise to salvation. The great end of revelation is to lay before men things necessary to salvation in the plainest and most easy way of conveyance, supported by the argument of Divine authority; so that the unlearned may believe, and practise what is necessary to salvation, upon the authority of a THUS SAITH THE LORD, or IT IS WRITTEN; and not because such men or an Assembly agreed that this or the other was the sense of scripture, and ordained it as a test of orthodoxy, and the only credible profession of christianity.

I PRESUME the unprejudiced reader will see how weak the reasoning of this dreaming author is, and how little truth there is in the minor of his long-winded sylogism, which I have proved false: Hence the whole must be visionary and come to nought; with all other such attempts to bring the word of GOD into disrepute, which is the scope of this author's last pages, in which are not obscurely intimated, that the scriptures are obscure and unintelligible, till the sense be drawn out and summed up by men; that they do not sufficiently confute error, nor guard against it; that they do not clearly prove the truth, and therefore not a credible profession of christianity, &c. All which qualifications the *Westminster* Confession is endued with. This is the amount of these laboured pages, and if it is not *Deism*, I confess, I know not what *Deism* is.

I SHALL oppose this author's sylogism with another; and leave the christian reader to chuse which he thinks most agreeable to scripture.

WHAT was a credible profession, and distinguished between truth and error in the days of the apostles and first christians, must be so still; but adhering to the words of the HOLY GHOST were judged credible,

credible, and fit to diftinguifh between truth and error then : *Ergo*, they are fit for that purpofe ftill.—The denying the major, will lay the apoftles did not make a credible profeffion of religion. The minor is evident from the admiffion of members into the church thro' the whole New Teftament. Again, The words of fcripture have fufficient evidence in themfelves to make them a credible profeffion of chriftian religion ;

HE who adheres to them, makes a credible profeffion of chriftian religion. The firft is true, fo is the latter. To deny the antecedent, is to refufe the credibility of the fcriptures. To reject the confequence, is uncharitably to judge the heart of the profeffor. And " who art thou that judgeth another man's fervant ? To his own mafter he ftandeth or falleth."† But further,

WHATEVER is not authorized from precept or example, by CHRIST and his apoftles, as the right of chriftian focieties, is none of their chriftian privileges : But for a fociety to fix the fenfe of fcripture, and fet their fenfe of it up as a teft and ftandard of orthodoxy to other chriftians, cannot be proved from the New Teftament : Therefore it is not now the privilege of any chriftian fociety. To refufe the firft propofition, lands in fuperftition and willworfhip. The fecond muft hold, till precept or example from the New Teftament is produced.

ONCE more : What was fufficient to guard againft error in the times of chriftianity, muft be fo ftill ; but the word of GOD was then reckoned only fufficient : Therefore it muft be fo ftill. The firft muft be granted, or fuppofe that the care of CHRIST towards his church changes with times and circumftances ; and the means of his people's fafety are uncertain and changeable. The fecond muft hold, without accufing the fcripture of infufficiency, and maintaining there are more duties and fins than the fcripture hath told us of. Tho' heretics pretend to hold by the fcriptures, and fix a falfe meaning to them, may they not do the fame with every other fyftem ? Or, is it becaufe any number of men knows better how to guard their words againft mifinterpretations than the Spirit of GOD, that fyftems compofed by them are preferable to the fcriptures, to guard againft error ? But enough of fyllogifms.

THIS author hath been at great pains to difcredit revelation, and now he comes to finifh his laudable tafk. And fuppofing he had proved the *Weftminfter* Confeffion the *only credible* profeffion of chriftianity, he now makes his laft effort for an *only* title to it alfo. He cannot endure it fhould be called human, and the Bible Divine. There is fuch majefty in what is Divine, and fo wide a difference betwixt what is fo, and things human, that it muft be compromifed. Either the Bible muft be called human, or the other Divine. He therefore gives us a definition of human fyftems, which he prefumes

none

† *Rom.* xiv. 4.

none will apply to the Confeffion: But they muſt be much wiſer than me that can find any ſenſe in it: Tho' he ſays with an air of aſſurance, peculiar to himſelf, that the mind is bound up to it: But this I don't wonder at, for men that have a right to fix the ſenſe of Divine revelation for others, have certainly a power of determining the meaning of human ſyſtems infallibly. The ſubſtance of the definition is, "Human ſyſtems are collections of heterogenious materials, —" and owe their *all*, both as to matter and manner, unto the in-" vention and ſagacity of men." I can learn nothing from this deſcription but that no ſyſtem can be called human, which is not wholly made up of contradictory materials; and if any of the materials are Divine, it ceaſes to be human: So the citing a text will make a Divine ſyſtem; in this ſenſe the author's own performance, and that he animadverts upon, are both Divine. But let the author's meaning be what it will, his concluſion is in plain enough words, when he queſtions very much, " if the Confeffion can with " any modeſty, be called human in the ſenſe of the deſcription." So whatever this oracular definition means, it proves the Confeffion not to be human, conſequently it muſt be divine. That I do not miſtake his ſcope is plain, for he ſays before we can prove it to be ſuch, (viz. human) we " muſt make it good that *none* of the words of the Confeffion are the truths of the Bible." But if any thing therein is not truth, I would think it has little claim to the character of a Divine ſyſtem, and that it is not all acceptable even to ſeceders is plain, from the different ſenſes in which they take faith, aſſurance, &c. from what the Affembly did.

However, from this hypotheſis we have a multitude of Divine books; the Bible is no longer the *only* Divine ſyſtem; here is one ſpecial rival to it; and one which excludes it from being a credible profeffion of chriſtianity. What a ſtrange notion this author has of a Divine ſyſtem! He confeſſes the words of the Confeffion are not Divine, but the ſenſe. How ſhall he certify to us that all the words, as they ſtand there have a Divine ſenſe? A Divine ſyſtem muſt be as perfect in its words and ſenſe, as it ought, or can be, ſuitable to all times, and agreeable to all circumſtances poſſible, and which expreſſeth the mind of God perfectly to men. None of theſe can be ſaid of the Confeffion. Is it perfect? No. Then an imperfect Divine ſyſtem is a contradiction. Is it ſuitable to all times and circumſtances? No. He ſays it muſt change as theſe change. But a changeable Divine ſyſtem is alſo a contradiction. Does it expreſs the whole mind of God perfectly? Or can nothing be found of God's revealed will to men, that is not in the Confeffion? Many things. Then it is a very improper rival to the Bible. I refer it to the conſideration of the ſerious, if it does not ſavour of blaſphemy, to call any book Divine but the Bible? How daring muſt it be thus to defame the contrivance of Infinite
Wiſdom!

Wifdom! Could this author imagine (I do not fay believe, for he certainly believes nothing of religion that makes more Divine books than the Bible) that the whole fenfe of revelation, and no more than the fenfe of it, is contained in the Confeffion? This conftitutes an infinite difference betwixt the fcriptures and all other fyftems; for this reafon I call them human, becaufe not Divinely complete: Not becaufe men's judgments are taken up in methodizing them, but rather becaufe men's judgments cannot fully comprehend the fenfe and meaning of fcripture, and hold it forth to other's in their compofitions: In this refpect they are not perfect, therefore I call them human. But the word of GOD holds forth the full and perfect fenfe, which is beyond the capacity of the wifeft generation of men fince the creation, fully to know or underftand. The fcriptures were indited by the infallible direction of GOD infpiring the penmen, who fpoke not their own mind, but as they were moved by the HOLY GHOST. None will fay the Affembly was under the fame infpiration when they collected the fenfe of fcripture.

BUT I flatter myfelf that 'tis unneceffary to point out the difference to difcerning men. Tho' our author is certainly dreaming when he fays, "the truth is, if every fyftem is human about which "the underftandings of uninfpired men have been converfant, we "have nothing befides human fyftems." Thus, reader, rather than not have his favourite fyftem Divine, he will conclude all copies and verfions of the Bible to be human. I do not fay our verfion, confidered as fuch, is Divine, but it is a tranflation of the Divine original very near literally correfponding with the text; fo near, that our greateft critics have found no difference that affects things neceffary to falvation. And I cannot help thinking, that it was rather *exact copies or tranflations* that the apoftle *Paul* points at, when he commands *Timothy* to hold faft the form of found words, than the fenfe of fcripture collected by focieties into a Confeffion. For it muft eafily occur to the apoftle, tho' he had not been Divinely infpired, that to the univerfal ufe of the fcriptures in the churches, it was neceffary to have them copied and tranflated; without the chriftian world could have been always together, and of one language. And a tranflation of the fcripture is an *exprefs draught*, as our author defines this form of found words; but that no fyftem can be called, which is compofed in words of men's invention.

BUT if it be found that the word of GOD muft be kept *pure* and *complete*, the whole of this author's fcheme will fall at once. This I fhall next endeavour to prove.

THE promife of CHRIST, that the HOLY GHOST fhould guide into all truth,* fecures the word of GOD from being injured or adulterated. He hath promifed to be even to the end of the world with
those

* *John* xvi. 13.

those that teach and observe all things whatsoever he hath commanded.† Therefore the things which CHRIST hath commanded shall remain to the end of the world for the use of men. We are told by *Moses,* that " those things which are revealed, belong unto us and to our children for ever, that we may do all the words of this law."‡ So that as long as it is the duty of men to keep the law of GOD, so long must the word of GOD be continued as he hath revealed it; which will be while there is a man upon earth. Nay, our blessed LORD hath told us, that " till heaven and earth pass, " one jot, or one tittle, shall in no wise pass from the law, till all " be fulfilled."§

HATH he said his words shall not pass away? Hence it is plain the word of GOD is more firm than heaven or earth; so that it is easier to pluck the sun from his orb, and toss the earth from its centre, than change any part of the word of GOD. For as the apostle *Peter* saith, " The word of the LORD endureth for ever, " and this is the word which by the gospel is preached unto you."‖ But if it be corrupted it cannot be called the word of the LORD.

'TIS an imagination every way unworthy of GOD, to suppose that he would suffer his word to be corrupted. He who will not suffer a hair of our heads to perish without his permission; and takes care of the fowls of the air, and meanest reptiles of the earth, will he suffer the foundation of religion to be overthrown, of which his beloved Son JESUS CHRIST is the chief corner stone? Will he suffer the seals to be torn from his will and testament, the articles thereof changed, and the spiritual food of his people, the word of life, to be poisoned by the inventions of men? In short, is he willing to lose his word, and give up his claim thereto wholly? None but *Atheists* can imagine it. To suppose it in any respect corrupted, is to question the whole. If in any thing, why not in fundamentals? There is nothing in it but what became the wisdom of an infinite GOD to dictate, and as well becomes his honour and glory to preserve pure and entire. Tho' all the legions of hell, and wicked on earth, should conspire to corrupt, add to, or diminish from this word of GOD, it would remain impossible while he continues a faithful GOD.

THE word of GOD is that appointed mean for bringing about the great purposes of JEHOVAH's love in the converting, comforting, &c. of the chosen vessels of his mercy, and must in spite of all opposition be kept pure and complete, as the foundation of their faith, the rule of their conduct, and store-house of all their comfort. Could the saint be once persuaded that the word of GOD is corrupted, his faith must stagger, hopes languish, comforts sink, and his soul faint. For, saith CHRIST, " Man shall not live " by bread alone, but by every word that proceedeth out of the
" mouth

† *Matth.* xxviii. 20. ‡ *Deut.* xxix. 19. § *Matth.* v. 18. ‖ 1 *Pet.* i. 25.

" mouth of God."* What faith the Pfalmift, " Thy word is very pure: therefore thy fervant loveth it. This is my comfort in all my affliction: for thy word hath quickened me. Mine eyes fail for thy falvation, and for the word of thy righteoufnefs."† We may therefore conclude with the great Dr *Owen*, " That the whole word of God in every letter and title, as given from him by infpiration, is preferved without corruption."‡

But why fhould I detain the reader to prove that which none but *Deifts* deny? And it is no fmall evidence of this author's being too much inclined thereto, in his ufing the very arguments which they place their greateft confidence in againft revelation: And goes fo far, as not only to difcard tranflations, but the originals themfelves: Yea, the very autographs of the infpired penmen; which he fays are human, " without we can prove that every one who had a hand in tranfcribing, and reprinting the originals, was infpired!" This is in plain language telling us, that the Divinity of the fcriptures ceafed with the apoftles, when infpiration ceafed, and chriftians in all ages fince have been believing they know not what. As if the faithfulnefs of God were not fufficient ground of affurance, that whatever means were ufed, his word fhould remain pure; which is abfolutely neceffary, in agreeablenefs to the plan God had eftablifhed, for bringing about the confummate felicity of his chofen. No matter who were employed as inftruments; it is the promife of an All-fufficient God that makes it fure to us, that none of his words fhall be loft; but there can be no reafoning from the Almighty's interpofition in favour of his own word, to the compofing a Confeffion.

And tho' we fhould not argue from the Divine care in this refpect, yet there is no comparifon betwixt *tranflating* and *explaining*, or *illuftrating*. The former is only to find fit words in one language to anfwer the fame words in the other language, and which bear the fame idea: But to explain, is to impofe a particular fenfe or meaning upon the text according to the judgment of the author: In the one cafe the primary fubject is not changed, it is ftill the fame tho' in another language, and this only can be called the " exprefs draught of the wholefome doctrines of chriftianity." It neither changes its fenfe nor its author. But illuftrations cannot be the fame with the primary fubject; and as to the fenfe, the moft perfect comment is not only liable to, but hath imperfections in it: Befides it conftitutes a new author. The tranflators cannot with propriety be called authors of the Bible; nor can comments claim God for their author; but if they were Divine they might.

Though we have not the fame fcrolls and paper the prophets and apoftles ufed, yet there are all the evidence and certainty the

cafe

* *Matth.* iv. 4. † *Pfa.* cxix. 140.—50.—123. ‡ *Pa.* 14. of the Divine original of the fcriptures.

case will admit of or requires, that we have the same words. And much more certainty than we can even have that the same words are transmitted to us, which *Adoniram Byfield* and other scribes wrote in the first copy of the Confession. There are many advantages in favour of the one case, that cannot be supposed in the other, or any one else.

THE scriptures carry their own pure evidence in themselves, which is plain, uniform, and simple in the greatest perfection. The convergent rays of scripture evidence coming into the soul, never fail to produce the same happy effects in the hearts and lives of thousands in every age, who are unacquainted with any confession. If other systems are profitable, it is from their agreeableness to this Divine one; they shine in borrowed robes. But the scriptures by their own internal light, worth, excellency, and Divine authority, bear the brightest and most convincing evidence in themselves, and clearly demonstrate what they are. Their innate beauty and superlative goodness powerfully persuades the mind to receive them, as in very deed they are the words of the Living GOD. They depend not upon men or any society for their authority, the faithfulness of GOD is engaged for them, and his Divine power never fails to make them effectual for the great purposes of salvation, which infinite wisdom provided them for. In this sacred volume is the majesty of GOD illustrious, the Sun of glory resplendent, and the word of the Divine Spirit infallible. To seek for more, or other evidence for the truth of the scriptures, than what is so conspicuous in themselves, is to set up a candle to behold the sun in his noonday splendor.

COULD it be possible to destroy this work of GOD by corruption or otherwise, it would long ere now been extinguished by the united powers and policy of hell and earth. What plots and machinations have been formed against it? Yet all over-ruled by Divine wisdom, for the spreading its light and displaying its glory: " Wherein they dealt proudly, GOD was above them."* He hath made it " mighty to the pulling down of strong holds, casting down imaginations, and every high thing that exalteth itself against the knowledge of GOD."† More quick and powerful in its own defence than the two-edged swords of combined enemies, bringing them in subjection to it, at the expence of confessing their deeds, and consigning their magical books, the contrivance of hell, to the flames. " So mightily grew the word of GOD and prevailed."‡— The word that bears the name of JESUS, which shall be continued to all generations in spite of all inventions from hell and earth, once to imagine it can be rendered of no effect by corruption or adulteration, is a thought equally false and ridiculous. Take away revelation, and there's an end of that common interest in which

* Exod. xviii. 11. † 2 Cor. x. 4. 5. ‡ Acts xix. 18, 19, 20.

which all the people of GOD are united, and ever will be, so far as they are guided by religion. Gospel churches are framed by rules upon record in the book of GOD, which make them golden candlesticks, among which the Divine Redeemer delights to walk.§

THE disquisitions of reason and philosophy, with the ingenious conjectures of exalted talents, tho' boasting of flights beyond the stars, and excursions into the invisible world of spirits, have thro' the prevalency of custom, or fashion, been esteemed and flourished for a season; but at last gave way to others in their turn. They acquired to their authors the reputation of subtle wits, discoverers of truth, irrefragable reasoners; but how are heaps of these curious volumes forgotten? And tho' they have escaped the ruins of time, yet they are turned over with the same smile of pity, which a few years hence, will be the only regard reckoned due to the admired works which have succeeded them. Revolutions of time terminate the glory of human systems. "For all flesh is as grass, and all the glory "of man, as the flower of grass: but the word of the LORD en- "dureth for ever. And his truth endureth to all generations."*— No process of time can alter the nature of the everlasting gospel: The same Divine evidence in itself thro' all ages inviteth to embrace it. When *Deists* have spent their sophistical wit, and metaphysicians lost themselves in the maze of abstractions, revelation will continue the sure pledge of JEHOVAH's love, the pure foundation of faith, the unerring rule of pure religion, the christian's comfort in life and death, and the same " power of GOD unto sal- " vation, to every one that believeth."†

WHAT was said concerning GOD's peculiar people, may with the utmost propriety be applied to his *sacred word*; " *Surely there is* " *no inchantment against Jacob, neither is there any divination against* " *Israel.*"‡

THIS author, Page 18th, wonders " how a doctrine is *Divine*, " so long as it is *standing* in the *words of scripture unknown*, and " *unthought of*; and becometh *human* as soon as it is conceived by " the human understanding, and is expressed in any *other words* than " those of scripture!" But who says that Divine words become human when conceived by the human understanding? Or that vitiated human minds can fully conceive the sense of them? This is an imagination to favour his own scheme. Divine words will be so, whatever the understanding conceives about them, or wherever they are put. But when men change the Divine words for others of their own, and call these the sense of scripture, which, tho' it may be, yet it is but imperfectly so, as men's understandings cannot comprehend the full sense, nor their words express it: And therefore may be justly called human. Does it not offer violence to the common sense of christians, to tell them, that the words contrived

by

§ Rev. ii. 1. * 1 Pet. i. 25. Psal. c. 5. † Rom. i. 16. ‡ Numb. xxiii. 23.

by any man or assembly, which they chuse to express scripture truth in, are *Divine words*? Can they be called the *words of GOD* which are not in *his word*? If they are *Divine words*, why is not the Confession called the *word of God*? It may be called the words of divines; but no more of it are *Divine words*, than what are taken from revelation in *express words*.

But here I must wonder in my turn, and I think every lover of God's word will join with me. However it entered into the mind of any christian, (if this author be one) that the Divine doctrines contained in the words of scripture as God hath expressed them, must continue *unknown* and *unthought of*, till their sense be collected by men, and written in a Confession of Faith!—Surprizing! This is at once rendering the Bible useless in itself, till manufactured by men. What a miserable condition must they have been in, who never saw the sense of scripture thus collected, without which the scriptures are *unknown* and *unthought of!* What a pity it is that the author should have spoke so much truth in his 8th Page, whereby he is so manifestly contradicted! What has now become of the perspicuity of the scriptures? How consistent with this is it to say, "The Bible is the catholic interpreter of itself, and
" sufficiently determines its own meaning? Yea, where is there
" any revelation at all? For an unrevealed revelation is a contra-
" diction." But may I not venture to ease this author's wondering mind, by informing him why doctrines as they stand in the scriptures are so little thought of? It is because other systems composed by men, are set up and countenanced by church authority, as tests of doctrine, standards of orthodoxy, rules for admitting into, and excluding from church communion; yea, made the *only* credible profession of christianity, preservative from error, and that which churches may, and ought to acquiesce in, and rest satisfied with, as the form of sound words, to conduct them in social worship with harmony. This is the reason why the Bible becomes of so little use, so much *unknown* and *unthought of*.

Though I value the *Westminster* Confession, as one of the best summaries of doctrine extant, I must be excused from admitting it into the place of revelation, as to authority, purity, perfection, title, use, &c. and must be still allowed to call it a *Human System:* In which I think I am countenanced, not only by the Assembly themselves, but also the best writers that have either defended or explained it; which I think are Mr *Erskine* and others, who, yet in their preface to the catechism explained, expresly call it a *Human Composure*. But speaking of the scriptures, quest. 14, they say, their authority cannot depend upon the church, " because the true
" church of Christ depends, in its very being, on the scriptures;
" and therefore the scriptures cannot depend upon it, as to their
" authority, *Eph.* ii. 22." And speaking of the incomparable excellency,

cellency, and usefulness of the scriptures, quest. 48, they say, "They
" are the well-furnished dispensatory of all sovereign remedies; the
" rich magazine of all true comfort; the complete armory of all
" spiritual weapons; and the unerring compass to guide to the
" haven of glory, *Psal.* cvii. 20. *Rom.* xv. 4. *Eph.* vi. 13,—18.
2 *Pet.* i. 19." These sentiments are clearly against the doctrine of
this performance of the Dreamer, and must be a just reproof to
both the author, and also the Replier as *imprimator*.

THESE who put the *Westminster* Confession in the place of the
scriptures, do it such a service as the friends of Lady *Jane Gray* did
to her, who, much against her own inclination, and those of her best
friends, but to favour their ambitious views, mounted her on the
throne of *England*, which soon became the means of taking off her
head. So the substituting this or any human system in the room of
the sacred word of GOD, is the most effectual way to destroy its reputation among all the lovers of the scriptures. If *Reuben* must
lose his birthright, if he goes up to his father's bed: Beautiful *Ab-
solom* be deemed a traitor when usurping the throne of his father:
And the handmaid dismissed when she becomes rival to her mistress:
Much more, whatever draws contempt upon the oracles of the Living
GOD, must be expected to have its glory stained, by him who is a
jealous GOD, and will not give his glory to another.

AND such as are for invading the prerogative of heaven, would
do well to remember how the Divine Author of revelation hath
fenced it against all such intrusions.—" If any man preach any o-
" ther gospel unto you, than that ye have received, let him be ac-
" cursed.* Add thou not unto his words, lest he reprove thee,
" and thou be found a liar.† Ye shall not add unto the word
" which I command you, neither shall ye diminish ought from it.‡
" For I testify unto every man that heareth the words of the pro-
" phecy of this book, if any shall add unto these things, GOD
" shall add unto him the plagues that are written in this book:
" And if any man shall take away from the words of the book of
" this prophecy, GOD shall take away his part out of the book of
" life, and out of the holy city, and from the things which are
" written in this book. He who testifieth these things, saith,
" surely I come quickly. AMEN. EVEN SO, COME LORD
" JESUS."§

* *Gal.* i. 9.　† *Prov.* xxx. 6.　‡ *Deut.* iv. 2.　§ *Rev.* xxii. 18, 19, 20.

ADDENDA.

AS the Replier has confidently engaged not to reply again, tho' a *thousand such scurrilous letters* as the Free Enquirer's should be written; and the Quaker has followed his dictator, and told us, that such *senseless epistles* as Mr *M—y*'s he will hold unworthy of his notice. Therefore, it may safely be concluded, whatever any of them replies to, will, in their own judgment, be neither *senseless* nor *scurrilous*. And if any thing I have done, get so far into their good graces, as to deserve their public notice, I may presume it will be the same as if they recommended it as a *sensible* performance; and which on that account, no doubt, will merit more regard from others. However, so many are the difficulties and contradictions that attend the human explications of the Trinity, that a fair resolution and reconcilement of them, upon a foundation that hath the authority of GOD, would, I own, be such a master-piece as I apprehend has no precedent. If this *mighty genius*, the Quaker, shall undertake this task, and acquit himself honourably, I shall no more account it strange that he thinks himself or others have a right to compose *Divine systems*; for nothing short of a new revelation can complete this discovery, as the volumes of revelation we are already blest with do not furnish us with any such accounts of that mystery, as the fertile inventions of men have annexed thereto. This would be an acquisition that might justly claim the regard of all, but especially these societies that have made these things terms of their communion; then they would know what better foundation they had to believe such things themselves, and impose them upon others, than the written word of GOD. This is intelligence extremely much wanted at this day, when the prerogative of societies, to make articles of faith, is so far extended, and the people taught it as their indispensible duty to submit to rules, framed by society, as the *only credible profession of christianity*.

I AM persuaded such adepts in demonstrating Divine mysteries, without the aid of revelation, will be at no loss for a clear resolution of all the difficulties that can occur. To such vast capacities as can with such ease demonstrate in what manner the three Divine persons subsist in one JEHOVAH—That the Divine Essence is communicated—That there are days in eternity, &c. &c. I say, to such, nothing can appear difficult. He must be wiser than mortals that can propose any thing, which such persons are not capable to investigate.

IF these eagle-eyed Theologists, that can see beyond the limits of revelation, give satisfactory accounts of what they pretend to be so well acquainted with, they may be certain the world will be *infidel enough* to give to their works that respect and reverence due to such *oracular discoveries*. Nay, such new information concerning
sacred

sacred mysteries, would even merit the attention of beings whose intellects are not encumbered with mortal bodies.

I SAID *infidel enough*, because, whoever pretend to teach more concerning the nature of GOD, than what he hath revealed in his word, they must be divested of christianity that will believe or regard them. All such attempts with this performance of the Quaker's (to borrow a favourite term of the Replier's) *tend* only to *deism* and *infidelity*. And if the Replier will employ an infidel amanuensis, and favour his excursions against christianity, by patronizing his deistical conceits, in publishing them to the world with comments, he cannot but expect to share with him in what he and his works only deserve, which at most is but satyr or contempt.

AFTER the Dreamer had said, Page 11th, that these men were " allowed to make the best of their belief in any society that should " please to join with them in it:" How much to the purpose must it be for the Replier, from the pulpit, to continue his railing against them, and any society that should receive them? May we not wonder what he has now to do with them, or any they may be connected with: But it is most likely, he and the Quaker (if they are different persons) have both adopted that *Popish* maxim, *Throw calumny enough, some of it will stick*.

BUT 'tis time enough to pronounce our principles *Sabellianism*, when he proves them to be such; and to find fault with other societies, when he accounts some better for the conduct of his own, than he has done in his Reply. One would think that society acted more like christians, in receiving one of us into communion with them, upon an explicit declaration of his adherence to the principles of truth as contained in Divine revelation; than the Replier's society, in receiving another (whom they had supposed guilty of the same errors) upon a bare subscribing an article of a human composition. This still shews that human systems, with them, are preferable to the scriptures: And that errors, which they reckon gross blasphemy when the person goes from their society, turn pretty innocent trifles if he will but return to it again.

F I N I S.

www.ingramcontent.com/pod-product-compliance
Lightning Source LLC
Chambersburg PA
CBHW032005300426
44117CB00008B/909